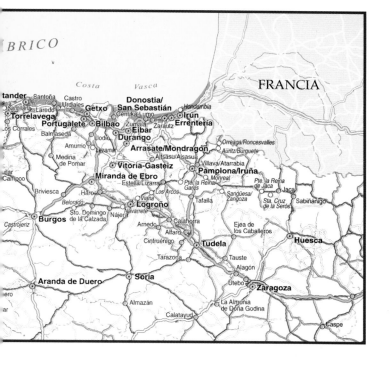

The road to Santiago
The Pilgrims' Practical Guide

José María Anguita Jaén

Editorial Everest would like to thank you for purchasing this book. It has been created by an extensive and complete publishing team made up of photographers, illustrators and authors specialised in the field of tourism, together with our modern cartography department. Everest guarantees that the contents of this work were completely up to date at the time of going to press, and we would like to invite you to send us any information that helps us to improve our publications, so that we may always offer QUALITY TOURISM.

QUALITY
TOURISM
WITH
EVEREST

Please send your comments to:
Editorial Everest. Dpto. de Turismo
Apartado 339 – 24080 León (Spain)
Or e-mail them to us at turismo@everest.es

Editorial director: Raquel López Varela

Editorial coordinator: Eva María Fernández

The team which has made this work: Centro de Estudios del Camino de Santiago. Sahagún

Coordination: José M. Anguita

Fieldwork: Francisca Anguita, José M. Anguita y Juan Alberto González

Documentation: José M. Anguita, Francisca Anguita

Cartographic sketches: Francisca Anguita

Photographs: Imagen MAS, Lucas Vallecillos, Miguel Raurich, Miguel Sánchez, Puri Lozano and Archivo Everest

Design: Luis Vallina and Gerardo Rodera

Production of title and half titles: Francisco A. Morais

Diagrams: Mercedes Fernández

Digital image processing: David Aller and Ángel Rodríguez

Cartography: Antonio Lopes © Everest

Translated by: Polaria

© José M. Anguita
    EDITORIAL EVEREST, S. A.
Carretera León-La Coruña, km 5 — LEÓN
ISBN: 84-241-0420-X
Legal deposit: LE. 196 - 2004
Printed in Spain

EDITORIAL EVERGRÁFICAS, S. L.
Carretera León-La Coruña, km 5
LEÓN (Spain)

www.everest.es
Customer Information Service: 902 123 400

Introduction

The *Liber Sancti Iacobi* Guide, the Modern Pilgrim Guides and the Current Road to Santiago Itinerary

Soon, 900 years will have elapsed from the time when a French pilgrim, who introduced himself as Pope Calixtus II and is now known by many under the name Aimeri Picaud, recorded a written description of the Road to Santiago. This work, known under the name *Liber peregrinations* or the "Mediaeval Pilgrim's Guide", is the fifth part of *Liber Sancti Iacobi,* an extremely famous compilation about the apostle St James written in the XIIth century.

This *Liber Sancti Iacobi* guide explained, among other things, the paths of the Road, its stages after reaching Spain, the names of the towns, the mountain passes and rivers through which it went, the sanctuaries, the hospitals and benefactors of the route... The information, therefore, combined practical data (such as day trips and distances, town names and characteristics of their inhabitants, and the quality of the water of their rivers) with information of a more cultural type (such as sanctuaries, relics, hagiographies and stories). For this reason, it is a noteworthy predecessor to our current tourist guides, especially within the modern guidebooks to the Road to Santiago.

Indeed, about thirty years ago, and coinciding with the revitalisation which the pilgrimages to Santiago de Compostela had been experiencing in recent times, a group of scholars lead by the parson of Santa María del Cebreiro, Mr. Elías Valiña Sanpedro, had the fortunate idea of thoroughly mapping and describing the whole of the French Road in Spain, always tracking the traces of the itinerary as described by the author of the *Liber Sancti Iacobi* guide. At the same time, several groups of pilgrims and lovers of the Road started to indicate the route to Santiago on the road itself by means of a conventional sign: yellow arrows painted on milestones, trees, tarmac, walls, traffic signs, lamp posts, etc., which has now gained worldwide fame. A new itinerary, as faithful as possible to the one reviewed in the XIIth century guide, was thus "invented". Although some stretches of the new track were debatable, the recovery of the route was permanently improved by the ever growing involvement of the local institutions affected (Autonomous Communities, Provincial Governments, Town Halls, Cultural and Friends' Associations).

The pioneering work of Elías Valiña's team, published by the publishing house Editorial Everest in the 1980's, was followed by other works which incorporated the successive and constant updates in the signalling of the route. Among these, I was lucky enough to take part in the *Practical Pilgrim's Guide. The Road to Santiago* (Guía Práctica del Peregrino. El Camino de Santiago), a publication born in the midst of the Road to Santiago Study Centre (Centro de Estudios del Camino de Santiago) in Sahagún and carried out by a team of enthusiasts who combined their status as pilgrims with their condition as scholars specialising in everything relating to St James and the pilgrimage. The leader of that work, which was also published by Editorial Everest in 1993, was the much missed Millán Bravo Lozano, professor of Latin Philology in the University of Valladolid; and founder of several Road to Santiago Friends' Associations, as well as of the Road to Santiago Study Centre in Sahagún and of its instrument of expression, the Magazine on Xacobean and Mediaeval Studies "Iacobus".

A decade later, the members of the Study Centre have again been honoured by Editorial Everest's request to write a new guide to the Road to Santiago. The constant updates to the route (modified by works, or improved by the finding of new alternatives), as well as the scientific innovations which affect the Road or its adjoining lands, have made it necessary to prepare a new edition faithful to the spirit of the two predecessors it is reviewing.

OUR GUIDE

• Aims and Contents

Indeed, this work does not profess to divert from the script which based the writing of those two publications, and whose aim was to help future pilgrims to prepare their St James adventure, as well as to assist pilgrims who were already on their way, and to provide historical illustrations of all the places through which the Road goes.

The itinerary described is still, as it was in the previous guides, the so-called French Road, i. e., the 800 km between Roncesvals and Somport in Santiago de Compostela. The criterion used to draw the itinerary to be followed by the pilgrims was the adaptation of the indications mostly signalled by the above mentioned yellow arrows.

In addition, this guide offers a new feature: the description of the two historic extensions of the Road to Santiago: the one to Padrón (Iria Flavia) and the one to Finisterre. The remaining historic Roads to Santiago, which are also going through a serious revitalisation process, have also been covered, although naturally in a much more summarised way. We will review four of the many roads to Santiago whose revival is currently being attempted: Vía de la Plata, the Northern Routes, the Portuguese Road and the English Road. We therefore leave the Levante Road, as well as the Catalonia and Madrid Roads and many others, untouched by our pen. This is not to say that we do not consider them worthy of our attention, but only that we do not want to fall into a level of thouroughness that leads us to comprehensively describe the roads to Santiago from each and every one of Spain's historic lands.

We believe that there were many roads to Santiago – it can even be said that there were as many roads as there were pilgrims –, but only one was lucky enough to be reviewed by a XIIth century author. In addition, many towns on the French Road owe their existence to the Road to Santiago, and many others were greatly affected by its vicinity, to the extent that it is difficult to find a town in its path that does not have a reference to the pilgrimage, whether this is a hospital, a dedication to a saint, an image, etc. As regards the other roads, the same can only be said of the Asturian stretches of the Northern Road, due to the very important sanctuary of Oviedo.

• Description

We have divided our work into chapters or stages, each of them corresponding to what could amount to a reasonable day of walking (between twenty and thirty kilometres). This distribution in stages corresponds, of course, to work organisation criteria adopted by the team that wrote this work, and makes no claims as to standardisation. The stages are distributed as follows:

1. A thirty-one-stage block to cover the approximately 800 km between Saint-Jean-pied-de-Port and Santiago de Compostela.

2. A six-stage block to cover the Aragonese Stretch, that is, the road between Puerto de Somport and Puente la Reina (approximately 170 km).

3. A two-stage block to review the extensions of the Road to Santiago to Padrón and Finisterre respectively.

4. A block of four chapters devoted to Vía de la Plata, the Northern Routes, the Portuguese Road and the English Road.

Each of these stages or chapters is divided into two large sections; a practical first section and a second historic and cultural section, supplemented by maps to scale, photographs and other illustrations.

Section 1: The road (including paths, milestones and references, distances, etc) is described in detail. The main services offered to pilgrims in that stage (such as food and accommodation) are also described in this section, and particular attention is paid to pilgrims' shelters. The section finishes with street and land height profiles and especially maps to scale containing, by means of symbols and illustrations, all the information developed in the text. The route to follow is of course specially highlighted on the map.

Cyclists wishing to follow the routes indicated will find additional information relating to viability and the difficulties of the road described for pedestrians.

– The Road to Santiago offers cyclists two alternatives: either to follow the pedestrian pilgrims' path, as marked by the yellow arrows, or to choose the roads and asphalted tracks parallel to them.

The advantage of using the asphalted road is that it is faster and more convenient; the disadvantage is that it must be shared with motorised traffic, with the risks and inconvenience which this poses.

The disadvantage of the dirt tracks is related to the impossible slopes and unworkable surfaces which are sometimes encountered; their advantage is that it is possible to quietly enjoy the landscapes along the "marked" route.

When making the choice, the cyclist pilgrim must be very aware of his or her physical possibilities and the qualities of the "mount". It is not advisable to venture into the tracks suggested by some stages on a bicycle with fragile mechanics or when carrying heavy weight.

Section 2: This includes a historic or cultural review, illustrated by many photographs, of all the towns and monuments along the Road to Santiago.

SOME KEYS TO THE MODERN PILGRIMAGE

The motives which lead hundreds of thousands of people to start on the great pilgrimage adventure in the Middle Ages were basically religious. Within the theocentric conception of the Universe, and full of the "contempt for the world" which reigned in those days, mediaeval pilgrims gave up the comfort and safety of their homes to set out on a journey full of fatigues and dangers, which even claimed some of their lives. The figure of the pilgrim who had willingly turned into a poor ascete is at the same time a heroic model of self-denial. For this reason, many institutions and people devoted themselves to alleviate the pilgrims' fatigues by offering protection, shelter, food and medical assistance.

The current road still retains much of such charitable institutions. In addition to the hospitality generated among the inhabitants of the towns along the Road, a network of semi-free or very cheap shelters exclusively for pilgrims (for one night only) have been created by institutions, associations and individuals.

The only essential requirement for a person to enjoy this hospitality is to prove that he or she is a pilgrim. This can be done by means of the pilgrim's passport or "credencial", or any other document which attests the pilgrimage. The "credencial" is a personal document: it includes the holder's personal data as well as a fold-out section for the stamps of all the places through which he or she has been, thus allowing the holder to prove that he or she is a pilgrim "en route". The accreditations can be obtained in many of the shelters on the Road to Santiago, as well as in episcopates and branches of Friends' Associations.

This is not, however, the credencial's sole aim. For many people, obtaining the "Compostela" once they have reached Santiago is as important, if not more, as enjoying the low cost hospitality. The Compostela is an old document issued by Santiago Cathedral municipal council. It is written in Latin and states that the recipient has made a *pietatis causa* pilgrimage to Santiago. Compostelas are currently given out in the Pilgrim Welcome Office (Oficina de Acogida del Peregrino), on no. 1, Rúa del Villar. They can only be given out if either 100 km on foot or horse or 200 km by bicycle have been covered *peregrinationis causa*.

GENERAL ADVICE

Starting out on a journey of several days either on foot or on bicycle does not require an extraordinary physical condition or any sophisticated materials. What it does require, however, is a certain level of preparation and some basic precautions, which can be summarised as follows:

> — Some previous training to measure your strength and gain some physical fitness. If you are not in good physical form, it is advisable to undergo a medical examination.

> — Use close-fitting, resilient, light, transpirable and waterproof shoewear. It is essential that the shoes are not worn for the first time when starting the journey, but that they are already sufficiently broken in. Socks are also important, since they can cause chafing marks or blisters if not worn properly.

> — The rest of the attire will vary according to the time of year in which the journey is undertaken. Sun lotion and a hat are essential in the summer, as are raincoats and warm clothing during the rainy seasons. It is always advisable to carry a waterproof cloak if carrying a non-waterproof rucksack.

> — The weight of the rucksack must be limited to the minimum essentials (sleeping bag, wash kit, several sets of clean clothes, washing soap, first aid kit), since excessive weight will certainly cause joint and muscle injuries.

— The first aid kit must contain everything necessary to treat blisters, sprains, chafing marks and burns; and alleviate the effects of tendonitis.

— Documentation: National Identity Card or passport and credentials.

Many of the recommendations for pilgrims on foot, in particular in relation to protection against the elements (such as the sun or rain), weight and essential luggage, also apply to cyclists. Cyclists must take care not only of themselves but also of their vehicle. This means that they will need some basic knowledge of mechanics, as well as suitable materials for any repairs that may be required.

And that's about it. We could fill several pages with a never-ending list of fatherly advice, typical of the "veteran" who knows everything there is to know and is offering his or her knowledge to the ignorant "newby". We understand that going on a pilgrimage is a rapidly acquired skill, and that taking in the non-written rules and the keys which govern the modern pilgrimages to Santiago is a none-too-difficult exercise in common sense. This guide only professes to make an introduction to that spectacular and massive world, so alive and varied, of the modern Road to Santiago, in a similar way to its old predecessors and most outstanding marks.

José María Anguita Jaén
ROAD TO SANTIAGO STUDY CENTRE (CENTRO DE ESTUDIOS
DEL CAMINO DE SANTIAGO). SAHAGÚN

The French Road

1 Saint-Jean-Pied-de-Port – Roncesvals

This stage, the first, could be viewed as the most difficult as it crosses the Pyrenees. The "Route de Napoleon" kicks off with a steep climb, passing by orchards and country houses and then, later on, through Alpine-style meadows, before weaving its way alongside leafy beech wood towards the border and the descent to Roncesvals. The Valcarlos route mainly sticks to the roadside, following the valley alongside the River Nive or the River Valcarlos.

Saint-Jean-Pied-de-Port. Church and river Neve.

From Rue de la Citadelle, the Camino goes down to cross the River Nive, going along the Rue d'Espagne and coming out of the city through the walls at the Port d'Espagne. From here you can either take the Napoleon Route or the Valcarlos Route, along the N-133.

A) If you chose the first option, veer to the left towards **Saint-Michel.** When you come to a fork in the road, follow the road-sign to the "Route de Napoleon et du Marechal Harispe". A little more than 5 km along the road, hidden amongst chestnut trees and the occasional oak, an asphalt track rises between meadows and country houses. After you pass through **Untto,** the last village before Roncesvals, the Camino follows the same road, (with one exception, where it veers off the track before joining it again further along). The track takes you through Alpine meadows surrounded by scrubland and bracken, and offers views of the hills and valleys covered in beech, conifer and oak trees. Fifteen kilometres in, the track goes off towards Organbide, but our grass trail continues on towards Bentartea. The route will take you through the Leizar Atheka valleys and, further on, alongside leafy beech woods and the border between France and Spain. Less than 1 kilometre away, beside the Roldán Fountain and on the border, a stone road marker proclaims: "Saint-Jacques de Compostelle - 765 km". After Bentartea, a paved road goes along the North face of Txangoa Mountain, passing by the ruins of Elizarra. Izandorre (on the Txangoa bluff), gives way to the

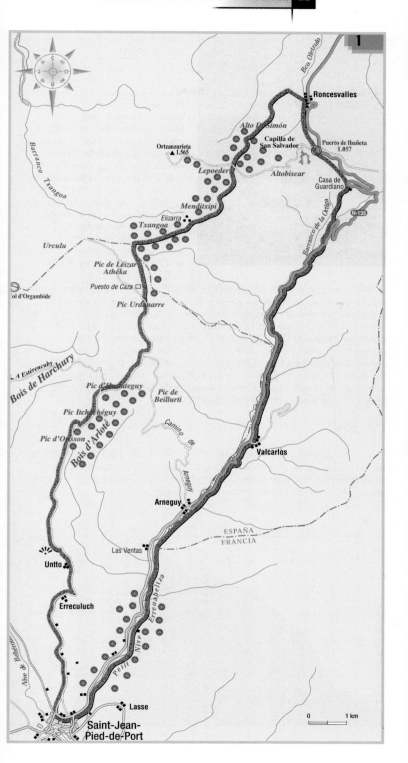

Stone of Roland on the mountain pass of Ibañeta.

eastern valleys of Aztobiskar. Once you pass by Lepoeder, you will cross a track that runs between Ibañeta and Ortzanzurieta, before facing 2 choices. On the one hand, you can take the **Ibañeta** route, which goes along a track to the port and then on to **Roncesvals.** Alternatively, you can take the so-called "old route", following the old Roman road through beech trees down a steep and dangerous hillside. Whichever route you chose, however, you will end up at the rear of the Collegiate Church.

B) Begin by coming out on the N-133 road. Cross the "Petite Nive", and follow its course to **Arneguy,** passing through a shady valley densely populated by typical riverside tree species, (ash, alder, willow, etc.). The Spanish border appears in **Las Ventas,** just before Arneguy. From here, continue alongside the road, going through **Valcarlos** and passing by numerous country houses. Follow the route up through oak and beech woods towards the Ortiga cliff, where you will leave the road to follow the Zabaleta route to Ibañeta. Once in **Ibañeta,** you will go through a beech wood down a path towards **Roncesvals,** where you will meet up with the "old Route" by the collegiate church.

CYCLISTS

Due to the steep inclines involved, it is recommended that cyclists go on the Valcarlos route, along the roadway. The other route takes an asphalt road almost all the way to the Spanish border, but then veers off into the grass, where the downhill sections are very dangerous.

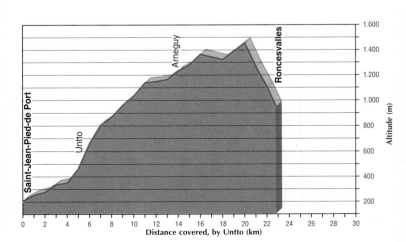

STAGE 1. PRACTICAL INFORMATION

SAINT-JEAN-PIED-DE-PORT

HOSTELS

Municipal shelter.
Rue de la Citadelle, 55. Next to "Porte de Saint-Jacques". It has 55 beds, a kitchen, washing machine and dryer. Pilgrims are taken in, at no. 39 of the same street, next to the "des evêques" prison, by the "Amis du Chemin de Saint-Jacques. Pyrénées Atlantiques" association.

Huntto hostel.

Saint Jean Pied de Port hostel.

MEANS OF TRANSPORT

There are two ways to get from Spain to Saint-Jean-pied-de-Port: buses leave from Pamplona (La Montañesa company, ✆ 948 221 584) to Roncesvals, where there is a taxi service. Trains leave Irún-Hendaya towards Bayone daily, and from there to Saint-Jean-pied-de-Port at various times.

SERVICES

It has all kinds of services: shops, restaurants, accommodation, tourism office, chemists, banks, etc.

VALCARLOS

HOTELS

HS** Casa Marcelino.
Calle Elizaldea, 1. ✆ 948 790 186.
18 rooms. 36 beds.
Double room: € 40; breakfast: € 3;
lunch/dinner: € 9,7.

H* Maitena.
Calle Elizaldea, 1. ✆ 948 790 210.
8 rooms. 16 beds. Double room:
€ 43/39; single room: € 37/36;
breakfast: € 3,5; lunch/dinner: € 12.

P* Andiko Berri.
Barrio Azoleta. ✆ 948 790 137.
4 rooms. 8 beds. Double room: € 23;
breakfast: € 2,4.

RESTAURANTS

Iñaki.
Calle Elizaldea. ✆ 948 790 001.
34 beds. € 6 / € 12.

Xaindu.
Barrio Pekotxea. ✆ 948 790 200.
Closed from 30/8 to 1/6 and on Thursdays.
International cuisine. Seats 45.
€ 12 / € 24.

RONCESVALS

HOSTELS

Roncesvals Pilgrim shelter (Refugio de peregrinos de Roncesvalles). The royal collegiate church chapter shelters pilgrims all year round. It has 100 beds. Bicycles are allowed. ✆ 948 760 000

Roncesvals Youth Hostel (Albergue juvenil de Roncesvalles).
✆ 948 760 302

HOTELS

HS* La Posada.
Collegiate Church of Roncesvals.
✆ 948 760 225. 18 rooms.
Double room: € 45/39;
single room: € 36/32;
lunch/dinner: € 10,94.

HS Casa Sabina.
Carretera Pamplona-Francia, km 48.
✆ 948 760 012 / 948 790 438.
5 rooms. Double room: € 37/31;
breakfast: € 3,01; lunch/dinner: € 9,02.

HISTORY AND WEALTH OF THE STAGE **1**

THE FRENCH ROAD. SAINT-JEAN-PIED-DE-PORT – RONCESVALS

Saint-Jean-Pied-de-Port is the starting point of our journey along the Spanish part of the Road to Santiago. If *Liber peregrinationis* (the fifth book of *Liber Sancti Iacobi),* the guide used by XIIth century pilgrims and which we will follow almost word for word, is to be believed, pilgrims from three out of the four French pilgrim routes of St James had already met up in Ostabat *(Hostavalla)* on previous occasions before reaching Saint-Jean. A large flow of pilgrims formed a thick network of

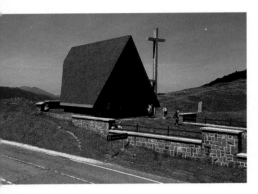

smaller roads which spread out across Europe and further, and then converged into these three routes which crossed the whole of France. According to *Liber peregrinationis,* these routes were:

– *Via Turonensis:* so called because it came from Tours and reached Ostabat via Poitiers, Saintes and Bordeaux. It was followed by pilgrims from Paris and Orléans, as well as by some Northern European ones who had entered France via the "Niederstrasse" or "low route", so called because it crossed the lower part of the Rhine Basin.

– *Via Lemovicensis:* its name derives from *Lemovicum,* the Celtic-Latin name which developed into Limoges, one of the cities through which this great route went and whose great meeting and departure point was the Abbey of Sainte-Madeleine-de-Vézelay. It then crossed France diagonally (from north-east to south-west) via Bourges,

Mountain pass of Ibañeta. Above, a chapel; below, crosses left by the pilgrims.

Vézelay, Perigueux, Bergerac and Agen. This route was followed by many Flemish and German pilgrims, as well as by more Eastern people.
-– *Via Podensis:* so called because it went through Nôtre-Dame-du-Puy. The French word "puy" and the Spanish "poyo" (meaning a stone bench or ledge) come from the Latin word *podium.* This explains why the adjective "podensis" was used for this route which went through Aurillac, Conques, Cahors and Moissac. This was followed mostly by travellers from Lyon and Grenoble, as well by a good number of Swiss, Austrian and Southern German pilgrims from the *Oberstrasse* or "high route" who had chosen this route over the more popular and southern *Via Tolosana.*

In spite of its long history as a meeting point for these three pilgrim "motorways", there are almost no remains left to indicate this privilege. This is also true for Saint-Michel-Pied-de-Port where, according to *Liber peregrinationis,* the starting point of the thirteen stages, approximately five kilometers from **Saint-Jean-Pied-de-Port,** was to be found. Both Saint-Michel and Saint-Jean are mentioned in *Liber peregrinationis* in the not too pleasant context of an anti-Basque tirade, condemning the unfair tolls and general bad treatment suffered by the pilgrims who went through this area. The book even goes as far as demanding that the King of Aragon, lord of that area at the time (1130-1134) be excommunicated as the person with ultimate responsibility.

Pilgrims' Cross in Roncesvals.

It wasn't until later that Saint-Jean-Pied-de-Port gained importance as the capital of Low Navarre and, later of the District of Ultrapuertos. The traces of the time when this city, which is still surrounded by its walls, was created, can still be seen in its rationalistic-style planning typical of those towns of the Road to Santiago and the Kingdom of Aragon which were either born or transformed in the late Middle Ages. Its high street, a genuine Pilgrim Road, runs from Puerta de Santiago in the North to Puerta de España in the South, dividing the city into symmetrical quadrangles. Saint-Jean most important monuments - the XIIIth century Gothic prison of the Bishops (prisión de los Obispos), the church of Nuestra Señora del Puente (Ama zubi buruko) and the arch of Saint-Jean which looks onto the Pont-de-Espagne over the river Nive - can be found in this straight axis.

Puerta de España is where the pilgrims first reached the Pyrenees. The most common route in the Middle Ages was the one we now know as "Route du Maréchal Harispe" or "de Napoleón", which more or less retraced the old *Via Traiana* between Bordeaux and Astorga. The *Itinerarium Antonini,* a sort of Roman Empire route map, mentiones two "mansiones" (stops) in this area: *Imus Pyrineus* and *Summus Pyrineus,* the highest and lowest points of the Pyrenean pass. The first one is usually associated with Saint-Jean-le-Vieux, whereas the second is believed to be located around the mountain passes of Aztobizkar or Lepoeder, although no archeological remains have been found to confirm this. Two hospitals, in this case supported by evidence, have been found between these two points, in **Untto** and **Erreculuch,** although they were built in later periods, as was the priory of **Orisson,** which depended on Roncesvals.

It is conjecturally - albeit reasonably - assumed that the *Summus Pyrineus* "mansio" was located at the top of the hill. The *Portus Cisere* mentioned in *Liber Peregrinationis* has also been conjecturally placed here, as has the now lost *Crux Karoli,* the first praying place of the Spanish Way and one of the monuments used to try to associate the

Collegiate Church of Roncesvals.

worship of St James with that of Charlemagne. According to *Liber peregrinationis,* after reaching that height with his army, Charlemagne drove a cross into the ground and, facing the grave of the apostle St James, entrusted himself to him. As much as a thousand crosses, stuck in the ground by as many pilgrims repeating the Emperor's gesture, could still be seen centuries later at that same spot.

On the opposite slope, a chapel and a monument in **Ibañeta** commemorate the old Benedictine monastery of San Salvador, which is older but definitely not a predecessor of Roncesvals. This is where the old (Roman and Mediaeval) route meets the one which follows the course of the river Petit Nive and whose journey includes another place whose name, **Valcarlos,** provides evidence of the worship of Charlemagne in this area. According to *Liber peregrinationis,* the Emperor was camping here when he heard about the tragedy suffered by the rearguard of his army. "Luzaide", the Basque name for this town, can be translated as "dark way" and seems to conjure up the narrow mountain passes in which, according to the *Chanson of Roland* (Song of Roland) and the *Annals* (Anales) of the time of Charlemagne, the French warriors were surprised. The parish of Valcarlos is dedicated to the apostle St James, and used to contain a pilgrims" hospital which depended on Roncesvals.

As we have seen throughout this stage, the long shadow of **Roncesvals** extends over this frontier spot. The hospital, protected by a community of Regular Canons of St Augustine, was founded in 1127 by the Bishop of Pamplona, Sancho Larrosa, and King Alfonso I of Aragon. Thanks to donations from all over Europe, it soon acquired, in addition to the fame it already had, a large amount of wealth, which allowed it to dominate the whole area with a large number of properties, and priories and hospitals which depended on it. The fame of the name "Roncesvalles" (Spanish for Roncesvals) which was, according to epic literature from Charlemagne's time, the setting for the defeat of Charlemagne's army and Roland's death (among other heroic couples), predates the collegiate church-hospital. In spite of this – or maybe it was even created for this purpose – the church successfully exploited the "trademark" and gave it a new dimension. Roncesvals is indeed the perfect synthesis between pilgrimage and epic, the bond which effectively links the worship of St James with that of Charlemagne. The pilgrims had in Roncesvals a sanctuary full of milestones and objects relating to Charlemagne and Roland, where they could – more or less surreptitiously – worship these

French epic heroes. Both *Pseudo-Turpin* (the fourth part of *Liber Sancti Iacobi*) and *Liber peregrinationis* carefully describe and accurately locate, among other things, the above mentioned Cross of Charlemange (Crux Karoli), the flat area where the great battle between Christians and Muslims took place, the large stone which Roland split with his sword Durendal, the punishment of Ganelon, and Valcarlos. That is, they create a perfectly adequate tourist guide of Roncesvals, which has made some people believe that there was an effective link between these books and the collegiate church. In fact, it was precisely this perfect synthesis of pilgrimage and epic, St James and Charlemagne which can be found in Roncesvals, that *Pseudo-Turpin* was aiming to achieve. The most noteworthy building from the royal collegiate church collection of buildings is the church itself, ordered to be built in the XIIIth century by Sancho VII *the Strong,* and its interior is dominated by a

Roncesvals. Museum and library façade.

beautiful Gothic-style sitting statue of the Virgin. A magnificent mausoleum is annexed to the church and protects the remains of the gigantic Sancho VII and his wife Clemencia. On one of the sides you can see the chains of the Almohad Caliph's tent, which the King of Navarre (one of three victorious Spanish kings over the Almohad power at Las Navas de Tolosa (1212)) ordered to be brought, and which became the heraldic motif of the small Kingdom of Navarre. Other points of interest inside the collection of buildings are the XIVth century cloister, the little chapel of Santiago dating from the same time, and the Sancti Spiritus chapel, which became an ossuary for many of the pilgrims who died in the hospital. In addition, the collegiate church museum houses some very valuable pieces such as Charlemagne's famous chess set.

Roncesvals. Santiago and Sancti Spiritus Chapels or "Charlemagne´s Silo (Silo de Carlomagno)".

2 Roncesvals – Larrasoaña

The Camino crosses two mountain passes through beech and oak woods and meadows, meeting up with the N-135 motorway on several occasions. Running alongside this part of the pilgrimage is the River Arga, its course continuing all the way to Larrasoaña.

Panoramic view of Espinal.

Upon leaving **Roncesvals,** a track on the right-hand side of the N-135 motorway heads off towards **Burguete,** passing through a wooded area containing, amongst others, beech, oak, maple, hazel and holly trees. Two kilometres into the track the trees give way to head towards some farm buildings, and the track turns left to join the road before arriving at Burguete. Once arriving in the village, you will carry on as far as the BSCH bank, before the route turns to the right and leaves the area. After crossing a ravine over the River Urrobi, you will follow an asphalt track through animal barns, passing a series of gates, streams, cultivated fields, beech woods and meadows. The track finally ends up in **Espinal** (6.5 km), in the Santiago quarter of the town. After passing a fountain, you will leave the town to the left to begin your climb towards Alto de Mezquíriz, going through meadows, coniferous forests and beech woods. The route then veers to the right and descends to cross the road, at the Trail of the Virgin of Roncesvals, before continuing downwards through the beech wood. At a curve about 8 kms later, it meets up with the road again, before going into a highly vegetated area. At the crossroads, you will re-join the N-135, before taking a path which goes into **Viscarret** in the Erro Valley. From here, a paved pathway goes up towards the graveyard, turning into a path that goes off between oak, maple and beech trees towards the N-135. After crossing the road, this time on the right-hand side, you come to **Linzoáin** (almost 19 km away). Leaving the town, you will go up a rocky incline, populated by boxwood, juniper and hawthorn, passing through more woodland before arriving at the Erro. A little past the "Pasos de Roldán" flagstones, you will cross the pathway, passing by Venta del Puerto on your way down to the Esteríbar Valley. Just 1 km further ahead, you will be able to

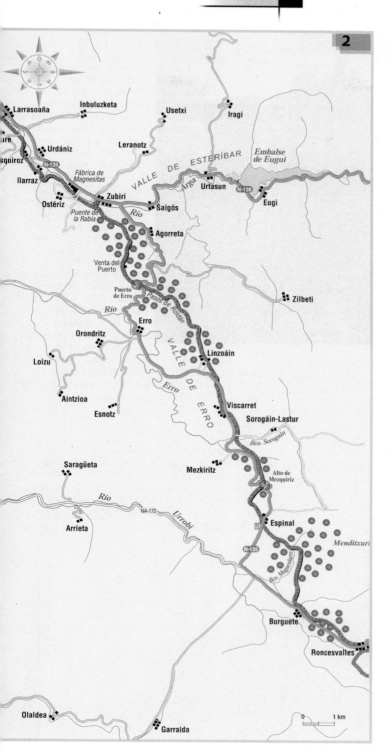

Zubiri. View of the river Arga from the mediaeval bridge.

see Zubiri. Leaving behind the thicket, 500 meters ahead, in **Zubiri,** you will come to the Puente de la Rabia bridge which spans the river Arga. The Camino does not cross the bridge, however. Instead, it goes up a street, then passing through oaks and shrubs alongside the meadows. Then, take a path which leads towards a factory, which eventually joins up with the Osteriz road. From here, a path runs parallel, eventually giving way to a series of steps, (23.6 km into the path), before crossing a watercourse. The ascent continues through a flagged path under the shade of oak, walnut, hazel and maple trees, before arriving at **Illaraz.** The road then descends to **Esquiroz,** where another path leads off through the trees. After passing by an animal feed factory and crossing the road, follow the path which crosses a bridge over the river Arga before coming into **Larrasoaña.**

CYCLISTS

Up to your arrival at Espinal, you will have little or no difficulty following the route. However, the ground gets very uneven from this point onwards, as two mountain passes have to be crossed. This can cause dangerous descents and paths that are not very suitable for cyclists. In this case, the N-135 is the best option.

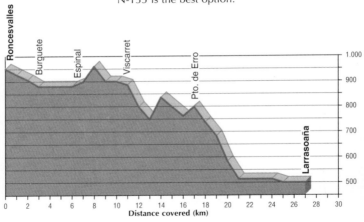

STAGE 2. PRACTICAL INFORMATION

BURGUETE

HOTELS

HS**Burguete. C/ San Nicolás, 71.
⌀ 948 790 488. Closed from 10/12 to
1/4. 20 beds. From 1/8 to 31/8 and
Easter Week: € 48,9 (double room); rest
of the year: € 39,9 (double room).
HS* Juandeaburre. Calle San Nicolás.
⌀ 948 760 078. Open from 1/5 to
31/10. 4 beds. € 25 (double room).

RESTAURANTS

Asador Aritza. C/ Kanaeleburua, 6.
⌀ 948 760 311. Home-made and
regional cuisine. Seats 42. € 12 / € 24.
Garage. Avenida Roncesvalles, 35.
⌀ 948 760 002. Home-made and
regional cuisine. Seats 30. € 12 / € 24.
Txikipolit. Avenida Roncesvalles, 42.
⌀ 948 760 019. Regional cuisine.
Seats 40. € 12 / € 24.

MEANS OF TRANSPORT

The Roncesvals-Pamplona line stops in
all towns included in this stage. La
Montañesa company, ⌀ 948 221 584

ERRO

HOSTELS

Casa Pablo Sorogain. ⌀ 948 768 095

HOTELS

HS** Erro. Carretera N-135, km 30.
⌀ 948 768 120. 4 beds. From 1/6 to
15/9: € 45; rest of the year: € 39
(double room).

RESTAURANTS

Casa Rafael. Ctra. Francia. ⌀ 948 768
002. Closed on winter Tuesdays. Seats 32.

ESPINAL

CAMPING SITES

2.nd C Cámping Urrobi. Carretera N-135
Pamplona-Valcarlos, km 42.
⌀ 948 760 200 / 696 463 609.
www.campingurrobi.com.
Open from 1/4 to 1/11. 400 places.

RESTAURANTS

Ederrena. Calle San Bartolomé, 29.
⌀ 948 760 121. Seats 28.

ZUBIRI

HOSTELS

Pilgrims' Hostel (Albergue de
peregrinos). ⌀ 948 304 262 /
948 304 114.

HOTELS

HS** Hostería de Zubiri.
Avenida Roncesvalles, 6.
⌀ 948 304 329. 10 rooms.
20 beds. Double room: € 65/62/59;
dinner: € 16,5.
P* Goikoa. Avenida Roncesvalles, 8-4°.
⌀ 948 304 067. 4 rooms. 8 beds.
Double room: € 28/24; single room:
€ 24/21; breakfast: € 3; dinner: € 9,5.

RESTAURANTS

Bar Gau Txori. Ctra. Francia. Crossroads
between N-135 Zubiri-Erro and NA-137
Zubiri-Urtasun. ⌀ 948 304 076. Open
12-17 h and 20-23 h. Seats 80. Excellent
Navarrese cuisine. 3 dining rooms.
Betargi. Avenida Roncesvalles.
⌀ 948 304 450. Seats 50.

LARRASOAÑA

HOSTELS

Located in the Town Council building, to
which it belongs. It has a kitchen. Good
facilities. 53 beds.
⌀ 948 304 242 / 616 972 455

HOTELS

P* El Camino. Calle San Nicolás, 100.
⌀ 948 304 288. 2 beds.
€ 32 (double room).

RESTAURANTS

Café-Bar Larrasoaña. Calle San
Nicolás, 16. ⌀ 948 304 250. Closed on
winter Tuesdays and in December. Home-
made and Navarrese cuisine. Seats 14.
€ 6 / € 12.

HISTORY AND WEALTH OF THE STAGE 2

Pilgrims entering Burguete.

THE FRENCH ROAD. RONCESVALS – LARRASOAÑA

Near the end of Roncesvals' collegiate church grounds there stands, at the edge of the road, a Gothic stone cross with a Calvary. The pedestal, finished with a Renaissance capital, holds a slender cross of St James generally known as "Pilgrims' Cross" ("Cruz de los Peregrinos"), and reported by local documents, which refer to it as "Old Cross" ("Cruz Vieja"), to have been moved to its current location in 1880.

The town currently known as **Burguete** (Auritz) is the old *Villa Runcievallis* mentioned in *Liber peregrinationis,* that is, the town (or Burg) of Roncesvals. Local and universal tradition set the "literary" battle of Roncesvals on the large high plateau where the city is situated, and which also covers the collegiate church and the town of Espinal. Its quadrilateral shape – bordered on by Alto de Ibañeta in the north, and Alto de Espinal and Alto de Mezquíriz in the south) – makes it the perfect meeting place for a direct and "sportsmanlike" confrontation of large armies of French and Saracen knights. This epic vision of the battle, however, bears little resemblance to the actual skirmish of 778, when the Pamplonese Basques, stationed behind the hills of the Pyrenees (Aztobizkar and Lepoeder) or in the narrow mountain passes of Valcarlos, surprised the French rearguard with their agility and knowledge of the terrain. The idealised epic version of the facts, however, was the only one accepted by thousands of people who only knew about them through the *Chanson de Roland* (Song of Roland). In this work, the historic Navarrese enemies were replaced by Saracens, fought against by the French with the noble aim of returning Spain to Christiandom. It was in this XIIth century epic/literary context that *Pseudo-Turpin* was created. This work adapts the episodes of the *Chanson de Roland* to the real geography of Roncesvals, turning each setting into a "tourist" place that the thousands of pilgrims to Santiago who can always be found around the pass can visit and remember. Thus, according to *Pseudo-Turpin,* in the great plain of Burguete, the French rearguard (composed of 20,000 men lead by Roland and Oliver) succumbs to the superiority of King Marsile of Saragossa's 50,000 Saracens. *Pseudo-Turpin* differs from other epic works in that it presents Roland and the other French heroes as martyrs for the Christian faith, dead in the crusade against Islam. The idea was to enable pilgrims visiting the hospital and Pyrenean sanctuary (which is actually dedicated to the Virgin) on their way to "legitimately" worship the relics and objects relating to their literary heroes fallen in Roncesvals, as if they were real martyrs for the faith. The tone used to describe the Passion of Roland's faithful companion Oliver, for example, is as gruesome as any martyrology or text of a Passion, which commemorated the passions of Paleochristian or early mediaeval martyrs:

> *"Oliver, who was already in a better place, was found lying on the floor, spread out in the shape of a cross, stretched by four strong ropes tying him to four sticks on the floor, skinned, from the neck to the nails on his hands and feet, with very sharp knives, his body roughly beaten and bruised and pierced with arrows, darts, spears and swords."*

After killing King Marsile of Saragossa to avenge the deaths and tortures of his 20,000 fellow warriors, a badly injured and exhausted Roland left the battle plain and headed up towards Ibañeta. And here it was, on the grounds of the collegiate church, that Roland hit a large stone with his sword Durendal, thereby shattering it, and then blew his oliphant with the full force of his lungs, causing both this and the veins on his neck to burst. He died of exhaustion soon thereafter. According to *Liber peregrinationis,* which was written by the same person as *Pseudo-Turpin,* a church was being erected at that time (c. 1130) on the great stone which Roland had split into three. This implicitly meant that it was consecrated to Roland or, at least, that when pilgrims went into it, they would be at the exact same spot of Roland's Passion where, in addition, the traitor Ganelon had been punished. In this sense, *Pseudo-Turpin* can be said to be the best publicist that Roncesvals has ever had, and its link with the collegiate church is beyond doubt, although this does not necessarily mean that its author was a canon of the church.

The name "Roncesvalles" itself seems to be the work of French jesters, possibly developed from the Basque name (of which we have no evidence), *Errozabal,* given to the plain in which the battle took place. The name can be translated as "plain of Erro", which would cover the county of Erro, whose boundaries matched those of this valley almost exactly. According to this theory, this was later distorted by French poets and jesters into *"Roncesvalles"*, "Valley of Thorns", with the aim of finding an "explicit" name full of negative implications, as befits the ill-fated place where Charlemagne's best knights, together with large numbers of Christian soldiers, met their deaths. The name **Espinal** (Auritzberri), the next town on the Road and still on the same plain, may be a Castilian version of the literary name Roncesvalles (the Spanish word "espino" means "thorn"). It was founded relatively late (1269) by

King Theobald II of Navarre personally, and is commemorated by a modern bust.

Viscarret, a town which still exists on the back (as suggested by its etymology – "bizcar" in Basque means "back") of Alto de Espinal, used to be a Stop on the Road, and is referred to in chapter II of *Liber peregrinationis,* under the names of *Biscaretus* y *Biscarellus,* as drawing to a close the first of the thirteen Spanish stages. However, no other documents or architectural remains have been found to confirm this status. Its Romanesque-style parish church of San Pedro was built in the XIIIth century.

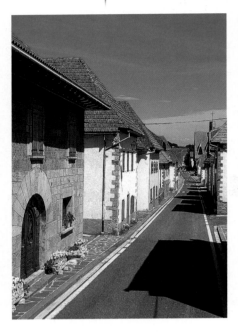

Espinal. Road and path for pilgrims.

The first clue to the importance of Tolosan presence in Navarre we find in our journey is the fact that the parish church of **Linzoáin** takes its name from St Saturnine. This Romanesque church, dedicated to the first bishop of Tolosa, dates from the XIIIth century.

Once you reach **Puerto de Erro** you find a large slab known as "Roland's Step" ("Paso de Roldán") which, according to folk tradition, represents the length of the French hero's step. We may find in this, for the first time in our journey, Roland's Basque counterpart, Errolán, a megalith-throwing giant and enemy of the Basque people. This may be a case of the real battle of Roncesvals surviving in popular Basque memory, having withstood the epic version created by French jesters and been spread from the collegiate church into this area. This Basque reflection of the Carolingian period will become clearer in later stages, especially when we reach the ledge of Roldán ("el Poyo de Roldán") in Nájera.

The modern "Venta del Puerto o del Caminante", an inn for pilgrims and passers-by, can be found further on in the same pass.

Most historic references to **Zubiri** mention its bridge. This suggests that the relatively late founding of this town (which is not mentioned in *Liber peregrinationis*) may be related to the great Gothic bridge over the River Arga. The name itself means "bridge town" in Basque. Arnold von Harff, a XVth century German adventurer, calls this town "Bridge of Paradise". Although the reason for this designation is unknown, it may related to the local tradition of forcing all beasts from the surrounding municipalities to cross it in order to overcome their hydrophobia. When this rite was Christianised, the bridge's power was attributed to the presence of a relic of St Quiteria, Gascon virgin and martyr, whose

Pilgrims on the bridge entering Zubiri.

worship in Zubiri may also have originated in Tolosa, where she was particularly worshipped.

Larrasoaña's long standing status as an important place is evidenced, in contrast with Zubiri, by a mention as a Stop on the Road *(Ressogna)* in *Liber peregrinationis*. Documentary references to its monastery of San Agustín, however, which depended on Leire in the early Middle Ages, are even older. We do not know whether that monastery's hospital, which existed at the time of *Liber peregrinationis* (1130), has anything to do with the building known as "cillería de Roncesvalles", a hospital which depended on the collegiate church since the XIIIth century and which continued in working order well into modern times. The existence of two brotherhoods, documented in the XVIIIth century and dedicated to St Blaise and St James and, through them, to the care of the pilgrims, provide evidence of continuing hospitality to pilgrims in Larrasoaña in contemporary times. Two chapels, each dedicated to one of these saints, are the living remains of this historic past. In addition, the great XIVth century bridge known as "puente de los Bandidos" (bridge of the bandits), the straight-line town planning and the fact that the parish church is dedicated to St Nicholas of Bari are due, to some extent, to the relationship between Larrasoaña and the Road to Santiago.

Larrasoaña. Bridge over the river Arga.

3 Larrasoaña – Pamplona

The Camino runs alongside the river Arga valley, at the foot of a group of hills covered in beech, oak and Scots pine, while the N-135 runs parallel to the river. As we approach Pamplona, the landscape becomes more obviously influenced by mankind, with its conifer reforestation and farmlands. Upon arriving at Villava, we once again rejoin civilisation.

La Trinidad de Arre and bridge over the river Ulzama next to Villava.

After crossing the bridge over the Arga which brought us to **Larrasoaña** in the last stage, we climb a winding path for 1 km, until we reach **Aquerreta.** From here, we descend once again, following a path through maple, walnut, boxwood, pine, and other types of trees. After passing the regional motorway, go through a pine grove and beech wood, both situated at the foot of Mount Maliturri, before descending once again to the river Arga. Passing through the riverside woods you will arrive at **Zuriáin,** where you will cross the river to meet up again with the N-135. 500 metres along, you will come to the turn-off for Ilurdoz. Following this road along the left-hand side of the river, you will pass by a few houses, (from where you can see an old quarry in the distance), and go by another pine grove, before joining up again with the Arga as it runs alongside cultivated land. After passing **Iroz,** you will cross the Arga yet again, (this time on the right-hand side), before carrying on for 7 km between the road and the river, finally arriving at **Zabaldica.** From here, take a path alongside the road until you reach a picnic spot, where you can cross the road. Then, follow a pathway which goes up the side of Mount Narval, (populated by boxwood and re-planted conifers), until you can see the Santa Marina hermitage in **Arleta.** After leaving Arleta, you will pass through oaks and maple trees, and will be able to see the old town of Burrín, a village which disappeared in the 14th Century. Just under 10 km further along, you will go downhill again to go through a tunnel, before continuing on between the road and Mount Miravalles, which is also planted with conifers. A little over 500 metres away, the

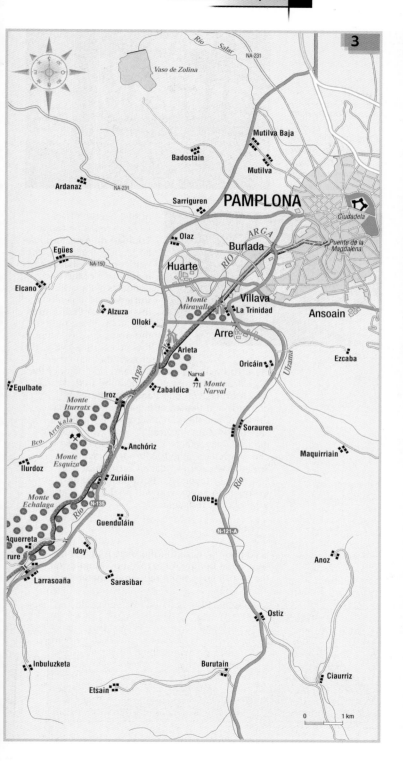

On the right, panoramic view of Pamplona from Cizur Menor. Below, pilgrims in Pamplona's high street (Calle Mayor).

bridge over the river Ulzama leads on to the **Trinidad de Arre** Basilica and, a few feet away, you will come to **Villava.** The main street of the town connects Villava to **Burlada,** and it is along this road that the Camino now goes. Head right at the Amor de Dios school, towards a tunnel which crosses the main road. Here you will see the right-hand side bank of the Arga, from where you will take the Burlada road which brings you into **Pamplona,** through orchards and houses and via the Magdalena Bridge. Once there, having gone through the "Puerta de Zumalacárregui", you will go along the following streets: Carmen, (from where you can reach the Cathedral through Navarrería Street); Mercaderes; Plaza Consistorial; San Saturnino; Mayor; and Bosquecillo. After Bosquecillo Street, you will finally arrive at the Citadel, (la Ciudadela).

CYCLISTS

If you do not wish to follow the rough and somewhat bumpy route taken by pilgrims on foot, the N-135 goes along the same itinerary.

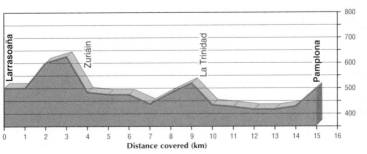

Distance covered (km)

Altitude (m)

STAGE 3. PRACTICAL INFORMATION

ZURIÁIN

MEANS OF TRANSPORT

The Roncesvalles-Pamplona bus line run by La Montañesa company stops in Zuriáin, Zabaldica, Villava and Burlada. The city bus goes all the way to Villava.

TRINIDAD DE ARRE

HOSTELS

The Marist brothers also take in pilgrims in a comfortable hostel with room for 34 people (including cyclists) in Arre basilica. It has a kitchen and washing machine.
∅ 948 394 378 / 948 332 941

VILLAVA

SERVICES

There are almost no services until Villava, where an urban area begins.

BURLADA

HOTELS

H** Tryp Burlada. Calle La Fuente, 2.
∅ 948 131 300. 53 rooms. 106 beds. Double room: € 127/67; breakfast: € 4; lunch/dinner: € 12,62.
HS** Casa Jacinto. Mugazuri Industrial Development (Polígono Industrial Mugazuri). ∅ 948 143 200. 22 rooms. 44 beds. Double room: € 112/47.

RESTAURANTS

Casa Jacinto. Mugazuri Development (Polígono Mugazuri). ∅ 948 143 290

PAMPLONA

HOSTELS

In San Saturnino parish church, on calle Ansoleaga. 20 beds and a kitchen. Run by the Navarre Road to Santiago Friends Association (Asociación de Amigos del Camino de Santiago en Navarra). Open from Easter Week to October. In June and July they adapt a school's sports ground, on Calle Fuente del Hierro, to make place for 100 beds.
∅ 620 573 074

HOTELS

HR** Eslava. Plaza Virgen de la O, 7.
∅ 948 222 270. 28 rooms. Double room: € 112/56; single room: € 61/33 breakfast: € 5.
P** Casa García. C/ San Gregorio, 12.
∅ 948 223 893. 9 rooms. Double room: € 26; breakfast: € 2; lunch/dinner: € 8.
P** Otano. Calle San Nicolás, 5.
∅ 948 227 036. Double room: € 70/45; breakfast: € 2,4; lunch/dinner: € 13.
HS** Abodi. Calle Sancho Ramírez, 15. 1° E. ∅ 948 272 975. 9 rooms. Double room: € 94/47; single room: € 76/38.
HS* Bearán. Calle San Nicolás, 25.
∅ 948 223 428. Double room: € 102/42/36; single room: € 96/37/30.
HS** Mesón del Barro-3. Calle Sancho Ramírez, 13-5°C. ∅ 948 256 366. Double room: € 105/45; single room: € 85.
HS** Navarra. Calle Tudela, 9.
∅ 948 225 164. 14 rooms. Double room: € 120/46; single room: € 75/37; breakfast: € 7.

RESTAURANTS

Acella. Travesía de Acella, 2.
∅ 948 265 460
Alsafir. Calle Castillo de Maya, 39.
∅ 948 243 193
Arangoiti. Travesía de Acella, 2.
∅ 948 271 969
Asador Olaverri. Calle Santa Marta, 4.
∅ 948 235 063
Asador Uslaer. Calle Tomás Burgui, 15.
∅ 948 122 106
Azparren. Avenida Zaragoza, 105.
∅ 948 151 743
Baserri. San Nicolás, 32. ∅ 948 222 021

MEANS OF TRANSPORT

Bus station. Calle Olivetos, s/n.
∅ 948 223 854
RENFE rail station. Avenida San Jorge, s/n. ∅ 948 130 202.
Noáin airport. ∅ 948 168 700

SERVICES

Tourism Office. C/ Duque de Ahumada, 3. ∅ 948 220 741

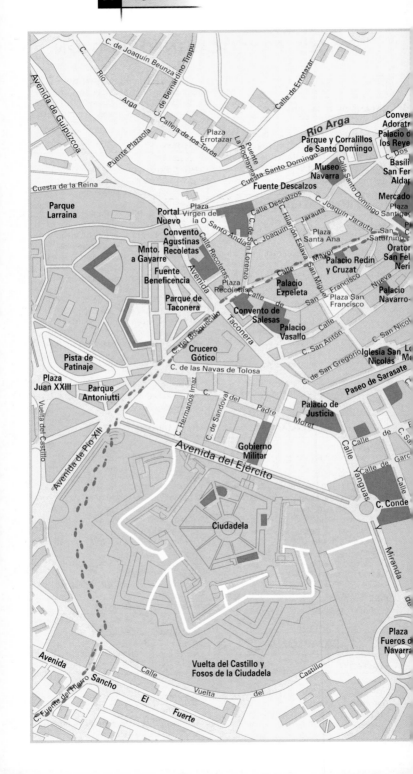

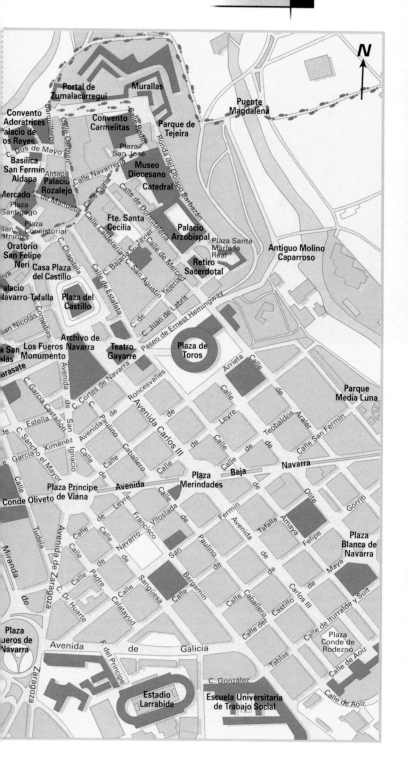

HISTORY AND WEALTH OF THE STAGE 3

Pamplona. View of the river Arga and city walls.

THE FRENCH ROAD. LARRASOAÑA – PAMPLONA

During most of the first part of this stage, the Road to Santiago runs next to the river Arga, through several small towns in the Esteríbar valley: **Zuriáin,** whose small mediaeval church, located in the high part of the town, is dedicated to the Castilian patron San Millán; **Iroz,** with its modern-time parish church of San Pedro; **Zabaldica,** with its Romanesque church dedicated to St Stephen, and the tiny house of Arleta, comprised solely of the majestic Palace of the Lords ("Palacio del Señorío") and the church of Santa Marina, which houses a Gothic sculpture of this saint.

However, as we have already mentioned, the main figure in the first part of this stage is the **river Arga,** which meets several mediaeval bridges on its way. It is when talking about this river in the chapter devoted to currents of water in the Road, that the author of **Liber Peregrinationis** makes the most serious geographical errors of the book, no doubt disoriented by the complicated Navarrese orography. First, labouring under the impression that the river and the Road have gone hand in hand all the way down the Pyrenees, he gets the Arga, Urrobi and Erro rivers, which he has come across on the way until now, mixed up. He then states that Pamplona has two rivers, the Arga and the *Runa,* when the two names in fact refer to one single river. The second name, *Runa,* has been found in many documents from that time, and is the name given, probably through the distortion of the city's Basque name, Iruña, by the mediaeval "Erdaldun" Pamplonese, that is, those who descended from the French. This is undoubtedly where it was taken from by the author of *Liber Peregrinationis.*

Before entering Pamplona, the Road parts company with the river Arga and meets the river Ulzama, a little tributary of the Arga, which can be crossed by means of a six-span Romanesque bridge leading directly to the famous **Trinidad de Arre basilica,** pilgrim assistance point since at least the XIIIth century, and later also to a hospital which depended on the all-powerful collegiate church of Roncesvals. In Arre, not far from here, the Knights of St John, a very important military order in the Navarrese and Riojan parts of the Road to Santiago, owned some properties.

The name of **Villava** (*Villa Nova*) is now famous as the hometown of great Spanish cyclist Miguel Indurain. The town's Basque name, "Atarrabia", should also be famous as the surname of one of the most distinguished Spanish mediaeval philosophers, Franciscan Pedro de Atarrabia (1275-1342), *Doctor fundatus,* teacher of theology in Paris and defender of his teacher Duns Scoto's gnoseologic theory in open

Romanesque bridge of La Magdalena over the river Arga.

disagreement with other great Franciscan teachers of the time, Pedro Auriol and William of Occam.

After crossing **Burlada,** the Road meets the Arga once again and crosses it via the Romanesque bridge of la Magdalena. The fact that the bridge is dedicated to this saint points to the existence of a pilgrim assistance institution in the area. At the bridge entrance, a stone cross with a stone sculpture of St James on its pedestal meets the pilgrims on their way to Pamplona, the first of the great historic capitals in the Spanish part of the Road to Santiago.

Pamplona is in all certainty the same place as *Pompaelo* or *Pompeiopolis,* mentioned by ancient geographers Ptolomaeus and Strabo and founded by Pompey the Great in his Pyrenean campaign against Sertorius (75-74 BC). The etymology of this name suggests that it is a strange Basque-Roman hybrid, composed of the founder's name, Pompey, and the Iberian-Basque word *ili-ilu,* a variant of *iri-iru,* meaning "city". Due to its location on the crossroads between the Bordeaux-Astorga and Oyarzun-Tarragona roads, this became the most important town of the Navarrese territory and was also, at least from Visigothic times, an episcopal see.

During his retreat to France after a failed expedition to Saragossa in 779, Charlemagne ordered Pamplona's walls to be destroyed. This seems to be what caused the Navarrese revenge at Roncesvals. This destruction of Pamplona was also sung by French jesters, who conveniently altered the historic truth to incorporate it into the Carolingian epic cycle. Thus, in the poem *La prise de Pampelune,* and the second chapter of *Pseudo-Turpin,* Pamplona is depicted as a city of impenetrable walls and Muslim inhabitants. After a fruitless three-month siege, Charlemagne prays to God and St James to conquer the city:

> *"And then, through the wish of God after St James' repeated requests, the walls crumbled from their foundations. The lives of those Saracens who agreed to be baptised were spared; those who refused were killed."*

The time of Sancho III the Greater (1000-1035), when the Kingdom of Navarre reached its maximum splendour, witnessed a great demographic

Pamplona. Town Hall façade.

and economic growth of its capital, Pamplona, due to the arrival of numerous craftsmen and traders from the other side of the Pyrenees, who were attracted by the "fueros", or charters, granted by the Navarrese kings. This economic boom, contributed to by the Road to Santiago, caused great tension to build up between the old Navarrese inhabitants, who inhabited the district or "burg" known as la Navarrería around the Cathedral, and the newcomers who settled into the new burgs around the fortress churches of San Cernín (Saturnine) and San Nicolás. Due to these tensions, the inhabitants of the three burgs deemed it necessary to protect themselves from others by building walls inside the city. This situation remained until the XVth century, when King Charles III ordered the walls to be demolished and a common defence system to be built.

The Road to Santiago enters the fortified enclosure through Portal de Francia or Zumalacárregui, and quickly reaches the Cathedral, the centre of the old Basque-Roman settlement and of the current district of la Navarrería. Here, in the church of San Miguel, which was later annexed to the Cathedral, was where the pilgrims found the largest lodging places in the city. It is known that master Esteban, who was master Mateo's co-worker in Santiago de Compostela and was mentioned in *Liber peregrinationis* among the famous builders of the Road, worked in the old Romanesque building of the Cathedral. After being destroyed by fire in the XIVth century, the Cathedral was sumptuously rebuilt in Gothic style. The works of art which can be found inside this temple, which has three naves and an ambulatory, include: Johan L'Homme de Tournai's magnificent mausoleum for Charles III and his wife Eleanor, which is located before the main altar; the famous Cristo de Caparroso in the chapel of San Juan Bautista; another magnificent Renaissance Christ in the chapel of El Santísimo; the Romanesque sculpture of Santa María Real in the Capilla Real chapel; the Puerta Preciosa door; the cloister; and countless works of art kept in other chapels such as La Barbazana, or in the Cathedral Museum.

The pilgrim route crosses the district of La Navarrería into that of **San Cernín** (Saturnine) around the fortified church dedicated to this saint, whose worship was brought by the important Occitan contingents who settled in this city in the Middle Ages. The patron saint of Navarre, the Virgin of the Way (Virgen del Camino), is worshipped here. A XVth

Pamplona. Charles III and his wife Eleanor's mausoleum in the Cathedral.

century reliquary-bust in the church of **San Lorenzo** in this burg contains the relics of San Fermín. This saint, the Pamplonese disciple of St Saturnine who was martyred in Amiens in Paleochristian times, is the object of a huge and festive popular devotion which results in the world famous San Fermín celebrations, or "Sanfermines", which start on 7th July. Another particularly important building in this district is the Chamber of Accounts (Cámara de Comptos), the administrative register of the Kingdom of Navarre and this autonomous region's most significant documentary treasure.

Another fortified church, like that of San Cernín, can be found in the district of **San Nicolás.** One of the must-sees of the many traces left in this city by the St James pilgrimage is the scalloping which decorates the church of Santo Domingo. The church's main altarpiece is dominated by a sculpture of St James in pilgrim attire.

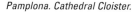

Pamplona. Cathedral Cloister.

4 Pamplona – Puente la Reina

When you leave Pamplona behind you, you are also leaving behind the Atlantic area of Navarra. From here onwards, the flora which will accompany you will mainly be cereal, holm oak, and Mediterranean brushwood. The Pamplona Basin is left behind when you cross the Alto del Perdón.

Sculpture of Larrea in Pamplona Citadel.

From the Ciudadela, carry on along Fuente del Hierro Street to the University Campus. Cross the pedestrian bridge over the river Sadar, then continue along the road to Campanas, passing by cultivated farmland until you reach a stone bridge which spans the river Elorz. After crossing this bridge, veer off the tarmac to the right towards some private farms. This section of road will also go on to cross the railway tracks, after which you should take a gravel path which runs parallel to, and eventually joins up with, the roadway. Following this path, under the shade of poplars, you will ascend to reach **Cizur Menor,** going by the Church of San Miguel Arcángel, (St Michael the Archangel), and its pediment. Pass through a housing estate that is currently being constructed to leave the area, before heading off between crop fields and houses, passing a new housing estate on the right-hand side. When the road turns to the right, the path will continue straight ahead towards Alto del Perdón, crossing the road to Galar en route. The Camino then goes through some poplar trees before crossing a small bridge over a stream. Here, the trees and a dam remain on the left-hand side, whilst the **Guenduláin** manor estate can be seen to the right. Just one kilometre further, you will pass by the graveyard before going up to **Zariquiegui,** situated on the lower foothills of the Alto. It is here that the remains of the Pamplona Basin are finally left behind. When you leave the area, you will begin a steep climb through boxwood and gorse scrubland. Before climbing the last slope and reaching the summit, you will come across the Reniega spring. Once at the peak, where there was once a hospital and a large church, Pamplona and the Pyrenees are left behind us, and the Valdizarbe Valley can be made out in the distance.

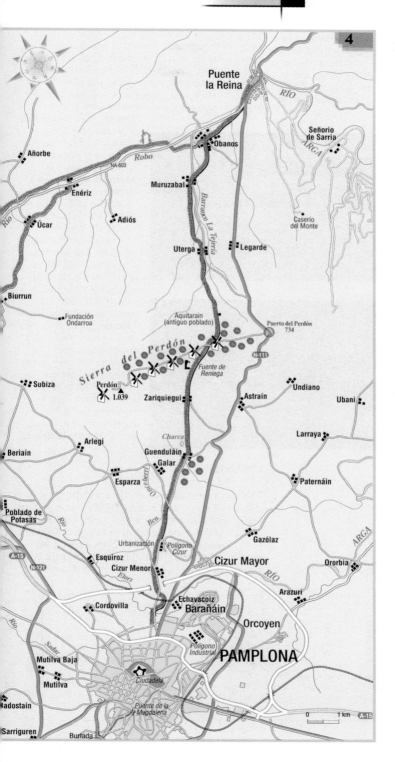

Upon crossing a service road, you will once again carry on downwards, through a very rocky path surrounded by dwarf oaks. Further along the path, you will cross a bridge over a small stream that runs through a group of poplars. The river Tejería runs off to the right, alongside cultivated farmland. The path makes its way through holm oaks to

Uterga, from where you will continue along a dirt track which turns into a rural path before making its way into **Muruzábal.** Next, you must leave the village along the motorway, before leaving the road via a path with veers off to the right. Following this path will take you across the river Tejería, and bring you through vineyards to the hill which will take you onwards and upwards to **Obanos.** Once there, go down along the NA-601 motorway to the Camino Aragonés, cross to the left-hand side, and head off between a few orchards, before rejoining the N-111 motorway which leads you to **Puente la Reina.**

CYCLISTS

This day's most difficult part is undoubtedly the Alto del Perdón, as it has a difficult ascent and an impossible descent, due to the rocky, uneven surface of the route. You can opt to go along the N-111 motorway for 15 kms, before taking the turn-off for Uterga. From this point onwards, you will be able to follow the route of the Camino.

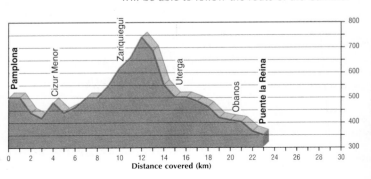

STAGE 4. PRACTICAL INFORMATION

CIZUR MENOR

Hostels

Municipal hostel (Albergue municipal).
The Order of Malta offers its hospitality
in this hostel with 27 beds and a
kitchen. Open from June to September.
∅ 948 221 479 / 600 386 891

Maribel Roncal Pilgrims' hostel
(Albergue de Peregrinos Maribel
Roncal). It takes in pilgrims (including
cyclists) all year round. It has 25 places,
a kitchen and good facilities.
∅ 948 183 885

Restaurants

Asador Martintxo-La Sidrería.
Calle Irunbidea, 1. ∅ 948 180 020

UTERGA

Hostels

Municipal shelter
Very small. Open all year round.
∅ 948 344 318

Camino del Perdón hostel
∅ 948 344 121 / 696 544 143

OBANOS

Hostels

Municipal Hostel (Albergue Municipal).
∅ 676 560 927

Restaurants

Ibarberoa.
Calle San Salvador. ∅ 948 344 153

Means of Transport

The Tafalla-Puente la Reina-Pamplona
line, which is run by the La Conda
company (∅ 948 221 026), stops at
Obanos and Puente la Reina.

PUENTE LA REINA

Hostels

Hotel Jakue.
Located at the entrance, on calle
Irunlarrea. It has 40 places, a kitchen
and a washing machine.

Priests of the Sacred Heart hostel
(Albergue de los PP. Reparadores).
They have an already traditional hostel
on calle Crucifijo. Open all year round.
It has 80 beds, a kitchen, dining room
and washing machine. Very good
facilities. ∅ 948 340 050

"Santiago Apóstol" hostel.
The owners of the camping site have
adapted this site on Paraje el Real with
100 beds. It has a washing machine.
∅ 948 340 220

Hotels

HR** Bidean.
Calle Mayor, 20. ∅ 948 341 156.
19 rooms. 38 beds. Double room:
€ 80/55/48; single room: € 50/40;
breakfast: € 6.

H** El Peregrino.
Carretera Pamplona-Logroño, km 23.
∅ 948 340 075. 14 rooms.
28 beds. Double room: € 180/144/72;
breakfast: € 9,02; lunch/dinner:
€ 48,08.

Restaurants

Hotel Jakue.
Calle Irunlarrea. ∅ 948 341 017

La Conrada.
Paseo de los Fueros. ∅ 948 340 052

La Plaza.
Plaza Mayor, 52. ∅ 948 340 145

Lorca.
Plaza Mayor, 54. ∅ 948 340 127

Means of Transport

The Pamplona-Puente la Reina –Estella-
Logroño line, which is run by the La
Estellesa company (∅ 948 222 223),
stops at Puente la Reina.

HISTORY AND WEALTH OF THE STAGE 4

THE FRENCH ROAD. PAMPLONA – PUENTE LA REINA

The knights of the Order of the Hospital of St John of Jerusalem (also known as the Hospitallers of Jerusalem, Knights of Malta and Knights of Rhodes) had a magnificent monastery in **Cizur Menor.** The current Romanesque parish church, dedicated to St Michael the Archangel, was part of this monastery. Pilgrims were protected by this Order all the way to Alto del Perdón, including not only Cizur, but also the next two towns before the woodland, **Guenduláin** and **Zariquiegui.** But this protection is not the only common feature of these two towns; in addition, their respective parish churches are dedicated to the same saint: St Andrew. Both the church and the palace of the Counts of Guenduláin, the other notable building of the now deserted Guenduláin, are now in ruins.

It is in this part of Cuenca de Pamplona, which includes the land between the city and Alto del Perdón, that the author of *Pseudo-Turpin* thought up one of the most outstanding episodes of his work, the definitive confrontation between Charlemagne and African leader Aigoland. According to the story, after pursuing Charlemagne all the way to France and then being rejected by him, Aigoland crosses the Pyrenees back into Spain and settles with his army in Pamplona which, according to this story, has been rebuilt after it was first destroyed. Charlemagne, on his part, gathers a huge army of 134,000 warriors, "who covered all the land between the river Arga and the hill three leagues away from Pamplona". Realising that he will be unable to defend the city from such force, Aigoland,

> "*left the city with his armies and, leaving the remainder close to the city, took sixty men from his General Staff and approached Charlemagne's tent, which was a mile away from the city. Charlemagne's and Aigoland's armies were thus arranged on the splendid plain next to the city, six miles wide and long, with the Road to Santiago between them.*"

Church of San Miguel in Cizur Menor.

Muruzábal. Parish church.

Charlemagne and Aigoland hold a religious-political discussion which is supposed to lead to Aigoland's conversion. However, seeing that this is not happening, Charlemagne and his men exterminate the Muslim army and its leader. As we saw earlier in the case of Roncesvals, the author of *Pseudo-Turpín* liked to place the French emperor's deeds at different points of the Road's geography, so that they could be recognised by pilgrims. There is no doubt that this fictitious battle in Cuenca de Pamplona was inspired by the impression made by the magnificent view, from Alto del Perdón, of the great plain with the city in the background. The chapel of Nuestra Señora del Perdón, which lent its name to **Alto del Perdón,** was found on one of the hilltops of the range, which today houses a row of gigantic wind mills which scan the wind and convert its force into the energy which supplies Pamplona with electricity. A modern fountain on the northern slope reminds the traveller of the old **fuente de Reniega,** associated with a typical pilgrimage legend in which the devil tempts the dehydrating pilgrim to give him his soul, in exchange for giving the pilgrim the location of the spring. The pilgrim rejects the offer and is rewarded by an offer of water from St James himself out of his own scallop shell.

The beautiful town of **Uterga** can be found along the way in Valdizarbe, on the southern slopes of the range. The parish church of La Asunción stands out among the large and solid houses.

A beautiful sculpture of St James in pilgrim attire, as he is usually depicted in this area, can be found in one of the chapels of the parish church of **Muruzábal,** which is dedicated to St Stephen.

Obanos is known with the nickname "Villa de los Infanzones" (Town of the Nobles) because the local nobles, resolved to uphold their rights against the foreign monarchy and the high nobility, met and associated here in 1323. Their Latin motto was *Pro libertate patriae gens libera state* (If you want a free fatherland, be free people).

Nowadays, Obanos is famous for the theatrical production it stages in August every second year. This has been declared an attraction of National Touristic Interest, and most of its neighbours (about 800

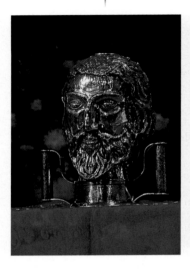 

Left, St William's skull in the parish church of San Juan Bautista in Obanos; right, St Mary of Arnotegui.

characters with roles) take part in it. The play, written by local author Santos Beguiristáin and first performed in 1965, tells an old story, which is both local and related to the pilgrimage: on returning from her pilgrimage to Santiago de Compostela, Felicia, daughter of the Duke of Aquitaine, decides to become a hermit and stay in Labiano, renouncing the rights and duties of her high social station. Her brother William searches for her but, when he fails to persuade her to change her mind, murders her in a rage of fury. In despair at what he has done, he makes the pilgrimage to Santiago himself and, when he returns, becomes a hermit in Arnotegui, near Obanos, devoting his life to penance and serving the pilgrims, and dying many years later as a saint. This plot is based on a local legend, based on the story of St William of Aquitaine, a relative of Charlemagne who became a hermit in the valley of Gellone (Saint-Guillaume-du-Désert, in the Departament of Hérault, Languedoc). We also find this story, possibly brought to Obanos by pilgrims or people of Occitan origin, in Finisterre where, according to whose local tradition, Duke William of Aquitaine spent the end of his life as a hermit in the chapel of San Guillermo Fisterrán. However, it is the story of Obanos which, embellished by literature, has reached us more strongly. The skull of St William can be found, protected by a silver reliquary representing his bearded head, in the early XXth century Neogothic parish church of San Juan Bautista. Wine which has been blessed in the relic's presence is distributed to the townspeople every Easter Thursday. This is said to protect the crop.

Next to road N-111 between Obanos and Puente la Reina, the wrought iron statue of a pilgrim marks the place where the roads from Roncesvals and Somport meet to enter Puente la Reina and continue, now merged into one single road, towards Santiago de Compostela.

Puente la Reina is now one of the best-known towns of the pilgrimage route. This is because the author of *Liber peregrinationis* publicised its status as a meeting of roads, although it is also mentioned under its old name Puente del Arga in *Pseudo-Turpin,* as the place where Charlemagne withdrew to rest after the great battle of Cuenca de Pamplona.

The perfectly regular layout of this town, born next to the Romanesque bridge which lent it its name, matches, almost exactly, the layout given to it when it was originally built. This was apparently done in one go, when Alfonso I of Aragon distributed identical pieces of land to all those who wished to inhabit the new town. Even today, you can see that all the High Street (Calle Mayor) façades have the same width. Interestingly, it was in 1122, at the time when its boundaries were drawn and its population established, that the city changed its old name of Puente de Arga in favour of the new Puente la Reina. No documents have been found to tell us who this queen ("Reina") in the name might be. It is, of course, possible that the name developed from a previous one, such as Puente del Runa, Runa being the river Arga's other name, or Puente de Larrain – "Larrain" being the Basque word for "plain", since the current city was built on one.

Just before the entrance to the city, where the church of El Crucifijo now stands, there used to be a monastery with a hospital. This belonged to the Knights of the Templar, yet another military order involved from its creation in protecting and assisting the pilgrims. When the Order disappeared, the Hospitallers of Jerusalem took over the facilities. Two works stand out from the treasures kept in this church: the Romanesque image of Santa María de las Huertas (the monastery's old name) and the Gothic crucifix on a furca, which may have come from the Rhine area, and which is dedicated to the same saint as the church itself.

On the High Street (Calle Mayor), the axis of the town and a stretch of the Pilgrim Road, we find the church of Santiago el Mayor, which still retains its original Romanesque façade. Inside it we find the "Beltza" or "Black One", one of the most famous Gothic sculptures of the Apostle in pilgrim attire. The High Street leads to the bridge on the river Arga. This Romanesque six half-point span structure is possibly the most beautiful and famous bridge in the whole of the Road to Santiago. There used to be, until last century, a little chapel on the parapet of the bridge, with an image of the Virgen del Puy or Virgen del Txori (meaning "bird"). According to tradition, a little bird used to appear every now and then to clean the Virgin's face with Arga water. This image is now in the church of San Pedro.

Puente la Reina. Gothic sculpture of the Apostle known as "Betlza", guarded in the church of santiago el Mayor.

5   Puente la Reina – Estella

The route to Estella is very uneven and quite agricultural, and is cultivated with cereals, vineyards and olive trees dotted out amongst small towns and villages.

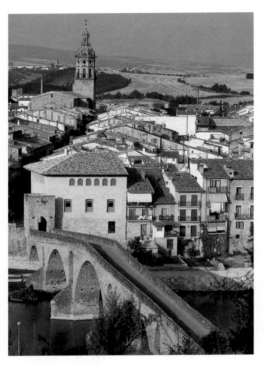

Panoramic view of Puente la Reina. Close up, the mediaeval bridge over the river Arga.

Travelling along the Calle Mayor, the pilgrim will come to the impressive medieval bridge. After passing the bridge, turn to the left and cross the road, before taking the turn-off that goes through a convent and various other buildings. The path carries on through crop fields, winding its way between the river Arga (passing close by the banks on several occasions), and the main road. Another 2.5 kms along into its route, the path heads off to the right, (leaving the water treatment plant behind), and goes up through pine trees and brushwood. Upon coming out of the vegetation and onto a pathway, you can see the township of Bargota, inhabited until the 11th Century by the mission of the Orden del Temple and, later, Hospital of St John. A small, shady path heads off through a woody area, running alongside the road to **Mañeru** through an agricultural landscape full of crop fields and vineyards. A small path heads downwards towards the village. Once there, Forzosa Street takes you out of the town and towards the graveyard. There isn't much change in the landscape until you get to **Cirauqui,** which is situated on a small headland. Go under the Puerta del Arco and head up through the town's streets before leaving the area via the roman road, surrounded by cypress trees. Next, head towards the Roman bridge which spans the river Iguste, before crossing the N-111 motorway and going through the river Salado valley, (crossing a gully on a small bridge en route). Continue along the path, passing alongside the old site of Urbe, advancing through the low hill and crop fields. Further down, you will come to the motorway, before taking the turn-off to Alloz. Go along this road until you get to an aqueduct and an old windmill,

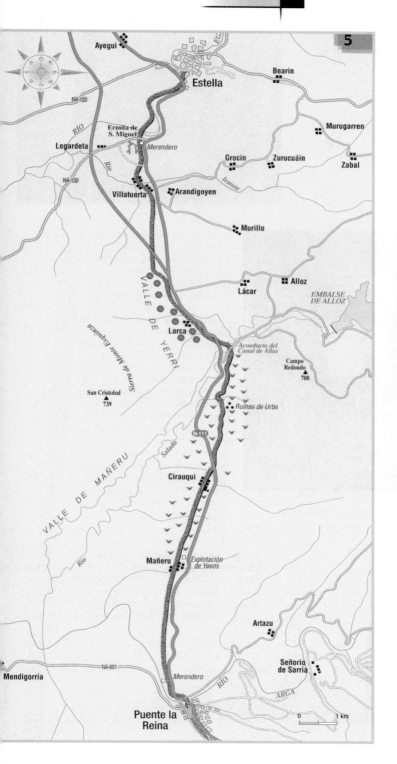

Panoramic view of Cirauqui, Roman bridge and road.

Estella. Calle de la Rúa and pilgrims' hostel.

from where you should head off towards the bridge which spans the river Salado. A tunnel which goes under the main road takes you off towards an old section of the road, from where you must head upwards to **Lorca,** your next destination. Once in Lorca, you will go through the main square, coming out at a laundrette and going alongside a few orchards towards the N-111 motorway, later continuing parallel to the road. Carry on along a few more paths before going through a tunnel under the path to Estella and coming out through orchards and fruit trees before entering **Villatuerta.** Once in the village, you will pass the river Iranzu and come out along Monasterio de Irache Street, heading towards the San Miguel hermitage. Cross the road to Oteiza and take a path on the right which will take you to a footbridge that crosses the Ega. From here, the Ordoiz path heads towards **Estella,** passing by orchards and factories.

CYCLISTS

The section of the Roman road which leaves **Cirauqui** and goes through the Urbe site presents some difficulties. It is important to take into account the state of the pathways in certain phases of this stage. The alternative is the N-111, which runs between Puente la Reina and Estella.

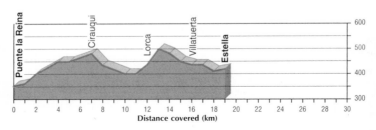

STAGE 5. PRACTICAL INFORMATION

MAÑERU

MEANS OF TRANSPORT

The Pamplona-Estella line, which is run by the La Estellesa company (∅ 948 222 223) stops at Mañeru, Cirauqui, Lorca, Villatuerta and Estella.
– Estella bus station:
∅ 948 550 127

CIRAUQUI

HOSTELS

Municipal hostel (Albergue municipal).
Town Hall. ∅ 948 342 080

LORCA

RESTAURANTS

Bodegón El Molino. Carretera Logroño, km 36. ∅ 948 551 103

VILLATUERTA

HOSTELS

Pilgrims' Hostel (Albergue de peregrinos). ∅ 948 640 083

RESTAURANTS

Asador Urpe. Carretera Pamplona-Logroño. ∅ 948 541 027
Lara. Ctra. Pamplona ∅ 948 541 016

ESTELLA

HOSTELS

Municipal Hostel (Albergue Municipal). On calle Rúa. Managed by the Estella Road to Santiago Friends Association (Asociación de Amigos del Camino de Santiago de Estella). ∅ 948 550 200 / 948 551 562. Open all year round. It has 114 beds, a kitchen, living room and dining room. Cyclists are welcome.

Oncineda Youth Hostel.
∅ 948 555 022

HOTELS

H** Yerri. Avenida Yerri, 35.
∅ 948 546 034. 24 rooms. 48 beds.
Double room: € 54/48; breakfast: € 4; dinner: € 9,26.
HS** Área 99. Calle Merkatondoa, 32.
∅ 948 555 287. 11 rooms. 22 beds.
Double room: € 42/36; breakfast: € 2,8; dinner: € 7,01.
HS* Cristina. Calle Baja Navarra.
∅ 948 550 772. 15 rooms.
30 beds. Double room: € 42.
HS San Andrés. Plaza Santiago, 58-1°.
∅ 948 550 448. 23 rooms. 46 beds.
Double room: € 30/27; single room: € 21.
P*** El Volante. Travesía Merkatondoa, 2. ∅ 948 553 957.
5 rooms. 10 beds. Double room: € 36; single room: € 18.

CAMPING SITES

1.ª C Lizarra. Calle Ordoiz.
∅ 948 551 733. 1.000 places.

RESTAURANTS

Asador La Tasca. Calle Navarro Villoslada, 1. ∅ 948 556 207
Astarriaga. Plaza de los Fueros, 12.
∅ 948 550 802
Cachetas. Calle Estudio de Gramática, 2. ∅ 948 550 010
China Town. Calle Fray Wenceslao de Oñate, 7. ∅ 948 552 988
La Cepa. Plaza de los Fueros, 18.
∅ 948 550 032
Merkatondoa. Calle Merkatondoa, 8.
∅ 948 554 951
Navarre. Calle Gustavo de Maeztu, 16.
∅ 948 550 040
Richard. Calle Yerri, 10.
∅ 948 551 316
Rochas. Calle Príncipe de Viana, 16.
∅ 948 551 040
Roma. Calle Chapitel, 17.
∅ 948 546 816

SERVICES

The **Tourism Office** is on plaza Mena.

HISTORY AND WEALTH OF THE STAGE 5

THE FRENCH ROAD. PUENTE LA REINA – ESTELLA

At the other side of the river Arga is the Puente la Reina district of Zubiurrutia (meaning "distant", or "separated by the bridge"), also known as the district of the nuns (barrio de las monjas), due to the Comendadoras del Espíritu Santo convent, which has been there since the XIIIth century.

After **Eunea,** which is close to the Road, lie the ruins of Bargota, another Templar dependency with a hospital for pilgrims. When the controversial Order of the Knights of the Templar disappeared, the Hospitallers of Jerusalem took over the facilities, just as they did with the church of El Crucifijo in Puente la Reina. The hospital of Bargota also belonged to the **Mañeru** Hospitallers. Its parish church, Baroque with Gothic traces, is dedicated to St Peter.

In spite of its etymology ("Cirauqui" means "snake nest" - "ziraun" in Basque, and "sirón" or "culebra ciega" in Spanish), **Cirauqui** is a cosy place. The Romanesque church of San Román, which crowns the rocky hill on which Cirauqui stands, forms the centre of this historic town. Its main feature is its ogival façade, with a waving arch very much resembling the one in the church of Santiago in Puente la Reina and the one in the church of San Pedro de la Rúa, in Estella. The votive altar inside it is one of countless Roman traces which can be found in Cirauqui, where a "mansio" of the great Bordeaux-Astorga road may have existed. Cirauqui's solid-looking houses center around the church of San Román, and include among their number the church of Santa

Catalina de Alejandría which, just like San Román, dates from approximately the early XIIIth century. The way leading out of Cirauqui meets a small segment of Roman road which disappears at a small one-span bridge, itself also partly Roman.

The remains of **Urbe** which, according to documentary evidence, has existed since at least the XIIth century but was abandoned in the XVIIIth, are now limited to a few stacks of stones and the humble foundations of some dwelling houses. A bit further on, one kilometre before reaching Lorca, runs the **river Salado** (meaning Salty River). This

Stretch of the Roman road in Cirauqui.

is where a scene, not so much dramatic as sensationalist, is set by *Liber peregrinationis* with the intention of giving the Navarrese rivers near Estella, as well as the Navarrese people, bad publicity:

> *"Next to a place called Lorca, on its East Side, runs a river called Salado. Once you get there, beware of drinking, or of your horse drinking, since it is a deadly river. When we were headed towards Santiago, we came upon two locals seated on its bank. They were sharpening the knives which they had used to skin those pilgrims" animals which had drunk from this water and died. When we asked, they lied and said the water was healthy and drinkable. So we let our horses drink from it. Two of them instantly collapsed dead and were skinned there and then".*

These words from *Liber peregrinationis* must of course be understood within their anti-Navarrese feeling, which may have been caused by the author himself having lived in Estella and identifying with his fellow Frenchmen who had settled there and who at that time (the XIIth century) lived in permanent conflict with the locals. Or he may have been using such negative publicity to encourage pilgrims to go through this area as quickly as possible and take refuge

Romanesque bridge of Villatuerta.

in heavenly (at least according to the author) Estella. So, for example, although the next town, **Lorca,** is not mentioned in the list of Stops of the Road, it is mentioned in reference to the alleged bad quality of the water of the river Salado, which means that the author of *Liber peregrinationis* knew the town well but was careful not to give it good publicity in his work. And this he did in spite of Lorca's old pilgrimage history, which can be seen in its layout, typical of pilgrimage towns, with the houses aligned on either side of the Road to Santiago, a stretch of which is also the town's High Street (Calle Mayor). The town had a hospital since at least the XIIIth century, and its parish church is dedicated to St Saviour. There is evidence dating from 1175 that there used to be another hospital, run by the Knights of Malta, in the segment of the Way between Lorca and Villatuerta, although its exact location is unknown.

In order to enter **Villatuerta,** you must cross the river Iranzu on a solid Romanesque two-span bridge. The parish church of la Asunción is the most outstanding building in this town. At the exit of the town you come across the chapel of San Miguel, built on the site of an old monastery which was also dedicated to St Michael ("San Miguel") and which depended on Leire, and in relation to which there is documentary evidence dating as far back as the Xth century.

Estella is, without a doubt, one of the towns most closely related to St James in the whole Road. It was founded in 1090 for the pilgrims by

Panoramic view of Estella. Close up, El Ladrón bridge *and, in the background, the church of San Miguel.*

wish of King Sancho Ramírez, and references to St James abound in it. Even the author of *Liber peregrinationis* himself temporarily inhabited, approximately in the first third of the XIIth century, the district or "burg" of San Martín, also known as "franco" (meaning French), which was built around the church of San Pedro de la Rúa. As well as making this the end of the third stage in his pilgrimage guide, the author strongly praises the town for its food and the water of its river, the Ega. The contrast between this and the insults he bestows on all other Navarrese rivers and the native population (albeit only implicitly in the latter case) is clear. By the time the author lived here, the old Basque name, *Lizarra* or *Lizarrara* (meaning "Ash tree" or "group of Ashes"), had already been lost to the new, and certainly promising, Latin name imposed by the French: *Estella* (meaning "Star"). It is possible that this creation - apparently nonsensical for the name of a place - developed from an earlier distortion of the Basque name consisting of omitting the initial "L", as if it was the Romance definite article. This would result in the name *Izarra* meaning, precisely, "the Star". There is only one step from this to the Latin translation, a step which was taken very often at this time. After the district of San Martín, other French districts or "burgs" such as the district of San Miguel, were created in Estella during the XIIth century. During the last third of the century, King Sancho VI "the Wise" granted "fueros", or charters, to two new burgs, San Juan and El Arenal, this time allowing the Navarrese population to settle into them under equal conditions. Estella prospered greatly during the Middle Ages: each burg had its own church and, more importantly, its own annexed pilgrims" hospital, with a brotherhood devoted to helping poor travellers. Rivalries between brotherhoods were not uncommon, and some were abolished as punishment for encouraging factions. Outside the city walls was the hospital of San Lázaro, reserved for pilgrims with contagious diseases.

Among Estella's mediaeval monuments is the church of San Miguel "in excelsis", in the old district with the same name. Its main feature is its magnificent Romanesque northern façade. In the castle of Lizarra, Estella´s early centre, stand the old churches of San Pedro de Lizarra and Santa María del Puy, the latter form of devotion having been brought by French people from the Midi region. The current parishes of San Juan Evangelista (which contains a Romanesque baptism font and a Gothic

*Estella. View and details
of the Romanesque cloister in the church
of San Pedro de la Rúa.*

crucifix) and San Salvador stand on the place occupied by the historic
burgs which gave them their names. The main burg, San Martín, can be
reached by crossing the one-span bridge known as La Cárcel, which was
blown up in 1873 and rebuilt in 1971. This bridge gave pilgrims access
to the burg of San Martín, Estella's political and economic centre, via
Rúa de las Tiendas (now called calle de la Rúa). Important buildings
within it include: the Gothic church of El Santo Sepulcro; the
magnificent Gothic convent of Santo Domingo; the remains of the castle,
at whose feet we find the church of Santa María Jus del Castillo, built on
the old Jewish synagogue from 1145; and the enormous church of San
Pedro de la Rúa, in which Navarrese Kings swore their "fueros". The
waved arch on its façade is reminiscent of the ones seen in San Román
in Cirauqui, and Santiago in Puente la Reina. Of particular interest
among its many treasures are the beautiful Romanesque cloister, which
was used as a cemetery for pilgrims and of which only two sections are
left, and the chapel of San Andrés (St Andrew being the patron saint of
Estella), which has a relic of this saint brought by the bishop of Patrás,
who died incognito in the city in the XIIIth century. Opposite this, where
the early church of San Martín (the centre of the burg) used to be, now
stands the palace of the Kings of Navarre (Reyes de Navarra), a rare
example of civilian Romanesque architecture and possibly a place where
king Sancho the Wise once lived. One of the capitals of the façade is
particularly noteworthy: this depicts the two stages of the fight between
Roland and Ferragut as told in *Pseudo-Turpin:* on horse and on foot. The
names of the sculptor, Martín, and the participants, *Ferragut* and *Rollán,*
can be read on the capital, and there is an indication that Ferragut came
from Logroño, as per the plot of the work on which *Pseudo-Turpin* is
based. As we will see later, this motif was also used in other parts of the
Road, such as Irache, Villamayor de Monjardín, Navarrete or San Juan
de Ortega. This provides evidence of a close relationship between the
author of *Liber peregrinationis* and *Pseudo-Turpin* with the French
people who settled in Navarre. Finally, on your way out of Estella, you
find the famous chapel of Rocamador, another French form of worship
brought to Estella in the Middle Ages.

6 Estella – Los Arcos

A new stage which goes through the Rioja area of Navarra: this route has ever-present vineyards, olive trees and cereals. From Villamayor de Monjardín to Los Arcos, you will cover 12 kilometres without coming across a single town or village.

Panoramic veiw of Villamayor de Monjardín.

After going along Rúa, San Nicolás and Camino de Logroño Streets, our route will take us out onto the N-111. When you reach the second petrol station, veer off along the Camino de Ayegui, passing between barns on the right and leaving **Estella** behind. Once in **Ayegui:**

A) if you want to take a small diversion to visit the Monastery of Our Lady of Real de Irache ("Nuestra Señora la Real de Irache"), you must cross the road. The Montejurra lies at the back of the Monastery. Pass alongside the "wine springs" of the wine cellars and, after visiting the monastery, cross the gardens to return to the N-111, crossing it again and rejoining your route.

B) Alternatively, continue alongside the N-111.

When you reach a hotel, the two different routes join up again and head off on the road towards Azqueta. After a tunnel which goes under the path, you will go deeper into an area forested with holm oaks. Coming out of this wooded area, you will pass between cultivated fields and through a small pine grove for about 5 kms, before reaching the hill that will take you on your ascent to **Azqueta,** situated on its summit. After coming down from this hill, you will pass by a livestock farm and a small stream. In the midst of vines and cereals, with the Monjardín hill in full view, the Camino approaches the "Moorish Fountain", a medieval tank structure which is situated just before **Villamayor de Monjardín.** From this village, you should head off via a path which leads towards the wine cellars. Before reaching them, however, you must go along a road flanked by walnut trees, passing alongside vineyards and crossing the regional motorway. The next 12 kms from this point go along a path with a very uneven surface, passing

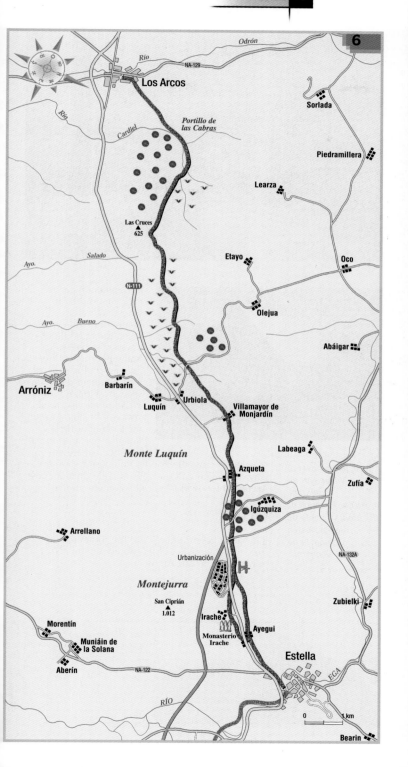

Above, pilgrim next to Villamayor de Monjardín. Below, Fountain of the Moors (Fuente de los moros) in Villamayor de Monjardín.

through countryside characterised by its vineyards, olive plantations and cereals, going through hillocks covered in pine trees. You will cross various ravines, on the sides of which tamarind can be seen growing. A further 18.5 km into the route, you will be able to see the Cogoticos de la Raicilla, rising up in the distance, where you must go to cross the Portillo de la Cabra. On the way down you will see your final destination, **Los Arcos,** which is situated one kilometre further on.

CYCLISTS

If it hasn't been raining, and the route is mud-free, this stage is feasible. Moreover, the N-111 joins Estella to Los Arcos.

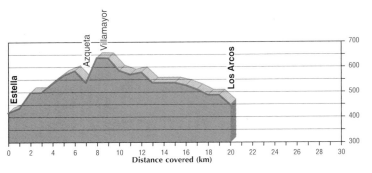

STAGE 6. PRACTICAL INFORMATION

AYEGUI

RESTAURANTS

Asador Urbasa.
Avenida Prado de Irache, 7.
✆ 948 551 150

Irache.
Carretera Pamplona-Logroño, km 43.
✆ 948 551 150

MEANS OF TRANSPORT

The La Estellesa company bus line stops at all these towns.

VILLAMAYOR DE MONJARDÍN

HOSTELS

"Hogar de Monjardín" hostel.
It has 12 beds, a kitchen, a stable and a place to keep bicycles. Open from May until the end of October.
✆ 948 537 136

RESTAURANTS

Castillo de Monjardín.
Viña Rellanada.
✆ 948 537 412

LOS ARCOS

HOSTELS

"Isaac Santiago de Los Arcos" municipal hostel.
Located on calle San Lázaro. Run by the Navarre Road to Santiago Friends Association (Asociación de Amigos del Camino de Santiago de Navarra). Approximately 70 beds. Cyclists are welcome, and there is a kitchen. Open from April until the end of October.
✆ 948 441 091

"Casa Romero" hostel.
Privately owned hostel located on calle Mayor. It has 28 places, a kitchen and a washing machine. Open between March and October. ✆ 948 640 083

"Casa Alberdi" hostel.
Another privately owned hostel, on calle Hortal. It has 17 places, a washing machine, a stable and room to keep bicycles. Open all year round.
✆ 948 640 764

HOTELS

H** Mónaco.
Plaza del Coso, 1. ✆ 948 640 000.
7 rooms. 14 beds. Double room:
€ 45/39; single room: € 32/29;
lunch/dinner: € 12.

HS** Ezequiel.
Calle La Serna, 14. ✆ 948 640 296.
18 rooms. 36 beds. Double room:
€ 33/28; breakfast: € 2,07;
lunch/dinner: € 9,02.

RESTAURANTS

Mavi.
Carretera Sesma, 2. ✆ 948 640 081

Sidrería Suetxe.
Calle Carramendavia. ✆ 948 441 175

Ezequiel.
Calle La Serna, 14. ✆ 948 640 296

HISTORY AND WEALTH OF THE STAGE 6

THE FRENCH ROAD. ESTELLA – LOS ARCOS

In **Ayegui,** now an industrial suburb of Estella, we find the parish church
of San Martín de Tours, one of the saints most commonly worshipped on
the Road and in Navarre. This XVIIth century Baroque church guards,
among other works, a XIVth century Gothic crucifix. Still inside the
town, at the foot of the hill of Montejurra - a Carlist pilgrimage
destination to this day - is the chapel of San Cipriano, a modest
mediaeval construction with a Gothic image of its saint, St Cyprian, the
old bishop of Carthage.

Irache. Wine and water fountain for pilgrims.

A bit later on, before reaching the famous monastery of **Irache,** there
stands, close to some cellars, a very special fountain. This dispenses not
only water – essential and refreshing –, but also wine, traditional pilgrim
fuel and provider of energy and comfort. After regaining your strength,
you can visit the impressive monastic complex of Santa María la Real de
Irache. This monastery, one of the best in the country, may have been
founded in Visigothic times, although the earliest documentary evidence
of it dates from 958. A pilgrims' hospital was set up in the monastery by
order of Navarrese King García III of Nájera in 1050, which makes it
older than the hospitals of Estella and Roncesvals, the other two great
references to the French Road in Navarre. This Benedictine monastery
saw its heyday in the XIth century when under the control of the abbot
St Veremundo, patron saint of the Road to Santiago in Navarre. Much
later, in the XVIIth century, the first university "studium" of Navarre,
specialising in Theology and in operation until the XIXth century, was
founded here. It is precisely here, in the monastery press, that the first
edition of father Yepes' *Crónica de la Orden Benedictina* (Chronicle of
the Benedictine Order) was first printed. The most important parts of this
magnificent collection are, of course, those which date from the
monastery's most prosperous times. Its Latin Cross-shaped church (three

*Villamayor de Monjardín.
Church of San Andrés.*

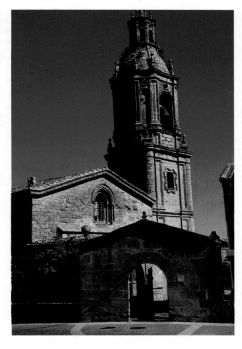

naves with their respective apses and two beautiful Cistercian façades) with a mighty octagonal dome on its transept, was built in the XIIth and XIIIth centuries. One of the capitals in the main chapel shows the fight on horse between Roland and Ferragut, narrated in chapter XVIII of *Pseudo-Turpin,* following the same pattern as the image seen in Estella although this one is less refined than the one in Estella. This motif, which we will encounter again - in Villamayor de Monjardín in this stage and in Navarrete a bit further on - proves the strong link between *Pseudo-Turpin* and Navarre. The refined Plateresque XVIth century cloister, built by, among others, masters Martín de Oyarzábal and Juan de Aguirre, is of particular interest from among its more recent parts. As regards even later constructions, the second cloister, solid tower and university outbuildings all date from the XVIIth century.

In **Azqueta** we find the parish church of San Pedro, whose main feature is the altarpiece on the high altar.

The stretch of Road just before **Villamayor de Monjardín** goes past a curious, recently restored, building. This is the Gothic-style XIIIth century fountain of the Moors (fuente de los Moros), a small quadrangular building topped with a gable roof, with an entrance formed by twin half-point arches separated by a central double column crowned with a capital. Inside it lies an underground well, with a remarkable barrel vault and a wide stone step which goes down to water level.

Villamayor is sheltered by the Colossus of Monjardín, which takes its name from the distorted version of *Mons Garsini,* which was mentioned in *Pseudo-Turpin* and is itself probably a distortion of *Mons Garseani* ("hill of García"), in relation to which there is no local documentary evidence. The top of the hill still holds the remains of the castle of San Esteban (note Villamayor de Monjardín's modern Basque name, *Doneztebe),* one of the fortress capitals of the old Kingdom of Deyo-Pamplona. Before being conquered during the emirate, this belonged to the powerful Muslim-Spanish Banu-Qasi family which owned the whole of the Ebro Basin. According to *Pseudo-Turpin,* Charlemagne snatched it away from a Muslim-Navarrese army lead by a Navarrese leader called Furre, after which "he seized the whole of the Navarrese territory".

View of Urbiola.

These words from Pseudo-Turpin ring of words from Spanish mediaeval literature according to which, after the conquest of Monjardín, the real conqueror, Navarrese King García Sánchez – who is buried there – ruled the whole of the Deyo-Pamplona territory. As in other cases, the author of *Pseudo-Turpin* attributed historic facts involving a Spanish king to his own hero. The name of Monjardín - *Mons Garseani* - could be explained by the fact that its conqueror King García was buried here.

The slender bell tower of the church of San Andrés, built in the XVIIth century following a common Riojan pattern, stands out from among Villamayor's houses. The Romanesque-style church has a single nave covered by a barrel vault, and a semicircular apse. The motif already seen in Estella's palace of the Kings of Navarre (palacio de los Reyes de Navarra) and in Irache (and which we will again encounter in Navarrete) appears once again on one of the capitals of its southern façade of half-point archivolts. Inside the church there is, among other works of great value, a beautiful XIIth century silver-plated Romanesque cross. This is one of very few Romanesque surviving silverware articles in Navarre.

In order to reach the town of **Urbiola,** the traveller must stray from the pilgrimage route, although not from the road. Historic pilgrims such as Arnold von Harff or Domenico Laffi visited this town. A pilgrims" hospital belonging to the Hospitallers of Jerusalem used to stand on the almost adjoining deserted spot of Cogullo.

Los Arcos, which forms the end of the sixth stage and spreads from Cerro del Castillo to the river Odrón, is another Navarrese pilgrimage town with great lineage. It is mentioned several times in *Liber Sancti Iacobi:* twice in *Liber Peregrinationis* - as a Stop of the Road and in relation to the "deadly" properties of its water -, and once in *Pseudo-Turpin,* according to a mysterious passage of which the city was also known as *Urancia* (its modern Basque name is *Urantzia),* a version of the name which may refer to the Cistercian monastery of Iranzu, not far from here. Los Arcos was founded in the Middle Ages on an originally Roman town (whose architectural remains may have something to do with its name): the "mansio" of *Curnonion,* which is situated on a crossroads. Due to its status as the most recent frontier stronghold (between the kingdoms of Navarre and Castille), Los Arcos became a thriving point for financial transactions, road toll collections and currency exchange in the Middle Ages. The Jews, who specialised in currency exchange, must have made up quite a large proportion of the population in the late Middle Ages, at least if we are to believe Künig von Vach, who calls it "City of the Jews" *(Juden stat)*. Another well known piece of information about this town relates to the "fuero", or charter, which Navarrese King Sancho VI granted and which made all inhabitants, whether they be Navarrese farmers or French craftsmen, equal before the law. The church of Santa María, next to the bridge over the river Odrón, stands out from Los Arcos' irregular layout. This church, built in architectural styles spanning from XIIth century Romanesque to XVIIth and XVIIIth century Baroque, is composed of a single nave lined with side chapels. Inside it, a lovely high altarpiece dedicated to the Visitation is dominated by the beautiful Gothic sculpture of

Church of Santa María de los Arcos. Above, a Renaissance bell tower; below, Baroque interior.

Santa María de los Arcos. A light effect similar to the one in San Juan de Ortega takes place once a year, shortly before the summer solstice, when the Visitation is lit by the sun. Other interesting features of the church include its octagonal tower – mighty yet slender and the best of Navarrese Renaissance –, the late-Gothic XVth century cloister, and the grand Plateresque façade - a beautiful stone work resembling an altarpiece which is also one of the best in this style in Navarre.

7   Los Arcos – Logroño

Today sees us leaving Navarra and moving into La Rioja. The first place that we come to in this region is Logroño, a city strategically situated on the border between Álava and Navarra.

Torres del Río. Chapel of Nuestra Señora de Poyo.

The Camino departs from the Arco de Castilla. Upon leaving **Los Arcos,** take the path which crosses the river Odrón, by the cemetery, towards Sansol, which will soon come up ahead. The N-111 motorway remains continuously on the left-hand side, running through cultivated fields. Before going up the regional road to the village of **Sansol,** you will cross the San Pedro river. Once in Sansol, you can see the village of **Torres del Río,** close by on the opposite hillside. To get there, you must go down the ravine, o through a tunnel under the Lazagurría road, and cross the river Linares. Coming into the town, you will pass by the Santo Sepulcro Church and take the road which leads to the graveyard. Go up a small hill near to the N-111, and continue along parallel to the road before crossing it. After passing through a small pine grove, you will come to the hermitage of Our Lady of Poyo ("Nuestra Señora de Poyo"). Shortly afterwards, you will leave the motorway to your left after reaching a cliff-face and, after a curve in the road, you will cross to the right-hand side of the road, before taking a pathway that leads up to, and crosses, the road to Bargota. Up ahead, you will be able to make out Viana and Logroño. Once again, you will follow the path downwards via the Mataburros ravine, which goes through the township of Cornava, and continues up and down ahead before crossing the road again by another curve. Until you get to **Viana,** the Camino alternates between pathway and hard shoulder. Upon reaching the site of the remains of a house and some palm trees, cross the road to go into the town, before leaving it again via San Miguel Street. Continuing downwards, cross the road and carry on through La Rueda and Fuente Vieja Streets, passing a school, some houses and several orchards, before crossing the Moreda motorway and

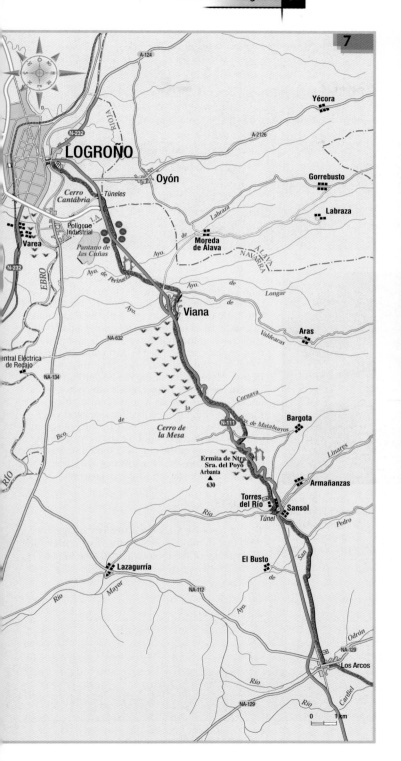

once again meeting up with the N-111. Take the path on the left which heads off towards the "Las Cañas" lagoon. When you reach the Hermitage of Our Lady of Las Cuevas ("Nuestra Señora de las Cuevas"), head off to the right, along a path which leads back to the motorway. After passing by a pine grove, cross the N-111 and continue through the pine grove until you are facing the paper factory. Here, you will see the beginnings of a tarmac path. After three tunnels which go underneath the bypass, you will go up to Cantabria Hill, covered in olive trees and vines. On your descent you will pass by the houses and gardens which make up the outskirts of Logroño. Before arriving in the city, you should pass by the graveyard before heading towards the stone bridge which leads the way into **Logroño.**

Above, pilgrims between Viana and Logroño; below, pilgrim's arc in Logroño's old quarter.

CYCLISTS

This stage of the Camino is totally manageable. With that in mind, however, those who prefer the firm surface of the motorway can take the N-111.

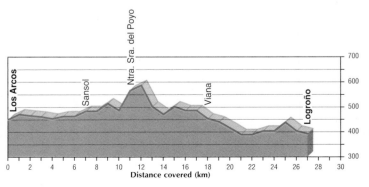

STAGE 7. PRACTICAL INFORMATION

TORRES DEL RÍO

HOSTELS

Torres del Río pilgrims' hospital (Hospital peregrino de Torres del Río). On calle Mayor. Open all year round. 32 beds. A portable stove is available for cooking. Bicycles allowed. ✆ 948 648 051

RESTAURANTS

La Pata de Oca. Calle Mayor, 3.
✆ 948 648 051

MEANS OF TRANSPORT

The La Estellesa company bus line stops at all the towns included in this stage.

VIANA

HOSTELS

"Andrés Muñoz" inn. On c/ San Pedro. Open all year round. It has 50 beds, a kitchen and a washing machine. There is room for bicycles. ✆ 948 645 530

HOTELS

P** Casa Armendariz (La Granja). C/ Navarro Villoslada. ✆ 948 645 078. 7 rooms. 14 beds. Double room: € 36/33; lunch/dinner: € 9.

RESTAURANTS

Bodegón Borgia. Calle Seraio Urra, 1.
✆ 948 645 781
Casa Armendáriz. Calle Navarro Villoslada, 19. ✆ 948 645 078
Pitu. Calle Medio de San Pedro, 9.
✆ 948 645 927

LOGROÑO

HOSTELS

Youth Hostel (Albergue juvenil).
✆ 941 291 145
Municipal hostel (Albergue municipal). On Rúa Vieja. Run by the Riojan Road to Santiago Friends Association. It has almost 80 beds as well as a kitchen, washing machine and room for bicycles.
✆ 941 260 234 / 947 229 201

HOTELS

H** Zenit Logroño. Carretera Pamplona, km 2. ✆ 941 271 555. 56 rooms. 112 beds. Double room: € 70; breakfast: € 4,51.
HR* Isasa. Calle Doctores Castroviejo, 13. ✆ 941 256 599. 30 rooms. 60 beds. 5 suites. Double room: € 55.
HSR*** La Numantina. C/ Sagasta, 4. ✆ 941 251 411. 17 rooms. 34 beds. Double room: € 43/41.
HSR** Mesón Pepa. Avda. Aragón, 9. ✆ 941 234 011. 19 rooms. 38 beds. Double room: € 47; breakfast: € 3,74.
HSR** Niza. Calle Gallarza, 13. ✆ 941 206 044. 16 rooms. 32 beds. Double room: € 47.

CAMPING SITES

1.st C La Playa. Avda. de la Playa, 6-8. ✆ 941 252 253. 248 places.

RESTAURANTS

Anzuelo de Oro. Calle Bretón de los Herreros, 62. ✆ 941 224 506
Asador La Gavilla. Plaza del Mercado, 25-bajo. ✆ 941 249 099
Avenida P21. Avenida de Portugal, 21. ✆ 941 228 602
El Fogón. C/ Peso, 6. ✆ 941 201 493
Florentino. C/ Milicias, 4. ✆ 941 260 714
Grand Canyon. C/ Vitoria, 1. ✆ 941 211 344
La Bombilla II. Calle Mayor. ✆ 941 224 523
Las Norias. Camino de las Norias. ✆ 941 263 117
Leito's. C/ Portales, 30. ✆ 941 212 078
Mesón Charro. Calle Laurel, 12. ✆ 941 224 663
Mesón Siglo XX. Calle Ingeniero Lacierva, 8. ✆ 941 238 078
Metropol. Avenida Jorge Vigón, 31. ✆ 941 253 136
Principal. Avenida Pérez Galdós, 3. ✆ 941 256 742
Trópico. C/ Salamanca. ✆ 941 201 254
Zubillaga. Calle San Agustín, 3. ✆ 941 220 076

MEANS OF TRANSPORT

Logroño bus station.
✆ 941 235 983

RENFE Logroño.
✆ 941 240 202

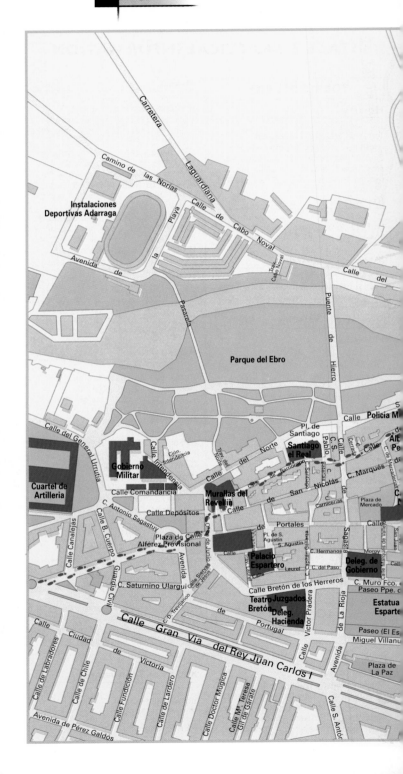

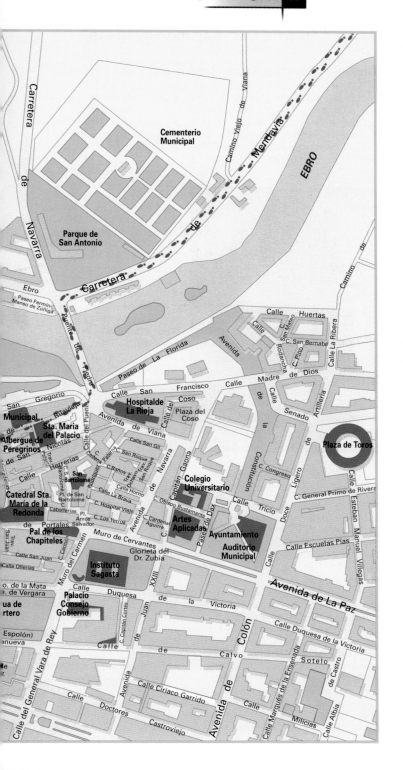

HISTORY AND WEALTH OF THE STAGE 7

THE FRENCH ROAD. LOS ARCOS – LOGROÑO

Just as you are leaving **Los Arcos** you cross the river Odrón, yet another river affected by bad publicity given to it by *Liber peregrinationis,* according to which its waters are as deadly as those of all other waters flowing on the Road between Estella and Logroño. Leaving the river behind you find, next to the cemetery, the chapel of San Blas, which used to have a hospital for pilgrims.

Sansol. Parish church central nave.

Its link to the monastery of San Zoilo in Carrión, of which it was a dependent territory, explains its name, **Sansol.** In addition, its parish church, a Baroque XVIIth century building, is dedicated to San Zolio. The unnamed hospital mentioned in *Liber peregrinationis* in reference to yet another poisonous river for men and animals alike, may also have been here.

Torres del Río is also mentioned in that work in relation to the harmful waters of its river Linares. The beautiful church of El Santo Sepulcro, a small Spanish Romanesque masterpiece, was built a few years later. The church has an octagonal layout is crowned with an also octagonal lantern, and has a semicircular apse and a small circular tower attached. Inside, a beautiful groined vault reminiscent of the "mihrab" in the Mosque of Cordoba crowns the octagon. No documents regarding its origins have been found, and it is dedicated to this particular saint because the Order of the Holy Sepulchre had a particularly active presence in this stretch of the Road to Santiago. However, its octagonal bases have caused some academics to link it to the Knights of the Templar, whose presence along the Road is equally strong.

Later on, the way goes past the ruins of **Cornava,** one of eight hamlets (the other ones are Longar, Tidón, Prezuela, Piedrafita, Soto, Gorano and Cuevas) whose inhabitants were gathered in 1219 to populate **Viana,** a newly created stronghold on the frontier with Castille. The main features which set Viana apart are related to its location on the Road to Santiago and to the fact that it was created for defense reasons. These features are: firstly, its location high up and enclosed within a solid wall; and secondly, its magnificent examples of civil and religious architecture (the churches of Santa María and San Pedro), made possible by the commercial prosperity of a village located on a great route (the name Viana derives from "vía", meaning "way" or "route"). By reason of its association with the pilgrimage, it boasted four hospitals in the XVth

Viana. Church of San Pedro.

century, which were mentioned by the German pilgrim Künig von Vach. In addition, its quadrangular layout, typical of the towns set up in the Middle Ages by the Kings of Navarre and Aragon, and which we have already witnessed in Puente la Reina and Sangüesa, gives away its royal origin. Sancho VII, founder of Viana, provided the town with an advantegous "fuero", or charter, which, together with its location, helped it become one of the most prosperous and powerful cities of Navarre, to the point that it was granted the honorific title of Principality by King Charles III in 1423, thus becoming part of the domain of the heir to the Navarrese Crown. In the XVth century, rivalries between the Navarrese nobility gave rise to bloody fights in Viana. The famous César Borgia died in one of these and is now buried in the atrium of the church of Santa María, probably the most noteworthy building in Viana. The most interesting aspects of this Gothic building are its later additions, such as its tower or the stone structure resembling an altarpiece, on its XVIth century southern façade. The most important treasures kept inside the church are the main altarpiece, the organ and the frescos by Luis Paret in the chapel of San Juan del Ramo.

Viana Frescoes by Paret in the church of Santa María.

The modern chapel of **Trinidad de Cuevas** gets its name and location from the old town of Cuevas, one of the eight hamlets from which Viana was formed, and which is also mentioned in *Liber peregrinationis* in relation to the health risks posed by its river, a stream by the name of Hormazuelas. Monks from the Order of the Trinity settled here as early as the XIIIth century to look after the pilgrims, a fact we are reminded of by the current name of the XVIIth century chapel.

After circumventing **cerro de Cantabria,** where the Celtic-Roman city of the same name used to stand

Logroño. Stone bridge over the river Ebro.

(Cantabria means "next to the Ebro") before being destroyed by Visigoth King Leovigild in the late VIth century, the traveller must cross the fast-flowing Ebro in order to enter Logroño. Until the XIXth century this was done via one of the most interesting bridges of the Road to Santiago: "Puente de Piedra". This was built by Alfonso VI (according to his chronicler Pelayo de Oviedo) at about the same time that Count García Ordóñez and himself were rebuilding and granting "fueros", or charters, to Logroño (1096), after it was destroyed by El Cid in 1092. The two great builder saints, Santo Domingo de la Calzada and his disciple, San Juan de Ortega, carried out subsequent repairs to the bridge. **Logroño** is mentioned in *Liber peregrinationis* as a Stop of the Road. Although no special treatment is given to the city in this work, its river, the Ebro, is mentioned for having "healthy waters" and being "rich in fish". The comment is rendered even more significant by the fact that every river on the Road between Estella and here has been described as poisonous. It is difficult to lay down the exact history of Logroño before the "fuero", since it seems to have been little more than an agricultural settlement. Even the structure of its name (composed of the Romance definite article and the name of an owner), seems to take us back to an early Middle Age *fundus*. In spite of this, the place where the city now stands may have been the location of *Vareia,* a Celtiberian city mentioned by the ancient geographers which was either abandoned or destroyed, as suggested by the loss of the name, in late ancient or Visigothic times. The planning of the city centre, with two streets, Rúa Vieja and Rúa Mayor, running parallel to the river and to each other, dates from the time of the García Ordóñez and Alfonso VI reconstruction. Next to the former stands the oldest church in Logroño, the imperial church of Santa María del Palacio, so called due to its having previously been part of Alfonso VII *The Emperor's* palace. The church, together with a hospital for pilgrims, was built by the knights of the Holy Sepulchre, to whom the King gave the palace after bringing the Order into Spain in 1155. Although its oldest parts are built in Cistercian style, the main structure is Baroque. Without leaving Rúa Vieja, we find the XVIIth century fountain of Los Peregrinos. At the end of the street is the church of Santiago el Real, a one-nave building dating from the XVIth century although, according to some in an attempt to link it to the legendary battle of Clavijo, it is as old as the IXth century. With the exception of a Romanesque sculpture of the Virgin of Hope (Virgen de la Esperanza), the patron saint of Logroño, all the iconographic elements in the parish are dedicated to the Apostle, depicted either as a pilgrim or as a killer of Moors ("matamoros"), symbol of the Christian Reconquest against Islam. The door known as Puerta del Camino or Puerta del Revellín, through which the pilgrims would leave Logroño, can still be found in what today is Calle de Barrio Cepo, which follows on from Rúa Vieja. The origin of the convent of San Francisco is also related to the Road to Santiago, since the convent may have been founded by St Francis himself during his pilgrimage to Santiago de Compostela. According to local legend, the saint performed a miracle on the Lord of Agoncillo's son who, in gratitude, supported the Franciscan foundation in Logroño. Lastly, we must note that the current Hospital Provincial, located at the end of Puente de Piedra, is built on the old pilgrims' hospital of Roqueamador or Rocamadour.

Other relevant buildings in the city are the XVth century concathedral of Santa María la Redonda, built on the small Romanesque octagonal church from which it got its name, and the XIIth century church of San Bartolomé, built in the centre of the early city. Its Gothic façade stands out for the beauty of its statues.

Ruins of Clavijo Castle.

Away from the Road, about 20 km south of Logroño, are the ruins of the **castle of Clavijo,** also related to the worship of St James although in its war, rather than its religious, facet. It is here, according to a later legend created to promote the idea of the Apostle protecting the four peninsular Christian kingdoms in their fight against Islam, that the Apostle appeared as a knight on a white horse and took part in the 844 battle between King Ramiro I of León and Emir Abderramán II, tipping the scales in favour of a Christian victory. This victory lead to the abolition of the also legendary tribute "of the hundred maids", to which the Christians were shamefully subject from the time of King Mauregato, and to the introduction of the St James tax (voto de Santiago), under which each city and village subject to the above tax (as well as many cities and villages which were later reconquered), had to pay a levy to the church of Santiago de Compostela, to show their gratitude for being released from the other tribute.

8 Logroño – Nájera

*From Logroño to Nájera, you will follow the routes of the
N-232 and the N-120 motorways, which go through
landscapes which are dominated by vineyards. All in all,
this is a relatively easy stage.*

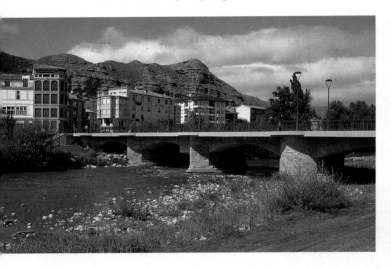

Nájera. Bridge over the river Najerilla.

To leave **Logroño,** you must begin by going along the Rúa Vieja and
Barriocepo Street. Cross the Puerta de Revellín, (otherwise known as the
"gate of the Camino"), before going along Once de Junio Street, Alférez
Provisional Square, Marqués de Murrieta Avenue and Burgos Avenue,
passing finally through the city's industrial estate. When you reach a petrol
station, veer left along Entrena Street and Rodejón Street, continuing your
route via Prado Viejo Street and Arco Street. Follow the route downwards
until you reach a tunnel which crosses the bypass and, upon coming out the
other side, you will find yourself on a green belt which lies in the shade of
many different types of ornamental trees (paradise trees, mimosas, poplars,
cypress trees, etc.). This green belt will eventually lead you to the Grajera
reservoir, situated some five kilometres from the city. Here, in amongst the
trees of a pine grove, you can find a park area. To leave the reservoir area,
head to the left towards the N-232. The Camino continues parallel to the
road, reaching the Alto de Grajera, the point where the N-232 meets up
with the N-120. From this point, the route will take you downwards towards
Navarrete. Just under one km away, it crosses the N-120 and a service road.
The Camino continues on through crop fields towards a bridge on the A-68
which leads the way to the entrance to the borough, just at the point where
you can see the ruins of the old Hospital of Saint John of Acre. Go along the
N-120 to leave the area, passing en route by the cemetery, whose XIII
Century façade once belonged to the aforementioned hospital. When you
arrive at a farm, the route begins to suffer from a lack of trees. However,
there is the possibility of deviating from the track along a rural pathway,
passing trough vineyards, olive trees and cereal fields. Upon arriving at the
wine-growing co-operative of Sotés, you must cross the road that leads to

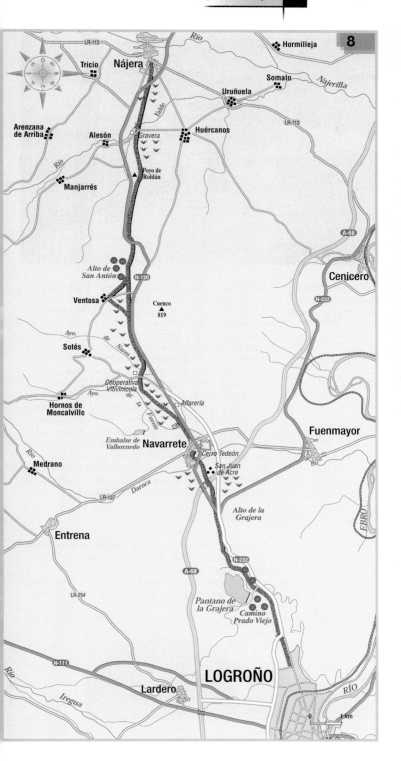

Pilgrims between Navarrete and Nájera near Poyo de Roldán.

the village, taking a tarmac path that leads back to the N-120. If you follow another section of the path linked to this one, it is possible to visit **Ventosa,** situated just over a kilometre away, where, you can stay at the hostel. Alternatively, you can proceed directly to Alto de San Antón. After climbing alongside vines, thickets and kermes oak to a certain height, you must descend the hill again to cross to the right-hand side of the N-120. One kilometre further along, you will pass on the left the legendary *poyo de Roldán,* now sadly topped with an unsightly antenna. Another 2 kilometres along will see you pass the Huércanos road, before you continue on your way by crossing a footbridge over the river Yalde. A little further on, you will find yourself in a rest area next to a factory, before you pass by some orchards and, after crossing the N-120 once again, you will finally enter **Nájera.**

CYCLISTS

Practically this entire section of the Camino is easily accessible to cyclists, thus avoiding the need to cycle along the main motorway, (the N-120). However, please note that you may encounter some difficulty when cycling through Alto de San Antón.

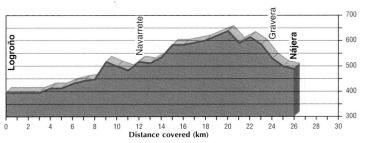

STAGE 8. PRACTICAL INFORMATION

NAVARRETE

HOSTELS

Municipal hostel (Albergue municipal).
Located on calle San Juan and run by
the Riojan Road to Santiago Friends
Association (Asociación Riojana de
Amigos del Camino de Santiago).
Approximately 40 beds. It has a washing
machine and a kitchen. Open all year
round.
∅ 941 440 776 / 941 440 776

RESTAURANTS

El Molino.
C/ Coso, 6. ∅ 941 440 364

Los Murales. Ctra. Burgos, km 8.
∅ 941 440 753

MEANS OF TRANSPORT

The Grupo Jiménez company buses stop
at Navarrete. ∅ 947 266 930

VENTOSA DE LA CUESTA

HOSTELS

"San Saturnino" shelter.
Run by the San Saturnino Pilgrims'
Association (Asociación de Peregrinos
San Saturnino). It has approximately 25
beds. It is open all year round and has a
kitchen and washing machine.
∅ 941 441 899

SERVICES

Although it is a small town, it has a
café/bar and a shop.

NÁJERA

HOSTELS

Municipal hostel (Albergue municipal).
It is located in the monastery of Santa
María la Real and is run by the Nájera
Road to Santiago Friends Association
(Asociación de Amigos del Camino de
Santiago de Nájera). It has 60 beds and
a kitchen.
∅ 941 362 121 / 607 487 591

HOTELS

HS* Hispano.
C/ Cepa, 2. ∅ 941 363 700.
22 rooms. 44 beds. Double room: € 33;
breakfast: € 3; lunch/dinner: € 9.

CAMPING SITES

3.ª C El Ruedo.
Carretera Nájera. ∅ 941 360 102.
154 places.

RESTAURANTS

El Mono.
C/ Mayor, 6. ∅ 941 363 028

Los Parrales.
C/ General Franco, 52.
∅ 941 363 735

Asador El Trinquete.
C/ Mayor, 8. ∅ 941 363 539

Bodegón de Judería.
C/ Constantino Garrán, 13.
∅ 941 361 138

Duque Forte.
C/ Calvo Sotelo, 15.
∅ 941 363 784

Hispano.
C/ Duques de Nájera, 2.
∅ 941 362 957

Royalty.
Paseo San Julián, 2. ∅ 941 363 302

MEANS OF TRANSPORT

The Grupo Jiménez company buses stop
at **Nájera**. ∅ 947 266 930

HISTORY AND WEALTH OF THE STAGE 8

THE FRENCH ROAD. LOGROÑO – NÁJERA.

In the time of *Liber peregrinationis* (c 1130), the Road to Santiago between **Logroño** and Nájera was not laid out like it is today: the definitive path was set a few years later. In fact, between these two towns, our mediaeval guidebook mentions *Villa Rubea* (a name which hardly appears in other texts), instead of Navarrete, as a Stop of the Road. Villa Rubea was on what is

now the deserted spot of Villarubia, in the district of Fuenmayor. This is no more than a few kilometres north of Navarrete, where a hospital managed by the Knights of the Holy Sepulchre, who had a strong presence in La Rioja, was built. It must have been during the last third of the XIIth century that the pilgrimage route between Logroño and Nájera was slightly diverted south, causing it to go through Navarrete. Before entering this town, post- *Liber peregrinationis* pilgrims would come across a dependency of the Order of St John, which had a magnificent hospital funded by doña María Ramírez around 1185. Some ruins can still be seen today on the place where it used to stand. Other ruins, spread out in the vicinity of Navarrete, are also still there to be admired. The magnificent Romanesque portico, now moved to the cemetery at the town exit towards Nájera, is one such example.

The first documentary evidence of **Navarrete** dates from 1175 and uses its current name *(Navarret)* which may have replaced the old name of *Corcuetos*. This is the name under which it appears, as one of the "Villas de Campo" (together with Fuenmayor, Hornos, Medrano, Velilla de Rad and Entrena) in a document relating to a donation made by Queen Estefanía – Navarrese King García of Nájera's wife – to the monastery of San Julián de Sojuela in 1060.

Navarrete. Exterior and Baroque main altarpiece in the church of La Asunción.

Panoramic view of Nájera.

The town, situated on the frontier, witnessed confrontations between Navarrese and Castilians and eventually ended up in the hands of the latter, whose king, Alfonso VIII, granted it a "fuero" (charter) in 1195. Navarrete preserves its Renaissance layout, which was adapted to the harsh topography of the hill on which it stands. The magnificent XVIth century three-nave church of Asunción is located on the higher part of the hill, which is also Navarrete's town centre. An enormous Baroque high altarpiece dedicated to the Assumption can be found among the treasures. A small XIVth century statue of Santiago Matamoros (killer of Moors) can be admired in a niche in the façade of one of the town's old palaces, on Navarrete's Pilgrim Road. On the outskirts of the town, on the way to Nájera, we can admire the concentric arches on the beautiful portico of the San Juan de Acre hospital, which was moved here in the XIXth century and which now forms the entrance to the cemetery. The fight on horse between Roland and Ferragut makes its appearance, yet again, on one of its ten capitals. This version follows the same pattern as the ones seen in Irache and Villamayor de Monjardín; all three were copied from the magnificent capital sculpted by Martín in the palace of the Kings of Navarre (palacio de los Reyes de Navarra), in Estella.

On a hill by the name of **Alto de San Antón,** between Navarrete and Nájera, stand the ruins of a convent of the same name, the remains of a convent belonging to the Order of St Anthony. This order, created in Viennois, stood out for its special assistance to pilgrims, especially in sanitary matters. There is no explanation, other than helping the pilgrims, for its presence in this desolate area.

Only a few meters from these ruins, we find another set which, according to local tradition, belonged to the Templars, and which ensured the safety of pilgrims in this remote place.

A similar hill, **Poyo de Roldán** in the vicinity of Nájera, brings back to memory the literary confrontation between the French hero and pagan giant Ferragut, a topic which, as we have seen on the Navarrese section of the Road in the form of icons and names, was very popular in this area. According to local legend, Roland went to Nájera to release the Christian knights locked up there by Ferragut. He climbed up the hill which today bears his name, glimpsed the giant in the distance and split his head open with a stone. Another version has it that the hill is the

Façade of the church of Santa María la Real in Nájera.

actual stone with which Roland squashed the giant. In any case, the local legend has picked up and combined two traditions: the one involving giant Errolán (Roland's Basque form), an enemy of the Basque people whom he attacked by throwing large stones, and the one found in several different literary sources, among which *Pseudo-Turpin* (c. 1140) stands out for its antiquity and the development of the plot, and for narrating it for the first time: after his great victory over Aigoland in Pamplona and Furre in Monjardín, Charlemagne reaches, via the Road to Santiago, the town of Nájera, which is ruled by Syrian giant Ferragut *(Ferrum acutum,* "sharp iron", or *Ferrea cutis,* "skin of steel"). The giant defeats Reinaldos de Montalbán, Constantine of Rome, Hoel de Nantes, and another twenty warriors in a single combat, and locks them all up in his castle. But at that moment Roland steps forward to defy the giant. After the first few inconclusive encounters, both on foot and on horse, the two participants strike up a conversation, during which the naïve giant gives away his only weak spot: his navel. The Frenchman makes a mental note of this and kills the giant by stabbing him with a dagger, after which he frees his fellow Frenchmen.

These stories, spread by *Pseudo-Turpin* throughout the whole of Europe, were so successful that they were recreated in hundreds of songs and poems, forever linking the name of **Nájera** to that of the Syrian giant to the point that a XIVth century Italian pilgrims' guide referred to this Riojan city as *Lazera di Ferrau.* We have already seen the iconographic representation of this story in various places, especially in the magnificent capital sculpted by Martín in the palace of the Kings of Navarre in Estella. This capital depicts both stages of the fight: firstly on horse (on the front of the capital) and then on foot (on the side). A piece of writing explains that Roland has come from Logroño (Rollan de Logrono) to meet the giant. The latter's animal features are depicted in a very expressive way when, having dismounted and taken off his helmet, he fights Roland with his hands. We have already seen several representations of the story on the Road to Santiago. These include, in addition to the one in Estella, the works in Irache, Villamayor de Monjardín and Navarrete. As well as being of lower quality, the latter three versions only depict the battle on horse. The motif can also be found on capitals of the Old Cathedral of Salamanca (Catedral Vieja de Salamanca), Sainte-Madeleine in Vézelay, Saint-Romain de Drayes-les-Belles-Fontaines, and Cunault, among others. It all provides evidence of the spread of *Pseudo-Turpin* in that time. Although the importance of Nájera does not stem exclusively from its status as a Stop of the Road, its location on the pilgrims' route favoured its mediaeval boom to a great extent. Built on the grounds of old Tricio, Nájera was founded by the Arabs, who gave it its name (meaning "place among crags"), and was taken away from the Muslims in 923 in a joint action of the Kings of Navarre and León. Sancho III *the Greater* of Navarre made it the capital of his kingdom, and diverted the Road to Santiago from its more rugged Northern path to go through it. Christian Spain's first coins were minted in Nájera at this time. Sancho's son, the unfortunate García IV *of Atapuerca,* was responsible for the city's most important historic building, the monastery of Santa María la Real, a magnificent collection built on the entrance to a cave. According to the legend linked to the monastery, it was King García himself who, having followed one of his falcons here while hunting, found in this cave an image of the Virgin lit by a lamp and adorned with a "terrace" of lilies. As well as building the sanctuary in honour of the Virgin, the King founded the first order of knights known in Spain, which he called

Monastery of Santa María la Real in Nájera. Above, Gothic cloister "de los Caballeros"; below, Romanesque sepulchre of Doña Blanca in Navarra.

the Order of the Terrace in honour of the flower pot found next to the Virgin. King García entrusted the care of the church to a religious community of canons which followed the community of St Isidore and which, in addition to its worshipping duties, took up the job of helping the pilgrims in the hospital annexed to the church. After La Rioja was conquered by Castille and León, Alfonso VI gave Santa María to the French Cluny monks as part of his methodical cultural and religious plan to make his kingdoms more European. This church is now run by a Franciscan community. The most spectacular parts of the monastery are of Gothic style. Some examples include the XVth century church, the impressive royal pantheon of the Kings of Navarre and the Cloister of "Los caballeros".

Alfonso VI's activities in Nájera consisted mostly of providing the church with facilities for assisting pilgrims: these included several lodging places and hospitals, as well as the bridge - later repaired by San Juan de Ortega - over the river Najerilla, which evidence the king's concern with Nájera and the Road to Santiago.

9 Nájera – Santo Domingo de la Calzada

Country roads dominate this stage, which runs through the Cantabria mountain range to the North, and the La Demanda mountain range to the South.

San Millán de la Cogolla. Yuso Monastery and valley.

You should leave **Nájera** via Rey Don García Street and Costanilla Street, moving on to a steep incline which makes its way upwards through a pine grove. Carrying on upwards you will reach a plain that has been converted into vineyards, through which runs a rural track which turns into a tarmacked pathway after 3.5 kilometres. From this point onwards, you should be able to make out **Azofra,** our next destination. To the left of the village you should also be able to see Cordovín. The Camino reaches Azofra through fields of irrigated land, going through the town along Mayor Street and Virgen de Valvanera Avenue, coming out the other side to pass by the "Romeros Fountain" on the right-hand side. The Camino then crosses the road which runs to San Millán de la Cogolla, (20 kilometres away), passing through Alesanco and the Cañas monastery. Continue on along a dirt track, where a marker shows the location of the border between Azofra and Alesanco. A section

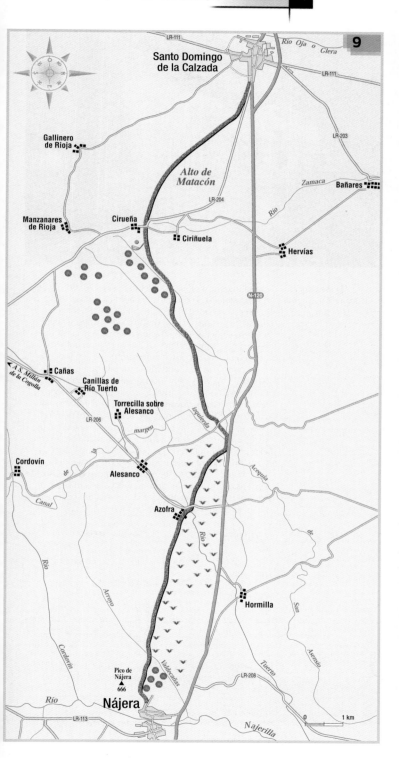

*Monastery of
Valvanera in Sierra
de la Demanda.*

of the road runs along parallel to the N-120, from where it is possible to go onwards to Santo Domingo. However, it is recommended to take the much more attractive option of getting away from the roadway and walking towards Cirueña. To follow this alternative route, begin by heading upwards through the vegetation until you reach a plateau, on which an extremely alien-looking golf course can be found in the middle of a holm oak wood. To the right of here, you will be able to see Ciruñuela, and then **Cirueña,** a village you will soon reach along the pathway. From here, and indeed until you reach Santo Domingo, the track is full of ups and downs, (the Matacón hills). From a viewpoint along the way, you can see as far as the foothills of the La Demanda mountain range to the South, and the Cantabria mountain range to the North. Straight ahead, you should be able to see **Santo Domingo de la Calzada,** your next stop. The entrance to the town is in between several barns, from where you must join the pavement again to go into the village along Doce de Mayo Street.

CYCLISTS

This is a fairly easy stretch, and should present no difficulty.

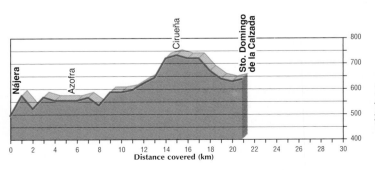

STAGE 9. PRACTICAL INFORMATION

AZOFRA

HOSTELS

"Herbert Simón" hostel.
The parish offers shelter next to the church all year round. It has 16 beds and a kitchen, as well as room for bicycles. ∅ 941 379 057

"Roland Kalle" hostel.
Private. ∅ 941 379 096

RESTAURANTS

Camino de Santiago.
C/ Mayor, 24. ∅ 941 379 239

El Peregrino.
Plaza de España, 17.
∅ 941 416 041

SANTO DOMINGO DE LA CALZADA

HOSTELS

"Casa del santo" hostel.
This hostel, which has a great tradition, is run by the "Fraternity of the Saint" (Cofradía del Santo). It has 70 beds, although there are more in the summer, and a kitchen. Open all year round. It has room for bicycles and a stable.
∅ 941 343 390

Abadía Cisterciense "Nuestra Señora de la Anunciación" hostel.
On calle Mayor, the Benedictine nuns offer approximately 30 beds. In addition, they have a kitchen, a stable and room for bicycles. ∅ 941 340 700

HOTELS

HS* Rio.
C/ Etchegoyen, 2. ∅ 941 340 005.
12 rooms. 24 beds.

HS Hospedería Cisterciense.
C/ Pinar, 2. ∅ 941 340 700.
79 rooms. 111 beds.

Albert guest house.
Plaza Beato Hermosilla.
∅ 941 340 827. 5 rooms.
10 beds.

Miguel guest house.
Avda. Juan Carlos I, 23-3°.
∅ 941 343 252. 6 rooms.
12 beds. Double room: € 22.

RESTAURANTS

Casa Sarmiento.
Avda. de Haro, 5. ∅ 941 341 572

El Rincón de Emilio.
Plaza Bonifacio Gil, 7.
∅ 941 340 990

Hidalgo.
C/ Hilario Pérez, 6.
∅ 941 340 227

Los Arcos.
C/ Mayor, 68. ∅ 941 342 890

Mesón del Abuelo.
Plaza Alameda. ∅ 941 342 791

Mesón El Peregrino.
C/ Mayor, 18. ∅ 941 340 202

Mesón Los Caballeros.
C/ Mayor, 56. ∅ 941 342 789

MEANS OF TRANSPORT

The Logroño-Burgos, line, which is run by the Grupo Jiménez bus company, stops in **Santo Domingo de la Calzada**.

HISTORY AND WEALTH OF THE STAGE 9

THE FRENCH ROAD. NÁJERA – SANTO DOMINGO DE LA CALZADA

For many pilgrims, leaving **Nájera** involves technically straying from the Road to Santiago for a few moments, in order to take a detour to Valvanera and San Millán de la Cogolla.

The patron saint of La Rioja is worshipped in the form of a beautiful XIth century Romanesque-Byzantian image in the enormous monastery of **Valvanera.**

The detour leads to the monastery of **San Millán de la Cogolla,** where not only the patron saint of Castille but also the Castilian language - the first known examples of Castilian and Basque ballads were found in this monastery's large library - were born. The pieces of literature found in the monastery include the very famous *Glosas Emilianenses,* now kept in manuscript 60 in the Academy of History, and the older *Glosarios,* a

type of encyclopaedia kept in the same institution in Madrid. The development in San Millán consists of two parts: the older one, Suso (from *sursum,* meaning "up"), includes the caves dug into the mountain, where the hermit saint and his followers lived since the VIth century, and the more recent parts, which were built and annexed later: these include the Mozarabic church, the famous atrium where the Seven Infants of Lara are buried, and the impressive

San Millán de la Cogolla. Left, interior of Suso monastery; below, Baroque vestry in Yuso monastery.

XIth century lying statue of St Millán on the place where he was once buried. By the XIth century, due to the vicinity of the pilgrimage route, some elements typical of the worship of St James had been added to the worship of St Millán. Two examples are the St James tax (voto de Santiago) that all Castilian towns up to the river Pisuerga had to pay, and the fact of St Millán himself becoming the patron saint of the Christian Reconquest (he too appeared in a battle or two riding a white steed). Another consequence of the Road to Santiago was that a lodging place and pilgrims' hospital, with its own infirmary and doctors, were built in the valley where Yuso (from *deorsum*, "abajo") can be found today. The monks eventually moved here, bringing from Suso the library and the remains of St Millán. The impressive monastic complex which now stands here was built in the XVIth century.

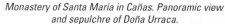

Monastery of Santa María in Cañas. Panoramic view and sepulchre of Doña Urraca.

Returning to the route while avoiding a second visit to Nájera, you reach **Cañas,** the hometown of St Dominic of Silos (1000-1073), founder of the Benedictine monastery in Burgos, which today bears his name (Santo Domingo de Silos). A community of Cistercian nuns occupies, since it was founded, the monastery of Santa María in Cañas, whose architectural style is also Cistercian. Of particular note are the church and the chapter house (sala capitular), which houses a small museum with high-quality pieces such as the XIIIth century Gothic sepulchre of the blessed Urraca López de Haro. In addition, local tradition has preserved the memory of St Francis of Assisi going through Cañas in his journey to Santiago de Compostela.

If you leave Nájera via the official way, the first town you encounter is **Azofra,** a small town with the typical pilgrimage town layout: houses lined along the Pilgrim Road. There is some XIIth century documentary evidence that there once stood, adjoined to a church dedicated to St Peter, a pilgrims' hospital and cemetery. A statue of St James depicted as a pilgrim is preserved in the current parish church of Nuestra Señora de los Ángeles, which dates from the XVIIth century.

*Santo Domingo de la Calzada.
Cathedral Renaissance façade.*

Rather than to the pilgrimage, the name of **Cirueña** is bound to Castilian count Fernán González who, according to the poem which bears his name, was locked up here by Navarrese troops after the battle of Valpierre. Close to **Ciriñuela** and **Hervías** used to be the hospital of Valleota or Bellota, run by the Knights of the Order of Calatrava in the late XIIth and early XIIIth centuries.

Santo Domingo de la Calzada, a city founded by and for pilgrims, is another great milestone in the Road to Santiago. Its name comes from its founder, Dominic, who was born in the XIth century in neighbouring Viloria de Rioja, also on the Road. According to his hagiography, after trying, to no avail, to be admitted into the monasteries of Valvanera and San Millán, he settled as a hermit in a forest on the bank of the river Oja. Feeling sorry for the pilgrims he saw struggling to cross the river, he first built a bridge for them. He later built a lodging place and, finally, a church which was consecrated in 1106 and which became a cathedral see towards the end of the XIIth century. Although he began this important personal project with very precarious means, St Dominic was supported by successive Lords of La Rioja - Alfonso VI of León and Castille to start with and Alfonso I of Aragon later -, as well as by the Bishopric of Calahorra, which had jurisdiction over the area where he carried out his activities. At the time of *Liber peregrinationis,* the saint's activities had already resulted in a flourishing town whose main monuments, which were dedicated to the pilgrims, included a bridge, a hospital and the church of San Salvador, where St Dominic was buried in the middle of the road which he built. In the chapter devoted to saints whose relics must be worshipped by pilgrims on their way to Santiago we mention, in relation to Navarre, "the remains of St Dominic, confessor, who built the Road between Nájera and Redecilla, where he now rests". At the beginning, the worship of St Dominic, supported by a diligent brotherhood devoted to assisting pilgrims, was very active. Among the many miracles attributed to him is the universally famous miracle of the chicken which crowed after being roasted, which is in fact no more than an enriched appropriation of the story of the unjustly hanged pilgrim who was kept alive by a saint supporting his feet. The earliest documentary reference to this miracle, which is repeated in several parts of the route in the whole of Europe, can be found in the *Book of Miracles in Liber Sancti Iacobi.* According to this, the miracle took place in Toulouse, the pilgrim was German, and the saint in question was, of course, the apostle St James. Both Jacobo di Voragine in his *Golden Legend,* and Vincent of Beauvais in his *Mirror of Stories,* follow *Liber Sancti Iacobi* very closely. Cistercian monk

Henhouse in the Cathedral of Santo Domingo de la Calzada.

Caesarius of Heisterbach introduced a few variations in his *Dialogue of Miracles:* instead of one pilgrim there are two: a father and son from Utrecht. Alfonso X the Wise replaced St James with the Virgin Mary, although other versions place St Giles or the bishop of Utrecht, St Amand, in this role. However, the addition of a second part, in which the subject of the action is a group of birds who, roasted and moments away from being eaten by the judge of the place, miraculously come back to life, relates to Santo Domingo de la Calzada, where a mid-XIVth century document tells this part of the story for the first time. The picturesque motif (taken from a passage from the *Apocryphal Gospels)* was so successful that it was depicted in many churches of the route in the whole of Europe, and even became the emblem of some of them, such as "o Galo" in Barcelos, Portugal. In any case, as was mentioned earlier, since Santo Domingo de la Calzada has the most documentary evidence, the legend of the miracle is deemed to belong to it. According to the version of this city, a whole family of pilgrims from Cologne – mother, father and son (by the name of Hugonel) – are staying at the hospital in Santo Domingo. A maid propositions the boy and, on being rejected by him, hides a silver goblet among his clothes and reports him as a thief. Hugonel is arrested and executed but, just before his parents are due to leave, they hear him say, from the gallows, that he is alive because St Dominic is holding him by his feet. The parents speak to the chief magistrate of the town, who is sitting at the table about to eat a roast rooster and hen and who, on hearing the story, sceptically replies that the boy is just as alive as the birds on his plate. At that moment, the birds jump off his plate and start flying around, thus proving the youth's innocence.

Since the XVth century, all pilgrims who have left a written account of their pilgrimage have included a version of the miracle of the birds, and have never failed to mention that the transept of the cathedral has, in its memory, a rooster and a hen. Even today it is possible to admire them in a beautiful Gothic niche called "el Gallinero" (the Henhouse). The cathedral, dedicated to the Saviour and the Virgin Mary, is one of the earliest Gothic buildings in Spain. The church has a Latin Cross base, a central body with three naves, a groined vault and a Romanesque ambulatory. In spite of their variety, the style of the capitals shows the relationship between their sculptors and the cities of Nájera, Moissac and Pamplona. Among the church's valuable works are Damián Forment's high altarpiece and the Romanesque lying statue of St Dominic. This saint, as explained in *Liber peregrinationis*, was buried in the middle of the road, which is why the cathedral has invaded and broken the Road to Santiago's straight line through the city. Both of Santo Domingo's two other great works, the bridge and the hospital, are still standing. The former has been totally rebuilt, and the latter is part of the current Parador Nacional de Turismo (national inn for tourism).

10 Santo Domingo de la Calzada – Belorado

Once again we are back alongside the N-120. With scarcely the time to take in the trees, the Camino takes us off through lots of crop fields, interspersed with small brooks and oak woods. This landscape warns us of the approaching mountain range and, indeed, we can soon see the Oca Mountains looming on the horizon.

Bridge over the river Oja in Santo Domingo de la Calzada.

In **Santo Domingo de la Calzada,** the Camino will take you through the main street and Palomarejos Street, before rejoining the N-120. After crossing the bridge which spans the river Oja, (a bridge built by Saint Dominic himself), you will take a shady path which leads off to the left, passing between the motorway on one side and cereal fields on the other. The Camino continues on its gentle incline until, 3 kilometres in, it reaches the *Cross of the Brave* (Cruz de los Valientes), where it crosses the bypass. After covering a further 5 kilometres, you will be faced with two options: to go along the road towards Grañón, which is 1.9 km away, or to stick to the pathway, which will take you to the same destination, but covers 3.2 km of pathway.

If you chose the second alternative, you will come into **Grañón** after passing through the cemetery and crossing the road that leads to Morales. You will continue on through the main street and Cercas Street before coming down an incline and leaving the area. When you come to the last building you should turn to the left, taking the rural path which then veers to the right before crossing the river Villar. You must then walk towards the border between La Rioja and Burgos, situated just 2 km away. From here, you will be able to make out the river Reláchigo on the other side of the road, and Redecilla and Castildelgado ahead of you, with the Oca Mountains away off in the distance. Just a little under 2 kms further on, you will come to **Redecilla del Camino,** after passing by a Camino information point crossing over to the left-hand side of the road. Continue via El Cristo Street and Mayor Street, next to the church,

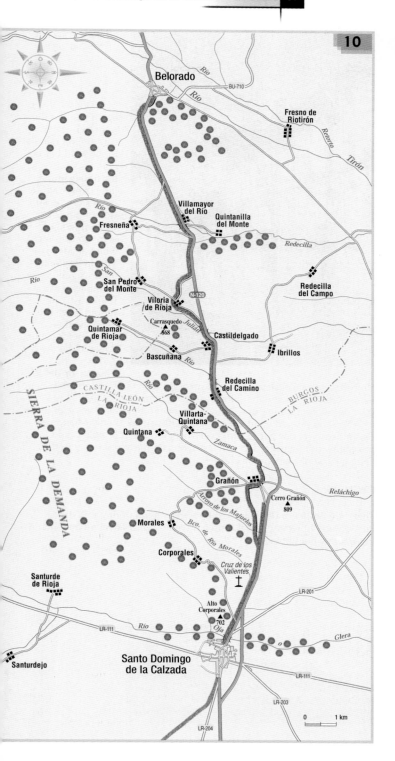

Pilgrim on his way through Grañón.

before following the path's descent yet again to cross the river Reláchigo, carrying on parallel to the road before coming to **Castildelgado.** A little over 500 metres on the far side of this town, you will come across a turn-off which leads to **Viloria de Rioja,** birthplace of Saint Dominic of the Walkway. You should leave this town via Bajera Street, before going down along the N-120 towards **Villamayor del Río.** Here you will take Mayor Street to meet up with the Camino once again, before covering the final 5 kilometres which remain before you reach your destination for the day. At the entrance to **Belorado,** you can leave the road and instead continue along a pathway on the right-hand side. This means you can avoid some very ugly industrial buildings and, passing by a hill covered in conifers, you can make your way to the church of Saint Mary and its hostel.

CYCLISTS

There are no major difficulties to be encountered during this stage. Please note, however, that the stretch which runs between Grañón and Belorado is not tarmacked.

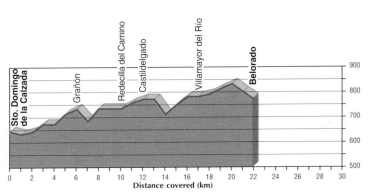

STAGE 10. PRACTICAL INFORMATION

GRAÑÓN

HOSTELS

"Virgen de Carrasgueda" Youth Hostel.
℘ 941 746 000
"San Juan Bautista" pilgrims' hospital.

MEANS OF TRANSPORT

The Grupo Jiménez Logroño-Burgos
buses stop here.

REDECILLA DEL CAMINO

HOSTELS

Municipal Hostel (Albergue Municipal).
C/ Mayor. In the old San Lázaro
Hospital. 24 beds, kitchen and patio.
Cyclists welcome. ℘ 947 588 078 /
947 580 283

MEANS OF TRANSPORT

The Grupo Jiménez Logroño-Burgos
buses stop here.

CASTILDELGADO

HOTELS

HS** El Chocolatero.
Carretera Logroño, km 57-58.
℘ 947 588 063. 50 beds. Double room:
€ 44/39; single room: € 24/21;
breakfast: € 5,9; lunch/dinner: € 12.
HSR* Club.
Carretera Logroño-Vigo.
℘ 947 580 699. 8 rooms. 15 beds.

RESTAURANTS

El Chocolatero. Carretera N-120, km
14. ℘ 947 588 063

VILORIA DE RIOJA

HOSTELS

Private pilgrims' hostel (Albergue
privado de peregrinos). ℘ 646 364 037

VILLAMAYOR DEL RÍO

HOSTELS

Villamayor del Río hostel (Albergue de
Villamayor del Río).
℘ 639 350 272 / 659 967 967

RESTAURANTS

Casa León. Carretera Logroño, km 90.
℘ 947 580 237

BELORADO

HOSTELS

Parish hostel (Albergue parroquial).
Next to the church of Santa María. It
has approximately 30 beds and a
kitchen. It also has a garage which
provides more places in the summer.
Cyclists welcome. ℘ 947 580 085
"Cuatro Cantones" hostel.
C/ Hipólito López Bernal, 10. It has 46
beds, a kitchen, washing machine and
garden. Room for bicycles. Open all year
round. ℘ 947 580 591 / 696 427 707

HOTELS

H* Belorado. Avda. Generalísimo, 30.
℘ 947 580 684. 20 beds. Double room:
€ 40; single room: € 25; breakfast:
€ 2,5; lunch/dinner: € 9.
Ojarre guest house. C/ Santiago, 16.
℘ 947 580 223. 7 beds.
Double room: € 27.
Toñi guest house. C/ Redecilla del
Campo. ℘ 947 580 525. 10 beds.
Double room: € 45.

RESTAURANTS

Etoile. Plaza Mayor, 26. ℘ 947 580 246
Goya. Avda. Generalísimo, 8.
℘ 947 580 344
Picias. Avda. Generalísimo, 8.
℘ 947 580 325
Tizona. Avda. Generalísimo, 10.
℘ 947 580 390

MEANS OF TRANSPORT

The Grupo Jiménez Logroño-Burgos
buses stop here.

HISTORY AND WEALTH OF THE STAGE 10

THE FRENCH ROAD. SANTO DOMINGO DE LA CALZADA – BELORADO

After crossing the bridge, built by St Dominic over the river Oja just outside his city, the road (also laid by him) lead pilgrims to the outskirts of **Grañón,** a town built on Mirabel hill and born as a stronghold of the large, moving and beaten down frontier which divided Castille and Navarre for centuries. Some of the remains of the city wall enclosure can still be seen on the street surrounding it. The earliest documents relating to Grañón date from the Xth century, and bind it to Castilian count Fernán González. It later appears as part of the Kings of Navarre's domain. It also appears later still, at the very end of the XIth century, in relation to King Alfonso VI and his faithful lieutenant and great rival of El Cid, García Ordóñez, who held, among others, the title of Count of Grañón, and who enforced Alfonso VI's policies in the Riojan territory, as we saw earlier in the case of the repopulation of Logroño. Due to Grañón's military and political importance, together with its position close to the Road to Santiago, some religious institutions, such as the monasteries of Santo Tomé and San Miguel, became established in its district. A pilgrims" hospital, which was active for a very long time, depended on the latter monastery, which was added to San Millán de la Cogolla in the XIth century. However, the religious institution which appears to have the strongest link to Grañón from its birth is the monastery of San Juan Bautista, on the Eastern part of the town. At the beginning, it depended on Santa María de Nájera, and it may have included a pilgrims' hospital. The large parish church, which inherited the monastery's location and form of worship, is a XIVth century Gothic building to which some additions were made later. Within it is an extremely valuable altarpiece by Natuera Borgoñón and Bernal Forment. The monastery was a central part of the town, whose grid-like structure may be related to the town planning model spread along the Road to Santiago for the creation and repopulation of towns which was carried out along its route, especially in Navarre and Aragon. Even though Grañón was relatively important and had the necessary means for

Grañón. XVIth century altarpiece in the church of San Juan Bautista.

Redecilla del Camino. XIIIth century baptismal font, in the parish church of La Virgen de la Calle.

hospitality, it is not mentioned in *Liber peregrinationis*. This may be because it was slightly away from the route planned and laid by St. Dominic of the Walkway (Santo Domingo de la Calzada, assuming that this coincided with the current road). In 1258, Alfonso X the Wise incorporated Grañón into Santo Domingo, which gave rise to some local conflict. The "Cruz de los Valientes" (Cross of the Brave Ones), dedicated to the rivalry between Grañón and Santo Domingo, was erected in an intermediate point between the two towns, where a trial by ordeal in relation to the ownership of a field took place.

Even today, the name of the victor, Martín García, who represented Grañón and asked the neighbours of his town to pray the Lord's Prayer Father and the Hail Mary for him every Sunday, is still remembered.

Unlike Grañón, **Redecilla del Camino** is mentioned in *Liber peregrinationis* as a Stop of the Road within St. Dominic of the Walkway's radius of activity. This is also a typical Road town, laid out along a Pilgrim Road with two hospitals facing each other at the ends: the XIIth century pilgrims' hospital of San Lázaro (the current refuge was built on the same spot), and the parish church of La Virgen de la Calle, whose name unequivocally refers to the Road or Way to Santiago ("calle" means "street"). One of the most famous pieces of the Road, a XIIth century baptismal font carved out of a large stone, can be found in this modern church. It is a half-spherical cup, standing on a solid pillar with a polylobulated circular base. The eight vertical lobes simulate a group of columns attached to a central pillar. These false columns reach the cup in the shape of four-storey towers adorned with doors, balconies and windows. The spaces between columns are similarly adorned. This very original decoration is evidently an attempt to represent a great building or, even better, a city: heavenly Jerusalem, the ultimate goal for anyone who has been baptised. On the bank of the river Relachigo in the outskirts of Redecilla there used to be, until the late XIIth century, a hospital dedicated to St Christine and which depended on San Millán de la Cogolla.

Castildelgado, which appears in mediaeval documents as *Villaipún,* also had a pilgrims' hospital, founded by Alfonso VII. The current name, which has only recently prevailed over the old one, honours its most famous son, don Francisco Delgado, bishop of Lugo and Jaén, the archbishop of Burgos elect, one of the greatest theologians of the Counterreform and an active participant of the Council of Trento (1564). He is now buried in the parish church of San Pedro.

———— *Belorado. Main square* (Plaza Mayor) *and church of San Pedro.* ————

Viloria de la Rioja was St. Dominic of the Walkway's hometown, and the Romanesque baptismal font with which the saint was allegedly baptised can still be found in the parish church. The land where his family's home (still there until relatively recently) was built is likewise suitably marked.

After **Villamayor del Río,** a small town on the bank of a meager stream, the traveller reaches **Belorado,** another historic stop of the Road to Santiago. The layout of Belorado, which may have been a Roman settlement, looks more like a North-South axis than a hypothetical East-West stretch of the Pilgrim Road. This may be due to the fact that the town was already relatively developed by the time St Dominic of the Walkway channelled the Road to Santiago through it. The reason for the North-South axis is Belorado's position: it extends along an old road which came from Briviesca and followed the narrow valley of the river Tirón from North to South. The town is built on a gully of the river Tirón, under the shadow of a limy reef on which a castle, now in ruins, stands. Belorado, mentioned in *Liber peregrinationis* as one of the Stops of the Road to Santiago, had already been repopulated in 1116 by Alfonso I of Aragon, as part of the series of acts he performed to consolidate his position in La Rioja against his stepson Alfonso VII of León and Castille who would ultimately regain that place for his kingdom. Belorado - a town at the edge of the county ("villa en cabo de condado"), as it is referred to in the *Poem of Fernán González* – had previously belonged (in succession) to the County of Castille (Fernán González), the Kingdom of Navarre (Sancho III) and the Kingdom of León and Castille (Alfonso VI). In fact, Belorado's vicissitudes during the Middle Ages are common to the whole of the Riojan territory, a large, rich and disputed frontier always shifting between the kingdoms of León and Navarre. Belorado contains many references to St James, although the oldest ones are rare and somewhat obscure. Among the most interesting and original ones is the worship of St Caprasio. Its history, associated with that of the Holy Faith, is partly narrated in *Liber peregrinationis:* St Caprasio, bishop of Agen (in French Gascogne), hid in a cave during the persecution ordered by Emperor Maximin in the last third of the IIIrd century. Following the example of a young girl called Faith who openly and bravely confronts martyrdom, he leaves his hiding place, goes to the place of her martyrdom, and meets the same glorious death. In the wall of the gully at whose feet we find Belorado, there is a cave with the name of San Cabrás, in memory of the bishop of Agen, who also hid in a cave before his martyrdom. It seems reasonable to believe that this form of devotion was brought to Belorado by pilgrims or colonists, maybe even the same ones brought by Alfonso I *the Warrior* to repopulate the town in 1116. The statue of St Caprasio, originally placed in the cave itself, can now be found in the church of San Nicolás. It seems that the cave, one of the many which perforate the gully of Belorado, effectively served as a dwelling place for hermits in

Belorado. Above, altarpiece of the church of Santa María; below, detailed view of the pilgrims' shelter.

Visigothic times, when the anchorite movement was particularly strong, as we already saw in the case of St Millán. Another striking reference to St James is the 1408 document – now kept in the town hall – whereby the king confirms Belorado's exemption from paying the church of Santiago de Compostela the levy known as "voto de Santiago" (tax of St James). According to this curious document, the dispute, which was resolved in 1408, started when, after his legendary victory at Clavijo, King Ramiro I demanded the town to pay the tax, to which the latter refused arguing that it did not belong to his kingdom. A beautiful stone altarpiece entirely dedicated to St James can be found in the church of Santa María. The piece depicts him, as we have already seen in other Riojan temples, in his two great iconographic versions, the Moor-killing knight and the peaceful pilgrim. In addition, the church's main altarpiece is dominated by a beautiful Romanesque sculpture of the Virgin. The only part of the old hospital of Santa María de Belén, which was run by the bishop of Burgos, which has survived is a chapel just outside the town. Other surviving monuments from Belorado's prosperous past are the churches of San Pedro and San Nicolás.

11 Belorado – San Juan de Ortega

Up until you get to Villafranca Montes de Oca, this stage is similar to the previous one. However, after a short while you will have to go deeper into the dense woods of the Oca Mountains.

Parish church of Espinosa del Camino.

Go along Camino de Santiago Avenue on your way out of **Belorado,** joining a tarmacked path that goes past St Claire's Convent before joining up with the N-120. Cross to the left-hand side of the road, where you can stop for a rest in a park area on the banks of the river Tirón before coming to a wooden footbridge. Just as in the last stage, your route will take you alongside the roadway, passing by cereal fields. After passing by a service station, a Red Cross point, and the turn-off which leads to San Miguel de Pedroso, the path separates itself from the N-120, (thought it remains in view all the time), and heads towards **Tosantos.** The Camino goes in through the back of the village, from where you can still see the hills, one of which houses the Hermitage of the Virgen of la Peña. Near Tosantos you will come to **Villambistia,** from where you will head off through rows of poplar trees. Further on you will be able to see **Espinosa del Camino,** situated on a hill. This is your next destination, and you must cross the road on your way to the village. After passing the village, you will now be faced with the valley of the river Oca. Continue along a dirt track which winds between crop fields and takes you first up, then down, towards the San Felices Monastery. The path will then veer off to the left and head towards **Villafranca Montes de Oca.** To get to this village, you must go along the road, which can prove to be quite dangerous, so take care. When you reach the San Antonio Abad Hospital,

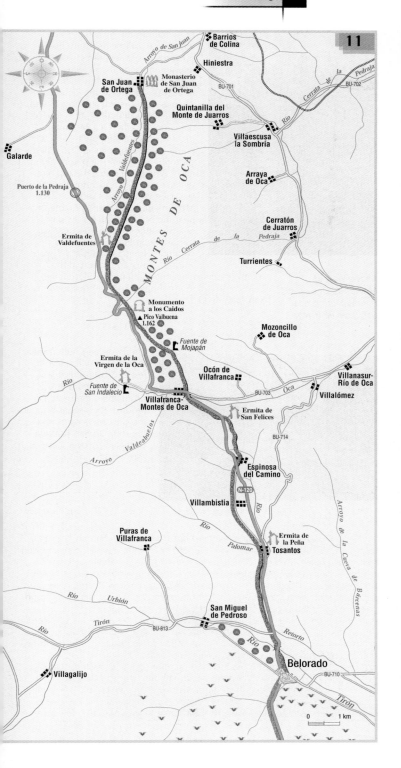

11

Barrios de Colina
Hiniestra
BU-701
Cerrata de la Pedraja
BU-702
San Juan de Ortega
Monasterio de San Juan de Ortega
Quintanilla del Monte de Juarros
Villaescusa la Sombría
Galarde
Arraya de Oca
Puerto de la Pedraja 1.130
Cerratón de Juarros
Ermita de Valdefuentes
Río Cerrata de la Pedraja
Turrientes
MONTES DE OCA
Arroyo Valdefuentes
Monumento a los Caidos
Pico Valbuena 1.162
Mozoncillo de Oca
Fuente de Mojapán
Ermita de la Virgen de la Oca
Ocón de Villafranca
Villanasur-Río de Oca
Río
Fuente de San Indalecio
Villalómez
Villafranca-Montes de Oca
BU-703
Oca
Ermita de San Felices
BU-714
Arroyo Valdeabuelos
Espinosa del Camino
N-120
Villambistía
Río
Puras de Villafranca
Río
Ermita de la Peña
Tosantos
Palomar
Arroyo de la Cueva de Bárcenas
Río Urbión
San Miguel de Pedroso
Río Tirón
BU-813
Río
Belorado
BU-710
Villagalijo
Retorto
Tirón
0   1 km

cross over to the right-hand side, where you will begin your climb upwards. Signs will direct you to the left, going round the cemetery, but there is a slope which is much easier to access, leading to the same point. Keep going upwards, (at times, with considerable difficulty), through thick oak woods to the Oca Mountains. Just over a kilometre away, you will come to the Mojapán spring, a pretty spot where you can stop and take it easy. When you reach the top, you will see conifers appearing next to the oaks. At the Los Caidos Monument, you should be able to hear the N-120, which runs past nearby. After crossing the river Cerrata de la Pedraja, you will continue along a forest path. If you want to, you can turn off at the MP-61 milestone to visit the Valdefuentes hermitage, before carrying on to the end of the forest towards **San Juan de Ortega.**

Above, view of Montes de Oca. Below, pilgrims near San Juan de Ortega.

CYCLISTS

Until you pass **Villafranca,** the surface will present few difficulties, but you may encounter a few problems if the route is muddy. The ascent through the Oca Mountains and the route to **San Juan de Ortega,** however, can prove quite arduous.

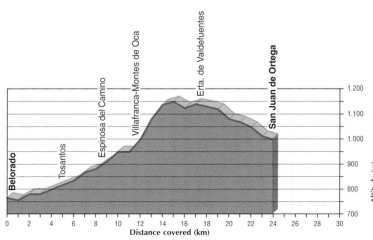

STAGE 11. PRACTICAL INFORMATION

TOSANTOS

HOSTELS

"Camino de Santiago" hostel.
℘ 947 580 250

VILLAFRANCA MONTES DE OCA

HOSTELS

"San Antonio Abad" pilgrims' hostel.
It is located on carretera Burgos. It has 20 beds, a kitchen, living room and hot water. ℘ 947 460 922 / 947 582 000

HOTELS

El Pájaro guest house.
Carretera Logroño-Vigo.
℘ 947 582 001. 7 rooms.
12 beds. Double room: € 30;
single room: € 16.

RESTAURANTS

El Pájaro.
San Roque housing estate.
℘ 947 582 029

MEANS OF TRANSPORT

The Grupo Jiménez buses stop here.

SERVICES

There is a shop, cafés/bars and a chemist.

SAN JUAN DE ORTEGA

HOSTELS

Albergue del Monasterio.
This hostel with a great tradition is run by the parish priest, who has been offering his hospitality for many years. It has 60 beds and is open all year round. ℘ 947 560 438

SERVICES

There is a café/bar on the other side of the monastery.

HISTORY AND WEALTH OF THE STAGE 11

THE FRENCH ROAD. BELORADO – SAN JUAN DE ORTEGA

When you leave **Belorado,** the way crosses the river Tirón by means of a little bridge attributed by tradition to San Juan de Ortega, and which still retains some elements from his time. Very close by, a chapel dedicated to St Lazarus reminds us of the old pilgrims' and patients' hospital that used to be there.

The peculiar cave hermit of Nuestra Señora de la Peña, dug into a perforated limy hill similar to the one in Belorado, can be glimpsed from the road in **Tosantos.** A Romanesque image of the Virgin is kept in it.

Near **Villambistia** (meaning the town of Laín el Bestia, the Beast – its first owner) a section of the old road still remains, and a sculpture of St Indalecio – whose worship is widespread in the region of Oca (as will be seen when we get to Villafranca) - depicted as a bishop can be found in the parish church of **Espinosa del Camino.** Later on, the Road leads the traveller to a simple country chapel known as Ábside de San Felices, the worn remains of the ancient Mozarabic monastery dedicated to St Felix, teacher of St Millán, where Castilian count Diego Porcelos, founder of Burgos, is said to have been buried.

Villafranca Montes de Oca is located on the old territory of *Oca (Auca,* which was an episcopal see at least between the IVth and VIth centuries), which was destroyed after the Saracen invasion and, although Alfonso I soon retrieved it from Muslim power, was never rebuilt. Old *Auca* itself was in Pago del Llano, in the current district of Villafranca, where the chapel of Santa María de Oca, possibly a vestige of the old and unknown saint to which the cathedral was dedicated, stands today. Behind it is the well of San Indalecio, a spring claiming to be on the spot where the bishop saint was martyred. According to local tradition, Indalecio evangelised the Oca region and was its first bishop. Although his worship is fairly widespread in the region, as we saw in Espinosa del Camino, it did not become established during his time but more recently: in pilgrimage times, if not later. But who was this Indalecio person, anyway?

According to a IXth century Mozarabic text from Southern Spain, he was one of seven apostolic men who, consecrated by St Peter and St Paul in Rome, were given the task of evangelising Spain. At the end of his mission (still according to this text), Indalecio had founded the diocese of *Urci* (Pechina, Almería), of which he was the first bishop. Already in the XIth century, as we find out from the third book of *Liber Sancti*

Ruins of Ábside de San Felices in Villafranca de Montes de Oca.

Iacobi, a text which reconciled the tradition of the apostolic men with that of Santiago's preaching in Spain was written in Santiago de Compostela. In this new text, instead of apostolic males we have the Apostle's Spanish disciples. According to another text also written around this time, the remains of St Indalecio were taken to San Juan de la Peña and, subsequently, to Jaca, where they now rest in its cathedral. The worship of St Indalecio in Oca, which is related to the old and important hospital

Chapel of Valdefuentes.

of Santiago, also created in the XIth century and very closely linked with the city's second birth, may have originated at this time.

Indeed, in 1075 Alfonso VI decided, firstly, to move the old and much reduced episcopal see of Oca to Burgos and, secondly and possibly as compensation for the first, to rebuild the city near its original place, with an advantageous "fuero", or charter, and a new name: Villafranca. The reconstruction was carried out in the relatively new diversion of the Road to Santiago, opened by Sancho III of Navarre and made possible by the builder saints, Dominic of the Walkway (Santo Domingo de la Calzada) and San Juan de Ortega, with Alfonso VI's support. The above mentioned old hospital of Santiago, Villafranca's main mediaeval institution, disappeared with no other trace than the current parish church's name, whose current building dates from the XVIIIth century and houses two good quality sculptures of St James as a pilgrim. Villafranca's other pilgrimage monument is another hospital, San Antonio Abad or hospital of La Reina. In contrast with the one discussed above, many important parts of this hospital, such as the spectacular elliptical arch on its façade, have been preserved. In spite of the large coat of arms of the Reyes Católicos (the Catholic King and Queen – Ferdinand and Isabella) sculpted on this building, the hospital's name actually refers to doña Juana Manuel, Henry II´s wife, who in 1380 donated it to the Antonites, a religious community with a particularly strong presence on the Road to Santiago which specialised in the treatment of some illnesses, such as erysipelas. Medical instruments from that time have been found in the hospital.

At rugged Montes de Oca, before the San Juan de Ortega sanctuary which marks the end of this stage, we find the chapel of **Valdefuentes,** now dedicated to St James, and the only remains of the old hospital church run by a Cistercian community in the XIIth century. We know that Montes de Oca used to have other hospitals as well, such as the hospital of Valbuena or the hospital of Muñeca, which were established there to assist pilgrims in this area, considered to be one of the most dangerous parts of the Road due, not only to its dense vegetation and rough terrain, but also to the many pests and bandits that lived in it. The latter used this area to hide from the Castilian and Navarrese authorities,

San Juan de Ortega. Mausoleum with lying statue.

and earned their living by attacking the most vulnerable pilgrims, whose sole hope of avoiding robbery was to gather in large groups. This was the main reason that prompted Juan de Quintanaortuño, follower and collaborator of St Dominic of the Walkway, to carry out some work here. He cleared up paths and founded a pilgrims' hospital, a chapel and a religious community in Ortega (from Latin *urtica*, "nettle"), one of the most inhospitable parts of the area. This development is known, since the XIIIth century, after its founder's name: **San Juan de Ortega.** Born in 1080 in nearby Quintanaortuño, St John was a follower of St Dominic of the Walkway from an early age, and worked with him in the building of hospitals, churches, roads (such as the road between Agés and Atapuerca) and bridges (including Logroño, Nájera, Santo Domingo de la Calzada, Belorado and Agés), among others. After his aged master's death in the year 1109 and, since the territory was in the middle of a damaging civil war between doña Urraca and Alfonso I the Warrior which destroyed a large proportion of the work carried out by the builder saints in La Rioja, he resolved to make a pilgrimage to the Holy Land. After entrusting himself to St Nicholas of Bari and narrowly missing death in this hazardous journey, he swore to dedicate a chapel to this saint. On his return, he started work on repairing some of the bridges built by his master but destroyed by the war. He concentrated mostly on Montes de Oca, where he built a hospital and a chapel dedicated to St Nicholas of Bari (as promised) and founded a community of Regular Canons of St Augustine. This involved, of course, cleaning up the surroundings and providing ways in and out of this inhospitable area. It seems strange that *Liber peregrinationis,* which describes a journey made approximately in 1130, does not mention the San Juan de Ortega complex. This omission may be due to the development not having been finished at the time. The first important document relating to the San Juan de Ortega hospital, whereby Pope Innocent II placed it under his direct protection, dates from 1138. Both St Dominic of the Walkway and San Juan de Ortega were supported by the king, to the point that the latter eventually became confessor to Alfonso VII who, in 1142, granted him a sizeable proportion of the Crown's properties in Montes de Oca. During the saint's life, the institution flourished as a sort of Castilian Roncesvals but, after his death in 1163, it lost a lot of the prestige it had acquired. However, it did remain active for the whole of the Middle Ages and recovered part of its old lustre in the XVth century under the powerful church of Burgos. Its renewed success was due to a community from the

Church of San Juan de Ortega.

Order of St Jerome, whom the famous bishop of Burgos Pablo de
Santamaría had placed there. The most famous virtue among the ones
attributed to this saint was his ability to cure infertility. This was the
reason Isabella the Catholic visited the sanctuary in 1477 and, if the
important and magnificent works which she ordered to be carried out in
his church are anything to go by, the results were satisfactory. The
Gothic chapel of San Nicolás de Bari, which replaces the one built by
San Juan himself, dates from this time, as does the magnificent
mausoleum and lying statue of San Juan de Ortega, the work of John of
Cologne and Gil de Siloé. Most of the original church (which was begun
in 1150) or, at least, the three apses and the transept, are also from San
Juan de Ortega's time. The magnificent Romanesque sepulchre of San
Juan de Ortega is slightly more recent, and most of the capitals are also
from the XIIth century. Among them we find a new depiction of the
battle between Roland and Ferragut, to be added to the ones already
seen in Navarre and La Rioja. But we also find a capital with a brilliant
squeezed in version of the Annunciation, Visitation, Joseph's Dream and
Nativity sequence. The capital's worldwide fame is due to a simple yet
wonderful combined effect of light, architecture and sacred history,
which takes place in the evening of every equinox: when the church
falls in darkness, a ray from the dying sun falls on the capital, making
the sunlight a visible symbol of the impregnation of the Virgin by the
Holy Spirit.

12 San Juan de Ortega – Burgos

After the quiet and peaceful spots of the Atapuerca Mountain Range, you will make your way down into the valley of the Pico river. Here, the tranquil agricultural landscape disappears, and you will begin travelling through the traffic and industry which is characteristic of the entrance to Burgos.

From **San Juan de Ortega,** your route will take you along the road which heads toward Santovenia de Oca and the N-120. If you prefer to continue along the roadway, there is a path which goes directly along the roadside to Burgos. Shortly afterwards, you will come to a wooden cross which will direct you into a pine and oak wooded area. After you pass by a fenced-off area for livestock, the wood comes to an end, and you will come across an old mining railway cutting. A further 500 metres along will bring you to

Bridge between Agés and Atapuerca.

another cross. To the right you will be able to see the Church of Santovenia, and **Agés** should lie straight ahead. Go down to the village, passing by the Hermitage of Our Lady of Rebollo. A small road leads out of Agés, going directly to **Atapuerca,** passing alongside the bridge over the river Vena that was built by St John of Ortega. From this point, the Camino continues uphill through holm oaks towards the Atapuerca mountain range. Shortly afterwards, you will see the barbed wire boundaries of a military base. Almost 2 kilometres further along, you will come to another huge wooden cross. Looking to the right from this point, you will be able to make out in the distance a quarry and some radio antennae. On your way down you will see a series of crossroads, the first of which will take you to either **Cardeñuela** or **Castañares:**

A) If you choose to go to Cardeñuela, the Camino heads down to the village through **Villalval** and, once in **Cardeñuela,** the route leaves to head towards **Orbaneja.**

B) If you opt for the **Castañares** route, you will come to another fork in the road. Here, you must choose between Castañares and Orbaneja:

A) if you choose to head for Orbaneja, head down towards the village to rejoin the road to Cardeñuela. From Orbaneja you should head towards the A-1 motorway, crossing over the road via a bridge and heading onwards on a tarmacked path towards **Villafría de Burgos.** Cross the railway line and, once in Villafría, you should carry on through the industrial estate, following the route of the N-120. Close by, you will find the area of Gamonal, which leads the way into **Burgos.** After entering the city, head towards the cathedral along Calzadas Street, San Juan Street, Avellanos Street and Fernán González Street.

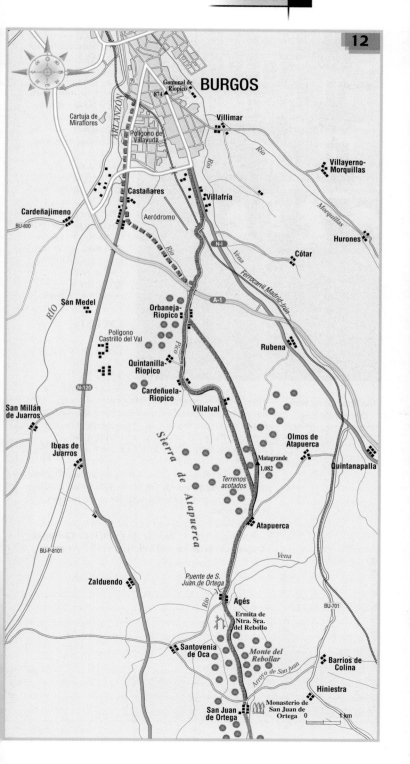

B) if you choose the Castañares route, you will find it much longer and much more difficult than the other route, with less road-signs to guide your way. Follow the motorway, as above, to Castañares, before taking a path that leads off to the left through dumps and fenced-off areas. After you pass **Castañares,** the route continues to follow the roadway, before joining up with the course of the Arlanzón as you come into **Burgos.**

CYCLISTS

When you come out of San Juan de Ortega, you can either:

A) opt to take the

The Road on its way through Burgos.

same route as pedestrians, although the section of the route that goes through the Atapuerca mountain range is extremely difficult. From **Atapuerca,** you can take the road which runs to **Olmos de Atapuerca,** from where you can carry on along the N-1;

B) or, head off to the left to take up the N-120 after passing by **Santovenia,** which will take you all the way to Burgos, via **Zalduendo, Ibeas de Juarros** and **San Mendel.**

C) or, alternatively, take the right-hand side route, which leads you to **Barrios de Colina** via **Olmos de Atapuerca, Rubena** and **Villafría.**

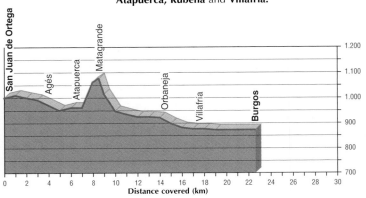

STAGE 12. PRACTICAL INFORMATION

ATAPUERCA

HOSTELS

"La Hutte" pilgrims' hostel.
C/ En Medio, 36. Approximately 20 beds. It has a meeting room and hot water. ⌀ 947 430 320

OLMOS DE ATAPUERCA

HOSTELS

Municipal hostel. (Albergue municipal) C/ La Iglesia. It has 32 places, a kitchen and hot water. ⌀ 947 430 328

IBEAS DE JUARROS

RESTAURANTS

Cantina de Ibeas. ⌀ 947 421 230
Los Claveles. Carretera Logroño, 31. ⌀ 947 421 230

MEANS OF TRANSPORT

The Continental bus company stop here. ⌀ 947 267 001.

RUBENA

HOTELS

Salo guest house. Carretera N-I Madrid-Irún, km 251. ⌀ 947 431 065. 13 beds. Single room: € 36.

VILLAFRÍA DE BURGOS

HOTELS

H** ABC Aduana. Carretera N-I Villafría, km 245. ⌀ 947 484 252. 22 rooms. 30 beds. Double room: € 53; single room: € 40; breakfast: € 3,15; lunch/dinner: € 7,5.

HR** Buenos Aires.
Carretera N-I, km 245. ⌀ 947 483 770. 140 beds. Double room: € 48.
HSR** Iruñako.
Carretera N-I Madrid-Irún, km 245. ⌀ 947 484 126. 52 beds. Double room: € 44-41; single room: € 27/25.

CAMPING SITES

$2.^{nd}$ C Río Vena. Ctra. N-I Burgos-Irún, km 245. ⌀ 947 484 120. 240 places.

MEANS OF TRANSPORT

The Logroño-Burgos buses stop here.

BURGOS

HOSTELS

Hostel set up on prefabricated huts on El Parral park, next to the King's Hospital (Hospital del Rey). It is run by the Burgos Road to Santiago Friends Association (Asociación de Amigos del Camino de Santiago de Burgos). 90 beds. Open all year round. In the summer it can accommodate people in the sports centre. ⌀ 947 460 922

HOTELS

Punta Brava guest house.
Pº Fuentecillas, 3-5º. ⌀ 947 208 211. Double room: € 30; single room: € 20.
Victoria guest house. C/ San Juan, 3-2º. ⌀ 947 201 542. 27 beds. Double room: € 30/25; single room: € 20/16.
H* Joma. C/ San Juan, 26-2º. ⌀ 947 203 350. 7 rooms. Double room: € 21/19; breakfast: € 1,87.
HS** Juarreño. C/ Santa Clara, 29. ⌀ 947 265 038. Double room: € 28.
HSR* Hidalgo. C/ Almirante Bonifaz, 14. ⌀ 947 203 481. Double room: € 30/20.

CAMPING SITES

$1.^{st}$ C Fuentes Blancas.
Ctra. Burgos-Cartuja de Miraflores, km 3,5. ⌀ 947 486 016. 1,200 places.

MEANS OF TRANSPORT

Bus station. ⌀ 947 288 855
RENFE rail station. ⌀ 947 203 560

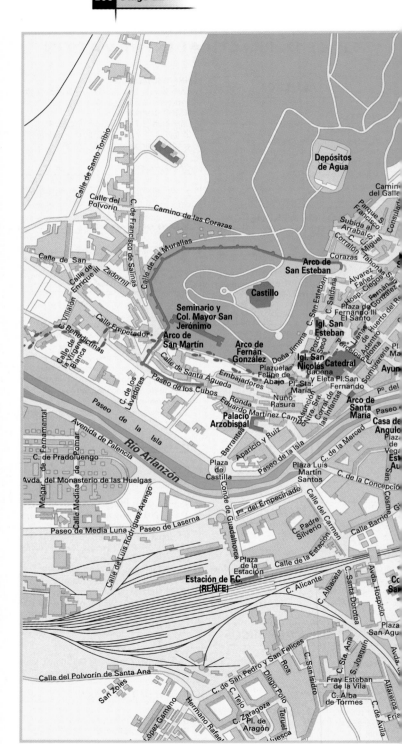

HISTORY AND WEALTH OF THE STAGE 12

THE FRENCH ROAD. SAN JUAN DE ORTEGA – BURGOS

According to the *Liber Sancti Iacobi* pilgrims' guide (c. 1130), the frontier between Navarre and Castille was precisely on Montes de Oca. Although this observation is probably more valuable as an ethnographic-linguistic note than as a description of the political situation of the time, it may also be a late echo of its old frontier status, narrated in the famous lines of the *Poem of Fernán González:*

> *Entonces era Castiella un pequeño rincón,*
> *Era de castellanos Montes de Oca mojón*
>
> *(In those days Castille was a small corner,*
> *Montes de Oca was the Castilians' frontier stone)*

The traces of San Juan de Ortega's activity can still be seen in the vicinity of **Agés,** just outside Montes de Oca, in the surroundings of its foundation, in the form of a small one-span Romanesque bridge over the river Vena. Agés' other historic reference, related to the events to which its status as a frontier gave rise, is an old sepulchral tombstone in the parish church, which local tradition claims to have something to do with the temporary burial of Navarrese King García *of Nájera,* before he was moved for good to the royal burial place in Santa María de Nájera, which he had founded.

La Gran Dolina archaeological site.

Indeed, the chronicles tell us that don García died in 1054 near Agés, in the field of **Atapuerca,** where a bloody battle for Montes de Oca and La Bureba had taken place between the armies of Sancho III the Greater of Navarre's two sons: the victor Ferdinand of Castille, and the unfortunate García. A boundary stone known as "the end of the king" ("el fin del rey") in the middle of the field before Atapuerca reminds us of the battle.

In 1992 the name of Atapuerca, hitherto no more than a reference to Spanish mediaeval history, became one of the most extraordinary milestones of the country's contemporary culture: the remains of *Homo antecessor,* humans' and neanderthals' common ancestor, was found in the archeological site of Gran Dolina. Its age is estimated at over 800,000 years old, which makes it the first human "European" that we know of.

After **Orbaneja** and **Villafría,** the Road enters Burgos via **Gamonal,** which is now merged with the capital. Opposite the magnificent XIIIth century church of Santa María la Real y Antigua, a relief of St James the

Panoramic view of Burgos and the cathedral.

Pilgrim on a Gothic stone cross shows the route's old path.

It is by no means an exaggeration to say that **Burgos** is one of the Spanish cities most closely associated with St James. Even though its foundation – which took place in 884 during King Alfonso III's plateau repopulation campaign – was unrelated to the Road, Burgos' development into a great economic and political centre was partly due to its location on the path of the pilgrims, which at this point met another important route: the one which joined the sea with the landlocked territories. Before the Road to Santiago was put through here, Burgos was no more than another defence bastion (as suggested by its originally Visigothic name, Burgos, meaning "fortified towers" in reference to the towers of Cerro del Castillo) in the first years of the fight against Islam. With the arrival of the Road to Santiago and the frontier with Navarre being moved further away (after La Rioja was annexed to Castille), the county's old capital became the capital of the whole kingdom and, from 1075, a bishopric. Burgos' prestigious mediaeval *status* is, as one might expect, reflected in its fantastic architectural heritage from this time which is, to a large extent, related to the assistance of pilgrims who reached the city via the current calle de las Calzadas, so called ("calzadas" means "roads") because this was where the Road to Santiago came together with the road for Bayona and the sea. Before reaching the city itself, the traveller encountered the monastery and hospital of San Juan Evangelista, one of the Road's great hospitals at the time. It was founded by Alfonso VI in 1074 for a Benedictine community and run by abbot Adelelmo. The devotion of this abbot, a contemporary of St Dominic of the Walkway and St John of Ortega, to the sick, the poor and the pilgrims, made him a great symbol of Burgos' hospitality. For this reason he was canonised and made the patron saint of Burgos, where he is known as San Lesmes. Although there are some surviving Romanesque remains of this old institution, its memory is kept alive in the church of San Lesmes, a XIVth century Gothic building erected next to the old hospital.

After crossing the XIIIth century door of San Juan and heading towards the centre on the street now known as calle de San Juan, pilgrims encountered a great many hospitals and lodging places in Burgos. Late

Burgos Cathedral.

XVth century German pilgrim Künig von Vach talks of 32 charitable institutions, of which some names are known today including, among others, the hospitals of El Emperador (founded by Alfonso VI), San Juan de Ortega, Malatos and San Lucas. In addition, there were the city's religious institutions, such as Las Huelgas or the convent of San Agustín, which devoted some of their activities to assisting pilgrims.

However, Burgos' visual point of reference, both for pilgrims and for all other visitors of all times, is its magnificent cathedral of Santa María, one of the most important Gothic cathedrals in Spain. It was started in 1221 on Ferdinand III the Saint's and bishop Maurice's initiative, although it was not consecrated until 1260 and it was not finished until the XVIth century. Its grandiose external appearance, characterised by its grand façade, its different portals and the spectacular top with the dome and two needle towers, matches the magnificence of its interior. Some examples of its long list of treasures are the chapel of El Condestable, the Holy Christ of Burgos (Santo Cristo de Burgos), the Golden Staircase (Escalera Dorada), the chapel of San Nicolás, the sepulchre of El Cid in the transept, and the chapel of Santiago. Within this motley group of statues and paintings from all time, it is hardly surprising that we often find the apostle St James (Santiago), depicted either as a pilgrim or as a knight (for example, in the chapel which bears his name, in the chapel of Santa Tecla, in the seat of honour of the choir, on the door of La Pellejería, in the cloister, or in the Cathedral Museum).

The cathedral surroundings are full of outstanding constructions, either from mediaeval or later times, including the old castle on the hill that overlooks the city; Santa Gadea (Águeda), the old church where Alfonso VI swore before El Cid and the Castilian nobility; the XVth century Gothic church of San Nicolás; the church of San Gil; the doors of San Juan, San Esteban (XIIIth century) and Santa María (XVIth century); and the palace of El Condestable (Casa del Cordón), to name but a few.

Many important religious institutions famous for the good quality of the assistance they offered pilgrims, such as the monastery of Las Huelgas or the convent of San Agustín, settled outside the old city.

In addition to these is the magnificent Carthusian monastery of Miraflores, built under the orders of Isabella the Catholic as a royal burial place for her parents, John II and Isabella of Portugal. Even in this secluded place we find another outstanding reference to the pilgrimage, this time in the form of an excellent wooden carving of St James the Pilgrim in the altarpiece of the high altar.

After leaving Burgos and crossing the river Arlanzón, pilgrims would find the most important hospital in Burgos, as well as one of the best of the whole Road: the King's Hospital (Hospital del Rey), founded in 1195 by Alfonso VIII, who entrusted its running to a religious community from the Order of Calatrava. This building, which was seriously modified in later times, now looks like a basically Renaissance building.

Burgos. Carthusian Monastery of Miraflores.

The Renaissance relief depicting a family of pilgrims and carved on one of the wooden doors by Juan de Balmaseda is possibly the most famous image of the place. The writings left behind by Laffi, a XVIIth century pilgrim, provide evidence of this institution's moments of splendour during the Counterreform.

The King's Hospital – now the University of Burgos' Law faculty – originally depended on the magnificent monastery of Las Huelgas Reales, which is almost next to it. It too was founded by Alfonso VIII, and was run by a community of St Bernard nuns of royal or noble ancestry. This institution, which had very strong links to the Castilian monarchy, witnessed the coronations of several kings. Before the coronation, the king to be was knighted by the apostle St James himself, who is here represented in a sitting statue holding a sword in his right arm, which is articulated to enable him to give the future king the gentle blow that was an integral part of the ceremony.

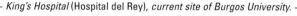

King's Hospital (Hospital del Rey), *current site of Burgos University.*

13 Burgos – Castrojeriz

During this rather long stage you will go through the stepped crop fields which are typical of the region, covered in little streams and separated by bleak plateaux. There are not very many trees in this section of the Camino: riverside species, groups of holm oaks which serve as memories of the time when woods existed on these lands, and young conifers on the hills.

Typical view of the Burgos plains.

Crossing the Malatos bridge over the river Arlanzón, you will leave **Burgos,** passing by the El Parral park en route. The Hospital del Rey and the Faculty of Humanities are on your left as the Camino continues alongside the N-620. Cross the railway line and go over to the right-hand side of the road, taking Pérez Galdós Street. From here, you should go along the path which goes by the Castilla y León Council tree nursery, before arriving at the Alameda rest area before arriving at **Villalbilla de Burgos.** If you do not wish to go into the village, you should continue along the path through poplars and fruit trees. Crossing the motorway will bring you back onto the N-120, from where you should cross the Arzobispo bridge which spans the river Arlanzón. A path next to the road will take you to **Tardajos** from where you should follow the tarmacked path towards **Rabé de las Calzadas.** Following this section of the Camino will take you through a valley with several riverbeds. After you cross the bridge over the river Urbel, you will arrive at the village. Leaving the village will take you past several barns, and will eventually lead you to a fork in the road by the cemetery next to the Hermitage of Our Lady of the Monastery. The signposts point to the left, but the tracks run parallel and end up running into each other after 3 kilometres in an area of countryside covered in cereal crops and protected by small hills. Head up to the plateau, and go along it for more than 1.5 kilometres. When you reach the "Matamulos" Hill, there is a bit of an abrupt turn downwards to the river Hormazuelas valley, where you should cross the road to Estepar and the river and make your way into **Hornillos del Camino.** After passing the hostel and the church, you will make your way along the road to the right, lined with poplar trees, to leave the village. Once again, you will follow the trail

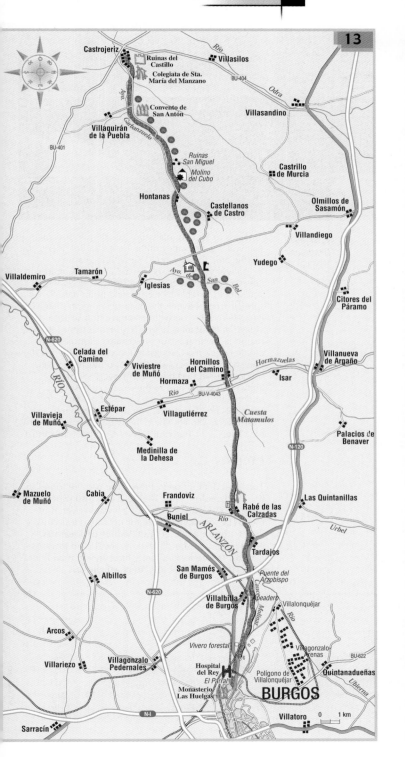

13

Castrojeriz
Ruinas del Castillo
Colegiata de Sta. María del Manzano
Convento de San Antón
Villaquirán de la Puebla
BU-401
Ruinas San Miguel
Molino del Cubo
Hontanas
Castellanos de Castro
Villasilos
Río
Odra
BU-404
Villasandino
Castrillo de Murcia
Olmillos de Sasamón
Villandiego
Yudego
Tamarón
Villaldemiro
Iglesias
Ayo. de San Bol
Citores del Páramo
N-620
Celada del Camino
Viviestre de Muñó
Hormaza
Estépar
Hornillos del Camino
Río BU-V-4043
Villagutiérrez
Hormazuelas
Isar
Villanueva de Argaño
Río
Villavieja de Muñó
Cuesta Matamulos
N-120
Palacios de Benaver
Medinilla de la Dehesa
Mazuelo de Muñó
Cabia
Frandoviz
Buniel
Rabé de las Calzadas
ARLANZÓN
Río
Las Quintanillas
Urbel
Tardajos
Albillos
San Mamés de Burgos
Puente del Arzobispo
N-620
Villalbilla de Burgos
Apeadero
Villalonquéjar
Río
Molina
Arcos
Vivero forestal
Villagonzalo-arenas
BU-622
Villariezo
Villagonzalo Pedernales
Hospital del Rey
El Parral
Monasterio Las Huelgas
Polígono de Villalonquéjar
Quintanadueñas
Ubierna
BURGOS
N-I
Villatoro
Sarracín
0   1 km

Outskirts of Castrojeriz.

upwards to another plateau and, on your descent, you will see the valley of the river San Bol. Here, you will be able to see a building with the Cross of Jerusalem, which is a refuge. Yet again, the road will take you up to another plateau, at the top of which you should be able to see the odd holm oak springing up between the pasture and crop fields. On its western hill, you will be surprised to see the village of **Hontanas,** whose Real Street turns into the main road which heads off towards Castrojeriz. A parallel track runs alongside the valley, following the course of the river Garbanzuelo, protected by the shade of reforested hillsides. About 4 kilometres ahead you will return to the roadway, passing underneath the Arch of the Convent of San Antón. From this point onwards you should be able to see **Castrojeriz,** a town where the entrance is guarded by the Collegiate Church of Santa María del Manzano.

CYCLISTS

The most difficult part of this stage is to be found in the "Matamulos" Hill. The stage can also prove to be quite tricky if the paths and tracks are covered in mud. The alternative route for cyclists is to follow the N-120 until you get to **Olmillos de Sasamón.** From here, you should take the local road towards Iglesias, before leaving the village by the road that heads off to the right towards **Castrojeriz.**

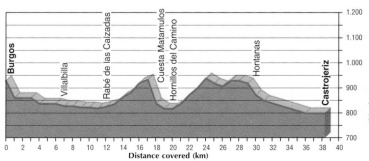

STAGE 13. PRACTICAL INFORMATION

VILLALBILLA DE BURGOS

HOSTELS

Municipal hostel. (Albergue municipal)
Villalbilla Arts Centre (Centro Cultural
de Villalbilla). 10 beds. ∅ 947 291 210

HOTELS

HSR* San Roque. ∅ 947 291 229.
Double room: € 33; single room: € 25.

RESTAURANTS

Los Brezos. Ctra. Valladolid.
∅ 947 291 010
La Forja. C/ Sagrado Corazón, 22.
∅ 947 291 279
La Tomasa. C/ Estación. ∅ 947 204 829

TARDAJOS

HOSTELS

Municipal hostel (Albergue municipal).
C/ Asunción. Open all year round. 20
beds. Kitchen for heating food.
∅ 947 451 189

HOTELS

Mary guest house. C/ Pozas.
∅ 947 451 125. 6 rooms. 11 beds.
Double room: € 24; breakfast: € 2,4.

RESTAURANTS

Los Pececitos. Avda. General Yague, 7.
∅ 947 451 060
Ruiz. C/ Pozas, 10. ∅ 947 451 125

RABÉ DE LAS CALZADAS

HOSTELS

"Virgen de la Guía" pilgrims' hostel.
30 beds. Dinner and breakfast. Room for
keeping bicycles. Open from 1/3 to 31/10.
∅ 947 451 341

HORNILLOS DEL CAMINO

HOSTELS

Municipal hostel (Albergue municipal).
Plaza de la Iglesia. Open all year round.
40 beds, kitchen and a patio for leaving
bicycles. In very good condition.
∅ 947 411 220
"La Escuela" hostel. ∅ 947 377 436.
Arroyo San Bol

ARROYO SAN BOL

HOSTELS

Next to the stream is a shelter, with a
large Jerusalem Cross on its façade,
which takes in pilgrims in the summer
season. Approximately 20 beds. A good
poplar grove, a fountain and the
manager's hospitality.

HONTANAS

HOSTELS

Municipal hostel (Albergue municipal).
C/ Real. In the same building as the old
pilgrims' hospital, this is the now
renovated "Mesón de los Franceses"
(Inn of the French). It has a kitchen and
room for bicycles. There are also other
places adapted for taking in pilgrims,
with a total of 50 beds between them.

CASTROJERIZ

HOSTELS

Municipal shelter (Refugio municipal).
C/ El Cordón. Under the responsibility of
the Shelter Friends Association. 32 beds.
Open all year round.
"San Esteban" municipal hostel.
Plaza Mayor. It opens when there is the
highest influx of pilgrims. ∅ 947 377 001

HOTELS

HS** Puerta del Monte. P.º Puerta del
Monte. ∅ 947 378 647. 14 rooms.
24 beds. Double room: € 44/39;
breakfast: € 3; lunch/dinner: € 7,81.

CAMPING SITES

2.ⁿᵈ C Camino de Santiago.
∅ 947 377 255. 150 places.

RESTAURANTS

La Taberna. C/ General Mola, 43.
∅ 947 377 120

HISTORY AND WEALTH OF THE STAGE 13

THE FRENCH ROAD. BURGOS – CASTROJERIZ

After crossing the district of San Pedro, where the Emperor's Hospital (Hospital del Emperador), which was founded by Alfonso VI, used to be, you must cross the "bridge of Malatos", over the river Arlanzón. Its name refers to a hospital for patients with contagious diseases which was there as early as 1165, as well as to the King's Hospital (Hospital del Rey), founded by Alfonso VIII. There was still one more pilgrims' hospital after Burgos: the hospital of San Juan del Puente, owned by the Burgos mitre, which could be reached after passing **Villalbilla** but before entering Tardajos, on the bank of the river Arlanzón. The bridge referred to in the name of the hospital must be the one we now call Puente del Arzobispo and which, as its name suggests, was also owned by the bishopric ("arzobispo" means "archbishop"). According to a little anecdote without much evidence of being true, while pursuing his enemies on horse, Alfonso VI had a serious fall. We must remember however, that in spite of its Burgos origins, local tradition regards King Alfonso VI as the enemy of the local hero – El Cid. This may explain little stories such as this one, with unfortunate endings for the King.

Just after crossing the bridge, you enter **Tardajos,** a small town with an ancient St James tradition, built on the road between *Clunia* (Coruña del Conde, Burgos) to *Juliobriga* (on the frontier between Cantabria and Palencia). Due to the fact that Tardajos had some hospitals in the Middle Ages, *Liber Sancti Iacobi* highlights it as a Stop of the Road. The name with which it refers to it, Alterdallia, is related to Oter de Aliis or Uter de Alios, found in local documents and meaning "Garlic Hill". These local documents always mention a pilgrims' hospital which was transferred to the Bishopric of Burgos by its founders. However, whether this is the above mentioned hospital of San Juan del Puente or not, is not clear. In any case, this was not the bishops (subsequently archbishops) of Burgos' only property in Tardajos; they also had a residential palace on the spot where the St Vincent de Paul monks' convent now stands.

The short and pleasant journey from Tardajos to Rabé has traditionally been glossed by an almost dramatic popular song

> *De Rabé a Tardajos, no te faltarán trabajos;*
> *De Tardajos a Rabé, ¡libéranos, Dominé!*
> *From Rabé to Tardajos you'll have plenty to do;*
> *From Tardajos to Rabé, the Good Lord spare you!*

rendered almost nonsensical now that the muddy Urbel valley has been cleaned up.

For the same reasons as Tardajos, **Rabé de las Calzadas'** status as a stop in the Road also goes back a long time. Just like the surname which goes with its old owner's Mozarabic name, Rabé used to be on the crossroads of the *Augustobriga-Clunia* Roman road and the Road to Santiago. Alfonso VI included it as part of his gift to the Emperor's Hospital (Hospital del Emperador), which he founded in Burgos. The most noteworthy of its old features is the Romanic façade on the parish church of Santa Marina.

Ruins of the convent of San Antón.

The name **Hornillos del Camino** is also very closely bound to the Road to Santiago, and the layout of the town itself provides one of the purest examples of a Pilgrim Road-town. It is mentioned in the *Liber Sancti Iacobi (Furnellos)* guide as well as in *Anseïs de Carthage,* a French epic poem from Charlemagne times, written in 1200 and set on the Road to Santiago, which explains at length the name of the town: according to its fictitious plot, the emperor Charlemagne found an oven next to the river Hormazuelas, and used it to bake bread for his army. The fact that, from 1151, Hornillos belonged to the monastery of St Denis of Paris, which had a great interest in encouraging the worship of Charlemagne, is very likely to have something to do with the origin of this pseudo-historic anecdote. A French Benedictine community, which depended directly on the French sanctuary of Rocamadour, later settled in Hornillos by licence of King Alfonso VIII in 1181. The legacy left in Hornillos by this community consists of an image of Our Lady of Rocamadour (Nuestra Señora de Rocamador – which was moved out of here a long time ago) and the name of its Gothic church. In addition to Benedictine hospitality, Hornillos could offer sick travellers a quarantine centre and lepers' hospital.

In the middle of the solitary way between Hornillos and Hontanas was the Antonite house of San Baudilio or San Boal, which depended on the nearby convent of San Antón de Castrogeriz and which has lent its name, Sambol, to the stream and valley in which its ruins are still to be seen. Although the Spanish worship of Baudilio de Nimes predates the Antonites' arrival from the French Dauphin, it is stronger in places where the order's presence was strong, such as Catalonia and Castille (and, in particular, Burgos).

In addition, **Hontanas** had a pilgrims' hospital in the building which, for that same reason, is now called "Mesón de los Franceses" (Inn of the French). Its XIVth century Gothic parish church is dedicated to the Immaculate Conception.

Two kilometres before Castrojeriz are the ruins of the convent of San Antón, the Hospital Brothers of St Anthony's main building in Castille and León, which was founded and supported by Alfonso VII in 1146. This Order, which originated in the French Dauphin in 1095 and took its

Panoramic view of Castrojeriz and its collegiate church.

name from the fact that it had a relic of St Anthony, the IIIrd century Egyptian hermit, rapidly spread throughout Europe and had an exceptional presence in the Road to Santiago. It took on responsibility for medical assistance and became famous for its ability to cure erysipelas, a gangrenous ergotism also known as "St Anthony's fire" or "holy fire", whose symptoms consisted of burning rashes and reddening of the skin. In addition, Antonites could cure a type of swine fever with similar characteristics to erysipelas, known in Spain as "pigs' red disease". These activities gave rise to the two symbols with which St Anthony Abbot is often depicted - fire and a pig, and to his becoming the patron saint of animals. The third symbol associated with St Anthony and the Antonites was a cross in the shape of a "tau" (the letter "t" in the Greek alphabet) which was embroidered in their habits and which can still be seen on the mullions in the convent of San Antón. This badly preserved Gothic ruin's most noteworthy feature is a double arch over the way, the church's doorway and the strange cupboard where food and drink was left by the Antonites for pilgrims arriving at the convent after hours. Tradition has it that these hospitable monks used to meet pilgrims on the way and encourage them with the "Eultreia, esuseia" chant, the great hymn of the pilgrimage and of the crusades.

Castrojeriz is another outstanding example of a Pilgrim Road-town, i.e.: a single street with all the houses aligned along it. In this case the street was full of monuments – which have unfortunately not been well preserved –, and it was so long that German pilgrims referred to the town as *die lange Stadt* (the long city). Castrojeriz's origin and early development are not well documented, but they may be similar to those of Burgos: both cities started off with a castle on a hill, possibly as a result of the Castilian frontier policy of consolidation from Alfonso III's times; Sigerico (from its name: Castrojeriz > *Castrum Sigerici),* an Asturian or Castilian noble ignored by other sources, may have been the founder of Castrojeriz. Castrojeriz's long layout, consisting – like Burgos – of a street surrounding the southern foot of the castle hill, was determined by the Road to Santiago.

Castrojeriz's most splendorous time was during the Middle Ages. This was due to a great extent to the constant flow of pilgrims, who could find accommodation in several hospitals (four at the end of the XVth century). Another symptom of Castrojeriz's limited mediaeval urban splendour was the existence of convents of mendicant orders such as the Franciscans and the Dominicans. The worship of St Dominic is still preserved in the current church of Santo Domingo. French pilgrims referred to Castrojeriz as the "castle of the mice" or "four mice" *(Castra Sorecia, Castrum Soricis, Quatre Souris, Castre Soris),* a play on words based on the sound of the name, which reminded them of the word *souris,* meaning "mouse".

At the town entrance is the magnificent Gothic collegiate church of La Virgen del Manzano or Virgen de Almazán, with the works of important artists, such as Mengs, Bronzino and Carduccio, inside it. In his *Cantigas* (songs or poems), Alfonso X sang to the virgin who lends her name to the church, and of whom there is a beautiful XIIIth century sculpture. Other important buildings in the town are the elegant church of San Juan,

St James the Pilgrim in the collegiate church of La Virgen del Manzano or Virgen de Almazán.

also Gothic but with some Romanesque elements, and there used to be two other churches, dedicated to St Stephen and St James respectively, which have unfortunately not been preserved.

Collegiate church of La Virgen del Manzano.

14 Castrojeriz – Frómista

After Castrojeriz, situated on the hillside between the valleys of the river Odrilla and the Pisuerga, is Mosterales, the last plain in the Burgos area. The river Pisuerga brings you into the province of Palencia, and on into the Tierra de Campos, with its immense plains.

Itero Bridge over the river Pisuerga.

Go along Cordón street, which will take you out onto the road to Villasilos, which you must cross before taking a path which leads off between some barns. After crossing the road which leads to Melgar de Fernamental, leaving behind you the hill with the castle on it, take a dirt track which crosses the valley of the river Odrilla towards a plain. After crossing a medieval bridge over the river, you will begin your ascent up the craggy side of the Mostelares hill. Carrying on along the plateau you will come to the end, from where you will be able to make out the valley of the river Pisuerga. You should also be able to see the Tierra de Campos to the West, and the Cantábrica mountain chain to the North. Continue downwards by the "Colada del Camino Francés". The descent is slightly abrupt at the start, but eventually evens itself out until you are walking on a more-or-less straight path. You will pass a rest area near to "Fuente del Piojo" and, shortly afterwards, will arrive at the path which comes from Pedrosa del Príncipe. However, another path will take you off to the left, leaving **Itero del Castillo** to the right, passing by the valley of the river Pisuerga. Before you get to the Itero bridge, you will go alongside the San Nicolás Hermitage. The river course marks the border between Burgos and Palencia, and crossing it will take you into the Tierra de Campos. The Camino follows the course of the river, passing alongside vibrant riverside forests. Once you pass the graveyard and the rest area, you will arrive at **Itero de la Vega** (originally off to one side of the Camino). To leave the village, you must go along the following streets: Onésimo Redondo, Emilio Ibáñez, Santa Ana and Comandante Ramírez. You should carry on along a shaded track to come out onto the road to Osorno, which you should cross before going on to cross the Pisuerga Canal. A gentle incline leads the way to the "Alto del Paso Largo", before you see Boadilla coming up in the distance. You should see several small hills on both sides, with forested hillsides and several pigeon lofts. A small stream is the last

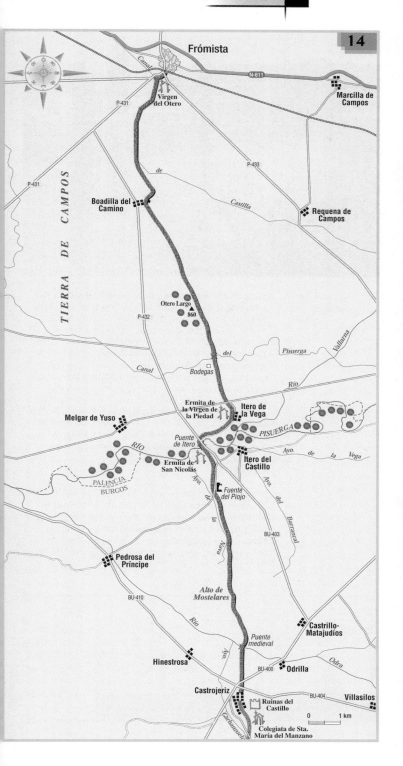

14

Frómista

N-611

Marcilla de
Campos

P-431

Virgen
del Otero

de

P-433

Requena de
Campos

Castilla

Boadilla del
Camino

P-431

TIERRA DE CAMPOS

Otero Largo
860

P-432

del

Pisuerga

Vallarna

Canal

Río

Bodegas

Ermita de
la Virgen de
la Piedad

Itero de
la Vega

Melgar de Yuso

PISUERGA

Puente
de Itero

Río

Ayo.   de   la   Vega

Ermita de
San Nicolás

PALENCIA
BURGOS

Itero del
Castillo

Fuente
del Piojo

Ayo.

del

Barranco

BU-403

Pedrosa del
Príncipe

de

la

Nava

BU-410

Alto de
Mostelares

Castrillo-
Matajudíos

Río

Puente
medieval

Hinestrosa

Ayo.

BU-400   Odrilla

Odra

Castrojeriz

Ruinas del
Castillo

BU-404   Villasilos

0   1 km

Colegiata de Sta.
María del Manzano

Castille Canal floodgate near Frómista.

thing you will meet before arriving in **Boadilla del Camino,** at the entrance of which you will find the town's hostel. Passing behind the Church of Santa María, you will go alongside the original route, coming out next to some vegetable patches. When you come across an irrigation ditch you will see a fork in the road. You should head off to the left, carrying along a path lined with poplars which will lead you to the Castille Canal, along which you must keep walking until you reach the outskirts of Frómista. After crossing the lock across the canal, a tarmacked road will take you towards the road to Astudillo, along which you will pass through a tunnel under the railway line and into Frómista.

CYCLISTS

Mostelares can prove to be an insurmountable obstacle to some cyclists. If you want to avoid it altogether, you should take the road that leads towards Melgar de Fernamental until you reach Castrillo de Matajudíos. From there, you should follow the BU-403, which will join up with the huge Itero bridge.

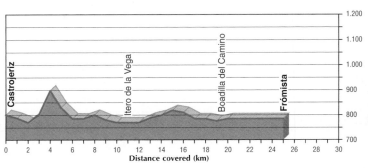

STAGE 14. PRACTICAL INFORMATION

ITERO DEL CASTILLO

Hostels

Pilgrims' Hostel (Albergue de peregrinos)
Located on plaza Mayor. It has 8 beds and is open all year round.
∅ 947 377 337

Chapel of San Nicolás.
Camino de los Peregrinos. It has 8 beds, a kitchen and a meeting room. Closed from October to May.
∅ 947 377 359

ITERO DE LA VEGA

Hostels

Municipal hostel (Albergue municipal)
Plaza del Generalísimo, s/n. It has 20 beds and is open all year round.
∅ 979 151 826 / 979 151 905

BOADILLA DEL CAMINO

Hostels

Municipal hostel (Albergue municipal).
C/ De las Escuelas, s/n. It has 12 beds and a patio with a garden. Open all year round. ∅ 979 810 776

Pilgrims' Hostel (Albergue de peregrinos). ∅ 979 730 579

FRÓMISTA

Hostels

Municipal hostel (Albergue municipal).
Located on calle del Hospital. It has 55 beds and a patio for leaving bicycles. Open all year round. ∅ 979 810 001

Hotels

H* San Martín.
Plaza San Martín, 7. ∅ 979 810 000.
12 rooms. 23 beds. Double room: € 36; single room: € 30; breakfast: € 3,9; lunch/dinner: € 7,8.

Camino de Santiago guest house.
C/ Las Francesas, 26.
∅ 979 810 053. 12 rooms.
24 beds. Double room: € 30/25; single room: € 21/18; breakfast: € 3; lunch/dinner: € 8.

Marisa guest house.
Plaza San Martín, 3.
∅ 979 810 023. 5 rooms.
10 beds. Double room: € 22; single room: € 14; breakfast: € 2,5; lunch/dinner: € 10,22.

Restaurants

Hostería de los Palmeros.
Plaza San Telmo, 4. ∅ 979 810 067

Villa de Fromista.
Avda. del Ejército Español, 22.
∅ 979 810 409

Van-Dos.
C/ Ingeniero River, 10.
∅ 979 810 861

Means of Transport

The Burgos-Frómista bus line is run by Amaya buses.
There is a RENFE rail station.

Services

There is a café/bar with a shop, and the hostel belongs to a country house that has a restaurant.

HISTORY AND WEALTH OF THE STAGE **14**

THE FRENCH ROAD. CASTROJERIZ – FRÓMISTA

Just before leaving Castrojeriz, pilgrims must cross the river Odrilla on a small Romanesque bridge. This is the only significant monument in the more than ten kilometres between Castrojeriz and **Itero del Castillo.** Itero is on the bank of the river Pisuerga, on the frontier between Burgos and Palencia, and used to be the frontier between the historic regions of Castille and Campos, as recalled by the famous verses of the *Poem of Fernán González:*

> *Entonçe era Castyella un pequeño rincón*
> *Era de castellanos Montes d'Oca mojón*
> *E de la otra parte Fitero el fondon.*

> *(In those days Castille was a small corner*
> *Montes d'Oca was the Castilians' frontier stone*
> *And the other part was the hollow of Fitero.)*

The name Itero refers to its frontier status. It is an adjective cognate with the Spanish "hito" ("milestone"), which comes from the late Vulgar Latin secondary participle *ficto,* created from the verb *figere,* (to "drive in" or "pierce" - the correct classical Latin participle would be fixus, i.e., "fixed"). This participal adjective, ficto, which appears in the phrase *mojone fito* in a document from the year 1100, was abbreviated into the noun "hito", which means precisely "stone driven into the ground" and, by extension, "frontier indication" or simply "frontier", (and Itero, spelt as "Fitero" until the XIXth century). Strangely enough, XVIIth century Italian pilgrim Domenico Laffi refers to the bridge as *ponte che si chiama della Mulla,* possibly reflecting the hypothetical name of "puente de la Muga" (*muga* or *muria* means "heap of stones" and "frontiers" in many Spanish dialects) which the locals may have given this border post.

The *Liber Sancti Iacobi* guide mentions this town under the name *Pons Fiterie.* This is in keeping with

other documents from that time *(Pons Fiterii* or *Pontefitero)* and may be related to the town having been born at the start of the great eleven-span Romanesque bridge built by Alfonso VI, the great benefactor of the Road to Santiago. Itero del Castillo used to have an important Order of the Hospital of St John of Jerusalem building, devoted to assisting pilgrims, as well as a hospital belonging to Castilian noble Nuño Pérez de Lara. The now restored chapel of San Nicolás may be the surviving remains of one of these.

Boadilla del Camino. XIVth century baptismal font, in the church of La Asunción.

Gothic pillory in Boadilla del Camino.

On the other bank of the river Pisuerga is **Itero de la Vega,** a town which, judging by the names it is given in mediaeval documents (simply *Fitero,* with nothing else) is older than Itero del Castillo. Before entering the town, you come across the XIIIth century chapel of La Piedad, where a beautiful image of St James the Pilgrim is kept. The parish church of San Pedro, although still retaining its mediaeval façade, was almost completely rebuilt in the XVIIth century.

As mentioned above, this is where the historic region of **Tierra de Campos,** a region whose name tells us of its great geophysical uniformity, with an endless straight horizon and very few trees, begins. The impression made by this landscape was summarised by Jorge Guillén in this watercolour-like poem which, from the observation point of Montealegre, captures it in four lines which are characteristic of his very precise genius:

> *El castillo divisa la llanura*
> *Tierra de Campos, infinitamente*
> *Todo en su desnudez así perdura*
> *Elemental planeta, frente a frente*

> *(The castle glimpses the plain*
> *Tierra de Campos, infinitely*
> *Everything continues thus, bare*
> *Basic planet, face to face)*

The XIth century work *Crónica Albeldense* referred to this region as "Gothic Fields" *(Campi Gothorum), campus* being the Romans' translation for the very old vernacular expression *paramus* (this is reflected in a late Roman Latin inscription which mentions this land). Although all descriptions of this region, from those of ancient geographers to *Liber Sancti Iacobi,* mention these physical characteristics, Liber Sancti Iacobi also mentions the fact that this territory had great wealth in its time (c. 1130):

> *"Es una tierra llena de tesoros, de oro, plata, rica en paños y vigorosos caballos, abundante en pan, vino, carne, pescado, leche y miel. Sin embargo, carece de arbolado".*

> *(It is a land full of treasures, gold, silver, rich in cloths and strong horses, plentiful in bread, wine, meat, fish, milk and honey. However, it has no trees).*

But the wealth of Tierra de Campos is not limited to that derived from its own resources (such as bread and wine). The churches of that time contained large amounts of gold, silver and other riches, a large proportion of which came from war booties and tributes of the Spanish Taifa kingdoms.

The first town after Itero is **Boadilla del Camino,** whose characteristics – few houses, a (growing) scarcity of people and a very rich heritage – are typical of many towns in this region. Its church of la Asunción, originally

Romanesque but almost completely rebuilt in the XVIth century, contains, among other noteworthy works of art, a large XIIIth century Romanesque baptismal font carved out of a single large stone. It is a half-spherical cup, standing on a solid pillar and surrounded by twelve small columns. The cup is decorated with small roses, crosses and intertwined arches, which make it look slightly Celtic. Boadilla's other great monument is a large XVth century Gothic stone column where serious criminals used to be tried and executed by the local authorities.

Frómista. Statue of St Telmo and old Hospital.

After Boadilla, the Road meets and, for a while, accompanies, the Canal de Castilla, built in the XVIIIth century to transport cereals and to irrigate and grind grain. Just after one of the locks is the town of Frómista, mentioned in the *Liber Sancti Iacobi* guide, not only as a Stop of the Road, but also as the end of one of its thirteen stages. The town of **Frómista,** whose name comes from a Visigothic person's name meaning "the first" or "the most important one", was founded in the Xth century, during the repopulation of the plateau. A person with this name *(Fromesta)* has been found in a Sahagún document from around this time (961), and it is possible that this was the person who repopulated the town and was its first owner. About a century later (approximately in 1066), Queen doña Mayor, widow of Sancho III of Navarre and mother of Fernando I, King of Castille and León, ordered the construction of the building which was later added, as a priory, to the Clunian monastery of San Zoilo de Carrión. All that remains of this is the current church of San Martín, one of the greatest exponents of Spanish Romanesque architecture, which is directly connected to the monuments – all of which date from the same time and are located on the Road to Santiago – of the cathedrals of Jaca, Santiago and Pamplona (although not much is left of the last of these), and of the collegiate church of San Isidoro de León. It has three naves with their respective apses, a dome erected on four conical columns on the transept and which looks octagonal from the outside, three portals and two cylindrical towers on either side of the western façade. This small church's sculptural wealth is impressive for its quality, quantity and variety: over 100 decorated capitals and over 315 projecting beams, 86 of which were unfortunately replaced (some of them for decency reasons!) during the radical and debatable restoration carried out in the late XIXth century. Apart from the sublime church of San Martín, Frómista has other monuments of great merit. Two examples are the great XIVth century Gothic church of San Pedro, which contains,

Frómista. Church of San Martín.

among other things, a beautiful XVIth century sculpture of St James the Pilgrim; and the church of Santa María del Castillo, erected on an old fortress, whose most outstanding item is a panelled altarpiece painted by Castilian artist Fernando Gallego. The chapel of Santiago or chapel of El Otero, in the outskirts of Frómista, contains a Romanesque sculpture of La Virgen del Otero. As regards Frómista's history of hospitality, we have only found (apart from references in the Liber Sancti Iacobi guide) relatively recent references to two hospitals, those of Santiago and Palmeros, as well as something called "Huerto del Francés" or "Huerto del Romero", which may have been a pilgrims' cemetery. Among the town's famous locals is Dominican monk Pedro González Telmo (1190-1246), patron saint of Tuy and of sailors; the expression "St Elmo's fire" ("fuego de San Telmo" or "de San Elmo" in Spanish) originates from the saint's second surname and refers to an optical phenomenon, famous since ancient times, consisting of a luminous apparition on the water which sailors attributed to supernatural causes.

15 Frómista – Carrión de los Condes

This stage of the Camino passes through areas that have been heavily influenced by man - so much so, in fact, that the only trees we are likely to see are those on the banks of the river Ucieza. The route for today carries on in a straight line next to the road, and offers little protection against the rain, wind and sun. However, because of this there have been special rest areas set along the path.

Población de Campos. Chapel of San Miguel.

Julio Senador street leads you onto the local motorway which, in turn, takes you out of **Frómista** and across the ring road. A special path which has been set out for pilgrims starts on the right hand side, while on the left you can see the course of the canal. Carrying on along this path you will pass by the Hermitage of San Miguel, next to which there is a picnic area in the poplar wood, before coming to **Población de Campos.** Upon arriving in the village, you will pass by the hostel and the Hermitage of Socorro. When you get to Corro Square, just before you leave the town, you are faced with two choices:

A) Heading to the left will take you out towards the C-980, first crossing the river Ucieza, before following the river in a more or less straight line towards **Revenga** and finally **Villarmentero.**

B) Alternatively, you can opt to leave the village via Cruz de Malta Street, continuing along a country lane to the right of the river Ucieza. This way will take you by Villovieco, passing the river and heading to the left before reaching Villarmentero.

From this point the two routes above meet up with each other again. There is, however, an old sign which points to the continuation of the route along an overgrown path which passes along the left-hand side of the Ucieza to the road to Arconado where, passing the Hermitage of the Virgen del Río, it then runs all the way to **Villalcázar de Sirga.**

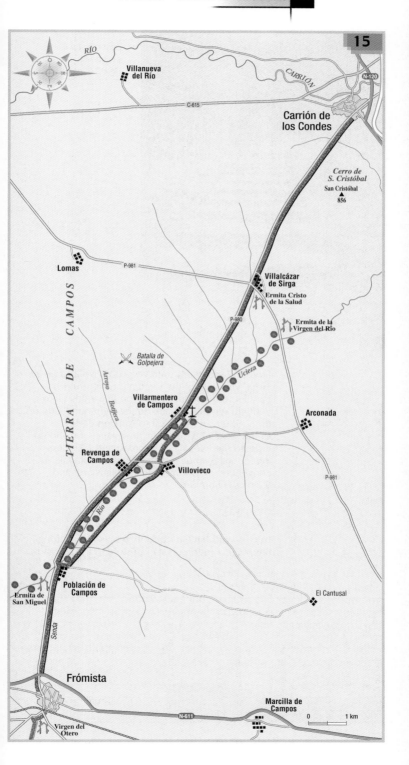

Conditioned path for pilgrims in the outskirts of Carrión de los Condes.

From Villarmentero until you reach **Villalcázar de Sirga,** you will follow the track which runs parallel to the road. When you leave this village, you will rejoin the track on the right-hand side of the C-980 as it heads off to **Carrión de los Condes.** When you enter the village, you should cross to the left side of the road and take Los Peregrinos Avenue, passing by the Santa Clara convent on your way to the Santa María and Santiago churches.

CYCLISTS

Cyclists will have no trouble whatsoever during this stage. Option (a) sticks firmly to the roadside.

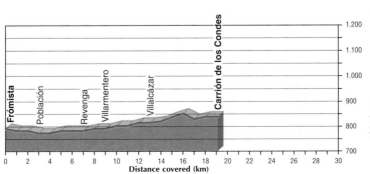

STAGE 15. PRACTICAL INFORMATION

POBLACIÓN DE CAMPOS

HOSTELS

Municipal Hostel (Albergue Municipal). Located on calle Francesa, 2. It has 16 beds, a kitchen, living room and hot water. Open from 1st April to 31st October. ✆ 979 810 293 / 979 810 738

VILLALCÁZAR DE SIRGA

HOSTELS

Municipal Hostel (Albergue Municipal). Located opposite the church and run by the parish priest. It has 20 places and a kitchen. Open all year round.
✆ 979 888 076 / 969 585 655

HOTELS

HS* Infanta Doña Leonor.
C/ Condes de Toreno, 1. ✆ 979 888 015. 9 rooms. 18 beds. Double room: € 37; single room: € 22; breakfast: € 3.
HSR* Las Cántigas. C/ Condes de Toreno. ✆ 979 888 015. 5 rooms. 9 beds. Double room: € 37; single room: € 22.

RESTAURANTS

Mesón Los Templarios.
Plaza Mayor. ✆ 979 888 089
Mesón Villasirga.
Plaza Mayor. ✆ 979 888 022

CARRIÓN DE LOS CONDES

HOSTELS

"Monasterio de Santa Clara" pilgrims' hostel.
30 beds. ✆ 979 880 134 / 639 919 875
"Parroquia de Santa María del Camino" pilgrims' hostel. The parish priest runs one of the most traditional - although recently renovated – hostels. It has 60 beds and is open all year round. ✆ 979 880 072

Youth Hostel (Albergue juvenil).
✆ 979 881 063

HOTELS

HSR* Hospedería Albe.
C/ Esteban Collantes, 21. ✆ 979 880 913. 8 rooms. 14 beds. Double room: € 24; single room: € 24.
HS* La Corte. C/ Santa María, 34.
✆ 979 880 138. 20 rooms. Double room: € 48/42; single room: € 39/33; lunch/dinner: € 9.
HS* Real Monasterio de Santa Clara.
C/ Santa Clara, 1. ✆ 979 880 134.
9 rooms. 15 beds. Double room: € 32; single room: € 16; breakfast: € 2,5.
HS* Santiago. Plaza de los Regentes, 8. ✆ 979 881 052. 16 rooms. 35 beds. Double room: € 46; single room: € 25.
P* El Resvalón. C/ Fernán Gómez, 19-1°. ✆ 979 880 433. 6 rooms. 14 beds. Double room: € 19.

CAMPING SITES

2.nd C El Edén. Carretera Logroño-Vigo, km 200. ✆ 979 881 152. 289 places.

RESTAURANTS

Abel. C/ Esteban Collantes, 11.
✆ 979 880 325
El Edén. C/ El Plantío. ✆ 979 880 185
La Corte. C/ Sta. María, 36.
✆ 979 880 138
Las Vigas (Hotel Real Monasterio San Zoilo). C/ Souto. ✆ 979 880 049
Los Condes. Plaza Mayor.
✆ 979 880 136
Mesón El Portón. C/ José Antonio Girón. ✆ 979 880 407
Mikus. C/ Conde Garay, 1.
✆ 979 880 018

MEANS OF TRANSPORT

ALSA buses go through Carrión on their way to Leon. ✆ 979 749 840.

HISTORY AND WEALTH OF THE STAGE 15

THE FRENCH ROAD. FRÓMISTA – CARRIÓN

On a pleasant landscape on the bank of the river Ucieza before **Población de Campos,** is the isolated XIIIth century chapel of San Miguel. The name Población refers directly to the repopulation of small settlements, hamlets, villages and towns such as this one which took place in the Xth and XIth centuries. Its relationship with the Road to Santiago is very old, since there was already a building belonging to the Knights of St John in the Middle Ages. It is not clear whether these Knights have anything to do with the fact that the parish church, in spite of its clear character as an assistance institution and its close links with the worship of St James, is dedicated to the Magdalene. The Romanesque chapel of El Socorro, which contains a Romanesque

Façade of the church of Santa María la Blanca in Villalcázar de Sirga.

sculpture of La Virgen del Socorro ("socorro" means "aid" or "assistance"), also reminds us of providing assistance to those in need.

Revenga and **Villovieco,** which face each other, are also the result of a repopulation from the same time as Población. The name Villovieco is formed in the usual way: the designation of "villa" ("village" or "hamlet"), and the name of its founder or first owner, in this case someone by the name of Oveco, also a typical name in Campos in the early Middle Ages. In addition to these two off-shoots of the French Road (the name given to this part of the Road to Santiago), important Jacobean traces can be found in more distant towns, such as Arconada.

The structure of the name Villovieco also applies to **Villarmentero,** whose founder was one of the several Armenteros or Armentales (meaning "rich in cattle") referred to in documents from that time. The parish church, which is dedicated to St Martin of Tours, has a beautiful Mudejar coffered ceiling. It is interesting to see that in this town, as well as in some neighbouring ones, the festival of the patron saint of St Martin is not celebrated on the traditional autumn date of 11th November (the traditional date of his death) or on the old Spanish calendar's summer date (11th August), but on 4th July. This was the second St Martin celebration (commemorating his election and the moving of his relics) under the Roman calendar, and the fact that this date prevailed in Villarmentero must be an indication of the strong influence exercised by Clunian orders (established in Carrión, Frómista and Sahagún) on this region and of their great interest in replacing the Spanish-Mozarabic calendar with the Roman one.

Villalcázar de Sirga. View of the church of Santa María la Blanca.

Following the thread of local oral tradition rescued by the late historian Lourdes Burgos, it has recently been found out how the battle of Golpejera (1071), in which El Cid and King Sancho II of Castille defeated and imprisoned King Alfonso VI of León and which is narrated in countless chronicles from the time as well as in (now lost) epic poems and ballads, took place in Villarmentero. The various aspects of the battle, as told by chronicles and poems, are reflected almost step by step in several place names in the area of Villarmentero and Lomas, slightly south of the Road to Santiago. The tents in which the armies camped - Reyerta, Matanza, Mortera, Botijera (a modern corruption of the old name Golpejera) - as well as Senda del Obligado, the track on which Alfonso VI was lead towards Burgos as a prisoner, are some such names which evoke the scenes of the battle and which have been preserved as the names of some small places in this area. It is even possible that the famous stone cross erected in the middle of the cereal field and placed on the precise spot where the old Road to Santiago used to meet the Road of Las Tiendas, is a visible reference to this memorable event.

Villálcazar de Sirga (or "Villasirga") is another good example of a Campos village: few houses and people, but an impressive church full of treasures: this is the magnificent church of Santa María la Blanca, famous among other things for the various cantigas (songs or poems) that King Alfonso X the Wise dedicated to the saint that lends the church her name. Alfonso X was one of the best sources of publicity for this sanctuary, whose Virgin he claimed had cured several pilgrims of their ailments. The church has a fortified shape because it used to be a house-fortress of the Knights of the Templar, an order with a significant presence on the Road to Santiago, particularly in Tierra de Campos and in the stretch between Astorga and Galicia, and whose task was to protect pilgrims at a time when there were many and very varied dangers.

The church of Santa María is a late Romanesque building with three vaulted naves and a double transept. Oustanding features of its exterior include the large rose window and the collection of sculptures on its façades covered in porticos. Inside is a beautiful Gothic sculpture of the White Virgin (la Virgen Blanca), who is the same virgin that the Wise King sang to. The beautiful chapel of Santiago contains the tombs of prince don Felipe and his wife doña Leonor Ruiz de Castro. The fact that Felipe, Fernando III the Saint's fifth son and King Alfonso X's brother,

*Panoramic view of
Carrión de los Condes.*

belonged to the Order of the Templar, explains the presence of his mausoleum in Villasirga. The chapel is dominated by a XVIth century sculpture of St James in pilgrim attire, whereas the church itself is dominated by a large altarpiece, dedicated to the Virgin and composed of panels and reliefs depicting some of the miracles which Alfonso sang about in his cantigas.

Due to its history and central location, it can be said that **Carrión de los Condes** is the capital of Tierra de Campos. *Liber Sancti Iacobi* reflects this important status and bestows on it the sort of praise which it denies cities such as Burgos:

> *"Viene luego Carrión, que es una villa industriosa y excelente, abundante en pan, vino, carne y todo tipo de productos"*

> *(Then comes Carrión, an industrious and excellent village, rich in bread, wine, meat and all types of products)*

The name Carrión de los Condes, which replaces the old Ciudad de Santa María or Santa María de Carrión (the river Carrión) is related to the important Banu-Gómez family, a noble family from León who ruled over the area from this city. One of its members, Count Gómez, ordered the remains of Paleochristian martyr Zoilo to be brought from Córdoba and, together with his wife Teresa, ordered a church and hospital to be built and then donated it to Cluny in 1076. This soon became, together with the one in Sahagún, the most important sanctuary in the region. In spite of this, the *Liber Sancti Iacobi* guide does not mention it in its chapter about saints of the Road, possibly because, by the time it was written, San Zoilo had lost importance under the dominance of the close-by and all-powerful monastery of Sahagún. Few Romanesque traces remain in the current building, although new things appear every now and then, such as the arch supported on four marble columns which was discovered in 1994.

In addition to San Zoilo, Carrión had quite a few hospitals and religious institutions devoted to hospitality. If you follow the Road to Santiago route along this town you will find the convent of Santa Clara, founded in the XIIIth century and related to St Francis of Assisi's undocumented pilgrimage to Santiago de Compostela. Among other treasures that can be admired in its museum is a *Piedad* sculpture by Gregorio Fernández. The church of Santa María del Camino or of la Victoria which, in early days, lent its name to Carrión, is adjoined to the city wall. The current building dates from the XIIth century and has three vaulted naves culminating in apses. A

Romanesque image of the saint to whom the church is dedicated is kept here. The main façade – located on the side of the building and protected by a portico supported by two solid flying buttresses – is decorated by a rich and varied set of sculptures which have, however, been slightly disfigured by the passing of time. Among these is a group of bulls' heads linked by local tradition to a legend under which, thanks to the miraculous apparition of a group of bulls which attacked the collectors, Carrión was freed from the yearly obligation (which had bound them since Mauregato's times) to give one hundred maids to the Moors. This legend, which matches the one relating to the battle of Clavijo, must be read as a local attempt to be spared from what is known as the "voto de Santiago" (St James tax).

The church of Santiago de Carrión was originally another settlement of the Knights of the Templar. Its façade, which miraculously saved from the fire and devastation it was subject to during the French invasion, has one of

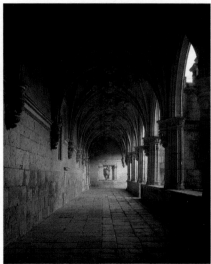

Different aspects of the monastery of San Zoilo in Carrión de los Condes. Above, sepulchres of the Counts and Infants of Carrión; below, monastery cloister.

the most beautiful collections of Spanish Romanesque sculptures. Of particular note are the archivolte's 24 figures depicting several everyday figures (such as craftsmen, artists and warriors), the frieze with the apostolate and, above all, the "Phidian" Pantocrator surrounded by the Tetramorph which is, without a doubt, one of the high points of Romanesque sculpture.

16   Carrión de los Condes – Sahagún

*For 13 kilometres you will follow the historical Aquitana
route through isolated countryside, before arriving at
Calzadilla. Here, the surface ceases to be so flat, when the
"cuezas", or "little valleys", start to crop up between small
hills. If you opt to take one of the alternative paths, you will
leave the roadside to head through an oak wood, before
coming back to the familiar cereal fields and crossing the
river Valderaduey on your way into the countryside of León.*

Pilgrims crossing the bridge to enter Sahagún.

After crossing the river Carrión, you will pass alongside the San Zoilo
monastery, and cross the road to Saldaña before heading off towards
Sahagún. When you come to another crossroads, go straight ahead along
the path that leads to Villotilla, also known as the "carretera del Indiano".
En route, you will pass by several poplar woods and cross over a few
irrigation channels. About 4 kms into the journey, you will come across
Benevívere Abbey, situated in a very leafy part of the route, before crossing
the Molino river. A further kilometre ahead, you will come to a bend, on
which you should leave the path to go off straight ahead. This will take
you 13 kilometres along the old Aquitana route, hidden away amongst
trees which provide little or no shade. Continuing along this route, you
will pass by the "Fuente del Hospitalejo", also known as "Santa María de
la Fuente". If you look to the North, parallel to the Roman road, you
should be able to see the motorway running past, along with a few solitary
holm oaks which appear between the crop fields. Crossing the road to
Bustillo del Páramo, you will go on to cross several streams which run
perpendicular to the Camino, as well as crossing the Cañada Real. A few
steps ahead you will be able to see the tower of **Calzadilla de la Cueza's**
church on the horizon. Upon leaving the village, you have several choices:
A) Carry on along the path which runs parallel to the N-120, passing
through **Ledigos** before arriving at **Terradillos de los Templarios.**
B) Head off to the left of the path, along the so-called forest path which,
after crossing the Fuente Arriba river, carries on through an oak wood

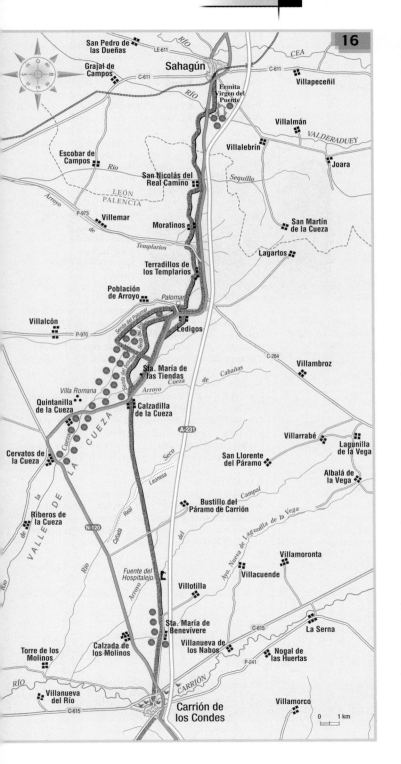

16

San Pedro de
las Dueñas

LE-611

RÍO

CEA

C-611

Grajal de
Campos

C-611

Sahagún

Villapeceñil

Ermita
Virgen del
Puente

RÍO

Villalmán

VALDERADUEY

Escobar de
Campos

Río

Villalebrín

Joara

San Nicolás del
Real Camino

Sequillo

LEÓN
PALENCIA

Arroyo

de

P-973

Villemar

Moratinos

San Martín
de la Cueza

Templarios

Lagartos

Terradillos de
los Templarios

Población
de Arroyo

Palomar

Villalcón

P-970

Senda del Palomar

Ledigos

C-264

Villambroz

Senda de bosque

Sta. María de
las Tiendas

Cabañas

de

Cueza

Villa Romana

Senda del río

Arroyo

Quintanilla
de la Cueza

Calzadilla
de la Cueza

A-231

Villarrabé

Lagunilla
de la Vega

Cervatos de
la Cueza

Cueza

VALLE DE LA CUEZA

Seco

San Llorente
del Páramo

Albalá de
la Vega

Leonesa

Riberos de
la Cueza

N-120

Calzada

Real

Bustillo del
Páramo de Carrión

Campal

Ayo. Nueva de Lagunilla de la Vega

Villamoronta

Villacuende

Río

la

de

Río

Fuente del
Hospitalejo

Arroyo

del

Villotilla

Sta. María de
Benevívere

C-615

La Serna

Villanueva de
los Nabos

Torre de los
Molinos

Calzada de
los Molinos

Nogal de
las Huertas

P-241

Villanueva
del Río

C-615

RÍO

CARRIÓN

Carrión de
los Condes

Villamorco

0   1 km

before rejoining the N-120. At the 222 km marker, the route then follows a rural path parallel to the road, heading off to the right towards **Ledigos.**
C) Follow the river path, which comes after the previous option and, after passing between the Cueza river and the road, takes the road to **Población de Arroyo** at **Ledigos,** before it reaches a dovecot and joins up with the next route.

D) Cross the river Cueza and follow the path until it leads you to a dovecot, just off the road to Población de Arroyo. From here, a country path avoids the road altogether and heads towards **Terradillos de los Templarios.**
You will leave this village via a path that goes on to take you to the road to Villada, heading off towards the

Interior of the Sahagún municipal shelter.

right. Cross the river Templarios and pass by the medieval settlement of Villavieja. From **Moratinos,** another path takes you to **San Nicolás del Real Camino,** after which you should cross the river Sequillo. As soon as Sahagún appears on the horizon, you will find yourself at the border between the provinces of Palencia and León. You will then pass the river Valdereduey and find yourself back on the road again. From here, you will take a path that leads to the Hermitage of Virgen del Puente, before carrying on along a path which runs parallel to it on your way into **Sahagún.**

CYCLISTS

As soon as you leave the "Carretera del Indiano", the difficulty of the route to Calzadilla de la Cueza depends entirely on the state of the paved pathway.

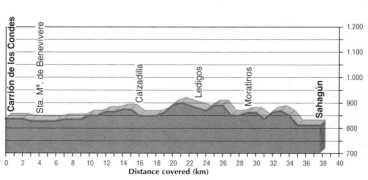

STAGE 16. PRACTICAL INFORMATION

CALZADILLA DE LA CUEZA

HOSTELS

"Camino Real" pilgrims' hostel.
Segunda Travesía Mayor. It has 100
beds, a kitchen, washing machine, patio
and swimming pool. Closes at Christmas.
✆ 979 883 187 / 676 483 517
Pilgrim shelter (Refugio de peregrinos)
✆ 979 803 050

HOTELS

HS* Camino Real. C/ Trasera Mayor, 5.
✆ 979 883 072. 10 rooms. 18 beds.
Double room: € 38; single room: € 25;
breakfast: € 3,25; lunch/dinner: € 9,6.

LEDIGOS

HOSTELS

"El Palomar" pilgrims' hostel.
✆ 979 883 614

TERRADILLOS
DE LOS TEMPLARIOS

HOSTELS

Terradillos de los Templarios hostel.
C/ La Iglesia, 18. It has 55 beds, a
washing machine, a shop and a garden.
Breakfast, lunch and dinner are served.
Open all year round. ✆ 979 883 679

SAN NICOLÁS
DEL REAL CAMINO

HOSTELS

"Laganares" inn. C/ Nueva, 1. Next to
the church. It has 21 beds and is open
from 1st March to 31st October.
✆ 629 181 536

SAHAGÚN

HOSTELS

"La Trinidad" pilgrims' hostel.
Magnificent municipal hostel located in
the church of La Trinidad. It has 104
beds, kitchen and a patio for leaving
bicycles and horses. Open all year round.
Computers connected to the Internet.
✆ 987 780 001 / 987 782 117
In the summer, the **Benedictine nuns**
also take in pilgrims.

HOTELS

HS** Alfonso VI. C/ Antonio Nicolás, 4.
✆ 987 781 144. 14 rooms. Double
room: € 40/33; single room: € 33/27;
breakfast: € 2,5; lunch/dinner: € 8.
HS** La Codorniz. C/ Arco, 84.
✆ 987 780 276. 37 rooms. 74 beds.
Double room: € 48/42; breakfast: € 4;
lunch/dinner: € 10.
HS* El Ruedo. Plaza Mayor, 1.
✆ 987 781 834. 4 rooms. 8 beds.
Double room: € 62/59/54; breakfast:
€ 2,95; lunch/dinner: € 10,5.
HS* Hospedería Benedictina.
Avda. Doctores Bermejo y Calderón, 8.
✆ 987 780 078. 21 rooms.
HS* Pacho. Avda. Constitución, 86.
✆ 987 780 775. 8 rooms. 13 beds.
Double room: € 35/27; breakfast: €
1,75; lunch/dinner: € 7.
La Asturiana guest house. Plaza Lesmes
Franco, 2. ✆ 987 780 073. 9 rooms.
12 beds. Double room: € 18; breakfast:
€ 1,5; lunch/dinner: € 6.

CAMPING SITES

2.nd C Pedro Ponce. Ctra. N-120, km 2.
✆ 987 781 112. 600 places.

RESTAURANTS

Asador El Ruedo. Carretera Mayorga.
✆ 987 780 438
Camino de Santiago. Avda. Conde
Ansúrez, 3. ✆ 987 780 177
Luis. Plaza Mayor, 4. ✆ 987 781 085
El Cepo. Avda. Constitución, 43.
✆ 987 781 136
El Peregrino. Avda. Fernando de Castro,
78. ✆ 987 780 372
Mesón El Húmedo. C/ Flora Flórez, 6.
✆ 987 781 213
San Facundo. Avda. Constitución, 99.
✆ 987 780 276

MEANS OF TRANSPORT

The train to Leon goes through Sahagún.
ALSA goes through Sahagún on its way
to Leon. ✆ 987 260 500

HISTORY AND WEALTH OF THE STAGE 16

Chapel of Nuestra Señora del Puente, near Sahagún.

THE FRENCH ROAD. CARRIÓN – SAHAGÚN

Very close to Carrión are the deteriorated remains of the **abbey of Santa María de Benevívere.** This was founded in 1189 by Castilian noble Diego Martínez to aid the poor, the ill and the pilgrims, as we are told by his biography in Latin verse. It was run by a community of regular canons and was, together with San Zoilo de Carrión and Sahagún, one of the great hospitals of the Road in this area.

From here, the Road to Santiago follows the paving of the old Via Trajana, which used to communicate Bordeaux with Astorga. The splendid late Roman villa of Quintanilla de la Cueza is close to here.

It dates from the IVth and Vth centuries, when the cities of the Empire were being abandoned by their most prominent inhabitants to move to well-communicated self-sufficient country villa such as this one.

The name **Calzadilla de la Cueza** is an example of the old Roman road's importance in the Middle Ages. Calzadilla's parish church of San Martín is full of St James crosses, which evidence the Order of St James' great presence in this area. Indeed, there were two important houses belonging to this Spanish order of knights in Villamartín (on another branch of the Road just outside Carrión) and especially in **Santa María de las Tiendas** just outside Calzadilla. The latter was famous for its dimensions and munificence towards pilgrims and, although it was in operation until the XIXth century, nothing but a building in ruins now remains of its old splendour. One of its treasures, the altarpiece that once dominated the church's high altar, can now be found in the church of San Martín de Calzadilla.

The fact that the parish church of **Ledigos** is dedicated to the apostle St James may be related to the strong presence of the Order of St James in the area. Inside the church is a beautiful image of the saint depicted as a pilgrim.

From the next town, **Terradillos de Templarios,** we enter a territory which was once protected and cared for by the Knights of the Templar. Its parish church of San Pedro contains a Romanesque crucifix.

Moratinos was, as indicated by its name ("moros" means "moors"), repopulated by Mudejars (Muslims living in Spain under Christian rule) who may have been builders specialising in brick work, and who were responsible for some of the famous mudejar-style buildings in Sahagún and its surroundings.

The Templars had some properties in **San Nicolás del Real Camino,** but there is no evidence to suggest that they had a settlement here. The

Romanesque sculpture of the Virgin which can be found in its church may be related to them.

A community of regular canons did, however, have a hospital here, starting off as a lepers' hospital but later expanding to offer its services to all pilgrims.

Before entering Sahagún, a Roman bridge allows you to cross the river Valderaduey, whose name may be the old Iberian name for the flat region of Campos. Since Menéndez Pidal, its etymology is usually explained as being based on the Iberian-Basque word ara, meaning "flat", plus the suffix *toi,* which adds a measure of abundance or augmentation. As we saw earlier, before the Roman form *campos* prevailed, there was a genuinely peninsular designation for the same flat plain, *paramus,* whose etymology is unknown but which has some Indoeuropean resonances. This would suggest that, before the Romans arrived, the great plain of Campos was shared by peoples of different origins and languages.

Pilgrims resting in Sahagún's main square (Plaza Mayor).

At the other side of the river is the chapel of La Virgen del Puente built, like most other mediaeval churches in Sahagún, in brick. An old pilgrims' hospital run by a religious brotherhood of which we know neither the origin nor the order, used to be here.

Sahagún is one of the most frequently mentioned towns in *Liber Sancti Iacobi*. Not only does the fifth book of this pilgrims' guide mention it as the end of a stage, but it praises it in terms which can only be compared with the ones bestowed on Santiago de Compostela, Estella, León and Carrión. It also recommends a visit to the local martyrs' (Facundus and Primitivus) sanctuary, an honour only received, apart from by Santiago, by Santo Domingo de la Calzada and San Isidoro de León. As if this wasn't honour enough, *Pseudo-Turpin,* the famous fourth book of *Liber Sancti Iacobi* which narrates Charlemagne's fictitious feats in Spain, grants Sahagún the honour of having been founded by the Emperor himself.

As regards Sahagún's historical origins, it is possible (although not certain) that the current town is located where *Camala* used to be, next to the Bordeaux-Astorga road according to IVth century road map *Itinerario de Antonino.* Even if this is the case, nothing – not even the name – remains from the old Celto-Roman city.

The origins of Sahagún itself (as well as those of its name - Sahagún < Safagún < Sanfagund < Sanctus Facundus) go hand in hand with its sanctuary which, according to local tradition, is where saints Facundus and Primitivus were martyred in the IIIrd century. These saints – whose hometown is claimed by both Sahagún and Orense– must have been fairly important in Paleochristian and Visigothic times, since there is documentary evidence dating from the year 652 that some relics of theirs were taken to the distant church of Guadix. Two centuries later, in 872, the destroyed basilica dedicated to these two saints, which had

Sahagún. Church of San Lorenzo.

been destroyed by then, was bought and rebuilt by King Alfonso III and given to a community of Mozarabic monks who had fled from Córdoba. From then on, Sahagún's properties and prestige started to grow to the point of becoming self-sufficient. One sign of this growth was the *Pasión* of its two saints, a Xth century literary work whose pomposity and length, unequalled among the Passions of Spanish martyrs, must have been as magnificent as its sanctuary.

But Sahagún really peaked during Alfonso VI's time, who turned the abbey into one of Spain's cultural, spiritual and even political centres of the time. The King, who resided in Sahagún for long periods of time, turned it into the centre of the ambitious religious and cultural reform of his kingdoms, replacing the local (Spanish/Visigothic/Mozarabic) liturgy with the Gregorio-Roman one. The liturgy reform brought about some serious changes in the kingdom's and its people's lives. Everything changed, including the saints' days calendar, texts, music and other

Sahagún. Above, La Peregrina sanctuary; below, arch of San Benito.

liturgic customs, as well as the writing they used for the books. The King was assisted in these changes by the powerful abbey of Cluny in Bourgogne, which sent large numbers of well trained monks to Spain. Many of them spent some time in the cells of Sahagún, the most important Clunian building in Spain – it had over 50 monasteries and priories under its jurisdiction – before taking some of the most important Spanish bishop posts of the time.

There are now very few visible traces (including the arch and the chapel of San Mancio) of that amazing institution, although a great excavation campaign to bring out to light the foundations of its splendid church and other dependencies, among which there must have been a *scriptorium* and a library to match the abbey's wealth and the importance of its mission, has been planned.

Sahagún was also important in the Road to Santiago – which Alfonso VI had so lovingly tended – and had one of the most important hospitals in the whole route.

The wealthy village of Sahagún grew near the abbey (to which it belonged), to a great extent thanks to the pilgrimage, and was inhabited by people from all over Europe. The town's most typical and valuable monuments date precisely from the golden centuries of the pilgrimages, the XIIth and XIIIth centuries: the churches of San Tirso and San Lorenzo, whose spacious brick towers opened to the outside world by means of three rows of arched windows are Sahagún best known image; and the Franciscan convent of La Peregrina, where the Road to Santiago's document centre (Centro de Documentación del Camino de Santiago) will be as soon as it has been restored. Other noteworthy buildings include the XVIth century chapel of San Juan de Sahagún, La Trinidad (which now provides shelter for pilgrims) and the Benedictine convent of La Santa Cruz, which to a certain extent carries on the memory of the old abbey. The convent museum has some of its artistic treasures, such as the famous Baroque sculpture of the Pilgrim Virgin (la Virgen Peregrina) by Sevillian sculptress Luisa Roldán, or Enrique de Arfe's splendid Custodia, on display. The tombs of eloquent King Alfonso VI and his four wives can be found in the convent's church, which retains some Romanesque elements. Among the famous inhabitants to which Sahagún has dedicated something are St John of Sahagún, Bernard of Sahagún, Pedro Ponce de León and, more recently, pilgrimage historian Millán Bravo Lozano.

17   Sahagún – Reliegos

*In Sahagún, you will leave Tierra de Campos behind,
moving on through the cereal and grain-covered plateaux of
León. This part of the countryside is also characterised by
small valleys and riverbeds which began life when water
started collecting in the rocky surface of the terrain, and
remained there due to the high amounts of clay that lie
deeper underground.*

Pilgrims in Calzada del Coto.

Antonio Nicolás Street takes you on to the Del Canto bridge across the
river Cea which, in turn, will lead you out of the village of **Sahagún.** The
famous Meadow of the Spears, or "Prado de las lanzas", and the town's
campsite, can be see to your right as you leave. A poplar-lined pathway
heads off to the left of the N-120 until you cross to the right-hand side of
the road to pass by the Hermitage of San Roque. Here, you will come to
a fork in the road, where you must choose between heading alongside
the French "Real Camino" or opting to go for the "Via Traiana":
A) Without actually going into Calzada de Coto, you should take the path
that heads on to Mansilla de las Mulas. This path is lined with many
young, vibrant plane trees, and has quite a few rest areas along its course.
Continuing along this path you can hear the motorway, which runs
parallel along to the right. After passing by various seasonal lakes
surrounded by poplars, crossing the river Coso, and passing by the
Perales Hermitage, you will come to the first village along this route,
Bercianos del Real Camino. To the north of this area you should be able
to make out the woody area of Valdelocajos, where the alternative route
runs. Upon leaving Bercianos, you should go back onto the same dirt
track as before, and cross the Majuelos river. In amongst the poplars, a
sign points you to the "Fuente de los Romeros", and further along this
path you will pass by some more small lakes. To go into **Burgo Ranero,**
you should go under the motorway and, once in the village, you should
go all the way along Real Street. This will take you out on the other side
of the village, passing by a large pond on your way out. Once on the
pilgrims' path again, you should continue onwards.

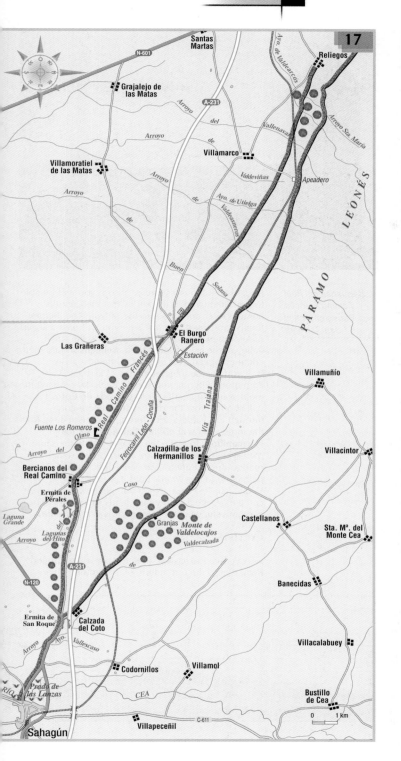

17

Santas
Martas

N-601

Reliegos

Grajalejo de
las Matas

A-231

Ayo. de Valdearcos

Arroyo

del

Vallenava

Arroyo

de

Villamarco

L E Ó N É S

Villamoratiel
de las Matas

Valdeviñas

Apeadero

Arroyo

Ayo. de Utielga

Arroyo

de

Valdeasneros

Buen

P Á R A M O

Solana

Las Grañeras

El Burgo
Ranero

Estación

Villamuñío

Real Camino Francés

Ferrocarril León - Coruña

Vía Trajana

Fuente Los Romeros

Olmo

Calzadilla de los
Hermanillos

Villacintor

Arroyo

del

Bercianos del
Real Camino

Coso

Ermita de
Pérales

Castellanos

Laguna
Grande

Granjas

Monte de
Valdelocajos

Sta. Mª. del
Monte Cea

Arroyo

del

Lagunas
del Hito

Valdecalzada

A-231

de

Banecidas

N-120

Ermita de
San Roque

Calzada
del Coto

Ayo.

Villacalabuey

Arroyo

Vallescaso

Prado de
las Lanzas

Codornillos

Villamol

Bustillo
de Cea

RÍO

CEA

0   1 km

Sahagún

Villapeceñil

C-611

Bercianos del Real Camino Francés. Parish church of San Salvador.

Roughly 8 kilometres further ahead, you will be able to see Villamarco to the left, whilst the Camino comes closer and closer to the railway line, before finally crossing it. On one side you will pass a group of reforested conifers, before going by the small valley of the river Santa María. **Reliegos** should then come up ahead, just over 12 kilometres away.
B) If you decide to go along the "Via Traiana" or Path of the Pilgrim, you should begin by crossing the motorway and heading into **Calzada de Coto.** You will shortly cross the railway line before going through the Valdelocajos forest. Upon emerging from the forest, you will go into **Calzadilla de los Hermanillos.** To leave the village, follow the same path which brought you in, which then crosses the road to Burgo Ranero and carries on forward. The path continues onwards until it reaches the Villamarco rest area. When you get to Reliegos, you can either take a path which leads straight there or, alternatively, you can carry on towards Mansilla.

CYCLISTS

For cyclists, the easiest route to take is the Camino Real, due to the firm nature of the terrain.

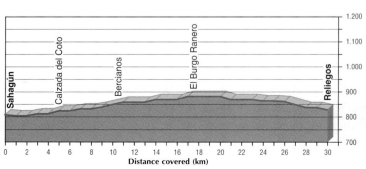

STAGE 17. PRACTICAL INFORMATION

BERCIANOS DEL REAL CAMINO

HOSTELS

Bercianos del Real Camino parish hostel (Albergue parroquial de Bercianos del Real Camino).
Located on calle Santa Rita. It has 38 beds, a kitchen and dining room. Open all year round. ∅ 987 784 008

HOTELS

HS* Riveiro.
C/ Mayor, 12. ∅ 987 744 287.
8 rooms. 16 beds. Double room: € 30.

RESTAURANTS

Rivero.
C/ Mayor, 12. ∅ 987 784 287

EL BURGO RANERO

HOSTELS

"Domenico Laffi" hostel.
It is one of the most beautiful hostels of the Road. It is made of adobe, like the traditional buildings of this area. It has a kitchen, chimney and and 26 beds.
∅ 987 330 154 / 987 330 023

HOTELS

HS* El Peregrino.
C/ Fray Pedro del Burgo, 30. 10 rooms.
∅ 987 330 069. 14 beds. Double room:
€ 34/31; single room: € 22/19;
breakfast: € 3; lunch/dinner: € 8.

RESTAURANTS

El Molino. Barrio Estación, 13.
∅ 987 330 031

MEANS OF TRANSPORT

The Valladolid-Leon **RENFE** train line stops here.

RELIEGOS

HOSTELS

Municipal Hostel (Albergue Municipal).
The Town Council has turned the old schools into a fairly big hostel, which has a kitchen and is open all year round. Good facilities.

CALZADA DEL COTO

HOSTELS

Municipal Hostel (Albergue Municipal).
It has 24 beds and is open all year round. ∅ 987 781 177

CALZADILLA DE LOS HERMANILLOS

HOSTELS

Calzadilla de los Hermanillos hostel (Albergue de Calzadilla de los Hermanillos).
∅ 987 330 023

HISTORY AND WEALTH OF THE STAGE 17

Bridge next to Chopera de las Lanzas.

THE FRENCH ROAD. SAHAGÚN – RELIEGOS

Just like the river Pisuerga marks Tierra de Campos' eastern boundary, the western boundary is marked by the river Cea. "Puente de Canto" ("Bridge of Canto", "canto" meaning "edge", "end" or "limit"), the name given in this area to the solid five-span bridge which Alfonso VI ordered to be built in 1085, may be a reference to this frontier status. However, it is more likely to refer to stone, the material with which it was built, in contrast to brick, the material which was typically used for Sahagún's other buildings.

Either **Chopera de las Lanzas,** the thick forests on the other side of the river or, at least something similar, must already have been there in the XIIth century. The author of the fourth part of *Liber Sancti Iacobi,* or *Pseudo-Turpin,* made up an amazing story, not only to explain the existence of this forest and the origins of Sahagún, but also to associate Charlemagne with one of the most important parts of the Road to Santiago. Among the false claims contained in this fictitious chronicle of the French Emperor's feats in Spain are the claims that he found the apostle St James' tomb and that he contributed to building the Road. At that time, Sahagún's importance on the Road was so great that the author felt compelled to attribute its origins to Charlemagne. This is how they are narrated in the eighth chapter, in the context of a campaign by Charlemagne against Muslim leader Aigoland, whose footprints he was following and whom he …

> *[…] found in the land of Campos, in a field next to the river Cea, a very fertile and flat place where Charlemagne would later order the building of the splendid basilica in which the bodies of martyr saints Facundus and Primitivus now rest; the abbey would be founded; and a large and wealthy town would be built […]*

After several single combats, Emperor Charlemagne and Emir Aigoland decide to have an open field battle. The miracle which takes place on the eve of the battle explains the origin of the large groups of trees on the river bank, which are now, in honour of *Pseudo-Turpin's* fiction, referred to as "Chopera de las Lanzas" ("lanzas" meaning "lances" or "spears").

> *"While preparing for battle the night before, some Christians drove their spears into the ground on the river bank, opposite the camp. The next day, the spears of those who would become martyrs in the battle were adorned with bark and luxuriant branches. In total wonder, and thinking that this was a divine miracle, they cut the spears at ground level. The extensive forest which can still be found there subsequently grew from the roots of the poles which remained buried as if they had been planted, since many of the spears were made of ash wood [...]. When the two sides joined in battle that day, 40,000 Christians, including Duke Milo (Roland's father), as well as Charlemagne's horse, died."*

Charlemagne is forced to continue the battle on foot, and heroically resists the Muslim assaults with only 2,000 warriors until, at the end of the day, four Italian marquis arrive to help him and Aigoland flees. These picturesque aspects, such as setting Duke Milo's and the horse's deaths in Sahagún, are part of the author's attempt to make of Sahagún a place of Charlemagne worship. For whatever reasons, however, the attempt was fruitless, unlike the one in Roncesvals, and nothing remains of this beautiful story in local tradition, either in the form of place names or of popular or literary stories or, in fact, any other form. The Sahagún episode itself, however, is depicted on one of the boards of the silver coffer with contains the remains of Charlemagne's chest in the cathedral of Aachen.

Calzada del Coto provides an example of a town turned into an important geographical point of reference, almost like an administrative district or region, by Vía Trajana's physical preservation in this area, between Carrión and Mansilla. The location of many places near it, such as Sahagún itself, Calzada del Coto, Calzadilla de la Cueza or Calzadilla

Chapel of La Virgen de Perales, near Bercianos.

de los Hermanillos, is referred to in mediaeval documents by reference to "a territory called Calzada" *(in loco Calzata)*. This description would later become part of some of these places' names. An obvious example of this process is Calzada del Coto, which went from being called *Villa Zakarias in loco Calzata* in the Xth century to simply "the village which was on the road" and finally "the village called Calzada" ("calzada" means "road") *(in villa que dicunt Calzata)*.

Between here and Reliegos, the Road splits into two parallel branches. The first and older one is the one on the right, which runs concurrently with the old "Vía Trajana" (A). The left branch is known as "Real Camino Francés" (Royal French Road). This is a combination of terms which include, firstly, the fact that it was a pilgrims' - and therefore, a foreigner's - road; and, secondly, its XVIIIth century classification, due to its quality and size, as one of the royal roads, the equivalent of a modern motorway in status (B).

A) The "Vía Trajana" branch, which still has some stretches of the old paving as well as some milestones (Dehesa de Valdelocajos), only goes through one town, expressively named **Calzadilla de los Hermanillos.**

Although lacking a priory, the town must have had a modest dependency of the abbey of Sahagún, established here to assist pilgrims. The modern town grew around this dependency, and its parish church (dedicated to St Bartholomew) contains some valuable pieces such as a XVIth century Calvary scene on the high altar.

B) In the "Real Camino Francés" branch we find, before reaching Bercianos, the Virgen de Perales chapel, which belonged to the hospital of El Cebreiro in the XIIth century.

Bercianos del Real Camino Francés. Interior of the parish church of San Salvador.

The most outstanding piece in **Bercianos del Real Camino Francés,** whose name refers to its mediaeval inhabitants' place of origin, Bierzo, is the image in its parish church of San Salvador, which contains a sculpture of St John the Baptist. A monument to the pilgrimage historian Millán Bravo Lozano has recently been erected next to Lake Valdematas.

This desolate landscape, before you reach **Burgo Ranero,** is the setting of the well known and gruesome episode, told by XVIIth century Italian traveller Domenico Laffi, of the dead pilgrim who was eaten by wolves. The Italian pilgrim himself describes Burgo Ranero as a sheep farmers' town, comprised of thatched huts. Burgo's name, together with other indications, seem to suggest that the town was not as humble when it was founded as it was in the XVIIth century. It is documented for the first time in 1126 as a "burgo" (burg) of Sahagún. Its one-street layout denotes the existence of "burghers", traders and craftsmen who practised their trade on the side of the Road, to which they owed their prosperity. Such prosperity is evidenced, for example, by the beautiful Romanesque sculpture of the Virgin, which until recently was kept in the parish church of San Pedro and is currently in León Cathedral Museum. Another indication of its prosperity was the fact that prominent people such as XVth century Pedro del Burgo, who was the mitred abbot of Sahagún for 20 years, was originally from Burgo Ranero. This abbot, also a sculptor and architect, was responsible for the restoration of important monuments such as the monastery of San Pedro de Cárdena. Its lying statue, which was sculpted by his own disciples, is in the Madres Benedictinas convent museum, in Sahagún.

The two historic roads, Vía Trajana and Real Camino Francés, meet again in **Reliegos.** The distances in *Itinerario de Antonino* suggest that the old mansion of *Pallantia* on Vía Trajana (Bordeaux-Astorga), where this road used to meet another Roman road – the road from León *(Legio VII Gemina)* –, used to be either on this spot or not far from it. Its parish church is – quite unusually – dedicated to St Cyprian of Carthage and Pope St Cornelius (IIIrd century), both of whom belonged to the early Christian church and fought against the heresy of the libellatici. But we needn't go that far to find the origins of this form of worship, which originated in the IXth and Xth centuries, when Reliegos was repopulated and it was usual for these two saints to be worshipped together.

18 Reliegos – León

You should go down from the plateau towards the capital of León, passing the valley of the river Esla and Mansilla de las Mulas. You will then continue alongside land that has been set aside for irrigated crop growing, before seeing the first signs of industrial activity up ahead. From Portillo Hill you should be able to make out the beautiful city of León.

Monument to the Pilgrims in Mansilla de las Mulas.

A) The French Real Camino goes through **Reliegos** along Real Street, and carries along past the pelota court and the football pitch. You should continue along the same tree-lined path that you were on yesterday as far as the Esla valley. Passing the Grande river, you will cross a bridge over the ring road and pass by a canal, before entering **Mansilla de las Mulas,** entering via what was once the Southern boundary gate of the city. B) The "Via Traiana" carries along a similar and almost parallel route before ending up in Mansilla de las Mulas, entering the village by the Santa María gate. You will leave the village via the N-601, crossing the medieval bridge which spans the river Esla. A little further ahead you will see a dirt track which runs parallel to the tarmacked path, hidden among the trees, and you should head off along this path. After passing by the graveyard and the river Moro, you will come to **Villamoros de Mansilla.** This village is situated alongside the motorway, on the other side of which is Lancia, situated atop a small mound. Leave Villamoros on the hard verge of the road, before taking a path a few metres ahead which heads off into a poplar wood. The river Porma runs along the left-hand side of this path, before eventually crossing the path. You should then cross the river over the huge bridge with twenty arches, carry along the leafy riverside, and then cross the road to San Miguel de Escalada. Next, go through **Puente de Villarente** and, coming out of the village, pass by a petrol station and take a path which leads off to the right of the N-601. Pass by the Porma Canal and head off towards a small hill on the top of which you will find **Arcahueja.** Just 1 kilometre further ahead you will come to **Valdefuente.** From here you should rejoin the main road which takes you upwards to Alto del Portillo, after which the city of León awaits your

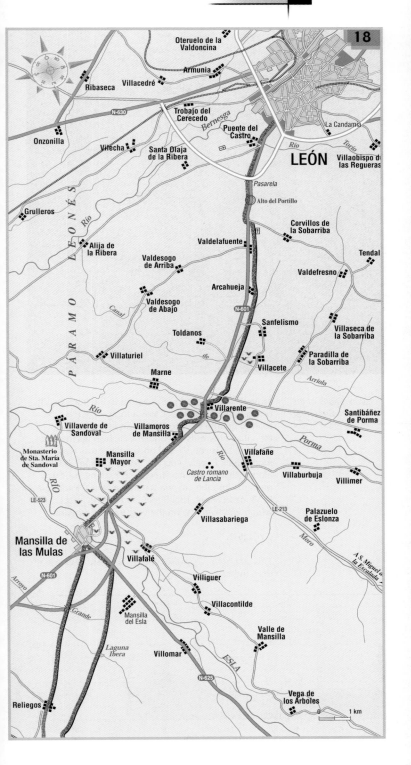

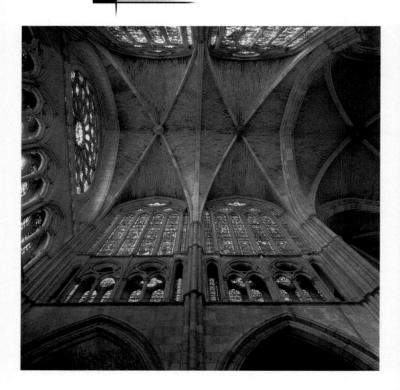

León. Vaults of the Cathedral.

arrival. A tarmacked path parallel to the track heads down towards the city. Cross a footbridge over the road to go into **Puente Castro,** and then head out of the village towards the bridge which spans the river Torío, (which you should once again cross via a footbridge). Finally, you will come to **León,** passing along Miguel Castaño Street, and making your way onwards into the city via Barahona Street, Puerta de la Moneda Street, Rúa Street, and Ancha Street, which will lead you all the way to the Cathedral.

CYCLISTS

This stage is a very easy one, as it rarely deviates from the N-120.

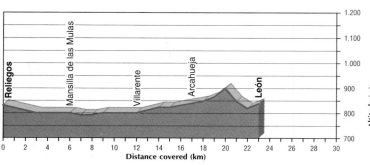

STAGE 18. PRACTICAL INFORMATION

MANSILLA DE LAS MULAS

HOSTELS

Mansilla de las Mulas hostel (Albergue de Mansilla de las Mulas).
Located on calle del Puente. The Leon Road to Santiago Friends Association (Asociación de Amigos del Camino de Santiago de León) takes in travellers all year round. It has a kitchen, washing machine and dryer. ∅ 987 310 068

HOTELS

HS** El Gallo. Carretera Cistierna, 17.
∅ 987 310 359. 7 rooms. 11 beds.
Double room: € 46; single room: € 27.
Breakfast: € 2; lunch/dinner: € 10.
HS* Las Delicias. C/ Los Mesones, 22.
∅ 987 310 075. 6 rooms. 11 beds.
Double room: € 35; single room: € 23;
breakfast: € 2; lunch/dinner: € 8.
HS* Los Faroles. Avda. Picos de Europa. ∅ 987 310 949. 12 rooms.
20 beds. Double room: € 32; breakfast: € 3; lunch/dinner: € 10.

RESTAURANTS

Alberguería del Camino.
C/ Concepción, 12. ∅ 987 311 193
Bahillo. Ctra. Cistierna. ∅ 987 230 839
Casa Marcelo. C/ Postigo, 1.
∅ 987 310 835
El Hórreo del Tío Faico. Avda.
Constitución, 58. ∅ 987 311 220

CAMPING SITES

2.nd C Esla. Fuente de los Prados.
∅ 987 310 089. 168 places.

MEANS OF TRANSPORT

Bus station, where ALSA buses stop on their way to Leon. ∅ 987 260 500

ARCAHUEJA

RESTAURANTS

Camino Real. Carretera Madrid N-601, km 320. ∅ 987 218 134
El Pradillo. Carretera N-601.
∅ 987 269 032

VALDELAFUENTE

RESTAURANTS

Cerro Alto. Ctra. Madrid.
∅ 987 258 357
Santa Fe. Ctra. N-601, km 321.

PUENTE DE VILLARENTE

HOTELS

HSR* El Delfín Verde. Ctra. Adanero-Gijón. ∅ 987 312 065. 23 rooms. Double room: € 33/32; single room: € 16/15.
Casablanca guest house. Ctra. Adanero-Gijón, km 314. ∅ 987 312 164. 8 rooms.
Double room: € 21; single room: € 12.

RESTAURANTS

Avellaneda. C/ Camino de Santiago, 139. ∅ 987 312 236
La Casona. C/ Camino de Santiago, 20.
∅ 987 312 474

LEÓN

HOSTELS

Benedictine Nuns Pilgrims' Hostel (Albergue de peregrinos "De las RRMM Benedictinas"). Pl. del Grano, 7.
150 beds. ∅ 680 649 289
"Consejo de Europa" Youth Hostel.
On Paseo del Parque, 2. Open in July, August and September. 90 beds and a kitchen. ∅ 987 202 969 / 987 200 206
"Ciudad de León" municipal pilgrims' hostel. C/ Campos Góticos, s/n. 64 beds for pilgrims and 75 as a youth hostel.
Washing machine. ∅ 987 081 833

HOTELS

HS* España. C/ del Carmen, 3. ∅ 987 236 014. 12 rooms. Double room: € 24.
Avda. guest house. Avda. Palencia, 4.
∅ 987 223 763. Double room: € 18.
Suarez guest house. C/ Ancha, 7-2º.
∅ 987 254 288. 7 rooms. Double room: € 18.

MEANS OF TRANSPORT

Bus station. ∅ 987 296 100

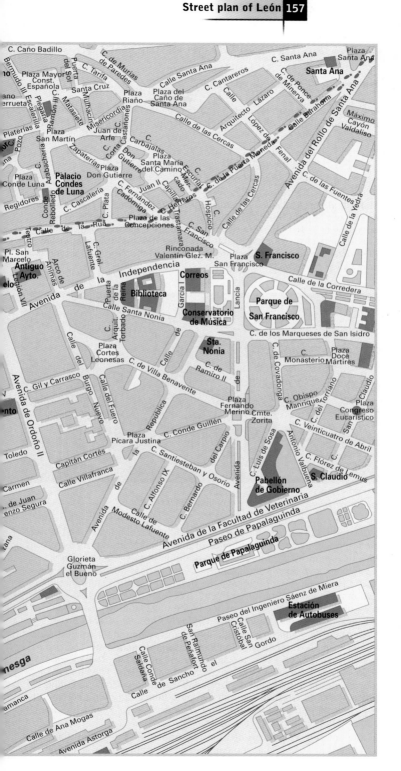

HISTORY AND WEALTH OF THE STAGE 18

THE FRENCH ROAD. RELIEGOS – LEÓN

The distance between Reliegos and Mansilla de las Mulas, exactly one Castilian league, is well known in the Road to Santiago thanks to the following couplet:

> *"La legua de Castilla / de Reliegos a Mansilla."*
> *"(The Castilian League / from Reliegos to Mansilla.)"*

Mansilla de las Mulas may be the *Manxilla* mentioned in *Liber Sancti Iacobi* as a Stop of the Road. Although at one point (1130) there were three towns called Manxilla within a small area, the mention of the river Esla running close to it has enabled us to be sure that it was *Mansilla de illa Ponte,* as mentioned in other documents of the time, and which is now called Mansilla de las Mulas.

Square in Mansilla de las Mulas.

Indeed, the bridge over the river Esla and the powerful wall are the two great monuments which remind us of mediaeval Mansilla. As regards its historical relevance on the Road, in addition to *Liber Sancti Iacobi,* references have been found to three good pilgrims' hospitals from the XVth century, and we even have the bylaws – dated a century later – of two of them, Sancti Spiritus and Santiago. Mansilla is also famous for providing the setting for part of one of the most famous picaresque novels of the Spanish Golden Age (Siglo de Oro): *La pícara Justina.*

Near Mansilla – although outside the route –, where the rivers Esla and Porma meet, is the **monastery of Santa María de Sandoval.** The current building dates from a bit later, since it was built in late Romanesque style in 1142 under Count Ponce de Minerva's orders. The famous monasteries of **San Miguel de Escalada** (Xth century Mozarabic) and **Santa María de Gradefes** (founded in the XIIth century for a community of Cistercian nuns, just like the monastery of Huelgas Reales in Burgos), can also be found outside the route.

Before entering **Villamoros de Mansilla,** one of the three Mansillas found in mediaeval documents, you can see, on the right hand side of the road, cerro de **Lancia,** which still has some remains of the old Celto-Roman city. Lancia was the last bastion of the *Astures cismontanos* – the Asturian people from the south of the Cordillera Cantábrica mountain range, who lent their name to the river Esla *(Astura* in ancient and mediaeval documents) – against the Romans, until its definitive conquest in 26 BC. *Itinerario de Antonino* highlights it as a Stop of the Road between *Pallantia* (Reliegos) and *Legio VII Gemina* (León).

The bridge over the river Porma, which we know today as **Puente de Villarente,** impressed the

León Cathedral.

author of *Liber Sancti Iacobi,* who describes is as "huge". It is, indeed, a large twenty-span structure. Although it has been completely rebuilt, its mediaeval design has been kept. On its left, almost at the beginning of the bridge, is a large and solid XVIth century house which was once a pilgrims' hospital and was founded by the archdeacon of Triacastela, a member of León town council.

After the villages of Arcahueja and **Toldanos,** the latter of which was populated with Mozarabic people from Toledo, you reach **Alto del Portillo,** where a beautiful stone cross marks the Road to Santiago. The cross we find there today is modern and replaces the XVth century one, which is now in San Marcos square. From here you can reach **Puente Castro,** a district of León on the bank of the river Torío. Both the district and the bridge owe their name to the old Jewish quarter, built on a pre-existing Asturian town on Cerro de la Mota. This fortified quarter is referred to in mediaeval texts as *castrum iudeorum* (for example in the *Liber Sancti Iacobi* guide and in Lucas de Tuy's work) or *castrum Legionis* (Rodrigo Jiménez de Rada).

León is also mentioned in the *Liber Sancti Iacobi* guide, not only as the end of a stage, but also as "the seat of the royal court, equipped with goods of all kinds". The guide also recommends a visit to St Isidore's relics and makes it evident that its author knew the city and its names well – it names the city's two rivers, the Torío and the Bernesga, as well as the Puente de Castro quarter). However, this is no more than a pale reflection of what the city was like in Alfonso VII's time when he was the most powerful king in the Iberian Peninsula, and León was the most important city in Christian Spain.

At that time (c. 1130), León was almost a thousand years old, since it was founded in 69 BC as a settlement of *Legio VII Gemina,* to which it owes its name *(Legionem > Leion > León),* and which explains why the original town layout was quadrangular in shape and had a structure

*León. Pantheon of the Kings (Panteón de los Reyes) in the Royal
Collegiate Church of San Isidoro.*

based around two perpendicular axes. After being invaded by the
Muslims in the VIIIth century, it was quickly recovered by Alfonso I.
In 914-915, in the time taken to repopulate the whole of the "Meseta
Norte" or Northern Plateau, King Ordoño II moved his court from
Oviedo to León and made it the capital of the Kingdom.

The golden age of the pilgrimage was also the city's most splendorous
time. León had many hospitals and charitable institutions to offer
pilgrims, as well as many sanctuaries in which to stop while visiting the
city. Before crossing the wall via the Arco del Rey archway or the Puerta
Cauriense door, the travellers encountered the church and hospital of
Santa Ana which, in the XIIth century, was run by a community of
Knights of the Holy Sepulchre. Inside the city they would come across
the church of Santa María del Camino, now Santa María del Mercado, a
Romanesque church with a Gothic image of the Patron Saint of León
inside. Following calle de la Rúa, the travellers reached the church and
hospital of San Marcelo. This was dedicated to a Paleochristian VIIth
legion centurion martyr from León, and was run by a community of
regular canons.

If you make a small detour, you find the cathedral of Santa María de la
Regla, one of the best Gothic churches in Spain. This piece of land has
supported, in succession, the Roman military settlement baths, Ordoño
II's palace from the time when he made León the capital of the kingdom,
and the early Romanesque cathedral, which was completely demolished
to build the Gothic building that we see there today. The most
interesting feature of this architectural gem is, without a doubt, the
multicolour brightness of its interior, achieved by over one hundred large
stained glass windows. The most interesting parts of the exterior are the
magnificent collections of sculptures around its main façade's three
doors. The apostle St James' presence is clear here as well as on the
main altarpiece and the many chapels and stained glass windows.

Not far from the cathedral and still within the old city, we find León's
other great architectural treasure, the collegiate church of San Isidoro,
which is practically adjoined to the city wall which marks the old city
limits. The current building dates from the middle of the XIIth century,
although it was the bringing of St Isidore of Seville's relics (VIIth century)

from Seville that definitely turned this collection of buildings into a great sanctuary. This saint was the author of *Etymologiae,* one of the most widely read works during the Middle Ages and which, together with Boethius' and Casiodoro de Reina's works, lay down the foundations of knowledge for the long mediaeval period. The move took place in 1063 at the special insistence of King Fernando I, who gave a community of regular canons the task of worshipping the relics. Some of this splendid construction's most noteworthy aspects are the sculptures on Puerta del Perdón, whose series of icons are based on Christ's Passion and resurrection; and those of Puerta del Cordero, dominated by *Agnus Dei,* the symbol of Jesus' sacrifice for humankind, and under which we find many other sacrifice scenes taken from the Old Testament and painfully crammed into the available space.

Inside the church is the famous Pantheon of the Kings (panteón de los Reyes), a vaulted crypt containing the remains of 23 monarchs of León. Its walls and ceiling are covered in beautiful tempera paintings depicting different scenes from the Gospels, as well as a Zodiac and a Calendar. Among the Romanesque treasures kept in this church are the chest containing the saint's relics, a Bible with miniatures painted by the great XIIth century Biblical scholar St Martin of León, the Cross of Peñalba and Doña Urraca's Chalice, among others.

Although, as befits such a flourishing institution, St Isidore made its mark in pilgrim assistance, the city's two great hospitals in the late Middle Ages were San Antonio and, especially, San Marcos. This institution belonged to the knights of the Order of St James from the late XIIth century, and became their main building in the XVIth century. The much loved Plateresque monastery, with its façade full of St James symbols, is also from this time. Its knighthood symbols (such as sword crosses and depictions of St James as the killer of Moor ("matamoros") are more numerous than its pilgrimage ones (such as scallops).

León. Night view of the façade of San Marcos "parador" (national inn).

19 León – Villadangos del Páramo or Villar de Mazarife

Leaving León, the urban area continues almost as far as Virgen del Camino. From this point onwards, however, you have 2 options: either stick close to the main road and follow the historical route, or stay away from the road and move along paths and local routes which make up a route that was devised a few years ago. Both routes, however, will pass through the plateau of León.

León. San Marcos Bridge.

Go along Renueva Street and Suero de Quiñones Avenue, before coming to San Marcos. From here, you will take the bridge which crosses the river Bernesga, continue straight ahead, and cross the footbridge which goes over the railway line. You should now be in **Trobajo del Camino,** which is part of León, where you should take a street to the left which heads to the N-120, crosses to its right-hand side, and heads up the path of the cross (el camino de la Cruz). You should follow this path along until you return to the main road, just before the petrol station. About 4 km ahead, you will arrive at **La Virgen del Camino.** Leaving the village, after passing by the Shrine to the Virgin, you will cross to the left-hand side of the N-120, before continuing parallel to the road and crossing the A-66 motorway. Here you will come to a fork in the road, and are faced with 2 possible choices:
A) The first option involves heading towards **Villadangos del Páramo** along a well-maintained path next to the N-120, passing through **Valverde de la Virgen** and **San Miguel del Camino** en route. After going through the latter

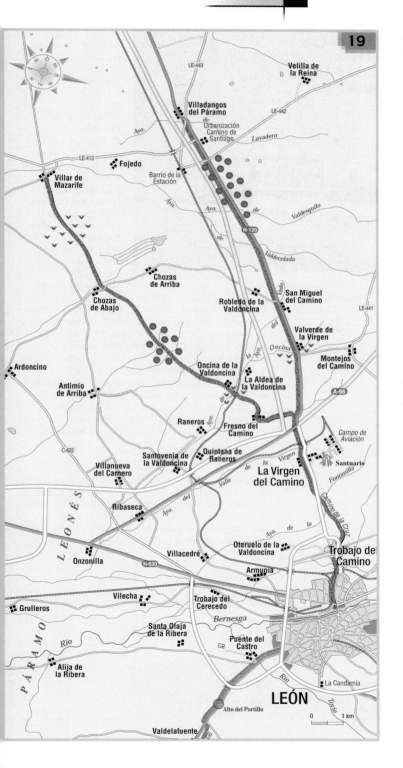

La Virgen del Camino sanctuary.

of the 2 villages, you will cross the road, but continue parallel to it, always keeping it in sight. A further 8 kilometres will bring you to **Villadangos del Páramo.**

B) Alternatively, you can head for Villar de Mazarife, crossing the motorway and heading towards **Fresno del Camino,** a village which nestles in the valley. You should leave this village to the right, along the road to **Oncina de Valdoncina,** which passes by a solitary spot covered in scrub and brushwood. Before reaching Oncina, you will cross the railway line and the river which shares its name. Upon arriving in the village, Real Street will lead you through and out the other side, where you should take a country path, dotted with oak trees, as it makes its way up to the plateau. About 5 kilometres further along, you will come to **Chozas de Abajo.** Leaving the village, you will pass by a poplar wood and cross a stream. Then, following a path which leads through irrigation ditches and crop fields, you will arrive at **Villar de Mazarife.**

CYCLISTS

Despite the traffic, it is easiest for cyclists to begin on the N-120 and take it all the way to **La Virgen del Camino.** From here, it is easier to take the first of the options outlined above, which heads towards **Villadangos del Páramo.** Having said that, however, the second of the two options is not overly difficult.

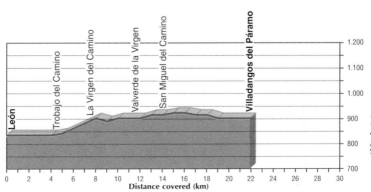

STAGE 19. PRACTICAL INFORMATION

TROBAJO DEL CAMINO

HOTELS

HS* La Gárgola. C/ Gran Capitán, 7.
✆ 987 806 180. 10 rooms. 21 beds.
Double room: € 29; single room: € 19.
Ancar guest house. C/ Menéndez Pidal,
16. ✆ 987 802 761. 5 rooms. 10 beds.
Double room: € 30; single room: € 15.

RESTAURANTS

Buenavista. Avda. Párroco Pablo Díez,
325. ✆ 987 802 982
Casa Talique. Avda. Párroco Pablo Díez,
240. ✆ 987 802 763
Mirador de la Cruz. C/ Cruz, 20.
✆ 987 802 439
Pata Negra. Avda. Párroco Pablo Díez,
289. ✆ 987 253 150

LA VIRGEN DEL CAMINO

HOTELS

H** Villapaloma. Avda. Astorga, 47.
✆ 987 300 990. 30 rooms. 57 beds.
Double room: € 63; single room: € 42.
HSR** San Froilán. Avda. Peregrinos, 1.
✆ 987 302 019. 22 rooms. 40 beds.
Double room: € 48; single room: € 42.
HSR** Soto. Ctra. León-Astorga, km 5.
✆ 987 802 925. 41 rooms. 46 beds.
Double room: € 48; single room: € 36.
HSR* Julio César. C/ Cervantes, 6.
✆ 987 302 044. 8 rooms. 14 beds.
Double room: € 18; single room: € 18.

RESTAURANTS

Asturias. C/ Cervantes, 5. ✆ 987 300 005
Central. Avda. Astorga, 85.
✆ 987 302 041
El Soto. Ctra. León-Astorga, km 5.
✆ 987 804 010
Miravalles. Ctra. León-Astorga, 34.
✆ 987 302 338

MEANS OF TRANSPORT

The city bus goes all the way to **La
Virgen del Camino**. The ALSA Group
Leon-Astorga-Ponferrada line, which
stops at **Trobajo del Camino**, **Valverde
de la Virgen**, **San Miguel del Camino**
and **Villadangos**, also goes through here.

VILLADANGOS DEL PÁRAMO

HOSTELS

Municipal Hostel (Albergue Municipal).
It has 80 beds, a kitchen and a place to
leave bicycles. Open all year round.
✆ 987 390 629 / 987 390 003

HOTELS

HR** Avda. III. Ctra. León-Astorga, km
17. ✆ 987 390 311. 40 rooms. 76 beds.
Double room: € 27; single room: € 17.
HS** Alto Páramo. Ctra. León-Astorga,
km 18. ✆ 987 390 425. 15 rooms. 26
beds. Double room: € 35.
HS** Libertad. C/ Padre Ángel Martínez,
25. ✆ 987 390 123. 23 rooms. 39 beds.
Double room: € 36.
HSR* Avda. II. Ctra. León-Astorga, km
17. ✆ 987 390 151. 10 rooms. 19 beds.
Double room: € 47/41.

CAMPING SITES

2.nd C Camino de Santiago. Ctra. N-120,
km 324. ✆ 987 680 253. 494 places.

RESTAURANTS

Avda. II. Ctra. León-Astorga, km 17.
✆ 987 390 081
Camino de Santiago. Ctra. León-
Astorga, km 18. ✆ 987 390 193
La Pradera. Ctra. León-Astorga, km 17.
✆ 987 390 017

SAN MIGUEL DEL CAMINO

RESTAURANTS

El Rincón de Julia. C/ La Fuente, 7.
✆ 987 303 266

VILLAR DE MAZARIFE

HOSTELS

Jesús hostel. Located on calle Orujo, 8.
It has 55 beds, a kitchen and a living
room. Open all year round.
✆ 987 390 697 / 686 053 390

History and wealth of the stage 19

The French Road. León – Villadangos del Páramo or Villar de Mazarife

A good example of the knowledge of León that the author of the fourth part of *Liber Sancti Iacobi* had is the fact that he recognises the existence of two rivers (which he does not do for any other city) and even explaining their location in relation to the city: the river Torío is where the Road of Santiago enters the city beside Puente Castro, and the river Bernesga is on the other side, on the Road exit towards Astorga. The

Image of St Saviour in Oviedo Cathedral.

guidebook only mentions two rivers (Pisuerga and Carrión) in the almost 250 km between Logroño (Ebro) and Sahagún (Cea), whereas up to nine rivers (Cea, Esla, Porma, Torío, Bernesga, Sil, Cúa, Burbia and Valcárcel) are mentioned by name in the space occupied by what is now the province of León (just over 200 km).

After one last glance at San Marcos, pilgrims crossed the bridge over the river Bernesga and then had to decide whether to follow the direct route to Santiago de Compostela, or to make a detour to the North, towards Asturias and **Oviedo.**

If they chose the latter option, they had to follow the Bernesga upstream to La Robla, and go up Puerto de Pajares where, from the XIIth century, there was an assistance institution available for pilgrims: the collegiate church and

hospital of Santa María de Arbas. The first sight of Oviedo was from mount Manjoya, whose name, just like Monte del Gozo in Compostela, refers to the pilgrims' joy at reaching a goal which took so much effort. A spectacular collection of relics, sacred objects relating to Jesus' life, the Virgin, the apostles, characters from the Old Testament and many other Paleochristian, Spanish and North African martyr saints awaited them there. These relics which, according to tradition, had been gathered by the apostles themselves and brought to Spain by their disciples, were kept in the holy chest of San Salvador cathedral – where they were supposedly brought after the VIIIth century Muslim invasion – and were venerated to an extent only exceeded in Spain by the worship of the remains of the apostle St James, just like the number of pilgrims to San Salvador was only exceeded by the number of pilgrims to Santiago. There was, in fact, a certain common audience for the two sanctuaries, fuelled particularly from Oviedo, as reflected in this famous old verse:

> *Quien va a Santiago / y no a San Salvador*
> *Visita al criado / y deja al Señor*
> *(If you go to Santiago but not to San Salvador*
> *You are visiting the servant and leaving out the lord)*

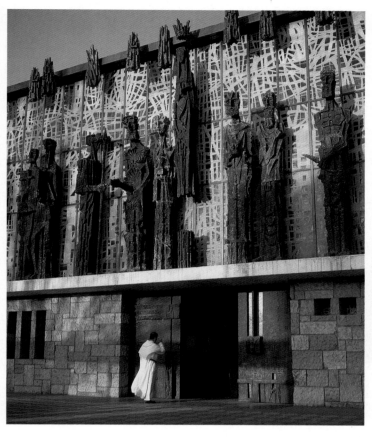

La Virgen del Camino sanctuary.

However, it seems that the Asturian pilgrimages owe their inspiration and existence to the Santiago de Compostela ones, since the former consisted mostly of Santiago pilgrims who, attracted by San Salvador's fame, decided to take the long and tiring detour that would take them from León to Oviedo. In a way, it could be said that Oviedo was the most important sanctuary of the Road, and that visiting it involved the longest detour from the French Road.

Many pilgrims weighed up the hardships and fatigue that awaited them on the way to Oviedo, and decided to follow the direct route to Santiago de Compostela. After leaving León, the first town they reached was **Trobajo de Camino,** which is now part of the capital. The image of Santiago Matamoros (the Moor Killer) which is kept in its parish church of San Juan Bautista was brought from the XVIIIth century chapel of Santiago. After Trobajo, pilgrims came up to a stone cross, of similar characteristics to that of Alto del Portillo, from which they could look at León for the last time.

Immediately after this came **La Virgen del Camino,** which had been created and had existed around the sanctuary dedicated to the Virgin and which housed an image of the patron saint of León, a XVth century

Right, view of Valverde del Camino; below, panoramic view of San Miguel del Camino.

Gothic Virgin Dolorosa. Tradition has it that the Virgin appeared to a shepherd in 1516, who subsequently had a chapel erected in her honour. The fame and importance acquired by the new sanctuary both in León and in its neighbouring regions caused this Virgin to be named Virgen del Camino ("Virgin of the Road").

This is the name under which she was known in León until it was changed to Virgen del Mercado.

The spacious building that we now find there is very recent (1961) and was built by architect Francisco Coello de Portugal. Its Art Nouveau-style apostolate which dominates the building's main façade is particularly famous. It consists of thirteen large bronze statues (six metres high and weighing seven hundred kilograms) sculpted by José María Subirachs and depicting the Virgin and the twelve apostles.

Since recent years, the Road divides into two parallel branches at the Virgen del Camino. The first branch goes through **Fresno del Camino, Oncina de la Valdoncina, Chozas de Abajo, Villar de Mazarife** and **Villavante,** all of which are small towns which already existed in the Middle Ages.

The first town on the second branch, better documented as Road to Santiago, is **Valverde de la Virgen.** This town on the varied Oncina valley is small but remarkably old, and was mentioned in documents as early as the Xth century. We do not know whether its uncommon parish church name may be related to its old age; it is dedicated to Paleochristian Saragossan martyr Engracia, about whom (together with her eighteen fellow martyrs) the great poet Prudentius sang in his IVth century collection of hymns *Peristephanon*.

The next town, **San Miguel del Camino,** had a pilgrims' hospital in the XIIth century, and its parish church of San Miguel used to house a XVth century sculpture of St James in pilgrim attire, which is now in León.

Villadangos del Páramo also had a pilgrims' hospital. As its name suggests, this town is in the middle of a group of municipalities known as "páramo Leonés", which includes the territory from the capital all the way to Astorga. The word "páramo" (meaning "bleak plateau" or "high moor") is a genuinely Spanish pre-Roman word used by the inhabitants of the current province of León and *Tierra de Campos* to refer to the large plains which are typical of this area.

"Santiago Matamoros" in the parish church of Villadangos del Páramo.

It is not clear whether Villadangos is the old *Vallata* which, according to Itinerario de *Antonino,* was on Vía Trajana. If it was, then this was where the Road to Santiago met the old Roman road from which it had parted company in Reliegos to go towards León. In any case, the first documents referring to Villadangos with its current or a similar name *(Angos, Viadangos, Fontedangos)* date from the XIIth century and appear in *Historia Compostelana,* which the great Compostelan archbishop Diego Gelmírez ordered to be written. According to this chronicle, Villadangos witnessed several brushes during the war which this prelate from Compostela held to fight for his godson's (the future King Alfonso VII) interests against the latter's stepfather, Alfonso I the Warrior who, after his marriage to doña Urraca, was attempting to gain power over the whole of Christian Spain. Although the Aragonese king won most of these skirmishes in Villadangos, the war resulted in the Compostelan mitre acquiring the place.

The fact that the parish church is dedicated to the apostle St James and that his depictions are more related to war than to the pilgrimage may be due to the area's war past and to its link to Santiago de Compostela. The altarpiece at the high altar, for example – which, if it wasn't for the sculpture of St Claudius, would be exclusively dedicated to the apostle –, is dominated by a well-known XVIIIth century sculpture which depicts St James charging against the enemy, riding his white steed and wearing the three-cornered hat which was typical of the time. The church door has some fun and slightly rough polychrome reliefs "illustrated" by illegible notices depicting the mythical battle of Clavijo. In this battle, King Ramiro I of León, with the Apostle's assistance, defeats Abderraman II's army, thus freeing the Spanish Christians from the onerous tribute of the hundred maids. As you may remember from previous stages, in gratitude for being freed from such oppression, all the towns in the kingdom had to pay Santiago a tax known as "voto de Santiago" (St James tax). Since Villadangos belonged to the Compostelan church, it wouldn't be too far-fetched to suggest that these depictions were a reminder of the obligation to pay the tax, which many of the towns affected (among which we have already mentioned Carrión and Belorado) tried to avoid.

20 Villadangos del Páramo or Villar de Mazarife – Astorga

In Puente de Órbigo, the two alternative routes which began during the last stage meet up again. From here, you will leave behind the León plateau, which is now not so stepped, due to the infiltration of irrigation farming methods which has heavily influenced this region. The León Mountains can be seen up ahead, and the end of this stage will bring you to Astorga, the capital of Maragatería.

Puente de Órbigo.

A) From **Villadangos del Páramo,** pass through a vibrant poplar wood and go by a stream before taking the path which runs parallel to the N-120. After **San Martín del Camino,** you should follow the Camino, passing through irrigation fields by the tarmacked path, heading towards **Puente de Órbigo.**

B) From **Villar de Mazarife,** you should head out on the local road between poplars and irrigated crops, (mostly maize and beetroot), passing through a part of the stage which is covered in canals and irrigation channels. Crossing the road to San Martín, with **Villavante** in view up ahead, you should take the turn-off to the village if you want to pay it a visit. Having left the town, and just before coming to **Puente de Órbigo,** you must cross the railway line, the Camino de Santiago motorway, and the N-120.

Once both routes come together as one again, you will cross the magnificent bridge into **Hospital de Órbigo,** passing by the town refuge as it nestles amongst the luxurious foliage surrounding the river Órbigo.

Camino de Santiago Street ends at a junction: the road heads off to the left and our route to the right, along a path which takes us to **Villares de Órbigo.** From here, a gentle uphill path heads towards the N-120 but, before reaching the road, you should head off on a path amongst the shrubs and bushes which will take you up, and then down, a hill which leads to **Santibáñez de Valdeiglesias.** From here onwards, a path goes up Colomba Mountain, which is covered in holm oaks, chestnut trees, and an oak forest. From here you can make out Teleno to the South-West,

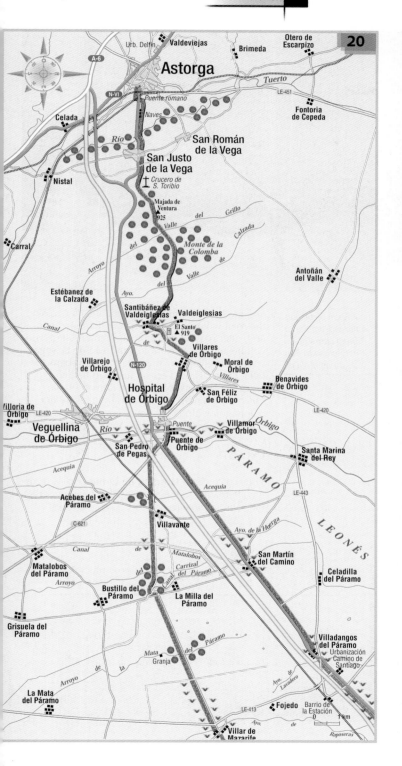

20

Urb. Delfin   Valdeviejas   Brimeda   Otero de Escarpizo

A-6

Astorga

Tuerto   LE-451

N-VI

Puente romano

Naves

Celada

Fontoria de Cepeda

Río

San Román de la Vega

San Justo de la Vega

† *Crucero de S. Toribio*

Nistal

Majada de Ventura
925

Valle   *del*   Grillo

Carral

del

Monte de la Colomba

Calzada

Arroyo

Valle   de

Estébanez de la Calzada

Ayo.

del

Antoñán del Valle

Canal

Santibáñez de Valdeiglesias   Valdeiglesias

† El Santo ▲ 919

de

Villares de Órbigo

Villarejo de Órbigo

N-120

Moral de Órbigo

Villares

Benavides de Órbigo

Hospital de Órbigo

San Féliz de Órbigo

Villoria de Órbigo   LE-420

Órbigo

Veguellina de Órbigo   *Río*

Puente

Villamor de Órbigo

LE-420

San Pedro de Pegas

Puente de Órbigo

P
Á
R
A
M
O

Santa Marina del Rey

Acequia

Acequia

LE-443

Acebes del Páramo

C-621

Villavante

Ayo. de la Huerga

L
E
O
N
É
S

de

Matalobos

San Martín del Camino

Matalobos del Páramo

Carrizal   del Páramo

Celadilla del Páramo

Arroyo

del

Canal

Bustillo del Páramo

La Milla del Páramo

Grisuela del Páramo

Villadangos del Páramo

Urbanización Camino de Santiago

Mata   *del*   *Páramo*

Granja

Ayo.   de   Lavadero

de   la   Arroyo

La Mata del Páramo

Fojedo

Barrio de la Estación
0   1 km

LE-413

Ayo.   de

Raposeras

Villar de Mazarife

Pilgrim glimpsing Astorga from Santo Toribio stone cross very close to San Justo de la Vega.

and the León Mountains straight ahead. Crossing the road will take you past a conifer plantation and, after passing the Santo Toribio crossing, you will begin your descent to **San Justo de la Vega.** Leave this village by the bridge which spans the river Tuerto. Next, veer off the road behind houses and barns, passing the Roman bridge. Once on the road again, cross the railway line, before going along the Travesía de Minerva and Puerta del Sol Street on your way into **Astorga.**

CYCLISTS

The N-120, from **Hospital de Órbigo** onwards, is the alternative to the routes which head over the hills and mountains.

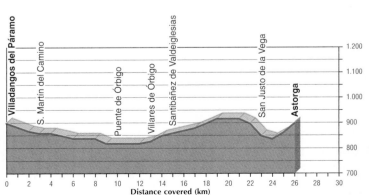

STAGE 20. PRACTICAL INFORMATION

SAN MARTÍN DEL CAMINO

HOSTELS

"Teleclub". Ctra. León-Astorga, s/n.
60 beds, kitchen and bar. ∅ 656 544 555

MEANS OF TRANSPORT

The **ALSA** Group Leon-Astorga-
Ponferrada line goes through here.

PUENTE DE ÓRBIGO

HOTELS

La Asturiana guest house. Avda.
Constitución, 54. ∅ 987 388 425. 6
rooms. Double room: € 18.
José Luis guest house. Ctra. Villamor.
∅ 987 388 349. 3 rooms. 5 beds.
Double room: € 30; single room: € 15.

RESTAURANTS

Parrillada Puente del Paso.
Avda. Constitución, 124. ∅ 987 388 851

HOSPITAL DE ÓRBIGO

HOSTELS

Municipal Hostel (Albergue Municipal).
In "Casa de la Vega". 40 beds. Kitchen,
washing machine and a place for bicycles
and horses. Chiropody and physiotherapy
service in the summer. ∅ 987 388 206
"Karl Leisner" parish shelter.
C/ Álvarez Vega, 32. 100 beds. Kitchen,
chapel and a garden for tents. Open
from 15/3 to 31/10. ∅ 987 388 444 /
987 389 198

HOTELS

HR** Paso Honroso. Ctra. N-120, km
335. ∅ 987 361 010. 25 rooms. 47
beds. Double room: € 52/45.
HS** Don Suero de Quiñones. C/ Álvarez
Vega, 1. ∅ 987 388 238. 11 rooms.
Double room: € 55; single room: € 36.

CAMPING SITES

2.nd C Don Suero de Quiñones. Terrenos
de la Vega. ∅ 987 361 018. 350 places.

RESTAURANTS

La Encomienda. C/ Álvarez Vega, 30.
∅ 987 388 211
La Vega. C/ La Vega. ∅ 987 388 486

SANTIBÁÑEZ DE VALDEIGLESIAS

HOSTELS

Parish hostel (albergue parroquial).
C/ Carromonte, 3. 65 beds. Kitchen. From
1st May to 31st October. ∅ 987 377 698

SAN JUSTO DE LA VEGA

HOTELS

HSR* Juli. C/ Real, 56. ∅ 987 617 632.
8 rooms. 12 beds. Double room: € 28;
single room: € 25.

ASTORGA

HOSTELS

Municipal hostels. C/ Rodríguez, 24.
60 beds. Plaza de los Marqueses, 13.
162 beds. They have kitchens.
∅ 987 618 281 / 660 547 751
"San Javier" hostel. C/ Portería, 6. 110
beds, a kitchen and a washing machine.
Room for bicycles. ∅ 987 618 532

HOTELS

Fuertes guest house. Avda. Madrid, 54.
∅ 987 615 572. Double room: € 23.
Ruta Leonesa guest house. Ctra. León, 14.
∅ 987 615 037. Double room: € 27.

RESTAURANTS

Delfín. Ctra. Madrid-Coruña, km 326.
∅ 987 615 016
El Maragato. Ctra. Madrid-A Coruña,
km 386. ∅ 987 619 169

MEANS OF TRANSPORT

The **ALSA** Group León-Astorga-
Ponferrada line goes through Astorga.
Bus station. ∅ 987 602 423
RENFE rail station. ∅ 987 616 091

HISTORY AND WEALTH OF THE STAGE 20

THE FRENCH ROAD. VILLADANGOS DEL PÁRAMO – ASTORGA

The road between Virgen del Camino and Hospital de Órbigo is divided into two branches. The town of **Villavante** is on the first branch, where something resembling the remains of an old Roman road has been found.

After Villadangos, the second branch goes through **San Martín del Camino,** whose name stems from the fact that its parish church is dedicated to St Martin of Tours. The worship of this Panonian saint, a Roman legion soldier in his youth and bishop of Tours in later life (IVth century) was one of the most prestigious forms of worships in the Merovingian world, from which it spread to the whole of the Christian world. This saint was worshipped with particular fervour in Spain during the Suevan Kingdom (VIth century) and again in the Asturian Kingdom (VIIIth-IXth centuries), due to the contact between their respective kings and the Caroligian world. This worship was also definitively promoted by the pilgrimages to Santiago de Compostela (XIth-XIIIth centuries). The worship to St Martin in this specific place may have originated at any of the three stages mentioned, although the first is less likely. We also know that San Martín del Camino had a hospital for poor pilgrims since at least the XVIIth century.

Puente de Órbigo. Pilgrims crossing the bridge towards Hospital de Órbigo.

Liber Sancti Iacobi points out a town which it refers to as Orbega as a Stop of the Road. This clearly refers to one of the two towns over the river Órbigo – either Puente de Órbigo or Hospital de Órbigo –, or possibly even to both at the same time, included in a possible plural *(Orbega =* the "Órbigos"). Órbigo itself, as mentioned above, is the name of an important river which, strangely enough, is not mentioned by the author in the relevant section. This suggests that the author's journey through the "páramo leonés", from León to Bierzo, was fairly quick.

Although the first known documentary evidence of the town of **Puente de Órbigo** dates from the late XIIth century, it may have existed for longer. From a strategic point of view it was very important as an access point to North-Western Spain. Suevans and Visigoths had already fought here in the Vth century, as had Asturian King Alfonso III against the caliphs' armies in the Xth century. Due to its length and elegance, the bridge which has lent its name to the town since the XIIth century is one of the best erections of its kind on the Road. The main reason for its fame, however, is not its architectural merit but the facts of "Passo honroso", the "private" feat of a worthy predecessor to Don Quixot, the noble Suero de Quiñones from León. This is one of the most spectacular stories of the Road to Santiago, in which pilgrimage and knightly matters combine in a bizarre mix.

Don Suero, imprisoned by his love for a certain lady, put an iron ring on his neck every Thursday. In order to free himself from this ring, and with the apostle St James as his witness, he set his rescue from the "love prison" at three hundred spears, to be broken by him and eight friends in the jubilee year of 1434. He got a herald to publish his intention and to prepare a field next to

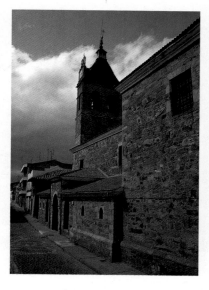

Hospital de Órbigo. Church and street.

Puente de Órbigo for the joust. From here, Suero de Quiñones and his eight squires would challenge any "adventurous" knight who went by and accepted the challenge to a single combat. The rules of the joust, broken down into twenty-two sections, were published and included, among others, the rule that no knight who did not want to fight would be forced to do so. However, any lady who did not have a knight to defend her would have to give up her right glove as a forfeit. The notary Pero Rodríguez de Lena certified the legitimacy of the contest and made a detailed notarial report of everything that took place here between 10th July and 9th August. Between those dates, don Suero and his squires defeated sixty-eight French, Italian, German, Portuguese and Spanish knights who accepted the challenge, and only one death – that of an Aragonese knight – was reported. Although nothing like the three hundred spears originally specified had been broken, Don Suero accepted his achievement as valid and set off, together with his helpers, on a pilgrimage to Santiago de Compostela, where he gave the Apostle a gold bracelet with the following French-Provençal rhyming inscription, undoubtably evocative of a "love prison".

> *Si a vous ne playst avoyr mesura /*
> *certes ie di que ie suy sans ventura.*

This bracelet can now be found sitting as a necklace on the Santiago Alfeo reliquary bust in the cathedral of Santiago de Compostela

On the other side of the bridge is **Hospital de Órbigo,** whose name is due to the presence (not confirmed by documents but transmitted by oral tradition) of an Order of St John pilgrims' hospital.

The parish church of **Villares de Órbigo** is dedicated to St James, who dominates the high altar on his horse. He is also depicted in this way in the church of La Trinidad in Santibáñez de Valdeiglesias, next to St

Astorga. Panoramic view of the Cathedral, the Episcopal palace (Palacio Episcopal) and the city wall.

Roque in Xacobean pilgrim attire. As we find in other places, St Roque seems to replace the Apostle himself in the pilgrim role. The dedication of this church to the Trinity (la Trinidad) may mean that a community of Trinity monks, who were fairly active assisting pilgrims from the XIIIth century, were established here.

Before reaching **San Justo de la Vega,** the Santo Toribio stone cross lets pilgrims know that they can catch their first sight of Astorga from here. According to local tradition, this is where St Toribio, a Vth century bishop from Astorga, set eyes on his city from the last time while shaking the dust off his shoes. This legend may be related to the widespread Priscillian heresy in the Astorgan diocese. We still have two letters from St Toribio dealing with this matter, as well as pope Leo Magnus' reply. The name of a street, calle Hospital, is one of the many references to the pilgrimage in the village.

Astorga is, together with Burgos, the only great city with an episcopal see whose educated Latin name *(Asturica)* was not known by the author of *Liber Sancti Iacobi,* who referred to it as *Austurga y Osturga,* and didn't even consider it the end of a stage. This fact, together with the small amount of information he offers about the El Páramo and La Maragatería territory, (as contrasted with the many references to the capital of León and El Bierzo), suggest that the author did not linger here for very long.

Had he travelled during Roman times, when Astorga was *Asturica Augusta,* head of the *Conventus Iuridicus Asturicensis,* the Asturian territory's administrative unit, things would have been different. Astorga was the capital of a region with legendary gold resources, where a *procurator metallorum* lead a special military unit. This explains why two Roman roads as important as Vía Trajana and Vía de la Plata met here. From St Cyprian of Carthage's letters, we know that Astorga had a Bishopric by the middle of the IIIrd century. The city was destroyed by Visigothic King Theodore (in the Vth century) and by Almanzor (in the Xth). Active hermit and monastic movements flourished in Visigothic and early mediaeval times. At one point, Astorga had ten monasteries which, added to its twenty-one hospitals, made it one of the most hospitable places of the Road.

The city was enclosed within a more or less quadrangular wall, which pilgrims crossed via Puerta del Sol. They then went past the stalls on Rúa de las Tiendas (now called calle de San Francisco) via San Francisco (which, according

—— *Astorga. Crocks in the Roman Museum.* ——

to tradition, was personally founded by St Francis of Assisi) and San Bartolomé (XIth century) until they reached the city's most important monument: the cathedral of Santa María. Although the current building is Gothic (from the XVth century), its stonework still retains something of the old Romanesque cathedral. Inside, we find works by Gregorio Fernández, a Romanesque statue of the Virgen de la Majestad and a magnificent altarpiece by Gaspar Becerra, on the high altar. Outside, on a pinnacle, is yet another reference to the mythical battle of Clavijo: the popular Pero Mato from La Maragatería, who took part as second lieutenant in the Christian army. Next to the cathedral is the old hospital of San Juan, which was founded in the XIIth century. Other Astorgan hospitals included San Esteban, San Feliz and Las Cinco Llagas, among others. Between the church of Santa María and the Gothic chapel of San Esteban was Celda de las Emparedadas where, according to tradition, women of ill repute were locked up and fed by pilgrims themselves on their way through the city.

In addition to Astorga's countless Roman remains (including a bridge, the Ergástula – a Roman slave prison – and furniture), the Museum of Los Caminos, whose headquarters are located in the Neogothical Episcopal palace (Palacio Episcopal) built by Antoni Gaudí at the beginning of the XXth century, is particularly worthy of mention.

—— *Astorga. Xacobean Room in the Museum of Los Caminos.* ——

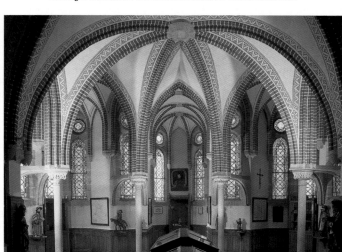

21   Astorga – Rabanal del Camino

*Now totally immersed in the region, yet hardly noticing it,
we gradually make our way up the first foothills of the León
Mountains. This part of the countryside is characterised by
broom, heather, oak trees and conifer plantations.*

Night view of Astorga Cathedral.

If you leave the village from the Cathedral, your way out of **Astorga**
should follow the following streets: Rúa de los Judíos, Poeta Leopoldo
Panero Street, Esteban Carro Celada Street, San Pedro Street and Rúa de
los Francos. Cross the N-VI as it heads towards Ponferrada, before heading
along the tree-lined pavements of the LE-142, making your way towards
Murias de Rechivaldo. On your way, you will see Valdeviejas to the right,
and will also pass by the "Ecce Homo" Hermitage. A bridge then crosses
the motorway and, after it, a crossroads leads you to a pilgrim path which
follows on by the roadway. Before you arrive at Murias, you will pass by a
polar grove and the river Jerga. Off to the left, a path goes behind the
village, passing along its Iglesia Street. When you leave the village, the
Camino carries on next to another path, going through a landscape with
small hills covered in holm oak, broom, conifers and oaks. To your right,
the road goes on towards **Castrillo de Polvazares.** If you want to, you can
make a detour to stop off and see some of this pretty village. When the
road heads off towards Santa Colomba de Somoza, you should cross to
the other side before continuing along a tarmacked path towards **Santa
Catalina de Somoza.** Go along Real Street, which will take you right
through the village and out the other side. Upon leaving the village, rejoin
the path parallel to the road, and 4.5 km further on, you will come to the
point where the village of **El Ganso** meets the roadway. As you leave the
town, you will notice that the landscape is densely populated by oak

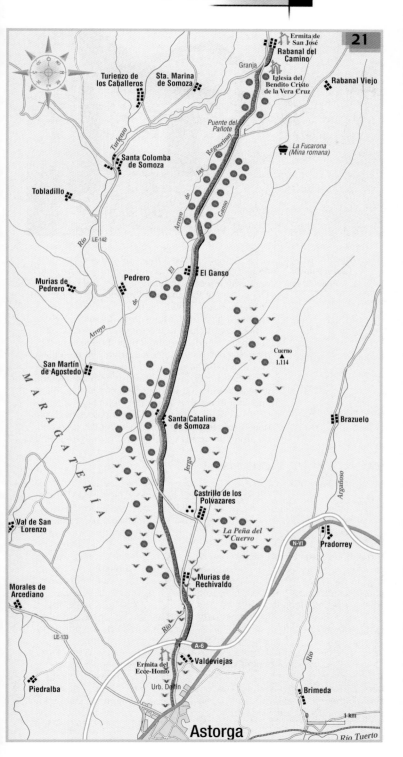

21

Ermita de San José

Rabanal del Camino

Granja

Iglesia del Bendito Cristo de la Vera Cruz

Rabanal Viejo

Turienzo de los Caballeros

Sta. Marina de Somoza

Puente del Pañote

La Fucarona (Mina romana)

Río Turienzo

Santa Colomba de Somoza

Tobladillo

Río LE-142

Murias de Pedrero

Pedrero

El Ganso

Cuerno 1.114

San Martín de Agostedo

M A R A G A T E R Í A

Santa Catalina de Somoza

Brazuelo

Jerga

Argañoso

Castrillo de los Polvazares

La Peña del Cuervo

Val de San Lorenzo

N-VI

Pradorrey

Morales de Arcediano

Murias de Rechivaldo

LE-133

Río

A-6

Piedralba

Ermita del Ecce-Homo

Valdeviejas

Urb. Delfín

Brimeda

0   1 km

Astorga

Río Tuerto

Typical street in Castrillo de los Polvazares.

trees. Two kilometres further on, our path comes to an end, and you must continue along a tarmacked path which passes through heather and conifers. The village of **Rabanal del Camino** then comes up on the horizon. However, before arriving there, you must pass by the turn-off to Rabanal el Viejo, which passes close to the roman mine of "La Fucarona". And cross the Pañote bridge over the river Reguerinas. Just before arriving in the village, you will pass the oak wood which is home to the "Oak of the Pilgrim", famous for both its size and its age. You are now at the entrance to the village, and should be able to see the Hermitage of Santo Cristo, as well as the LE-142 as it passes by. From here, cross to the right-hand side of the road and go along the roads which form the "pilgrims' trail".

CYCLISTS

All of today's itinerary is accessible to cyclists.

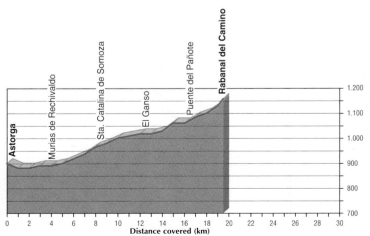

STAGE 21. PRACTICAL INFORMATION

MURIAS DE RECHIVALDO

Hostels

Albergue de Murias (Murias) hostel.
It has a small hostel with approximately 20 beds, which is open all year round and run by the Neighbours' Committee (Junta Vecinal). ⌀ 987 691 150

Restaurants

Mesón Asturum.
Ctra. Santa Colomba. ⌀ 987 619 270

CASTRILLO DE LOS POLVAZARES

Hotels

HSR** Hostería Cuca la Vaina.
C/ Jardín. ⌀ 987 691 078. 7 rooms.
Double room: € 55; breakfast: € 3.

Restaurants

Casa Maruja Botas.
C/ Real, 24. ⌀ 987 691 065

Casa Coscolo.
C/ El Rincón, 1. ⌀ 987 691 984

Mesón La Magdalena.
C/ Real, 21. ⌀ 987 691 067

Casa Juan Andrés.
C/ Juan José Cano, 16. ⌀ 987 691 971

Mesón del Arriero.
C/ Real, 4. ⌀ 987 691 047

La Peregrina.
C/ Real, 52. ⌀ 987 691 102

SANTA CATALINA DE SOMOZA

Hostels

Santa Catalina de Somoza Neighbours's Committee Hostel (Albergue Junta Vecinal de Santa Catalina de Somoza) ⌀ 987 691 819

EL GANSO

Hostels

Camino de Santiago hostel.
⌀ 987 691 088

RABANAL DEL CAMINO

Hostels

"Gaucelmo" shelter.
This is located in the old parish house, which was rebuilt thanks to the Confraternity of Saint James and is run by its members and by the El Bierzo Road to Santiago Friends Association (Asociación de Amigos del Camino de El Bierzo). Open from April to October.
⌀ 987 691 901

Municipal Hostel (Albergue Municipal).
Located on plaza del Pueblo. It has 40 beds, kitchen and laundry. Open from Easter Week to 15th October. Masseur available from 16:00 h. ⌀ 687 617 445

"Nuestra Señora del Pilar" hostel.
On plaza Gerónimo Morán, s/n. It has 72 beds, kitchen, chimney and a large patio. Open all year round.
⌀ 987 691 890

Hotels

HS* Hostería El Refugio.
C/ Real. ⌀ 987 691 274. 9 rooms.
14 beds. Double room: € 47; single room: € 32; breakfast: € 3,6;
lunch/dinner: € 9.

El Tesín guest house.
C/ Real. ⌀ 652 277 262. 3 rooms.
6 beds. Double room: € 40;
breakfast: € 2.

Restaurants

La Posada de Gaspar.
C/ Real, 24. ⌀ 987 691 079

History and wealth of the stage 21

View of Castrillo de los Polvazares.

The French Road. Astorga – Rabanal del Camino

From the cathedral, pilgrims left Astorga via Puerta del Obispo, where the Furriers' Guild ("pelliteros") had dedicated a chapel to the apostle St James. Once they had crossed the wall, they would cross the suburb of Rectivía until they reached a crossroads. At this point they had to decide whether to follow the Road via Puerto del Manzanal or go via Rabanal and "Monte Irago". XVth century German pilgrim Künig von Vach recommended the former because it was flatter. However, and in spite of the fact that the Manzanal route also contains significant references to St James – such as the Hospitallers of St John's hospital near the pass – we will follow the second route.

The town we now know as **Valdeviejas** appeared in mediaeval documents as *villa Sancti Verissimi*. Indeed, even today the parish church is dedicated to Lisbon martyr St Verisimo, which is another sign that we are approaching Galician land. Documents which mention a pilgrims' hospital since the XVth century provide evidence of Valdiviejas' pilgrimage-related past. Outside the town is the chapel of the *Ecce Homo*.

When we reach **Murias de Rechivaldo,** the Road to Santiago enters a new territory, La Maragatería. The first part of the town's name ("Murias") may be a reference to its frontier status. This exceedingly old Spanish word means "heap of stones" but can also mean "limit" or "frontier" due to the function such heaps used to perform.

Astorga is sometimes considered the capital of **Maragatería.** This had more to do with its character as a city centre in the surroundings of the group of municipalities, than with it actually belonging to it. Rather than a territory with exact geophysical characteristics, La Maragatería is a group of towns with old customs which set them apart from their close neighbours and which its inhabitants have kept until fairly recently. The expensive jewellery worn by some of the women in this area, pointed out by some XVth century travellers such as Arnold von Harff, has been interpreted by some as deriving from old Celtic customs. This may be right, since the gold mines in El Bierzo were not far from here, but the jewellery could also simply be a sign of prosperity resulting from the entrepreneurial character of this town of muleteers and traders.

A detour of less than one kilometre from the Road to Santiago will take you to **Castrillo de los Polvazares,** which is considered the most representative of the Maragatan spirit, and whose fame stems from the fact that it provided the setting to Concha Espina's famous novel *La Esfinge Maragata,* a beautiful portrait of the customs and manners of this region's people. Some famous aspects of Castrillo are its perfectly paved high street and its most typical dish, a stew whose ingredients are savoured in reverse order, starting with the richest part of the meal (the meat), then going onto the vegetables and pulses, and finishing with soup. The remains of a Celtic military encampment can be found near Castrillo de los Polvazares, on Cerro de la Mesa.

Santa Catalina de Somoza may be the town which Arnold von Harff referred to simply as "Hospitale". Apart from the writing of this pilgrim from the banks of the Rhine, there is other documentary evidence of a hospital dedicated to the Virgin of the Candles (Virgen de las Candelas). The parish church of Santa María, originally dedicated to St Catherine of Alexandria (where the name of the town comes from), houses a relic of St Blaise, the town's patron saint. The worship of the bishop of Sebaste (Armenia) appears in many parts of the Road which are associated with institutions which offered pilgrims medical assistance as well as hospitality. This may also have been the case with the hospital of Santa Catalina de Somoza. The second part of the name ("Somoza", from Latin *sub montia,* meaning "on the foot of the hill") defines and describes the features of this land, which is located on the slope before the steep ascent to the hill known as Rabanal, Foncebadón or "Irago".

Above, typical Maragatan wedding attire in Castrillo de los Polvazares; right, view of a street in Santa Catalina de Somoza.

*View of
El Ganso.*

Arnold von Harff, generally so careful to reflect the toponymy of the places he went through, didn't bother to collect the names of the small Maragatan towns of La Somoza. Not only did he call Santa Catalina "Hospitale", but he designated the next town, El Ganso, "Hospitale grande". The oldest documentary evidence of a hospital in **El Ganso** dates from 1142, when it started to depend on the cathedral of Astorga. Here, a community of Premonstratensian nuns looked after pilgrims from the XIIIth century. The fact that its parish church is dedicated to St James and has a depiction of the Apostle as a pilgrim provides further evidence of the town's pilgrimage-related past.

El Ganso is the first town on the modern Road where we find thatched houses, which are typical of the North-Western part of León and a section of Galicia. According to XVIIth century Italian pilgrim Domenico Laffi, it wasn't that long ago that this roofing technique was widespread in the province of León.

Slightly out of the way of the Road, to the right, is **Mina de la Fucarona,** one of the oldest gold mines which made a cliché of Astorga's wealth in Roman times.

Rabanal del Camino is mentioned a couple of times in *Liber Sancti Iacobi*. The first mention makes it the end of the ninth stage, a privilege which was not granted to the region's historic capital, Astorga. The guidebook mentions that it was also known as *Captivus*. This strange nickname, unheard of in toponymy, has been explained as originating from the Galician word "cativo", meaning "small". If so, the aim of this adjective would be to tell Rabanal del Camino apart from Rabanal Viejo, an older town located in the same area. Another theory is that Rabanal was hypothetically (there is no documentary evidence of this) related to a powerful Astorgan family which dominated this area in the mid-XIIth century and which had exactly the same nickname, *Captivus.* Centuries later, Bolognan pilgrim Laffi reported that in his time Rabanal was still known by a nickname, which he transcribed as *Ravancilla,* and which may be a distortion of the diminutive form "Rabanalcillo" (which would mean "little Rabanal").

The second mention of Rabanal in *Liber Sancti Iacobi* is a chapter regarding the good deeds performed by various people, such as Andrés, Roger, Alvito, Fortún, Arnaldo, Esteban and Pedro, who built the Road to Santiago between Rabanal and Puertomarín before 1120 during the reigns of Alfonso VII, Diego Gelmírez, Alfonso I of Aragón and Louis the Fat of France. Only one of these has ever been identified, although there is some evidence that they could all be related to the Knights of the Templar: both Rabanal and Portomarín had large Knights of the Templar settlements, and El Bierzo, which separates the two towns, also had a large and significant presence of this order, as we can see, among many other examples, in its impressive castle of Ponferrada. The Templars settled in Rabanal because of its proximity to Puerto de Foncebadón (whose mediaeval name was *Mons Iragus*) and the need to protect the mostly defenceless pilgrims from robberies, pillagings and other abuses which took place in these harsh areas.

The Templars' presence in Rabanal del Camino is related to its oldest and most noble building, the late XIIth century Romanesque parish church of Santa María, whose construction has some peculiarities. Although it has been greatly remodelled through the centuries, some surviving aspects of its early Romanesque construction,

Panoramic and detailed views of Rabanal del Camino.

such as the portal that allows access to the sacristy, can still be admired. This XVIIIth century portal probably stands where the Templar friars' dependencies used to be.

In addition to the church of Santa María, Rabanal had several hospitals and churches, such as the hospital of San Gregorio or the chapel of El Santo Cristo de la Vera Cruz (just outside the town). Inside the city is the XVIIIth century chapel of San José, which contains an image of the apostle St James.

Even the town layout, consisting of a long street, gives away Rabanal's origin as a town which developed on the Road to Santiago. Within the slightly neglected aspect of its houses, some signs of more prosperous times can still be observed. The most interesting of these is Casa de las Cuatro Esquinas, where King Philip II once stayed when going through the town.

22   Rabanal del Camino – Ponferrada

*Passing through broom, heather and other plant species
you will continue your ascent towards the famous "Mount
Irago". By the pass on the mountain you will see the "Iron
Cross", an age-old tradition, before making your way
downwards to the wealthy area of Bierzo.*

Manjarín shelter.

From the Church of the Assumption you will continue upwards before
leaving **Rabanal** and taking a path to the right of the road. One kilometre
later you will cross to the left-hand side and continue climbing upwards
along another track. After a bend in the track, you will come back to the
tarmacked route and go into the revived town of **Foncebadón** (spring),
before leaving it via a path and once again crossing over to the right-hand
side after another curve. You will then pass by a coniferous forest before
ariving at **Cruz de Ferro** and the Hermitage of Santiago. Next, you should
take a path which, due to the undergrowth, can prove quite difficult in
places. **Manjarín** is the next place you will pass through, with a spring at
the exit. A path carries on to the left of the road, from where you will be
able to see the valley floor and the hillsides of the León Mountains. Carry
along the roadside to a hill covered in conifers, with a huge radio antenna,
before descending towards Ponferrada in the distance. To the right, a small
path will save you from having to take a large bend in the road. A little
further on, and to the left, another path with a rather abrupt incline heads
towards **El Acebo,** passing along its Real Street. Take the road, (from which
you will see the turn-off to Compludo), before leaving it behind and
heading left through the scrub towards **Riego de Ambrós.** Once there, head
left along a path which will take you down through the chestnut trees to
the valley of the Prado Mangas river. Cross the river and return to the road,
but veer off it again, this time to the right, descending to the valley of the
Pretadura river. Climb upwards again up a hillside, before going down to
the road again. Take the road to **Molinaseca,** (passing by fruit trees and
orchards), entering the village via the bridge over the Meruelo river. Your
journey through the village will take you along Real Street, Rúa del Cristo,
(crossroads), and Santiago Street. Leave the village and meet up with the

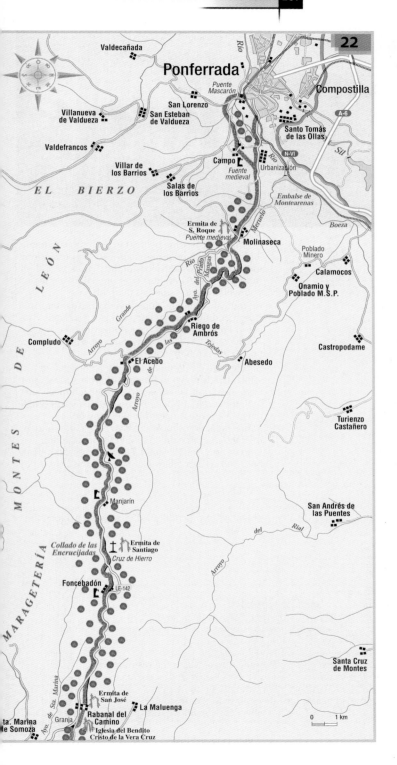

22

Valdecañada

Ponferrada

Puente Mascarón

Compostilla

San Lorenzo

A-6

San Esteban
de Valdueza

Villanueva
de Valdueza

Santo Tomás
de las Ollas

N-VI

Valdefrancos

Sil

Villar de
los Barrios

Campo

*Fuente
medieval*

Urbanización

E L   B I E R Z O

Salas de
los Barrios

*Embalse de
Montearenas*

Ermita de
S. Roque

Río Meruelo

Boeza

Puente medieval

Molinaseca

L E Ó N

Poblado
Minero

Río del Prado

Calamocos

Ayo. del Prado

Onamio y
Poblado M.S.P.

Grande

Riego de
Ambrós

Compludo

Arroyo

las

Tejedas

Castropodame

de

El Acebo

Abesedo

M   O   N   T   E   S

Arroyo

Turienzo
Castañero

D   E

San Andrés de
las Puentes

Manjarín

Rial

del

Collado de las
Encrucijadas

Ermita de
Santiago

Cruz de Hierro

Arroyo

L   E   Ó   N

Foncebadón

LE-142

M   A   R   A   G   A   T   E   R   Í   A

Santa Cruz
de Montes

0   1 km

Ayo. de Sta. Marina

Ermita de
San José

La Maluenga

ta. Marina
e Somoza

Granja

**Rabanal del
Camino**

Iglesia del Bendito
Cristo de la Vera Cruz

*Bridge over the
river Meruelo
in Molinaseca.*

LE-142, after passing by the Hospital de San Roque, which is now a pilgrim refuge. The river runs along to the right, and both sides of the path have walnut trees and grapevines. Just over one kilometre later, you will come to a fork in the road:

A) You can continue along this road, cross the river Boeza and the railway line, and carry on until you get to **Ponferrada.** Then, go along Molinaseca Avenue and Del Castillo Avenue, which will take you to the symbolic castle.

B) Alternatively, you can take the path to the left, which heads down to **Campo,** (Roman spring), and from there, join a tarmacked path which meets up with the road, just before crossing the Escaril bridge over the Moriscal river. You will now be in **Ponferrada,** and should cross the Mascarón bridge over the river Boeza, continuing along Camino Bajo de San Andrés Street. Finally, cross the railway line, and go along Hospital Street to the castle.

CYCLISTS

This stage can be followed in its entirety along the LE-142.

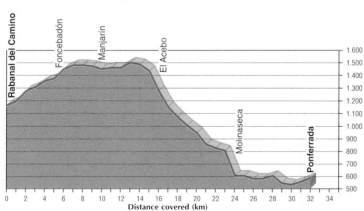

STAGE 22. PRACTICAL INFORMATION

FONCEBADÓN

HOSTELS

Shelter. The church has been adapted.

RESTAURANTS

El Convento de Foncebadón. Travesía
C/ Real. ∅ 987 691 245
La Taberna de Gaia. ∅ 987 691 079

MANJARÍN

HOSTELS

"Refugio de Tomás". Modest but fairly
willing to welcome tired pilgrims.

EL ACEBO

HOSTELS

"El Acebo" hostel. C/ Real, 16.
It has 24 beds, a washing machine and
room for bicycles. ∅ 987 695 074
"La Taberna de Josefina" hostel.
C/ Real, 16. 14 beds. ∅ 987 695 074
Neighbours' hostel (Albergue vecinal).
C/ Real, 16. 10 beds. ∅ 987 695 074

RESTAURANTS

El Acebo. C/ Real. ∅ 987 695 074
La Taberna de José. Pl. de la Peña, 4.
∅ 987 695 488

RIEGO DE AMBRÓS

HOSTELS

The neighbours' committee runs a hostel
which is open all year round. C/ Real,
s/n. 35 beds. Kitchen. ∅ 987 695 190

HOTELS

Riego de Ambrós guest house. Ctra.
Astorga, 3. ∅ 987 695 188. Double
room: € 20.

RESTAURANTS

Ruta de Santiago. Travesía Gutiérrez
Suárez, 1. ∅ 987 418 151

MOLINASECA

HOSTELS

"San Roque" hostel. Avda. Manuel Fraga
Iribarne, s/n. It has 80 beds in the summer
and 30 in the winter. Kitchen, chimney,
washing machine. ∅ 615 302 390

HOTELS

H** La Posada de Muriel. Pl. del Santo
Cristo. ∅ 987 453 201. 8 rooms.
Double room: € 59; single room: € 41.
HSR** El Palacio. C/ El Palacio, 19.
∅ 987 453 094. Double room: € 42/35.

RESTAURANTS

Mesón Real. Ctra. Ponferrada-Astorga.
∅ 987 453 166
Azar. C/ El Palacio. ∅ 987 453 100
Mesón Puente Romano. C/ La Presa.
∅ 987 453 154

PONFERRADA

HOSTELS

"Parroquia del Carmen" hostel.
100 beds. Open all year round. It has a
kitchen and a place for horses.

HOTELS

Casa Manolo guest house. Avda. Valdés,
35-4° Dch. ∅ 987 411 017. 5 rooms.
Double room: € 14; breakfast: € 1,5.
El Minero guest house. C/ Via Nueva,
17. ∅ 987 411 326. Double room: € 9.
HSR* Roma. Avda. Ferrocarril, 16.
∅ 987 411 908. Double room: € 16.

RESTAURANTS

Tresportiñas. C/ Lago de Carucedo, 13.
∅ 987 425 572
Burbia. Avda. Astoga, 9. ∅ 987 424 976
Mesón El Ancla. Avda. Galicia, 57.
∅ 987 416 954

MEANS OF TRANSPORT

ALSA buses. Leon-Ponferrada line.
Bus station. ∅ 987 640 080
RENFE rail station. ∅ 987 424 623

HISTORY AND WEALTH OF THE STAGE 22

Cruz de Ferro.

THE FRENCH ROAD. RABANAL DEL CAMINO – PONFERRADA

Foncebadón is the last town of the Road before leaving the territory of Astorga and entering El Bierzo. The oldest documents, which effectively place it *in confinio Vergidense,* give us a clue as to the etymology of its name, *Fons Sabbatonis,* which means "Fountain of a person called Sábado". This is a rare but not altogether undocumented name in the early Middle Ages. Its current abandoned state does not match the previous importance of this town, where a council convened by King Ramiro II was held in the Xth century. Documents from just over a century later provide evidence of at least three hospitality institutions. The first of these is related to the emblematic hermit Gaucelmo, a contemporary of St Dominic of the Walkway, San Lesmes de Burgos and San Juan de Ortega. Gaucelmo, just like his contemporaries, devoted his life to helping pilgrims. In his case the assistance provided consisted of helping them through Puerto de Foncebadón. Just like the saints mentioned above, he was protected by King Alfonso VI. Guacelmo, who was of French origin (if his name is anything to go by), had withdrawn into this rough area as a hermit but the daily sight of pilgrims in difficulties compelled him to help, in a similar way to St Dominic of the Walkway. Using crosses to mark the limits of an area around Guacelmo's lodging place, Alfonso VI granted him immunity in 1103, just like he did with the guardians of the church of San Salvador in Foncebadón.

In addition to Guacelmo's lodging place, Foncebadón had two other hospitals in the XIIth century: Santa María Magdalena and San Juan. Later, a community of hermits which depended on the church of Astorga followed in Guacelmo's footsteps and settled in Foncebadón. The old prosperity and importance of this sadly derelict town can still be seen in the length of its Pilgrim Road, as well as in the quality of some of its buildings.

Mediaeval Latin texts including *Liber Sancti Iacobi* refer to **Puerto de Foncebadón** as "Monte Irago" *(Mons Yragus)*. All foreign pilgrims, whether French, Italian or German, later called it "Monte Rabanal" *(Rabanel, Ravanel, Rauaneel)*. Such was the impression made on pilgrims by these hills that they captured them in the setting of part of their literary works. The role of Monte Rabanal in *Anseïs de Carthage*, written approximately in the year 1200, is of particular significance among French Charlemagne cycle poems.

In the highest part of the pass, on the vortex of a conical heap of stones, stands **Cruz de Ferro**, a five metre tall bare trunk crowned with a plain iron cross. The simplicity of its execution belies the intention with which this cross, one of the most significant monuments of the Road to Santiago, was started a very long time ago. This is a collective work, whose component stones were piled up by thousands of passers-by from time immemorial. What started off as yet another pile of stones indicating the frontier between two territories, became a large ever-growing heap, that passers-by kept adding to for votive or apotropaic reasons. The heap was finally christianised, at the beginning of the XIIth century, when Gaucelmo the hermit placed the cross which now crowns the monument.

View of El Acebo.

Manjarín, the first town in El Bierzo after Foncebadón, has also been almost abandoned for years. The hospitality which is currently offered there has at least one precedent, documented in the XVIth century.

In exchange for not paying tax, the inhabitants of **El Acebo** kept a lodging place for pilgrims from the time of the Reyes Católicos (the Catholic King and Queen – Ferdinand and Isabella). In addition, they had to drive 400 stakes into the path between their lodging place and the Hospital of Gaucelmo in Foncebadón. These tall stakes were particularly useful for showing the way in the winter, when paths would disappear under the snow and pilgrims were in danger of getting lost in the woods. The parish church of San Miguel houses a beautiful polychrome stone statue representing a bearded middle-aged man bearing only a book and a turquoise coloured tunic covered in golden irises. This mysterious image has been identified with St James, possibly because of its bare feet. The iris flower is referred to in *Liber Sancti Iacobi* as a symbol of the Apostle, but this is not supported by the icons, especially if we ignore this particular image. This flower is strictly speaking a symbol of the Saviour, although the book is typical of his apostles and disciples rather than of the Saviour himself.

When you leave El Acebo, a detour leads to **Compludo,** which is in a deep and almost inaccessible valley. This is where St Fructuosus founded

View of Molinaseca.

his first monastery in the VIIth century, the monastery of San Justo and San Pastor, which he consecrated with relics of the Alcalá de Henares (at that time known as *Complutum*, hence the name Compludo) child martyrs. This is also where he wrote his first monastic rule, which made him the main booster of the great Spanish monastic movement in Visigothic times. One of this movement's main centres was in Compludo and El Bierzo, but Compludo's fame really stems from its "ferrería", an early forge whose power-watered mechanism still works as it did in the Middle Ages.

The parish church of La Magdalena and a fountain of the same name in **Riego de Ambrós** may be the remains of an old pilgrims' hospital.

Molinaseca is the first stop mentioned in *Liber Sancti Iacobi* after Monte Irago. A document dating from 1188 confirms that *casa de Molina* belonged to the church of Astorga, which was the town's pilgrims' hospital. Other signs of a link with the Road to Santiago are the beautiful Romanesque bridge and the town's layout. The parish church of San Nicolás, which was rebuilt in the XVIIth century over an XIth century Romanesque church, houses a sculpture of St Roque in pilgrim attire. At the town entrance is the chapel of Nuestra Señora de la Quinta Angustia. Although it is Baroque, it was already documented in the XIth century and was an object of particular devotion among pilgrims. There was a lepers' hospital outside the town between the XIIth and XIVth centuries.

The fact that **Campo's** parish church is dedicated to St Blaise suggests that there may have been a pilgrims' hospital here.

Ponferrada is also mentioned a couple of times in *Liber Sancti Iacobi*. The first reference is as a Stop of the Road, between Molinaseca and Cacabelos, and the second is a reference to its river, the Sil, as one of the Road's largest rivers. This river has been linked to the birth of the city ever since the moment when bishop Osmundo de Astorga ordered a bridge, garnished with some iron supports which turned it into something typical (if the etymology of the name is anything to go by), to be built next to a church dedicated to St Peter. The old *Interamnium Flavium* mansion of the Astorga-Braga road may have previously stood on the place where the rivers Sil and Boeza meet, although this is not certain. The assumption is supported by the many Roman remains found in the area.

Pilgrims wishing to enter Ponferrada had to cross the river Boeza. At the beginning they did this by boat, as the name "paso de la barca" ("barca" means "small boat") suggests, subsequently by a bridge which was later demolished, and finally by the Mascarón bridge. The district or "burg" of Pomboeza was on the river bank, and several hospitality institutions could be found there.

Templars' Castle in Ponferrada.

The pilgrims went along what is now calle Hospital (after the Real Hospital de Santa Ana or de la Reina, funded by Isabella the Catholic). Later on, on a promontory next to the river Sil opposite the church of San Andrés, is the magnificent castle of the Templars (castillo de los Templarios), which was probably this military order's headquarters in El Bierzo, one of the parts of Spain in which it had the most power. Close by is the basilica of La Encina, which houses an image of El Bierzo's patron saint. A legend according to which the image was found by knights of this order on the trunk of a holm oak that was to be used for building the church links this to the Templars.

Some of the best examples of pre-Romanesque Spanish architecture, such as Santo Tomás de las Ollas or Santa María de Vizbayo, can be found in the area around Ponferrada. Not far from here are the ruins of the ancient abbey of San Pedro de Montes, founded by St Fructuosus and carried on by St Gennadius, and which later became one of the most important Benedictine monasteries in Spain.

23 Ponferrada – Villafranca del Bierzo

The region of Bierzo, situated in a ring of mountains and lying in a depression, is a fertile land, whose agreeable climate allows cultivation of many types of fruits and vegetables.

Villafranca del Bierzo. Portada del Perdón (El Perdón façade) in the church of Santiago.

From Paseo Huertas del Sacramento, follow the footpath until you pass the Endesa buildings. Next, go along the streets of Compostilla, before leaving the village and going through a tunnel. Walking through vines, you will come to **Columbrianos,** where you will cross the road which goes to Villablino. Go along Iglesia Street, then Real Street, passing by the Hermitage of San Blas y San Roque, before leaving the village and carrying on through irrigated farmlands. Go along a path before taking the road which brings you into **Fuentes Nuevas.** A little further on, you will come across **Camponaraya,** which you will enter and exit via the main road. Next, follow the road which leads off from the co-operative and the rest area, as it goes up a hill. After the bridge which spans the motorway, you will see the small valley through which the Magaz river flows. Pass through many vineyards and poplar groves before arriving in **Cacabelos** via the *Calle de los Peregrinos,* (the Street of the Pilgrims). Cross the Cúa river and leave the village, passing by the Church of Our Lady of Las Angustias, carrying on along the LE-713 through typical "wine" country. You will then come to **Pieros,** to the left of which is *Castrum Bergidum.* After this town, the road goes through the uneven valley, a valley dotted with buildings. After passing the Valtuilles river, take a road which leads off to the right through vineyards, fruit trees and a few oaks, passing by some headlands which have been replanted with conifers. To the left you can see the valley of the river Burbia. Continue along the Camino de la Virgen and,

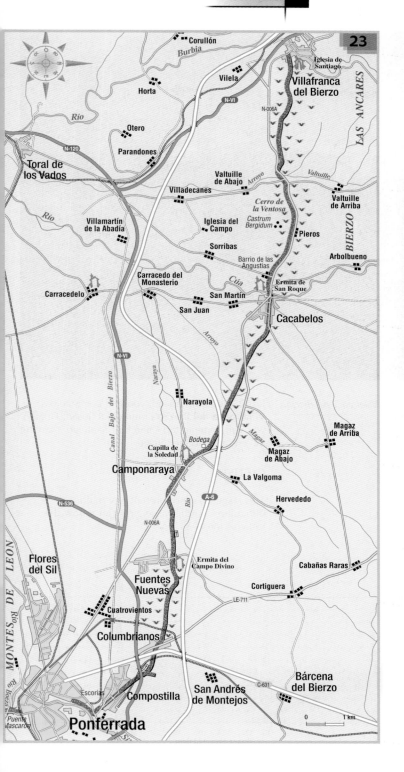

Villafranca del Bierzo.

just 2 kilometres ahead, you will come across **Villafranca del Bierzo's** municipal hostel. Finally, you will come to the Church of Santiago, marking the entrance to the village.

CYCLISTS

This stage does not present any major difficulties. Furthermore, you can follow the route of the N-VI.

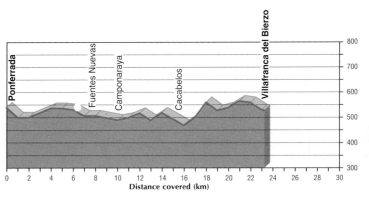

STAGE 23. PRACTICAL INFORMATION

FUENTES NUEVAS

RESTAURANTS

Monteclaro. C/ Antonio Cortés, 24.
✆ 987 404 814

CAMPONARAYA

RESTAURANTS

Gran Bierzo. C/ Tercera Paralela.
✆ 987 463 252
Naraya. Camponaraya Industrial
Development (Polígono Industrial
Camponaraya). ✆ 987 450 260
Riazor. Carretera N-VI, km 395,6.
✆ 987 463 142

CACABELOS

HOSTELS

Municipal Hostel (Albergue Municipal).
Located at the exit. Open from April to
October. It has 70 beds. When this is
closed, the teachers' old houses are used,
at least provisionally, for shelter.

HOTELS

HSR** Santa María. C/ Santa María,
20-A. ✆ 987 549 588. 32 beds.
Double room: € 36; breakfast: € 4.
P El Molino. C/ Santa María, 10. 5
beds. ✆ 987 546 829. Double room: €
18/16; breakfast: € 2; lunch/dinner: € 8.

RESTAURANTS

Casa Gato. C/ El Foyo, 2.
✆ 987 547 200
Casa Lázaro. C/ Santa María, 8.
✆ 987 546 247
El Refugio de Saúl.
C/ Calexa Sixtina, 4. ✆ 987 547 055
La Moncloa de San Lázaro.
C/ Cimadevilla, 99. ✆ 987 546 101
Mesón Apóstol. C/ Santa María, 29.
✆ 987 549 189
Mesón Los Arcos. C/ Alférez
Provisional, 23. ✆ 987 549 015
Villamaría.
Avda. Constitución, 98. ✆ 987 547 343

VILLAFRANCA DEL BIERZO

HOSTELS

Municipal Hostel (Albergue Municipal).
C/ Santiago, s/n. Next to the church of
Santiago. 78 beds and a kitchen. Open
from April to November. ✆ 987 542 680
Ave Fenix pilgrims' hospital.
C/ Santiago, 4. 77 plazas. Open all year
round. ✆ 987 542 655

HOTELS

HS** Casa Méndez. C/ Espíritu Santo, 1.
✆ 987 542 408. 21 beds. Double room:
€ 38; breakfast: € 4; lunch/dinner: € 10.
HS* Comercio. C/ Puente Nuevo, 9.
✆ 987 540 008. 25 beds. Double room:
€ 20; breakfast: € 2,5; lunch/dinner: € 8.
HS* El Cruce. C/ San Salvador, 37.
✆ 987 542 469. 22 beds. Double room:
€ 27/23; dinner: € 9.
HSR* La Charola. C/ Doctor Areen, 19.
✆ 987 540 200. 9 beds. Double room:
€ 21; single room: € 16; breakfast: € 4.
Venecia guest house. Ctra. N-VI, km
410. ✆ 987 540 468. 19 beds.
Double room: € 18; single room: € 9;
breakfast: € 1,8.

RESTAURANTS

Casa Goyo. C/ Antonio Pereira.
✆ 987 540 276
El Padrino. C/ Doctor Arén, 17.
✆ 987 540 075
La Charola. Ctra. N-VI, km 406.
✆ 987 540 200
La Escalinata. Pl. Prim, 4.
✆ 987 540 706
Mesón Don Nacho. C/ Truqueles, 1.
✆ 987 540 076
Panchi. C/ Las Vegas, 2. ✆ 987 542 004
Sevilla. Pl. Mayor, 13. ✆ 987 540 186
Venecia. Ctra. Madrid-A Coruña.
✆ 987 540 311
Viña Femita. C/ Calvo Sotelo, 2.
✆ 987 542 490

HISTORY AND WEALTH OF THE STAGE 23

THE FRENCH ROAD. PONFERRADA – VILLAFRANCA DEL BIERZO

The fact that the church of **Compostilla** (whose name is the Castilian equivalent of the Galician "Compostela" and which can be translated as "Little Beautiful" or "Beautiful Town or City") is dedicated to Our Lady of the Refuge (Nuestra Señora del Refugio) may be a reference to an old hospital, lodging place or refuge for pilgrims.

As its name indicates, **Columbrianos** was repopulated by Mozarabic people from the Portuguese city of Coimbra, although remains of much older settlements (from Asturian times) have been found here. The fact that one of its two chapels is dedicated to St Blaise must be related to the pilgrims' hospital whose remains were found in the area.

Very close to **Fuentes Nuevas,** next to the small river Naraya, is **Camponaraya,** which used to boast two pilgrims' hospitals. Its church was dedicated to St Ildephonsus (VIIth century), who was the archbishop of Toledo and one of the best considered intellectuals of his time. One of his works (all of which are still famous long after his death) is strangely linked to the documented origins of the pilgrimage to Santiago. Indeed, the first we hear about a pilgrim from the other side of the pyrenees (Xth century bishop Godescalco Le Puy) relates to the fact that, during his journey past the monastery of Albelda, in La Rioja, he ordered a copy of Ildephonsus' treaty about the Virgin (entitled *De virginitate perpetuae Sanctae Mariae*).

Cacabelos, just like its river Cúa, is mentioned in *Liber Sancti Iacobi*. In addition to this brief mention, other pieces of information contained in this book suggest, as we will see later, that its author knew Cacabelos and its surroundings well, a fact which may have something to do with Cacabelos belonging to the church of Santiago de Compostela.

According to *Historia Compostelana,* Diego Gelmírez ordered that the district or "burg" of Cacabelos – which he had found destroyed – be re-

---
Cacabelos. Las Angustias pilgrimage.

erected in 1108, and its church – the current church of Santa María de la Plaza – be consecrated with full honours. Cacabelos' mediaeval prosperity enabled it to grow, which in turn allowed the churches of San Bartolomé, San Esteban and San Lázaro, all of which have now disappeared, to be erected. The church of San Lázaro, originally outside the city walls, was linked to a hospital for sick pilgrims. The current chapel of San Roque, which stands close to where the church used to be, is a surviving part of it, and houses an image of this saint, depicted as the usual wounded pilgrim, which reminds us of the many sick pilgrims who went on the pilgrimage in order to recover their health. The current church of La Quinta Angustia near

Pottery sale in Cacabelos.

the bridge over the river Cúa is also erected on an old pilgrims' hospital. Inside it is a very interesting Baroque image with the very widespread representation of St Anthony of Padua and the Baby Jesus. The originality of the sculpture, however, lies in the fact that the Lisbon saint and the Baby Jesus are engrossed in a game of cards.

Many of the Pre-Roman and Roman remains which were found in the area around Cacabelos and which can now be found in the town's Archeological Museum came from **castro de la Ventosa,** where the old *Bergidum,* an Asturian fortress which later lent its name to the whole area of El Bierzo *(Bergidum > Bierçi[d]u >* Bierzo), was established. The peculiar story about this Celto-Roman ruin in *Pseudo-Turpin,* the fourth part of *Liber Sancti Iacobi,* gives away the author's knowledge of the land around Cacabelos. The story attempts to explain why *Lucerna Ventosa* – the ruins of Castro de Ventosa– was in ruins in the author's time (c. 1140) and why it should continue to be so forever:

> *All these cities [all cities in Spain] were conquered by Charlemagne, some without a fight and others after great battles, except for the above mentioned Lucerna, a very strongly fortified city in Valverde [ie, El Bierzo], which he was only able to take at the end. He finally went there and sieged it for four months. After he prayed to God and St James, the city walls fell, a pool of black water with large black fish rose from it and the city remains abandoned until this day [...] The cities of Lucerna Ventosa, Cáparra and Adania were cursed by [Charlemagne] because of the great effort he had to expend in taking them, and that is why they remain uninhabited until today.*

This legend, moved from Switzerland (hence the name Lucerna, or Luzerne, for the cursed city) to El Bierzo (not only to *Castro de Ventosa,* but also to the nearby lake of Carucedo, which is indeed full of large black fish) by the author of *Pseudo-Turpin,* fulfils two functions. The first of these is to contribute to *Pseudo-Turpin's* aim of filling the Road to Santiago with Charlemagne-related legends, which were an attraction point for the pilgrims, who were the "tourists" of the time (remember the cases of Roncesvals, Monjardín, Nájera or Sahagún). The second function was to support the church of Santiago de Compostela's (which owned Cacabelos) economic interests. During the XIIth and early XIIIth

Church of Pieros.

centuries, the kings of León repeatedly tried to rebuild and repopulate the old Castro de Ventosa. However, this could potentially ruin Cacabelos and adversely affect the nearby monastery of Carracedo. After taking the issue to the courts, the kings gave up on this idea, ordered the new village which had been built in

Castro de Ventosa (and which large numbers of Cacabelos inhabitants had moved to) to be demolished, and promised the church of Santiago de Compostela and the monastery of Carracedo never again to try to repopulate the old ruin. It must be noted, however, that this imported story did not take root in El Bierzo, although it did in Lake Sanabria (Zamora), which has a legend about a lake-submerged city called Villaverde de Lucerna.

The transplant of this legend was almost certainly caused by communication between **Carracedo** and its affiliated town San Martín de Castañeda, on the shore of Lake Sanabria. The old abbey of Carracedo had been founded in the Xth century and had been dedicated to the Saviour, but this was changed to Santa María in the XIIth century, and the abbey became one of the most important Cistercian centres in the whole region, although its battered ruins are now no more than a pale – albeit magnificent – reflection of its past splendour.

The inscription reporting the consecration by bishop Osmundo de Astorga can still be seen in the parish church of **Pieros,** which is dedicated to St Martin of Tours.

The fact that **Villafranca del Bierzo** is mentioned in the *Liber Sancti Iacobi* guide as the end of the tenth stage shows that, even then (1130), it was an important place. Its exact origin is undocumented, but both its name and that of its main church, Santa María de Cruñego, help solve the mystery. Although the first documentary references are from 1120, it is assumed that Villafranca's boundaries were drawn and its population established during the reign of Alfonso VI, who wanted to set up a checkpoint in this area. In order to achieve this, he supported the arrival of a Clunian community which settled in the area around the hamlet of Burbia. The monks took on the tasks of assisting pilgrims and taking over the worship in the church of Santa María de Cruñego (Cruñego comes from *Cluniacum,* Cluny's Latin name). The current late Gothic building replaces the old Romanesque erection. However, the Clunians were not the only people to assist pilgrims in Villafranca; the church of Santiago, at the city's entrance, was linked to a hospital of the same name which has now disappeared. The early Romanesque stonework of the church, finished in 1189, on the other hand, can still be admired. The fame of the chapel stems, not only from the sculptures on its capitals, but also for the privilege it enjoyed in XVth century: under a bull by Calistus III, any pilgrims who were unable to complete their pilgrimage due to illness could achieve the same plenary indulgence by crossing "Puerta del Perdón", the door on the church of Santiago de Villafranca's northern

"El Cristo (the Christ)" in Villafranca del Bierzo.

façade. This privilege was unique in the whole Road to Santiago. There was, in addition, a hospital of San Roque, on whose land the XVIIth century convent of La Anunciada (Order of St Clare) was later erected. The memory of St Francis of Assisi's passing in his journey to Santiago is kept alive both here and in the church of San Francisco. Other noteworthy buildings in Villafranca are the enormous XVIth century church of San Nicolás and the solid Marquis of Villafranca castle (castillo de los Marqueses de Villafranca).

Interesting buildings in the surroundings of Villafranca include the small Romanesque churches of San Miguel and San Esteban, in Corullón, and the church of San Fiz (Felix), in Visonia. The latter stands where one of St Fructuosus' foundations used to be, and which later belonged to the Hospitallers of St John. For this reason, it is also known as the church of San Juan.

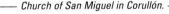

Church of San Miguel in Corullón.

24 Villafranca del Bierzo – O Cebreiro

The final day spent in the area of El Bierzo is both one of the most beautiful and challenging. You will pass through the narrow valley of the river Valcarce before tackling the ascent of O Cebreiro, situated between the ranges of los Ancares and la sierra do Courel. Although not the highest part of the trail, this stage involves a steep climb in the course of only a few kilometres.

Vega de Valcarce.

Villafranca del Bierzo is crossed by calle del Agua, which leads to the bridge over the river Burbia. At this point you are faced with two options:

A) Take the steep calle Pradela and begin climbing the Cerro Real, through woodlands of chestnut trees, conifers and holm oaks, common oaks, broom, heather, bracken and other flora. Along this route the bottom of the valley is always in sight, with the river Valcarce, the N-VI and the new route of the A-6 highway all running through it. After around 3 km, the route skirts the hill through thicket until you begin to descend through beautiful chestnut trees, with Trabadelo now on the horizon, Pereje left behind in the valley on the left, and Pradela on the right. You then come to the first fork in the path, where the path leading to Pradela branches off. You then have another choice of route. Although both paths eventually join the track which takes you down, the left-hand path, which is not very well marked out, is the most direct route. Once you reach the track, you follow it down, occasionally straying from it to cut across the bends. After 10 km you will come into **Trabadelo.**

B) Take calle Concepción to reach the N-VI, which leads directly to **Trabadelo,** via **Pereje.** This route meanders along the bottom of the deep and narrow valley of the river Valcarce, following its course. Whilst at one time this road may have been dangerous due to heavy traffic, it is now a much quieter route, thanks to the highway.

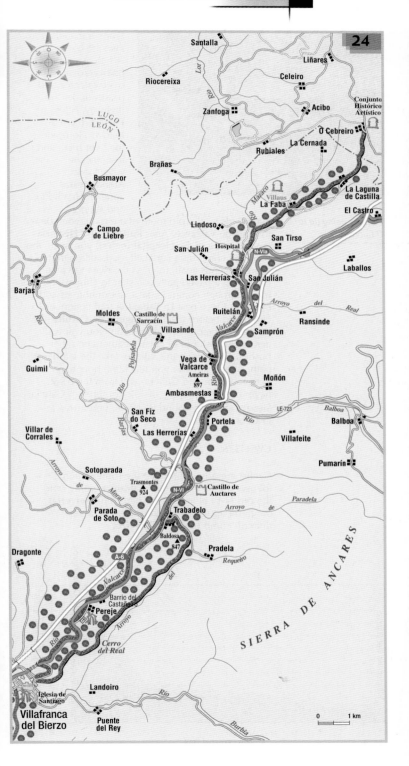

24

Santalla

Liñares

Riocereixa

Celeiro

Acibo

Zanfoga

Conjunto Histórico Artístico

O Cebreiro

La Cernada

Rubiales

Brañas

Busmayor

Mazaco

Villaus

La Faba

La Laguna de Castilla

El Castro

Campo de Liebre

Lindoso

San Tirso

Hospital

San Julián

Laballos

Barjas

Las Herrerías

San Julián

Moldes

Castillo de Sarracín

Villasinde

Ruitelán

Arroyo   del   Real

Ransinde

Valcarce

Samprón

Guimil

Vega de Valcarce

Ameiras
897

Moñón

Ambasmestas

LE-723

Balboa

San Fiz do Seco

Portela

Balboa

Las Herrerías

Villafeite

Villar de Corrales

Pumarín

Sotoparada

Arroyo   de

Moral

Trasmontes
924

N-VI

Castillo de Auctares

Paradela

Parada de Soto

Trabadelo

Arroyo   de

Baldosa
847

Pradela

Dragonte

Requeiro

A-6

Valcarce

del

Barrio del Castañeiro

Pereje

Arroyo

Cerro del Real

SIERRA   DE   ANCARES

Landoiro

Río

Iglesia de Santiago

Villafranca del Bierzo

Puente del Rey

Burbia

0   1 km

LUGO
LEÓN

Río   Lor

Pilgrims going up to O Cebreiro.

From Trabadelo you take the old N-VI, which at various points crosses the river Valcarce and passes under the highway. After **Portela,** the road follows alongside the river bank and its adjacent woodlands. **Ambasmestas** appears on a bend, and shortly afterwards by the old route of the road, you come to **Vega de Valcarce.** After **Ruitelán** and **Herrerías** (and the area of the **Hospital Inglés),** you begin the daunting climb up a surfaced road, although it soon descends again to cross the river Valcarce. On taking a paved path you start to climb once more, through common oaks, chestnut trees and bracken. Once past **La Faba,** the trail continues to climb and before reaching **Laguna de Castilla** (the last village before you leave León) you will walk across some slopes of grass, heather and other bushes. On leaving this village, take the left-hand path. After 1 km you will reach the boundary between León and Galicia, and from there you have in store a journey of 152 km through Galicia. Shortly after the boundary stone, you arrive at **O Cebreiro.**

CYCLISTS

Cyclist are advised to take the route which follows the N-VI out of **Villafranca,** going onto the old N-VI at km. 418. Then from **Herrerías** continue up the surfaced road, with a very difficult climb up to **O Cebreiro.**

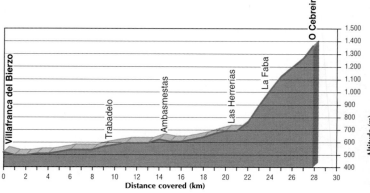

STAGE 24. PRACTICAL INFORMATION

PEREJE

HOSTELS

Municipal Hostel (Albergue Municipal). Camino de Santiago, s/n. It has 30 beds, a kitchen, washing machine and garden. Open all year round. ⌀ 987 540 138

TRABADELO

HOSTELS

Municipal Hostel (Albergue Municipal). C/ Camino de Santiago, s/n. 50 beds, a kitchen, laundry and library. ⌀ 629 855 487

HOTELS

HS** Nova Ruta. Ctra. Madrid-Coruña, km 414. ⌀ 987 566 431. 26 beds. Double room: € 44/37; lunch/dinner: € 10.

RESTAURANTS

Nova Ruta. Ctra. Madrid-Coruña, km 420. ⌀ 987 566 431
Trabadelo. Ctra. N-VI. Trabadelo (León). ⌀ 987 566 435

VEGA DE VALCARCE

HOSTELS

Municipal Hostel (Albergue Municipal). 60 beds. It has a kitchen and washing machine. ⌀ 987 543 192
"Sarracín" hostel. Ctra. N-6, km 426. 48 beds, washing machine and dryer. ⌀ 987 543 045 / 653 375 727

HOTELS

P Fernández. Plaza del Ayuntamiento. ⌀ 987 543 027. 10 beds. Double room: € 24; single room: € 12.

RESTAURANTS

El Español. Ctra. Antigua N-VI. ⌀ 987 543 113
Mesón Las Rocas. Ctra. Antigua N-VI. ⌀ 987 543 285

RUITELÁN

HOSTELS

"Pequeño Potala" hostel. Ctra. N-6. 40 beds, laundry and room for bicycles. Massages. ⌀ 987 561 322

LAS HERRERÍAS

HOSTELS

Camino de Santiago hostel.

LA FABA

HOSTELS

Municipal Hostel (Albergue Municipal). Shelter run by the German Road Association (Asociación del Camino Alemana). 35 beds.

LAGUNA DE CASTILLA

HOSTELS

Municipal Hostel (Albergue Municipal). 15 beds and a kitchen. Open in the summer.

CEBREIRO

HOSTELS

Municipal Hostel (Albergue Municipal). 80 beds, a kitchen, a washing machine and a stable. ⌀ 660 396 809

HOTELS

H* Santuario do Cebreiro. ⌀ 982 367 125. Double room: € 54; single room: € 36; lunch/dinner: € 12.
HS** Rebollal. Ctra. N-VI. Pedrafita do Cebreiro. ⌀ 982 367 115. Double room: € 45/37; lunch/dinner: € 11.

RESTAURANTS

Casa Carolo. O Cebreiro, 14. ⌀ 982 367 168
San Giraldo de Aurillac. ⌀ 982 367 125
Venta Celta. ⌀ 982 367 137
Hospedería O Peregrino. C/ Observatorio. Pedrafita do Cebreiro. ⌀ 982 367 164

HISTORY AND WEALTH OF THE STAGE 24

Panoramic view of Vega de Valcarce.

THE FRENCH ROAD. VILLAFRANCA DEL BIERZO – O CEBREIRO

Pilgrims crossed Villafranca via Calle del Agua, the town's Pilgrim Road to Santiago, until they reached the river Burbia, which they crossed near the place where it meets the river Valcárcel. Because of its location, on the mouth of the river Valcárcel, the *Liber Sancti Iacobi* guide refers to Villafranca del Bierzo with the descriptive name *Villafranca de Bucca Vallis Carceris* ("Villafranca of the river Valcárcel's mouth"). From here, the Road to Santiago penetrates the steep, narrow and deep valley of the Valcarce river. Its ominous name, **Valcarce,** meaning "Prison Valley", can be explained by the feeling of enclosure and narrowness that the valley gave both locals and travellers.

Ever since ancient times, criminals took advantage of the distress which the shape of this unavoidable part of the Galician route caused traders and travellers, and which made it the perfect place to make some money at their expense. Because of this, fortified posts were erected in this area from Roman times to ensure the safety in this thoroughfare *(Uttaris)*. In the early Middle Ages, however, it was the lords themselves who, instead of protecting the area as they were supposed to, and disguising their practice as rights of passage, excise and carriage, skinned the travellers, who were often poor pilgrims with no income from their journey. Although Alfonso VI issued a document in 1072 making such collections illegal, the archbishop of Santiago Diego Gelmírez reported, a few years later, that nobleman Nezano Gudesteiz was exerting complete control over the traffic which flowed through the valley. The need to put a stop to this situation in such an important thoroughfare may be the reason why Valcárcel's main fortresses (La Redoniña, Autares and Castrosarracín) were occupied – at least according to tradition – by the Knights of the Templar, who guaranteed the safety of the area during the pilgrimage's golden years.

Very close to La Redoniña we find **Pereje,** the first town on the Valcárcel after Villafranca. The abbot of Cebreiro built a church and a pilgrims' hospital here, which gave rise to a huge jurisdictional dispute with the Clunian community of Santa María de Villafranca.

Close to the next town, **Trabadelo,** on what is now known as Cerro de Aldares, was the old Roman *Uttaris* mansion from *Itinerario de Antonino.* After this, travellers reached the famous castle of Auctares, a sinister place where early mediaeval lords literally robbed pilgrims to collect rights of passage.

The name of the next town, **Portela,** refers to a particularly narrow pass in the already narrow Valcárcel valley. The river Valcárcel meets its tributary, the river Balboa, in **Ambasmestas,** where the remains of the Roman road, as well as those of a three-span Roman bridge, can still be found.

Vega de Valcarce, the most important town in the Valcárcel valley, stretches out across a fertile area of level ground near Castrosarracín, located on a nearby hill slightly away from the Road. The mention, in *Liber Sancti Iacobi,* of *Castrum Sarracenicum* as a stop in the Road to Santiago may be a reference, rather than to

Chapel of San Tirso in Vega de Valcarce.

the fortress, to Vega de Valcárcel (which hadn't yet changed its name), the town which grew at its foot. The fact that its parish church is dedicated to the Magdalene suggests that there may have been a hospital here. Although there are no reliable documents to support this, the castle of Sarracín must have been founded by Sarraceno, count of Astorga and El Bierzo, a powerful nobleman from Alfonso III's time (IXth century). According to tradition, the castle was under the Knights of the Templar's control between the XIIth and XIVth centuries. This is not surprising if we take into account the Order's widespread presence in El Bierzo, the area's traditionally dangerous nature and the Templars' main task in the Road of Santiago, which was to protect and look out for the pilgrims. The current building's reasonably well preserved stonework can't date from much earlier than the XIVth century.

According to another tradition, St Froilan – bishop of León and patron saint of his native Lugo – lived as a hermit in the area around **Ruitelán** (the next town) in the Xth century. Some pilgrims' stories refer to this town as "San Juan" because its parish church is dedicated to St John the Baptist (San Juan Bautista).

The name **Herrerías** is undoubtedly related to the iron and steel industry, which has existed in the area since the Middle Ages. The fact that written reports mentioning "fragoas" ("fraguas", meaning "forges") in the area around Villafranca go back to the early XIIth century, means that the industry must be much older.

XVIIth century pilgrim Domenico Laffi later described in detail the way the iron was melted and worked with. The remains of the iron foundry,

which was still in operation until the beginning of the XXth century, can still be seen today. You can regain your strength on Fuente de Quiñones, on an interesting place next to the river and which, according to local tradition, is on a piece of land which belonged to Suero de Quiñones' (the quixotic squire from Puente de Órbigo) family.

Walk up to O Cebreiro.

Towards the end of the town is the district known as **Hospital de los Ingleses.** It originated as a hospital, which was already documented with this name in 1178 *(In valle Carceris Hospitali quod dicitur Anglorum)* and whose birth has been linked to the pilgrimage planned by English King Henry II, who wrote to Fernando II of León to inform him of his intention in 1177.

It was recently found out that the town referred to in the *Liber Sancti Iacobi* guide as *Villaus* – one of the few names which hadn't yet been identified – is **La Faba.** By what can be gathered from the documents, the name must have changed in the XIIIth century. The place was well known by historians, who always referred to it as the end of El Bierzo. The second part of the name is the word "uz" or "urce" (from Latin *ulicem)*, which in the local dialect means "heather", the bush which dominates, unopposed, the slopes which ascend to El Cebreiro. In addition, the name of La Faba's parish church (San Andrés) is the same as it was before the town's change of name (a document from 1198 reads: *ecclesiam Sancti Andree de Villa Oxi).*

La Faba is no longer the last town before Galicia. This role is now fulfilled by the small village of **Laguna de Castilla,** whose (relatively recent) name is related to the proximity of the frontier with Galicia.

The first town of the Road in Galicia, the Apostle's Land, is also one of the most significant of the route: **O Cebreiro.** The town, which is near Puerto de Pedrafita, has a hospital which has been in existence since at least the XIth century although, just like in Roncesvals' case, tradition wants it to be earlier – as early, in fact, as the time when the apostle St James' sepulchre was found (the IXth century) – but the truth is that no documents dating before King Alfonso VI's time contain references to this institution.

The hospital was originally entrusted to a community from the French Benedictine abbey of Saint-Géraud d'Aurillac, from which it depended until at least the XVth century. Within a century, however, it became a priorate subordinated to San Benito el Real of Valladolid, head of the Spanish Benedictines from the reign of the Reyes Católicos (the Catholic King and Queen – Ferdinand and Isabella).

The way the town's buildings have survived from times immemorial, ignoring the passing of time in spite of its heavy traffic, is impressive. Two examples of this incredible survival are the church of Santa María la Real and the famous "pallozas" (thatched stone buildings for people or cattle to live in) which are typical of this area. The church of Santa María la Real is built in pre-Romanesque style. It has basilical layout and three naves, and its most noteworthy feature is the three

"Cáliz del Milagro" (the Miracle Chalice) in O Cebreiro.

rectangular apses at the front. Inside is a Romanesque image of Santa María la Real, as well as a goblet and paten from the same time. These two are associated with a wonderful event known as "the miracle of El Cebreiro" ("milagro del Cebreiro"), consisting of a visible transubstantiation during a communion. The two witnesses of the miracle, the officiant and a parishioner, are buried in the chapel in which these liturgical instruments are exhibited.

The constructive shapes given to the "pallozas", whose name comes from the word for "straw" (referring to the thatched roofs), by early pre-Roman inhabitants have hardly changed. O Cebreiro was the parish of Elías Valiña Sampedro, one of the pioneers in the recovery of the Road to Santiago and who is remembered here by means of a bust.

"Pallozas" in O Cebreiro.

25 O Cebreiro – Triacastela

*From O Cebreiro, surrounded by rounded peaks and
towering mountainsides, the trail passes through the sierra
of Rañadoiro and, after crossing the Alto do Poio, it
descends into the valley wherein lies Triacastela.*

*Monument to
the Pilgrim in
O Cebreiro.*

The descent from **O Cebreiro** begins at the rear of the hostel, along a
path which winds down through the pine covered slopes of Monte Pozo
e Aréa and comes out onto a track. This veers to the left towards **Liñares,**
where you cross the road to the right. You can either continue along the
surfaced road or descend for a while along a track and come back along
a path on the mountainside, passing meadows, holly bushes and hazels,
walking parallel to the road, until you come back out onto it at the **Alto
de San Roque.** By taking another path on the right you reach **Hospital da
Condesa.** From there you set off along the road, but after less than 150m
you turn off towards Sabugos and Temple, and turn off again after km.
144 to climb a path on the left. Once you have rejoined the road, you

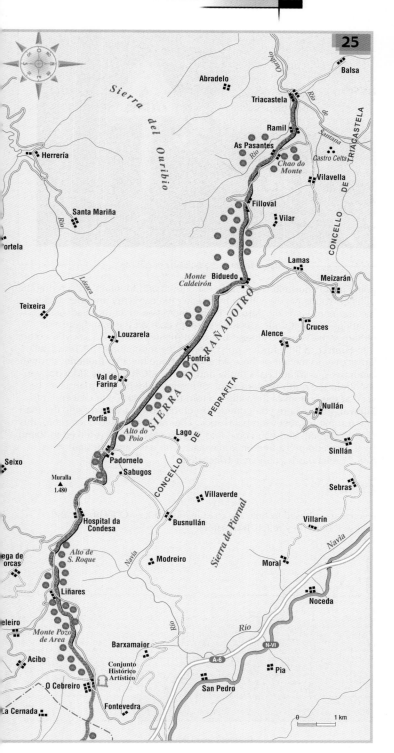

25

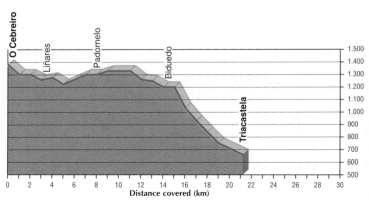

Pilgrim route in the outskirts of Liñares.

come into **Padornelo** (you will see a church and fountain on entering the village). You leave the village by passing the cemetery and then tackle the ascent towards the **Alto do Poio,** where you meet the road again. Continue along it until you see a parallel path on the right-hand side (where some young conifers have been planted). After 2.5 km you come into **Fonfría.** A little further on you enter the municipality of Triacastela. Cross over to the left of the road and continue towards **Biduedo,** through birch trees, common oaks, holly and bracken. On leaving Biduedo, you set off up the north-western slope of mount Caldeirón (a quarry can be seen at the bottom of the valley). From the mountain you descend into **Filloval,** from where you continue to climb down, after crossing the road and turning left, between oakwoods. The road is crossed once more, this time to the left, and you come into **As Pasantes,** which is linked to **Ramil** by a "corredoira", a tree-lined passage, with oaks and chestnut trees. Shortly afterwards you reach **Triacastela.**

CYCLISTS

Cyclist are advised to take the road leading out of **O Cebreiro** and follow it until they reach **Triacastela.**

STAGE 25. PRACTICAL INFORMATION

LIÑARES

RESTAURANTS

Casa Jaime. ✆ 982 367 166

HOSPITAL DA CONDESA

HOSTELS

"Hospital da Condesa" hostel.
Hospital da Condesa, s/n. It has 18 beds
and a kitchen. Open all year round.
✆ 660 396 810

FONFRÍA

RESTAURANTS

Casa Núñez. C/ Fonfría do Camiño.
✆ 982 161 335

ALTO DO POIO

HOSTELS

Municipal Hostel (Albergue Municipal).
✆ 982 367 172

HOTELS

HSR* Poio. Estrada Comarcal, km 21.
Padornelo. ✆ 982 367 167. 17 rooms.
Double room: € 27; single room: € 21;
breakfast: € 2,5; lunch/dinner: € 7,5.

RESTAURANTS

Santa María do Poio. Alto do Poio.
Padornelo. ✆ 982 367 096

VIDUEDO

HOSTELS

"Casa Quiroga" hostel.
✆ 982 187 299

RESTAURANTS

Mesón Betularia. ✆ 982 187 299

TRIACASTELA

HOSTELS

"Aitzenea" hostel.
Pl. Vista Alegre, 1. It has 38 beds, a
kitchen, heating, washing machine, dryer
and room for bicycles. Open from 1st
April to 30th October.
✆ 982 548 076 / 944 602 236
"Calvor" hostel. ✆ 982 531 266
Xunta hostel (Albergue de la Xunta).
Located at the entrance. It has 56 beds
and heating. Open all year round.
✆ 982 548 087 / 660 396 811

HOTELS

P** Albergue Turístico Aitznea.
C/ Vista Alegre, 1. ✆ 982 548 076.
4 rooms.

P* García. Rúa Peregrino, 8.
✆ 982 548 024. 3 rooms.

RESTAURANTS

Fernández. Travesía de la Iglesia, 3.
✆ 982 547 048

Mesón Os Tres Castelos.
Avda. de Castilla, 10.

O Peregrino. C/ Ramill.
✆ 982 548 024

O Novo. Avda. Camilo José Cela, 14.
✆ 982 547 005

Río. C/ Leoncio Cadórniga Carro.
✆ 982 548 133

Xacobeo. C/ Leoncio Cadórniga Carro, 4.
✆ 982 548 126

HISTORY AND WEALTH OF THE STAGE 25

Pilgrims among the "pallozas" of O Cebreiro.

THE FRENCH ROAD. O CEBREIRO – TRIACASTELA

San Esteban de Liñares, the first town of the Road after reaching the pass, is mentioned in the *Liber Sancti Iacobi* guide as a Stop of the Road, in spite of the short distance (3 km) between it and the hospital of El Cebreiro. The name given to it in this work, *Linar de Rege,* which can be translated as "the king's linen field", has caused modern scholars to conjecture about a possible linen plantation which the kings may have donated towards clothes to the Hospital of El Cebreiro. It must be admitted that the town's proximity to the hospital, together with the common history of the parish churches of San Esteban and Santa María del Cebreiro, make at least a link between this small town and the large hospital at the pass, possible.

At the end of the town, in a place known as **Alto de San Roque,** is a small chapel dedicated to St Roque. His worship originated in his native Montpellier and, even though he had not been canonised, his worship became one of the most popular of its time. St Roque was a historical character (1295-1327) who, according to his biography, became an orphan while still very young and, after donating his considerable inheritance to the poor, made a pilgrimage to Rome. On the way to Rome as well as in Rome itself, he cured many people of the plague simply by

——— *Church of San Juan in Padornelo.* ———

making the sign of the cross. On his way back, he contracted the disease himself, but miraculously recovered by divine intercession. When he reached his hometown of Montpellier, where his fame as a miraculous healer had preceded him, he was too humble to tell the guards who he was, so he was arrested for espionage and put in prison, where he died. His worship soon spread across Europe and become one of the most popular of its time. As we saw earlier, the Road to Santiago adopted him as one of its favourite saints (possibly from the XVth or XVIth century), and often depicted him with the icons reserved for pilgrims to Santiago. These depictions of St Roque are often modelled after those of St James when depicted as a pilgrim, only with two differences: the signs of the plague which can be seen on his bare legs, and a little dog carrying in its mouth a piece of bread which it offers the saint.

It is not clear from the documents who the noble unnamed lady, after whom the **Hospital da Condesa** is named, is: if it really was doña Eilo, the wife of count Gatón, who repopulated and was lord of El Bierzo in the IXth century, this could be one of the Road's oldest hospitable institutions. The Hospital da Condesa depended on the Priory of El Cebreiro, just like San Esteban de Liñares. The original church's archaic features are reproduced in the hospital's church.

As reported in *Historia Compostellana,* **Padornelo** was donated to the church of Santiago de Compostela by its owner Oveco Sánchez. Unless it is actually older, the fact that its church is dedicated to St John may be a sign that a territory belonging to the Order of St John, who ran a hospital dedicated to the Magdalene on the land where the cemetery can now be found, used to be here.

The Knights of St John's radius of activity in Pardornelo extended all the way to **Alto do Poio,** a place which was very difficult to get through in the winter, and where they probably had a post where the chapel of Santa María now stands.

Remains of the old paving have been found near **Fonfría** where, according to the documents, there used to be a pilgrims' hospital.

There was another Order of St John priory in **Biduedo,** which owes its name to the presence of a birch wood or patch. This military order was present on the descent from El Cebreiro for the same reason that the Templars were present in El Bierzo: because these hilly places with large amounts of traffic which central authorities had difficulty controlling were perfect for bandits (who were often local noblemen who felt they had the right to regulate traffic on their domains, even though the Road

Panoramic view of Triacastela.

to Santiago had been designated, at least partly for this reason, a "public highway"). The blooming of this type of military order, born to defend Christianity against Islam (especially in Holy Land), found that Spain and, in particular the Road to Santiago, offered another important front in which to carry out its mission, which was to protect and assist those Christians who were in most need of these things, the defenceless pilgrims, along a route with territories whose sometimes harsh orography made the journey through them gruelling and, more importantly, dangerous. Examples of such places were the Pyrenees, Montes de Oca and El Bierzo itself.

After Biduedo, the Road reached **Filloval,** whose name refers to the peculiar mediaeval institution of the collective wolf hunt. According to pilgrim Laffi on his way through Burgo Ranero (stage 17), the wolf was one of the inhabitants' biggest threats and an occasional enemy of weak and defenceless pilgrims. The pit where the natives positioned themselves or which served as a trap for the wolf must have been in Filloval. This is how the name evolved: *Fovea Luparia* ("wolf pit") > *Foya [lo]bar* > Foyllevar – Filloval.

After passing **As Pasantes** you reach **Ramil,** whose name is the result of the typical local evolution of its early owner's name, one Ramiro about whom we know nothing.

The sonorous Latin name of **Triacastela** seems to be related to the existence of three old Iron-Age settlements (in Galician, "castelos") located on different points of the peaks that dominate the deep valley which surrounds this town. It was first documented in the IXth century, when it was founded by count Gatón of El Bierzo.

The *Liber Sancti Iacobi* guide grants Triacastela the honour of deeming it the end of one of the thirteen stages of the Spanish part of the Road to Santiago. The book contains three other references to this town. Two of these relate to two peculiar customs associated with the pilgrimage. This is the first one:

> After this comes Triacastela, on the foot of the same hill
> [Cebreiro] on its Galician slope. Here, pilgrims pick up a
> stone and take it with them to Castañeda, where they use it
> to obtain lime for the building work of the Apostle's basilica.

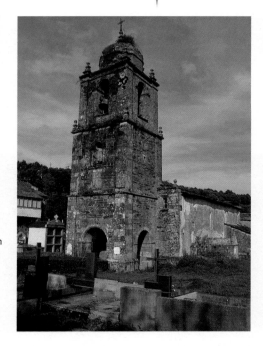

Triacastela. Tower of the parish church devoted to St James.

As we can see from this report from approximately the year 1130, the pilgrims' devotion to St James made them go as far as carrying heavy materials for the stonework of the great Romanesque cathedral of Santiago de Compostela, which at the time was still in progress. The quarry tradition of Triacastela, where some basic cement materials are extracted, is still alive to this day.

The pilgrims' sometimes disproportionate devotion must have been seen with some irony by those with a more material vision of life. The latter group must have included some of Santiago's innkeepers, whose behaviour is censured in a sermon in the first part of *Liber Sancti Iacobi*. According to this, in order to stay one step ahead of the strong competition in Santiago, they went all the way to Triacastela, 120 km away from Santiago, in a cunning early marketing technique. When they got there, they pretended to meet the pilgrims who were likely to reach Santiago within the next few days quite by chance, and then recommended their own house as accommodation during their stay there. They committed the naïve pilgrims by giving them a garment (such as a belt, key, ring or hat), and gained their trust by promising good board and lodging as well as other benefits. Once they reached Santiago, this trust turned into abuse, which materialised as extortionate prices for very low quality accommodation, food and other services.

From these two references in *Liber Sancti Iacobi,* we understand that Triacastela received many pilgrims and was a very important meeting point. From this we can deduce that there were several hospitable institutions, one of which would have been associated with the parish church, which was dedicated to the apostle St James. There is another institution which shows a slightly peculiar aspect of pilgrimage assistance: it is a prison for pilgrims, or rather for people who pretended to be pilgrims at a time when pilgrimage became almost a way of begging. On the walls of this hospital / prison you can still see the "graffitis" left by the troublesome travellers.

26 Triacastela – Sarria

*Of the two alternatives, the San Xil route offers scenery which
will uplift you and encourage you on your way. It has many
"corredoiras", with paved ways which go through leafy
oakwoods, so typical of Galicia. If you wish to visit Samos you
will need to pass through the narrow valley of the river Ouribio.*

"Corredoira" (stone pathway) from the monastery of samos to Sarria.

On leaving **Triacastela** there are two options to choose from:

A) On the right you can take the route to San Xil, proceeding along a
path beside the Valdoscuro stream, passing various kinds of riverside
plants, chestnut trees and common oaks. On arrival at **Balsa** the route
begins to climb. A fountain of St James can be reached by a surfaced
track and **San Xil** is to the left. Continue along the same track, climbing
up to the Alto de Riocabo. Once at the top, you take a "corredoira" to
the right, along which you make a gentle descent until you join a track
which leads into **Montán.** A few more metres will take you into
Fontearcuda, from where you continue down along *corredoiras* until
you cross a stream over a paved footbridge. The road takes you into the
municipality of Sarria and you reach **Pintín** (with Sarria visible ahead).
Further on, at km 117.5, the road reaches **Calvor,** where both routes
come together to continue onwards to Sarria.

B) If you wish to visit the monastery at Samos, you will need to go in the
direction of the road and follow it along the course of the river Ouribio,
through a valley wedged between mountains, passing through common
oaks, birch trees, broom and other plants typical of the riverbank, as
well as the odd chestnut tree. Less than 3 km on from the bridge, you
cross to the right of the road to go down a surfaced track to **San Cristobo
do Real.** You cross the river there and pass the cemetery to leave by a
path lined with chestnut trees and common oaks. You cross the water
several times as you pass through **Renche, Lastres** and **Freituxe.**

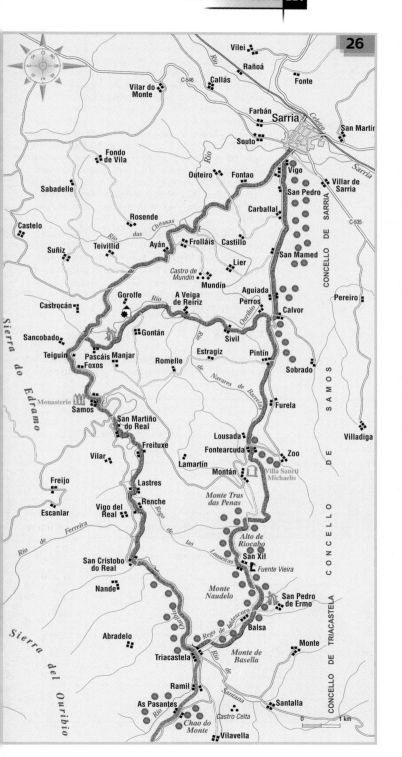

Then leaving **San Martiño do Real** on the right, you cross road LU-643 to go down a path to **Samos.** After visiting its monastery, proceed in the direction of the Ouribio riverside park and continue alongside the road, on a gravel path which is ideal for pilgrims, equipped with benches and lined with small trees. It has frequent rest areas. Foxos, Ferreira, Teiguín and Sancobade are all passed by. A road appears on the left-hand side which goes up to **Pascáis.** You now have to make another decision as to whether to continue alongside the road leading to Sarria, or whether to veer off along *corredoiras* through tiny hamlets **(Gorolfe, A Veiga de Reiriz, Sivil** and **Perros)** until you join the San Xil route at Calvor.

Out of **Calvor,** leaving the hostel at km 116.5, you walk along the route which passes through **Aguiada, San Mamede, San Pedro do Camiño** and **Vigo** before reaching **Sarria.** You then cross the bridge over the river Ouribio and via the Rúa do Peregrino and a flight of steps you come to the Rúa Mayor, the main street.

CYCLISTS

Cyclist should take the **Samos** route, and keeping to the LU-643 at all times is the most feasible route.

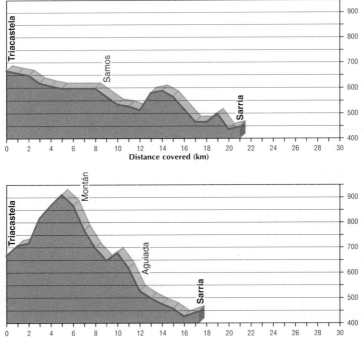

STAGE 26. PRACTICAL INFORMATION

SAMOS

HOSTELS

"Casa de Madera" hostel.
C/ Salvador, 16. Next to El Ciprés
chapel. It has 18 beds, a kitchen,
washing machine and library. Open all
year round.
℘ 982 546 189 / 653 824 546
"Monasterio de Samos" hostel.
The Benedictine monastery takes in
pilgrims. ℘ 982 546 046

HOTELS

HR* A Veiga. Estrada Sarria-Pedrafita.
℘ 982 546 052. 15 rooms.
Double room: € 30/24.
HSR* Victoria. Rúa Salvador, 3.
℘ 982 546 022. 4 rooms.
Double room: € 34/22.

RESTAURANTS

Hotel A Veiga. Ctra. Sarria-Pedrafita.
℘ 982 546 052
Paredes. C/ Paredes de Lóuzara, 1.
℘ 982 546 167
Pontenova. Ctra. de Pontevedra.
℘ 982 546 003
Resco. Avda. del Generalísimo, 34.
℘ 982 546 040
Victoria. C/ Salvador, 4.
℘ 982 546 022

CALVOR

HOSTELS

Municipal Hostel (Albergue Municipal).
Located in the old schools. 22 beds.

SARRIA

HOSTELS

Municipal Hostel (Albergue Municipal).
This is located in a beautiful adapted
large house on Rúa Maior. It has 40
beds. ℘ 686 744 047

HOTELS

H** Villa de Sarria.
C/ Benigno Quiroga, 49.
℘ 982 533 873. 23 rooms. Double
room: € 78/66; breakfast: € 4,8.
H* Roma.
C/ Calvo Sotelo, 2. ℘ 982 532 211.
18 rooms. Double room: € 37;
single room: € 26.
HS** Londres.
C/ Calvo Sotelo, 153. ℘ 982 532 456.
20 rooms.
HSR* As Rodas.
A Valiña. ℘ 982 546 749. 4 rooms.

RESTAURANTS

Estación de Autobuses.
C/ Lama de Gándara. ℘ 982 532 620
Litmar. C/ Calvo Sotelo, 141-143.
℘ 982 530 046
Londres.
C/ Calvo Sotelo, 153. ℘ 982 530 891
Mar de Plata. C/ Gran Via de Alfonso
IX, 29. ℘ 982 533 059
Mesón Camiño Francés.
C/ Mayor. ℘ 982 532 351
Mesón da Sardiña.
Estrada. Monforte. ℘ 982 546 636
Mesón O Tapeo.
C/ Calvo Sotelo. ℘ 982 534 040
O Camiño.
C/ Calvo Sotelo, 211. ℘ 982 532 612
Ponte Ribeira.
Rúa do Peregrino, 29. ℘ 982 530 005
Roma.
C/ Calvo Sotelo, 2. ℘ 982 530 570

MEANS OF TRANSPORT

In Sarria:
Bus station on Rúa Matías López.
℘ 982 531 901.
RENFE rail station on Rúa Estación.
℘ 982 530 787.

History and wealth of the Stage 26

The French Road. Triacastela – Sarria

There are two possible routes from Triacastela to Sarria: the straight one known as "Camino de San Gil" (A), and an alternative caused by the presence of an ancient institution, the monastery of Samos (B).

A) The first route, known as "Camino de San Gil", takes its name from **San Xil,** the first town after Triacastela. The cult of St Giles, a VIIth century Greek hermit established in Provence, became one of the most prestigious ones in the French world. Via Tolosana, one of the four French roads to Santiago, was also known as Via Egidiana because it included the abbey of San Gil *(Aegidius > Gil)* in its route. Although this worship is very old, its presence is thought to be related to the pilgrimage.

It has recently been discovered that the author of *Liber Sancti Iacobi* followed the first route going through several of its hamlets, and did not visit the great abbey of Samos, which would have involved a small detour. The reason we can be so certain of this is that one of the few place names mentioned in the guide which were yet to be identified has recently been identified as **Montán:** this is the mysterious *Villa Sancti Michaelis,* which the book mentions as a Stop of the Road between Triacastela and Barbadelo. The key to this discovery was in the reports of other pilgrims, such as Arnold von Harff (XVth century), who referred to *Sent Michel de la Costa* (the Galician word "costa" means "slope" or "mountain") between Triacastela and Aguiada, and an anonymous Italian pilgrim from the same time, who mentioned that pilgrims could find accommodation in *San Michele,* between San Xil and Furela, a mountain (cf. Montán). If you look in a map, you will see that the only place between San Xil and Furela – a very small area – is Montán.

General view of the monastery of Samos.

Gothic cloister in the monastery of Samos.

Even if these foreign pilgrims' reports were not enough, a document from 1068 from the nearby monastery of Samos says the following:

> *loco sancto isto Sancti Michaelis et Sancti Andree, quorum reliquie ibidem sunt recondite in villa vocabulo Montan*

> *(the sanctuary of San Miguel and San Andrés, whose relics are hidden in the village known as Montán)*

The existence of this sanctuary, which housed relics of saints of the calibre of the apostle St Andrew and St Michael the Archangel (probably brought from southern Spain after the Arabs' arrival) deserved a visit and some publicity, like that provided by *Liber Sancti Iacobi*. Between the XVIth and XVIIth centuries, however, the memory of these valuable relics was lost, the old monastery was reduced to a simple parish church, and the old name of San Miguel was changed to Santa María, which is the Romanesque-style church which we can see today.

As we mentioned above, shortly after Montán we reach **Furela,** referred to by the XVth century Italian pilgrim as *Finella*. After this we find **Pintín** and **Calvor,** whose parish church of San Esteban still retains some original elements of its early stonework. We know that it was founded in the VIIIth century in St Paul's and St Stephen's honour by a priest called Adilán and a few monks from the nearby monastery of Samos. Its remarkable baptismal font comes from a Romanesque capital which may have been part of the church. According to unconfirmed oral tradition, the last house towards Sarria may have been a pilgrims' hospital. There are also records of an old hospital in **Aguiada,** and the names of **San Mamed do Camiño** and **San Pedro do Camiño** tell us of a link to the Road ("Camiño" meaning "path" or "road"). Just before Sarria at the end of this stage is Vigo de Sarria. As its own name suggests *(vicus,* "village"), it was originally a town which depended on Sarria.

B) At the bottom of a deep steep valley between mountains on the other route, we find the great **monastery of Los Santos Julián y Basilisa de**

Pilgrim at Sarria entrance.

Samos, one of the oldest monasteries in Spain. It was founded in the VIth century by St Martin of Braga, who was also responsible for the Suevans' conversion to Catholicism. The unusual dedication to spouses Julián and Basilisa, two martyrs from the Egyptian city of Antinoe in Diocletian's time, is another sign of its age, since the popularity of their acts of martyrdom, a genuine ode to virginity even within wedlock, is related to the intensive monastic movement which took place in Spain in Visigothic times. The decision to dedicate the church to the chaste spouses may have been related, not only to the fact that the monastery had some relics, but also to it being a mixed-sex monastery, although the latter reason is no more than an assumption. An inscription from the VIIth century informing us that monastic observance was restored by Ermefredo, the bishop of Lugo, suggests that the worship may have been interrupted for a few years.

The relationship between Samos and the pilgrimage must have been quite strong, since the monastery is very close to the Road and Benedictines are famous for their hospitality. However, there aren't many documents to confirm this. What we do know, on the other hand, is that hospitality was offered here at later dates (XVIth-XVIIIth centuries).

Few mediaeval remains of the impressive monastic complex, which takes up over a hectare, are left, although the ones we have, such as the Mozarabic chapel of El Salvador or El Ciprés (dating from the IXth – Xth centuries), are really beautiful. Most of what is left in Samos is from Renaissance, Baroque or Neoclassical times. The church's enormous façade, for example, has images of the two saints to whom it is dedicated, together with one of St Benedict. The remarkably large church has a rectangular layout and dates from Neoclassical times. Of particular note within this collection of buildings is the XVIth century cloister of *Las Nereidas,* which provides direct access to the refectory and the library. The larger and more modern XVIIth century cloister of Feijoo is dedicated to the famous Benedictine writer Benito Jerónimo Feijoo y Montenegro (1676-1764), one of the most lucid minds in Spain in the disastrous late XVIIth and early XVIIIth centuries. The learned writings of Feijoo, who took his vows in Samos in 1688 and kept a close link to the monastery thereafter, are still remarkable for his intelligent and unprejudiced criticism and analysis of the possible causes and solutions to Spain's difficult situation.

Even the name **Sarria** provides a hint as to the age of this town, in which pre-Roman remains have been found. Its enviable location on a hilltop with a river on either side has given rise to the assumption that it has always been inhabited, although there is no documentary proof, and only very limited archeological proof of this. According to some documents of dubious antiquity, Sarria was populated by the mythical repopulator of the province of Lugo, bishop Odoario. What we do know for certain is that Alfonso IX re-founded and populated it around the year 1200 under the name *Villanova de Sarria*.

The whole of the pilgrims' journey across the village, on the foot of Cerro del Castillo, is uphill. Pilgrims would first reach the Romanesque church of Santa Marina, which has now been replaced with a modern church. The fact that the church was dedicated to this martyr saint from Antioque, whose relics were in circulation in early mediaeval Spain, is a sign of its antiquity.

Further on is the also Romanesque and very well preserved parish church of San Salvador, which is mentioned in XIth century documents, and which provides a good example of typical rural Romanesque art in Galicia. Its two front doors contain some sculptures and are slightly more modern, from the XIVth century. A nearby building is said by oral tradition to have been the hospital of San Antonio. If this is the case, it may be taken as evidence that the Order of San Antonio Abad, whose presence was so strong in the Castilian part of the Road, was also present in Galicia. The ruins of the castle, which was almost completely destroyed during the popular revolts known as "guerras dos irmandiños", in the XVth century, can be seen at the top of the hill.

The convent of La Magdalena, now run by a community of Mercedarians, is also close by. Its slightly hazy origin seems to revert to an old chapel of San Blas next to which an Italian congregation, which must subsequently have been replaced by the Knights of St John, settled. The mostly Plateresque current building still retains some of the old building's Gothic elements.

Sarria. Church of the convent of La Magdalena.

27 Sarria – Portomarín

Over the "Meseta lucense", the Lugo Plateau, you will pass through many hamlets dotted along areas of cultivated land, grazing pastures and woodlands, in the direction of the great river Miño.

Ponte Áspera.

You leave the Rúa Mayor towards the Convento de la Magdalena (Convent of Mary Magdalene) and from there walk down past the cemetery. Once you reach the road which runs between Monforte de Lemos and Lugo, follow it until you turn off to the left and cross the river Celeiro over the "Ponte Áspera" bridge. Follow alongside the river for a few metres. Cross the railway track (Sancti Michaelis) and then a stream shortly afterwards. Turn to the right and follow the course of the stream, steering away from the track. Climb up through ancient oaks, birch trees and chestnut trees until you reach the hamlet of **Vilei** which is next to **Barbadelo,** with its church of St James. Turn off to the right at km 100.5 to **Rente** and carry on by surfaced track to **Mercado da Serra.** Cross a track and the road which runs between Sarria and Portamarín, to come to **Mouzós** and on to **Xisto, Domiz** and **Peruscallo.** A little further along you reach **Cortiñas** and **Lavandeira,** from where you leave by a surfaced track. Cross the Cheto stream to reach **Brea** and continue along mount Mogarde to reach **Mogarde** itself at km 100. Once more start along a "corredoira", which crosses the Ferreiras stream and climbs up to Ferreiros, at which point you will be very near to the hamlets of **Mirallos** and **Pena.** Continue along the surfaced track towards **Couto** and **Rozas.** Take the right-hand path at km 96.5, which leads you through a pine grove and oak trees to the *Pena do*

27

Lombao

San Roque

San Martín

CONCELLO DE PORTOMARÍN

Portomarín

EMBALSE DE BELESAR

Torre

Vilachá

RÍO

Higón

Cortes

Loio

San Vicente

Castro

Monasterio de Sta. María de Loio

Tellada

Parrocha

Navallos

MIÑO

Santa Cristina

Suar

C-535

DE

PARADELA

Mercadoiro

Moutras

Vilar

Arroyo

Pacios

Loio

Francos

Moimentos

Grallas

Miral
los

Peña do Cervo

Castrelo

Villaragunte

Rozas

Couto

Guisande

CONCELLO

Adai

Vilar

Arroyo

Pena

Mirallos

Bocelo

Ferreiros

Friolfe

San Pedro

Brea

Mogarde

Monte Mogarde

de

Atelo

Cabana

Río

Rego

DE

Sierra del Páramo

Biville

Lavandeira

Cortiñas

Rego

de

Carna

SARRIA

Páramo 881

San Andrés

Iglesia románica de Sta. María de Velante

Peruscallo

Leimán

Baxán

Domiz

Xisto

C-535

Escarlán

Mercado

Mouzós

Outeiro

CONCELLO

DE

Rente

Barbadelo

Iglesia de Santiago

Rosende

Vilei

Río

de

Rañoá

Fonte

Argemil

Sanfiz

Callás

C-546

Rego

de

Vilar do Monte

Ponte Aspera

Farbán

San Martín

C-546

Vilar

Souto

Colmeiro

Sarria

Sarria

0   1 km

Outeiro

Fontao

Vigo

Villar de Sarria

Río

Bridge over Belesar reservoir.

Cervo. From there you go down to **Moimentos.** First by road, and then by path, you reach **Mercadoiro,** and then Moutras (river Bocelo) by surfaced road. This part of the walk is full of pine groves. The road leads out into another and you take the road towards Tellada, and then veer off to the right onto a path leading to **Parrocha.** Leave here by surfaced road, and then turn off to the right onto a path which leads to **Vilachá** after crossing the road. You are now in the vicinity of **Portomarín** and need to make your way to the bridge over the river Miño, on the banks of which you will see the remains of the old site of the village. Once in the village, climb up some steps or up the avenida de Sarria, to reach the carretera de Sarria (the Sarria road).

CYCLISTS

The stretches along the *corredoiras* can be dangerous when muddy. The alternatives would be either to take the various local tracks linking the hamlets, or to go round on the C-535 which leads directly to **Portomarín.**

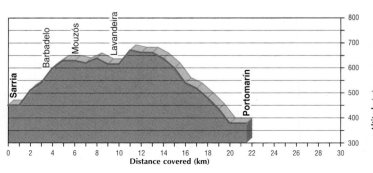

STAGE 27. PRACTICAL INFORMATION

BARBADELO

HOSTELS

Municipal Hostel (Albergue Municipal).
Ctra. Sarria-Lugo. It has 18 beds and a
kitchen. Open all year round.
∅ 660 396 814

RESTAURANTS

Casa Nova de Rente. Between
Barbadelo and Rente. ∅ 982 187 854

FERREIROS

HOSTELS

Municipal Hostel (Albergue Municipal).
The old schools have been adapted to
form this hostel. ∅ 982 549 894

RESTAURANTS

Mesón Casa Cruceiro. Ferreiros (Lugo).
∅ 982 541 240
O Mirallos. Ferreiros (Lugo).

PORTOMARÍN

HOSTELS

Municipal Hostel (Albergue Municipal).
It has 100 beds (40 in one building and
another 60 in a second one, which opens
in the summer only). On pl. dos Condes
de Fenosa, behind the church of San
Nicolás. ∅ 982 545 143

HOTELS

H* Villajardín.
Rúa do Miño, 14. ∅ 982 545 252.
36 rooms.

RESTAURANTS

Casa Ferreiro. Rúa do Progreso.
∅ 982 545 017
Casa Pérez. Praza Aviación Española.
∅ 982 545 040
El Labrador. Rúa Hospital, 2.
∅ 982 545 303
Mesón de Rodríguez.
C/ Fraga Iribarne, 6. ∅ 982 545 054
Pousada del Camino. Rúa de Lugo, 1.
∅ 982 545 007

MEANS OF TRANSPORT

Portomarín bus company.
∅ 982 530 132.
Lugo bus station.
∅ 982 223 985.

SERVICES

There is almost nothing before reaching
Portomarín but, once you get there, you
can buy anything you need.

HISTORY AND WEALTH OF THE STAGE 27

THE FRENCH ROAD. SARRIA – PORTOMARÍN

You leave Sarria via the district of St Lazarus (San Lázaro), outside the old city walls. Thanks to the district's name and the existence of a chapel dedicated to St Lazarus, we know that there used to be a lepers' hospital *(lazareto)* here. This is confirmed by documents from the XVth century.

Once you reach the Celeiro valley, you cross the river by means of a small one-span Romanesque bridge known as *Ponte Áspera*. Until recently, *Villa Sancti Michaelis,* which is mentioned in the *Liber Sancti Iacobi* guidebook, was thought to be here but, as we saw in the

Church of Santiago in Barbadelo.

previous stage (26), the place has now been identified as Montán.

After **Vilei,** you reach the parish church of **Santiago de Barbadelo,** which is the first stop after *Villa Sancti Michaelis* in *Liber Sancti Iacobi.* A mixed-sex Romanesque monastery which depended on Samos since the year 874 is said to have been here. This is confirmed by documents from Samos and even by the name of the district around the church of Santiago: Mosteiro (from Latin *monasterium*).

The current XIIth century church has some of the typical Romanesque features of this area, including a square tower with three sections, a single nave and the use of granite as the main building material. In spite of having been partly rebuilt, it is one of the best examples of its genre and style in the province of Lugo's stretch of the Road. The depiction, on the tympanum, of a tunic-covered person facing visitors with its arms spread out is a particularly striking part of the main portal´s already remarkable decoration.

The guide is not the only part of *Liber Sancti Iacobi* which mentions Barbadelo. Sermon no. 17 of part 1, for example, which aims to change the practices of all those (such as money changers, sellers, swindlers, prostitutes, rogues, fake cripples and innkeepers) who abused the pilgrims' defencelessness with their trickery, is vividly set in a picturesque scene in Barbadelo. It even includes a parody of the speeches with which innkeepers used to trick XIIth century pilgrims. Just imagine the scene: a group of rather absent-minded-looking pilgrims near the monastery of Santiago's pilgrims' hospital in

"Corredoira" (a stone pathway) in the outskirts of Brea.

Barbadelo. An affable and pleasant individual greets them, asks them about their pilgrimage and provides some local information, possibly with the help of a few glasses of wine, only to spring this on them:

> *"My brothers who are heading for Santiago de Compostela, I am a wealthy citizen of that place. I have not come to Barbadelo to find guests but to speak to a brother of mine who lives here. However, if you do want to stay in high quality accommodation in Santiago, stay at my house and tell my wife and family to treat you well for the sake of their love for me. I shall give you a garment for you to show them."*

He would then give them an item of personal property, thereby completely gaining the trust of the poor gullible travellers, who would turn up in Santiago thinking they were going to be treated like kings, only to be charged twice as much as usual for everything, including the candles which were essential for the festival of St James.

After Barbadelo, the Road goes through places such as Rente, Mercado and Mouzós. The *Liber Sancti Iacobi* guidebook does not mention any other places between Barbadelo and the end of this stage. Neither did later reports by pilgrims grant the almost continuous string of hamlets between here and Portomarín the honour of naming them. They are, admittedly, difficult to tell apart, since they are all very similar and blend into the dull landscape of meadows, "carballeiras" (oakwoods) and very small hamlets dominated by the grey granite which is typical of this region. Even their names are a sign of their modesty: for example, **Xisto** means "slate" in Galician and probably relates to a building or vein made of this material; **Domiz, Leimán** and **Peruscallo** are probably people's names; **Cortiñas** means small properties for ploughing; and **Lavandeira** is a place for washing clothes. Near these places, away from the straight Road, is the Romanesque church of Santa María de Belante. The name **Casal** refers to a small group of houses, while **Brea** (which will come up a few times during the Galician part of the journey) is a reference to the route itself, since it is a Galician word meaning "path" or "lane" (the equivalent of the Spanish "vereda").

Portomarín. Pilgrims in the main square (Plaza Mayor).

Once in the area of Paradela, you reach the town of **Ferreiros,** which takes its name from blacksmiths, a profession as necessary on old roads as petrol stations and garages are on modern ones, since smiths were the ones who repaired horse shoes and the metal reinforcements on pilgrims' shoes. Another territory belonging to the Order of St John, which was as important here as the Templars were in León, used to be here.

In **Mirallos** you will find the Romanesque church of Santa María de Ferreiros. The next towns are **Pena, Couto, Rozas** and **Moimentos.** The last of these names is a reference to an old monument. The long list of almost adjoining towns concludes with **Mercadoiro, Moutras, Parrocha** (parish) and **Vilacha** (which, as its name indicates, is a village on the plain). To the left, slightly away from the route, are the ruins of the old **monastery of Santa María de Loyo,** which was the original building of the Order of St James. It was donated to its founders in 1181 by King Fernando II of León, and it was here that the order's first rules were written.

If you stand on the modern bridge which crosses the wide and fast-flowing river Miño during a drought, you will be able to see the remains of old **Portomarín,** which are usually flooded by the modern Belesar reservoir. New Portomarín was built anew on a hill on the right bank of the Miño, and was inaugurated in 1962. The original town's most important monuments, which were moved stone by stone, can now be seen here.

Portomarín has a long history, since it was an important river Miño crossing since Roman times. The first part of its name, "porto-", means "river crossing" (among several possible meanings) in Galician. The second part, "-marín", relates to the presence, since the early Middle Ages, of a sanctuary dedicated to St Marina. The masculine ending ("marín" instead of "marina") is due to the fact that St Marina took her vows in a monks' monastery and was called "Marino" by everyone. Even her biographies and the reports of her martyrdom refer to her in the masculine form.

The *Liber Sancti Iacobi* guide, where Portomarín has a particular significance, always refers to the town as *Pons Minee*, "Bridge of the river Miño". This is due to the fame acquired by the building of another bridge, approximately in the year 1120, to replace the one which had been destroyed in the wars of doña Urraca and her husband Alfonso I of Aragon. It was built by one Pedro Peregrino, who is mentioned among seven other people as a mender of the Road to Santiago between Rabanal and Portomarín. The special presence of two great military orders – St John and the Templars – in this stretch of the Road has already been mentioned, as has the possibility that these seven people were associated with them. It seems that Pedro's link with the Order of St John can be proved, since the hospital he himself built at the head of the bridge (which was called *Domus Dei),* depended on the territory of the Order of St John which had settled in Portomarín. The old church of Santa Marina was also given to Pedro and, later, to the Knights of St John too. This church may – after a change of name – have become the church of San Nicolás which can still be seen in new Portomarín. It is a fortress church with towers and battlements, very typical of

Portomarín. Above, church of San Nicolás; below, steps and chapel of Las Nieves.

military orders. It was built in the XIIth century and has a rectangular layout, a single nave and a semicircular apse. Of particular note among its ornamental elements are the sculptures on its portals and the great rose window on the main façade.

Other monuments which have interestingly been moved from old to new Portomarín include: part of the old bridge, one of whose arches was used to build the chapel of Las Nieves; and the portal of the old church of San Pedro, which was on the left bank of the Miño, just like the Templars' territory in Portomarín, and which may have been associated with this order.

28   Portomarín – Palas de Rei

*Leave the modern town of Portomarín to continue through
an open and fairly humanized landscape, with a number of
pine groves, and also eucalyptus trees near Palas. On
crossing the sierra de Ligonde, on the Dorsal Gallega (the
Galician Ridge), separating the river Miño and the Ulla
stream, you enter the farming region of Ulloa.*

*Pilgrims leaving Portomarín via the bridge
over Belesar reservoir towards Gonzar.*

Walk down from **Portomarín,** once more towards the river Miño and
take a path off road C-135 to cross a footbridge over the Belesar dam.
Follow the course of the Torres stream along a surfaced track, climbing
up to the monte de San Antonio. Turn off to the left at km 89, onto a
path, continuing the climb through oaks, chestnut trees and pines. The
road passes nearby and you return to it after passing the turn-off to San
Mamed and walking parallel to the road until km 87. After this cross
over to the right (by a ceramics factory and a farm). There are pine
groves on either side of the road. Further on return to the left-hand
side, when you are level with a farm, and continue past cornfields and
pine trees, to arrive at **Toxibo.** Leave by the road for a few metres and
then turn off at km 83.5, through birch trees and oaks, as well as the
pine grove and cornfields. After a rest area with a fountain, you come
to **Gonzar,** which has a hostel located on the left of the C-135. From
here you take a left turn along a path and then turn right, where a track
leads you into **Castromaior.** You join the road at km 80 and continue
towards **Hospital da Cruz** which is reached by a path. From there you
climb a surfaced track and cross a footbridge over the N-540. Continue
towards **Ventas de Narón** (there is a rest area and fountain on the way
out). Climb up through pine groves to the sierra de Ligonde and from
there you begin to descend, passing through **Prebisa,** through oak trees
and meadows, **Os Lameiros** (with a cross on the left) and **Ligonde.**

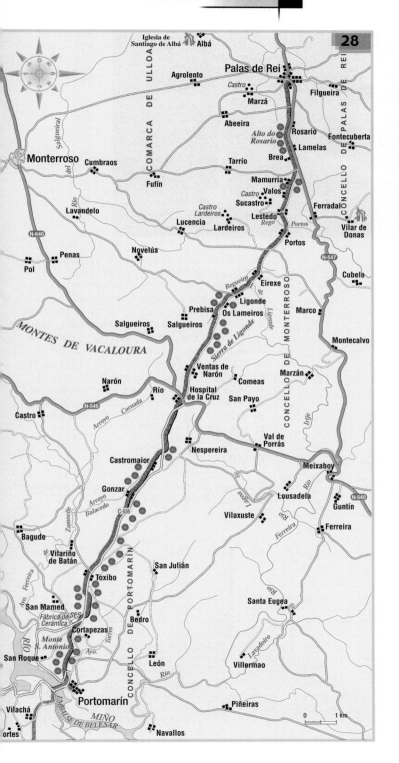

28

Iglesia de
Santiago de Albá   Albá

Agrolento

Palas de Rei

Filgueira

Castro

Marzá

Abeeira

Rosario

Fontecuberta

Alto do Rosario

Lamelas

Monterroso

Cumbraos

Tarrío

Brea

COMARCA DE ULLOA

Fufín

Mamurria

Castro Valos

Sucastro

Ferradal

Lavandelo

Castro Lardeiros

Lucencia   Lardeiros

Lestedo

Rego   *Portos*

Vilar de Donas

N-640

Penas

Novelúa

Portos

CONCELLO DE PALAS DE REI

Pol

Cubelo

Regueiro

Eirexe

Ligonde

Os Lameiros

Marco

Prebisa

MONTES DE VACALOURA

Salgueiros   Salgueiros

Sierra de Ligonde

Montecalvo

Ventas de Narón

Narón

Comeas

Marzán

Río

CONCELLO DE MONTERROSO

N-540

Hospital de la Cruz

San Payo

Arroyo   *Cornada*

Castro

Irije

Val de Porrás

Nespereira

Meixaboy

Castromaior

N-540

Gonzar

Lousadela

Arroyo Balacedo

Guntín

C-535

Vilaxuste

Ferreira

Bagude

Río Ferreira

Vilariño de Batán

Toxibo

San Julián

Santa Eugea

San Mamed

Fábrica de Cerámica

Bedro

Cortapezas

Monte S. Antonio

San Roque

León

Villermao

CONCELLO DE PORTOMARÍN

Portomarín

MIÑO

EMBALSE DE BELESAR

Vilachá

Piñeiras

ortes

Navallos

0   1 km

Pilgrims next to the Cruceiro (stone cross) of Os Lameiros.

Walk down towards the river of the same name, and cross it to then walk up to **Eirexe.** Cross the Monterroso road and descend. After leaving **Portos,** there is a turn-off leading to the beautiful Romanesque church of Vilar de Donas. **Lestedo, Valos** and **Mamurria** are the next hamlets along the route. At this point the first eucalyptus trees come into view. After **Brea,** follow the path which runs parallel to the road through **Lamelas.** Climb the Alto do Rosario and on descent, at km 66.5, you will come to a new rest area, next to the sports facilities and youth camp at **Palas de Rei.** Proceed into the town, towards the church of San Tirso.

CYCLISTS

This stage presents few difficulties, other than the ascent of Monte San Antonio.

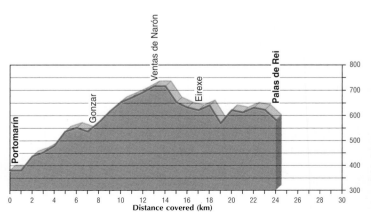

STAGE 28. PRACTICAL INFORMATION

GONZAR

HOSTELS

Municipal Hostel (Albergue Municipal).
Located in the old schools. It has 20
beds, a kitchen and heating. Open all
year round. ✆ 982 157 840

HOSPITAL DA CRUZ (VENTAS DE NARÓN)

HOSTELS

Municipal Hostel (Albergue Municipal).
Old school. It has 22 beds, a kitchen,
heating and a washing machine. Open all
year round. ✆ 982 545 232

LIGONDE

HOSTELS

Municipal Hostel (Albergue Municipal).
C/ Erixe, 14. It has 121 beds, a kitchen
and a living room. Open all year round.
✆ 982 153 483 / 679 190 796

MEANS OF TRANSPORT

Several bus lines go through **Palas de Rei.**

SERVICES

The villages the Road goes through are
very small and usually have no services,
but the influx of pilgrims has caused
some establishments to open: a café/bar
in **Castromaior**, a restaurant in **Hospital**,
café/bars next to **Eirexe** and **Lestedo**
respectively, and a traditional restaurant
in Brea. In **Palas de Rei** you will find
everything you need.

PALAS DE REI

HOSTELS

Municipal Hostel (Albergue Municipal).
A large adapted house is now used as a
shelter for pilgrims. Avda. de Lugo, s/n.
It has 60 beds. Open all year round.
✆ 982 380 090

HOTELS

HS* Vilariño.
Avda. de Compostela, 16. ✆ 982 380 152.
15 rooms. 30 beds. Double room:
€ 34/22; single room: € 22/17;
breakfast: € 3,5; lunch/dinner: € 7.

P* Arcos.
Auzo de Compostela, 6-1°C.
✆ 982 380 399. 4 rooms.

P* Maite.
Avda. de Compostela, 32-2°.
✆ 982 380 051. 6 rooms.

P* Ponterroxán.
Roxán. ✆ 982 380 132. 18 rooms.

RESTAURANTS

Guntina. Travesía do Peregrino, 4.
✆ 982 380 080

Mesón Casa Curro.
Avda. de Ourense, 15. ✆ 982 380 044

O'Portón. Travesía da Feira, 2.

Taberna Nosa Terra.
Estrada Santiago, 25. ✆ 982 380 361

Ultreya. Estrada Santiago-Estación de
Servicio. ✆ 982 380 097

Vilariño.
Avda. Compostela, 16.
✆ 982 380 152

HISTORY AND WEALTH OF THE STAGE 28

THE FRENCH ROAD. PORTOMARÍN – PALAS DE REI

After leaving Portomarín, you reach the hill of San Antonio. The name, the fairly isolated nature of the enclave and its location next to the Road to Santiago suggest that there may have been a hospital run by the Order of St Anthony. However, documents to certify this presumable Antonite presence are lacking both here and in Sarria.

After **Toxibo,** the Road enters **Gonzar,** whose church of Santa María used to belong to a priory which depended on the territory of the Knights of St John in Portomarín.

Castromaior also has a small Romanesque church dedicated to the Virgin. The name of the town, however, is related to the fact that there used to be a pre-Roman settlement here.

Façade of the church of Vilar de Donas.

The name **Hospital da Cruz** comes from an old hospitable institution which was still active in the XVIIIth century but of which no remains are left today. None are left either of the annexed chapel of San Esteban, which is mentioned in some documents. Almost immediately after Hospital is **Ventas de Narón,** whose name also rings of the old hospitality tradition. A church dedicated to the Magdalene in the area surrounding Ventas suggests that an undocumented hospital may have been here.

The *Liber Sancti Iacobi* guide mentions only one Stop between Portomarín and Palas de Rei, the beginning and end of this stage, and gives it the sonorous name of *Sala Regina,* "Sala de la Reina" (the Queen's room). This Sala de la Reina is not mentioned in any other local document or pilgrim's report. Its name suggests that it may be related to a hospitable institution founded by a queen, possibly one of Alfonso VI's wives or his daughter doña Urraca. If this was the case, however, we would probably have an official document of the fact or at least one that mentioned it. With absolutely no information to support this, we suggest that "Sala de la Reina" may have been a secular lodging place, connected to Palas de Rei, which the author decided to publicise for reasons unknown to us. The end of the "business", which can't have lasted too long, would have also been

Church of Vilar de Donas. Left, sepulchres; right, paintings.

the end of the name. If "Sala de la Reina" used to be where Ventas de Narón is today, the latter would also be, judging by its name, a lodging place or hospital.

After **Prebisa,** the Road reaches **Lameiros,** where a chapel dedicated to St Lazarus tells us that there used to be a hospital for infectious patients. In **Ligonde** we find a church dedicated to the apostle St James. The only part of the Romanesque construction to survive is the portal; the rest was replaced in the XVIIIth century. Both the church and the annexed hospital were run by the Order of St James, and we still know where the pilgrims' hospital used to be.

The remains of two settlements – Castro Lardeiros and Castro Simone – can be found close to **Eirexe** (whose name comes from the Latin *ecclesia,* "church") and **Portos.** Both are slightly away from the Road.

In **Lestedo** we find another church dedicated to St James. This may be evidence of the depth with which the military Order of St James had taken root in this area. In the same place but on the right side of the Road is the most valuable artistic monument of this stage: **Vilar de Donas.** Although the time of its foundation is unclear, we do know that it was originally a nuns' convent. This explains its name: "dona" in Galician, just like its Spanish equivalent "dueña", often means "religious woman". From 1184, Vilar de Donas depended on the Order of St James which, although recently created, was already gaining power, at least in the area close to Portomarín. This is when Vilar de Donas became the official burial place of this order's Galician knights.

It is a Romanesque church with a Latin cross layout and a single nave with a semicircular apse flanked by two smaller side apses. The layout of the church, together with the variety and quality of the sculptures outside, tell us that we are no longer under the influence of Cebreiro's Romanesque art and its strong and sober square shapes. Inside the church, however, a scene on the stone reredos on the high altar

El Cebreiro: the scene depicts an officiant raising the holy wafer before a single parishioner who is on his knees. The bleeding Jesus above the altar surrounded by all the symbols of the Passion represents the "physical" transformation of the items which that famous miracle consisted of. The beautiful XVth century Gothic mural paintings on the inside of the church represent an Annunciation. Among the witnesses to the scene are two characters who popular tradition used to call Bela and Elvira and who were thought to be the religious women who founded the church, although it now seems that they are actually a lady and a gentleman, dressed in clothes from the time. Since this church was a mausoleum, the sepulchres and tombstones of several knights of the Order of St James who were buried here are still preserved.

Galician raised granary.

Near **Valos,** on the left side of the Road, are the remains of yet another settlements. A sermon from *Liber Sancti Iacobi* is set somewhere before Palas de Rei, maybe where we now find **Brea** (another "vereda"), **Mamurria** or **Rosario,** or in any of the wild territories left behind. The sermon again uses a vivid scene to illustrate the author's disapproval of those who tried to damage the bodies, souls or pockets of the St James pilgrims. Just like Barbadelo and Triacastela provided the setting for the innkeepers' trickery, the stretch between Portomarín and Palas de Rei was the setting for another picturesque and sinful scene, in relation to which he launched another of his typical anathemas:

> *"The maidservants of the inns on the Road to Santiago who, either for money or for lust, and under the devil's inspiration, are in the habit of getting into the pilgrims' beds at night, are worthy of condemnation. And prostitutes who, for the same reasons, go to meet pilgrims in woody areas between Portomarín and Palas de Rei, should not only be excommunicated, but should also be stripped of all their possessions, have their noses cut off, and be exposed to public ridicule."*

Pilgrims in the outskirts of Avenostre.

Liber Sancti Iacobi mentions **Palas de Rei** several times, and even grants it the honour of considering it the end of the penultimate stage. Due to its sonorous and pretentious name as it appears in *Liber Sancti Iacobi* and some other later documents, *Palatium Regis* (royal palace) it has been thought to have been Visigothic King Witiza's residence as well as episcopal see in Suevan times (Vth century). However, no archeological remains or documents have been found to prove such an old age. The first documentary reference to Palas is in an XIth century forgery which only mentions its church of San Tirso de Ulloa. This suggests that Palas did not yet exist under this name. In addition, the Galician name which would have resulted from the early Visigothic or early mediaeval name *Palatium* would have been "pazo", not "palas". Lastly, most documents which mention this town (and which date from no earlier than the XIIIth century) call it *Palaz,* not *Palatium.* These are the reasons why we believe that Palas originated with this name about the time that the *Liber Sancti Iacobi* guide was written. To explain the name, we have recently suggested that it could be a direct import from the French "palais" ("palace"). The reason for this could be a secular lodging place founded by French people with this bombastic name: "Pala[i]s de Rei" (approximate XIIth century French pronunciation). This name, in contrast with the case of Sala de la Reina, would have become established as San Tirso de Ulloa's new official name. Palas' mediaeval monuments are precisely the Romanesque façade of the church of San Tirso, whose name is older than that of the town, and the also Romanesque façade of a house decorated with scallops. Could this be the old inn called "Palais de Rei", the Royal Palace?

Palas de Rei does not offer much more in terms of monuments. The area falling under the jurisdiction of its "concello" (town hall), however, has up to twenty Romanesque churches (including some mentioned in this stage) as well as famous castles such as Pambre and Felpós, or "pazos" (from Latin *palatium,* meaning "stately house") such as Pazo de Ulloa, made immortal by the writer Emilia Pardo Bazán.

29 Palas de Rei – Ribadiso

You now enter into the province of A Coruña before reaching Leboreiro by its old road. You pass through Melide, the main town in the municipality and the commercial heart of the area. The landscape begins to change, as the native woodlands full of bracken begin to disappear.

Furelos Bridge.

Descend from the church of San Tirso along the Travesía de la Iglesia and the Travesía del Peregrino towards road N-547. Continue along the pavement for around 100 m and take a path to the right which crosses the river Ruxián and rejoins the road at km 64. Soon after you arrive at **Carballal.** Descend along a *corredoira* which passes through **Alagua.** You then reach **San Xulián do Camiño** via a small road and then a path. Walk along a track to **Pallota,** and along a *corredoira* to cross the river Pambre at **Outeiro da Ponte.** Arriving at **Pontecampaña,** you climb a path up to Casanova, at km 60, from where you descend to the lowlands of the river Villar, passing through **Porto de Bois.** After 1 km you come to Campanilla, where you take the road and shortly enter into the province of A Coruña. A paved path takes you on to **Leboreiro.** Cross the river Seco at **Disicabo,** over the Magdalena bridge, and you will reach **Furelos** by walking along a track through a wooded area. In the direction of **Melide,** you cross the bridge over the river Furelos. Entering via the Barrio de San Pedro, and along the main street, calle Principal, you leave Melide by road N-547 which takes you to the Barrio de Santa María, from where you turn off towards San Martiño. Turn to the right at km 50 (there is a cross here), passing the river Lázaro in the direction of **Carballal.** You walk through a woodland of oaks, eucalyptus trees and pines and cross the river Barreiros. Shortly afterwards you come to **Raído** and the Trail then takes you back into the woods. You pass through **Paravispo** and over the Valverde stream, descending into **A Peroxa.** **Boente** is reached by a track, and you then cross the main road, an old road and, through a tunnel, the N-547 to descend to the lowlands of the

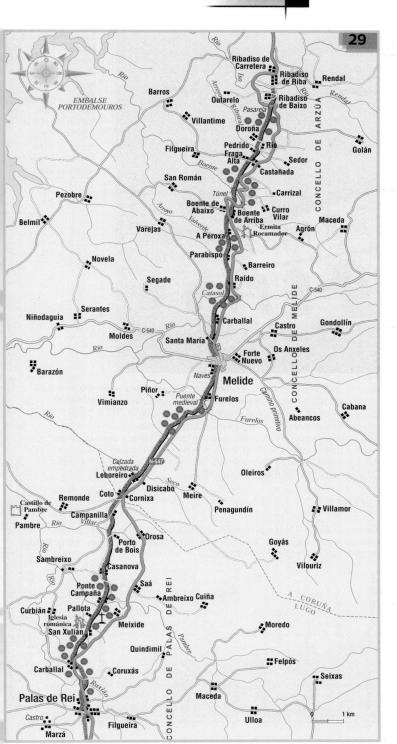

29

EMBALSE
PORTODEMOUROS

CONCELLO DE ARZÚA

CONCELLO DE MELIDE

CONCELLO DE PALAS DE REI

A CORUÑA
LUGO

Ribadiso de
Carretera
Ribadiso
de Riba
Rendal
Ribadiso
de Baixo
Barros
Outarelo
Pasarela
Doroña
Villantime
Golán
Río
Filgueira
Pedrido
Fraga
Alta
Sedor
San Román
Castañada
Túnel
Carrizal
Pezobre
Boente de
Abaixo
Boente
de Arriba
Curro
Vilar
Maceda
Belmil
Varejas
A Peroxa
Ermita
Rocamador
Agrón
Parabispo
Barreiro
Novela
Segade
Raído
Catasol
C-540
Niñodaguia
Serantes
Carballal
Castro
Gondollín
Moldes
C-540
Santa María
Os Anxeles
Barazón
Forte
Nuevo
Naves
Melide
Piñor
Puente
medieval
Furelos
Camino primitivo
Vimianzo
Furelos
Cabana
Abeancos
Río
Calzada
empedrada
N-547
Leboreiro
Oleiros
Remonde
Coto
Disicabo
Meire
Cornixa
Villamor
Castillo de
Pambre
Campanilla
Penagundín
Pambre
Villar
Orosa
Porto
de Bois
Goyás
Sambreixo
Casanova
Vilouriz
Ponte
Campaña
Saá
Curbián
Pallota
Ambreixo Cuiña
Iglesia
románica
San Xulián
Meixide
Moredo
Quindimil
Carballal
Coruxás
Felpós
Palas de Rei
Seixas
Castro
Maceda
1 km
Marzá
Filgueira
Ulloa

Sobrado dos Monxes monastery cloister. In the background, the church. Although it is not on the French Road, it is worth taking a detour of a few kilometers from Melide to see it.

river Boente. From there you climb up to **Castañeda** and continue past some meadows towards **Pedrido.** You descend towards **Río** (km 42), and there you cross the Ribeiral stream. After passing small orchards, meadows and cornfields you reach **Doroña,** from where you climb a hill, through eucalyptus trees, oaks and pines, to descend again and cross a bridge over the drop through which the road runs. As you descend you come to the river Iso, on the banks of which the old pilgrims' hospital of **Ribadiso** awaits you.

CYCLISTS

The route for this stage is quite negotiable for cyclists. If you prefer to ride on a surfaced road, you can take the N-547 on coming out of **Palas de Rei,** leaving it to go into **Ribadiso.**

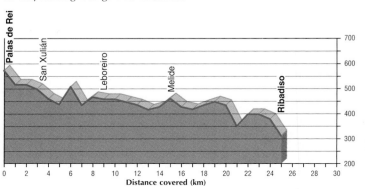

STAGE 29. PRACTICAL INFORMATION

MATO-CASANOVA

HOSTELS

Mato-Casanova hostel.
The old country school is now used as a shelter. It has 20 beds and a kitchen. Open all year round. ✆ 982 173 483

SERVICES

Pontecampaña has a country house, and there is a café/bar in **Furelos, Boente de Riba** and **Ribadiso de Baixo**. Melide has accommodation, restaurants, shops, etc.

LEBOREIRO

HOSTELS

Leboreiro pilgrim shelter (Refugio de peregrinos de Leboreiro).
This does not belong to the Xunta de Galicia hostel network. It has neither beds nor mats. Open all year round. ✆ 981 507 351

RESTAURANTS

Die Zwei Deutsch. O Coto. ✆ 981 507 337

FURELOS

HOSTELS

Pilgrims' Hostel
(Albergue de peregrinos)

MELIDE

HOSTELS

Melide pilgrims' hostel (Albergue de peregrinos de Melide).
C/ San Antonio, s/n. It has 215 beds and a kitchen. Open all year round. ✆ 981 506 266

HOTELS

HS ** Xaneiro II.** Avda. de la Habana, 43-B 1º, 2º y 3º. ✆ 981 506 140.

24 rooms. 48 beds. Double room: € 28/20; breakfast: € 3; lunch/dinner: € 6.

HR* Carlos. Avda. de Lugo, 119. ✆ 981 507 633. 12 rooms. 24 beds. Double room: € 33/27/21; single room: € 15/12/9; breakfast: € 2,5.

RESTAURANTS

Casa Ezequiel.
Avda. de Lugo, 42. ✆ 981 505 291

Coffee Center.
C/ General Franco, 7. ✆ 981 505 114

Continente.
C/ Luis Seoane, 8. ✆ 981 506 182

El Molino.
C/ Rosalía de Castro, 15. ✆ 981 506 048

Liñares.
C/ Alberto de la Fuente, 1. ✆ 981 505 184

Pilmar.
C/ Santa María de Melide. ✆ 981 507 617

Terra de Melide.
Ctra. de Lugo. ✆ 981 506 187

Xaneiro II.
Avda. de la Habana, 43. ✆ 981 506 140

Xoldra.
Avda. de Lugo, 25. ✆ 981 507 906

MEANS OF TRANSPORT

Several bus lines go through **Melide**.

RIBADISO DE BAIXO

HOSTELS

Ribadiso de Baixo Pilgrims' Hostel (Albergue de peregrinos de Ribadiso de Baixo) The old pilgrims' hospital has been adapted, thus recovering its original purpose. This is one of the most beautiful hostels. It has 62 beds, a kitchen, washing machine, a field for tents and room for bicycles. Open all year round. ✆ 981 501 185 / 660 396 823

HISTORY AND WEALTH OF THE STAGE 29

THE FRENCH ROAD. PALAS DE REI – RIBADISO

Just outside Palas, before and after **Carballal** and **Gaiola de Arriba,** the Road crosses two branches of a stream called Ruxián, a river of the **San Xulián do Camiño** parish (Ruxián < *rivu Julian[u],* "río Julián"). One of the twenty Romanesque churches falling under the jurisdiction of Palas de Rei's town council ("concello") is in San Xulián. It is a small church, with a single nave and a large semicircular apse. This San Julián (St Julian) must not be confused with the Egyptian martyr of the same name in the monastery of Samos. This one is St Julian the Hospitaller, a legendary character who, in order to expiate his parents' accidental murder, devoted his life to assisting pilgrims. His devotion got here via the Road to Santiago on the XIth or XIIth century and took root in Galicia. Although no documents supporting this have been found, a hospital associated with the parish church of San Julián may have existed.

In addition to Romanesque churches and settlements, the land under Palas' jurisdiction is full of mediaeval castles, stately fortresses which were not always a good sign for the pilgrims. For example, in the early XIVth century, the area around Palas was quite dangerous for pilgrims: a nobleman called Álvaro Sánchez de Ulloa would attack them from the nearby **castle of Felpós** to demand unjust rights of passage, sometimes even resorting to violence. With the help of some armed people, the illustrious archbishop of Compostela Berenguer de Landora put a stop to this by forcing the surrender of the castle in 1321.

A solid granite bridge over the river Pambre lends its name to **Outeiro da Ponte** and **Pontecampaña,** on either side of the river.

If you go upstream to the south, you reach the **castle of Pambre,** the best among the preserved fortresses not only in Palas but in the whole

View of the exterior of Pambre Castle.

Bridge at the entrance to Leboreiro.

province. Thanks to its solidity, it was able – in contrast to the castle of Sarria among others – to resist the attacks of the "irmandiños", peasants rebelling against the nobility in the XVth century just like the French Caboches and the British Lollards. Also on the left, you will pass **Pazo de Villamayor de Ulloa,** immortalised by Emilia Pardo Bazán's novel *Los pazos de Ulloa* (The House of Ulloa). From the pilgrims' point of view the Ulloas, the lords of the region, were successively tax collectors and benefactors. So, for example, don Álvaro Sánchez's (Lord of Felpós) abuses were later rectified by other members of the Ulloa family, who built and maintained pilgrims' hospitals in Leboreiro and Melide (on this stage of the Road).

The name **Porto de Bois** may be related to a ford over the river Villar on which oxen used to cross. In the XIVth century a battle took place here as part of the civil wars between Peter I *the Cruel's* supporters and those of his step-brother Henry of Trastámara, and was won by the latter.

The frontier between the provinces of Lugo and La Coruña is between **Coto** and **Cornixa.** A few hundred meters on a preserved (although renovated) stretch of the old mediaeval road will take you to **Leboreiro,** another Stop of the Road mentioned in the *Liber Sancti Iacobi* guide. The name used by that work to refer to it, *Campus Levurarius,* refers to the "gándara", i.e. a piece of uncultivated land, rich in hares, on which the burg of Leboreiro, a town born on and for the Road to Santiago, was built. Its parish church of Santa María is a small Romanesque church with a single nave and a semicircular apse. The saint to whom the church is dedicated is depicted, surrounded by angels, on a slightly coarse relief sculpted on the tympanum of the main portal. Opposite this is the old pilgrims' hospital; one of the ones founded by the Ulloa family. Proving this relationship are the powerful family's arms sculpted on two of the hospital's façades.

In nearby **Disicabo,** the Road crosses the river Seco by means of the small one-span Romanesque bridge of La Magdalena. An old pilgrims' hospital, also known as La Magdalena, used to be on the "gándara" (plain devoid of trees, uncultivated land) on the other side. On the journey to **Furelos,** a few sections of the old road lead to a beautiful four-span mediaeval bridge known as "Ponte Velha" ("Old Bridge") at the town entrance. A few meters away, next to the church of San Juan, is the building known as "casa do hospital", which was the town's pilgrims' hospital.

In spite of not being mentioned in *Liber Sancti Iacobi,* **Melide** was an important Stop of the Road to Santiago, as we can see from its two Romanesque churches as well as other monuments and references. Its name comes from *Mellitus* or Melito, which was the name of the first Visigothic or early mediaeval owner and which shows its modest origin. The pilgrimages, together with its privileged position on the Road, undoubtedly contributed to Melide's subsequent importance: this is where pilgrims who had avoided El Cebreiro by making a detour to Lugo – such as Künig von Vach in the XVth century – and the many pilgrims who, on reaching León, had decided to visit San Salvador in Oviedo, returned to the French Road. This explains the number and quality of Melide's hospitals, although the fact that the town belonged to the church of Compostela was another contributing factor. The church of San Pedro, which had a pilgrims' hospital which depended on it, was a Romanesque building with a single nave and a rectangular apse. It used to be at the city entrance but has now been moved to Campo de San Roque.

The monastery / hospital of Sancti Spiritus was later (in the XIVth century) erected on the spot where the French Road and the route from Lugo and Oviedo used to meet. It was founded by the knights of the Third Order, a congregation comprised of secular people who wished to follow St Francis' rules without withdrawing from the world and who naturally had very close links with the Franciscan Order. In the XVIth century Sancti Spiritus became the most important building of this order in Galicia, as well as a burial place for its members. It was completely rebuilt at the Ulloas' expense at the end of the XVth century, and the stones from the town's castle were used as building material. The inside is decorated with mural paintings, among which is one of St James the "Moor Killer" ("Matamoros"). This may be a sign of the knightly character of the members of the Third Order who founded the hospital. Pilgrims Arnold von Harff and Künig von Vach, both from the late XVth century, referred to Melide with a strange name: one of them called it *Villa rumpeta* (broken village), and the other called it *Zuobrochen stat* (destroyed city). These designations may be related to the fact that the castle was demolished to build the great Sancti Spiritus church. Two centuries later, when Italian pilgrim Domenico Laffi praised Melide's beauty, he placed particular emphasis on the Descalzos convent, ie the Sancti Spiritus building.

On the way out of the city is the Romanesque church of Santa María, which also had its own associated pilgrims' hospital. Outside the city, we know from the name of the river Lázaro that there used to be a lepers' hospital here, on the usual place for such institutions: outside the city walls, and generally on the exit that was closest to Santiago.

In the vicinity of **A Peroxa** is the chapel of Rocamador. This form of worship entered Spain strongly in the late XIIth century, imported by pilgrims from the French Midi and favoured by monarchs.

The fact that **Boente** is mentioned in *Liber Sancti Iacobi* suggests that it was a Stop of some importance on the Road. The name of its fairly old (the guide already refers to the town as *Sanctus Iacobus de Boento)*

Melide. Romanesque church of Santa María.

church is another sign of its importance. Inside the church is a strange image of St James, in that he is not represented as a "pilgrim" or as a "knight", but as a Majesty, that is, on a throne (just like in Santiago Cathedral).

Castañeda must have had some ovens in which to convert the stones from Cebreiro into lime, so they could be used to build Santiago Cathedral. As we saw in Triacastela, the pilgrims of that time had the pious custom of contributing to the building by bringing stones, which they carried for the full ninety kilometres between Triacastela and Castañeda.

On the bank of the river Iso is the town of **Ribadiso,** which had several pilgrims' hospitals. The most important of these was "Hospital de San Antón da Ponte de Ribadiso", which was founded by the Antonites in the XVth century and located at the beginning of a beautiful one-span bridge. Its management changed several times until it stopped operating during last century.

30 Ribadiso – Arca do Pino

On leaving Calzada you enter the municipality of O Pino, passing along a part of the Trail which constantly intertwines with the road.

Ribadiso Hospital.

You leave the bank of the river Iso and, passing **Ribadiso de Baixo** and **Ribadiso de Riba,** you go through a tunnel underneath road N-547, and come to **Ribadiso da Carretera** at the other end. You reach **Arzúa** along the N-547, and leave the village by Rúa do Carme. Through a landscape of meadows and small orchards you start to descend and pass through a wood of oak trees on the boundary of **As Barrosas.** The Trail winds through forests of eucalyptus and pine trees. You cross the bridge over the river Raído to reach the place of the same name. After **Perguntoño** you cross under the main road through a tunnel. Turn to the right and walk along a track to **Cortobe** and **Pereiriña,** then descend through the woods to cross the river Ladrón. A track will lead you to **Calzada** and **Calle** and after crossing several local roads you reach **Boavista.** On leaving **Salceda,** which comes out onto the N-547, you take a path which again leads back onto the road, which you cross to the left. The path carries on up through woodland to **Ras.** Leave on the surfaced track for a few metres and than go over again to the right-hand side, towards the houses of **Brea.** After **Rabiña** (km 23)

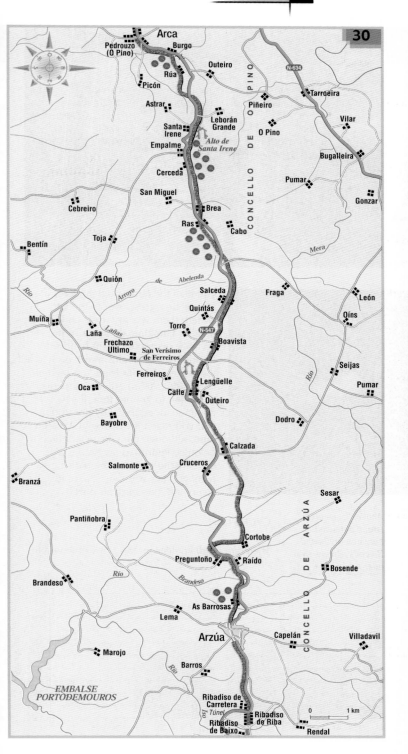

30

Arca
Pedrouzo (O Pino)
Burgo
Outeiro
Rúa
Picón
Astrar
Piñeiro
Tarroeira
Leborán Grande
Vilar
Santa Irene
O Pino
Empalme
Alto de Santa Irene
Bugalleira
Cerceda
Pumar
San Miguel
Gonzar
Cebreiro
Brea
Ras
Cabo
Mera
Bentín
Toja
de *Abelenda*
Quión
Salceda
Fraga
Arroyo
León
Quintás
Muíña
Oíns
Torre
Lañas
N-547
Laña
Boavista
Frechazo Ultimo
San Verísimo de Ferreiros
Seijas
Ferreiros
Pumar
Oca
Lengüelle
Calle
Outeiro
Bayobre
Dodro
Calzada
Branzá
Cruceros
Salmonte
Sesar
Pantiñobra
Cortobe
Bosende
Brandeso
Río *Brandeso*
Preguntoño
Raído
As Barrosas
Lema
Arzúa
Capelán
Villadavil
Marojo
Barros
Río
EMBALSE PORTODEMOUROS
Ribadiso de Carretera
Túnel
Rendal
Ribadiso de Riba
Ribadiso de Baixo

0   1 km

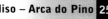

you take the tarmacked track for a few metres, cross over to the left (where there is a rest area) and, at the level of **Empalme de Santa Irene,** you go back over to the right-hand side. Beside the eucalyptus trees you reach the hostel of **Santa Irene** (on the left-hand side). At km 20 you cross over to the left to go into **Rúa.** If you continue along the verge for 200 m you will reach the hostel of **Arca do Pino,** although the village to which it belongs, **Pedrouzo** (as Arca is actually the name of the parish), is reached after you cross the road again and pass through **Burgo.**

Above, "corredoira"
(stone pathway)
between Arzúa and
Salceda. Below, river
near Arzúa.

CYCLISTS

There are no difficulties on this stage of the route.

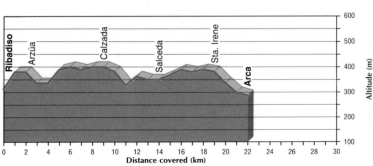

STAGE 30. PRACTICAL INFORMATION

ARZÚA

HOSTELS

"Casa Tarazona" hostel. An adapted old house, on Rúa Cima do Lugar, 6. It has 59 beds and a kitchen Open all year round. ✆ 660 396 824

HOTELS

H** Lar da Mota.
Outeiro,3. ✆ 637 779 739. 8 rooms. 16 beds.
HR** Suiza.
De Río Bello. ✆ 981 500 862. 10 rooms. 20 beds. Double room: € 54; breakfast: € 2,5.
HS* Mesón do Peregrino.
C/ Ramón Franco, 7-3°.
✆ 981 500 830. 5 rooms. 10 beds. Double room: € 30/24/18; breakfast: € 2,5; lunch/dinner: € 7,5.
HSR* El Retiro.
Ctra. Lugo. 12 rooms. ✆ 981 500 554. Double room: € 36/33; single room: € 23/21; breakfast: € 3.
HSR*Teodora.
Ctra. Lugo, 38. ✆ 981 500 083. 24 beds. Double room: € 31/28/25; breakfast: € 2.
P** Rúa.
C/ Rúa de Lugo, 130-1°. ✆ 981 500 139. 10 rooms. 20 beds. Double room: € 34/28; single room: € 22/19; breakfast: € 2.
Casa Milia guest house.
A Portela. 4 rooms. ✆ 981 515 241. 8 beds. Double room: € 40/31; breakfast: € 2,5; lunch/dinner: € 10

RESTAURANTS

El Retiro.
Ctra. Lugo. ✆ 981 500 554
Casa Carballeira.
C/ Ramón Franco, 14. ✆ 981 500 094
Mesón do Peregrino.
C/ Ramón Franco, 7. ✆ 981 500 145
O' Glomen.
A Quenlla. ✆ 981 500 585
Parrillada Europa.
C/ Luis Seoane, 3. ✆ 981 500 298
Parrillada Villanueva.
C/ Ramón Franco. ✆ 981 501 098
Suiza.
C/ Río Vello. ✆ 981 500 862
Teodora. C/ Lugo, 38. ✆ 981 500 083

SANTA IRENE

HOSTELS

"Santa Irene" hostel.
Ctra. Santa Irene-O Pino-A Coruña. It has 15 beds and serves dinner. Open from 1st April until the end of October. ✆ 981 511 000.
Xunta hostel (Albergue de la Xunta).
Ctra. Santa Irene-O Pino-A Coruña. It is run by the Xunta. It has 36 beds and a kitchen. Open all year round.
✆ 660 396 825

RESTAURANTS

Empalme. Santa Irene junction (Empalme Santa Irene).
✆ 981 511 109

SERVICES

There is a bar before Calzada, and restaurants or inns in Salceda, Santa Irene junction (Empalme de Santa Irene) and Pedrouzo, which also has some shops. Accommodation in Rúa.

ARCA DO PINO

HOSTELS

This is the last shelter before Monte do Gozo. It has capacity for up to 126 pilgrims and also has stables.
✆ 981 511 110

RESTAURANTS

Regueiro.
Avda. Santiago, 33. ✆ 981 511 109

HISTORY AND WEALTH OF THE STAGE **30**

Panoramic view of Arzúa.

THE FRENCH ROAD. RIBADISO – ARCA DO PINO

Ribadiso, the historical pilgrimage town on the bank of the river Iso, is now actually divided into two towns, one on each bank: Ribadiso de Baixo (Lower) and Ribadiso de Riba (Upper), and yet another Ribadiso, **Ribadiso da Carretera,** must be passed before reaching Santiago.

Soon after this is **Arzúa,** another important Stop of the Road in Galicia – that is, if it really is the town referred to as *Villanova,* between Boente and Ferreiros, in the *Liber Sancti Iacobi* guide. Although no reliable documents to support this theory have been found, there are some clues which point to this possibility: firstly, it is by far the most important town in this part of the Road and, secondly, we know that it was already important in the XIIth century, since it has two Romanesque churches from that time.

As was the case with Sarria, Villafranca del Bierzo and many others, there may have been a hamlet here first, Arzúa, on which a new town comprised of people from elsewhere, mostly craftsmen attracted by the constant flow of pilgrims, would have been superimposed in the late XIth or early XIIth century. For this reason, to tell it apart from the previous hamlet, it was given the unoriginal name of Villanova (meaning "new town").

The fact that *Liber Sancti Iacobi,* which usually attempts such precision in its topographic specifications, refers to it with such a vague name, suggests that this place had a particular connection with Santiago de Compostela, to the point that it was considered the Villanova by right, the Villanova that didn't need a second part to its name to tell it apart from the rest. *Historia Compostelana,* which was written in Santiago de Compostela at the same time as *Liber Sancti Iacobi,* mentions several

Villanovas, and all except one – a place donated by Pedro Arias to the Church of Santiago de Compostela – have a second part to their name (such as Villanova de Deza or Villanova de Magide). If this Villanova in *Historia Compostelana* was the same as the one in *Liber Sancti Iacobi,* the theory that Arzúa belonged to the Mitre of Santiago would be confirmed.

Also in support of this theory is the way the last chapter of the *Liber Sancti Iacobi* guide tells of three miracles relating to people who didn't assist pilgrims as they should. In two of them, many topographical specifications are added to the place where the miracle took place ("in Nantua, a city between Geneva and Lyon...", "in the city of Poitiers, between the house of Jean Gautier and the church of Saint Porcaire...") The third one, however, is referred to simply as *Villanova,* which means that, at least at that time, there was no possible confusion with other Villanovas. This is the miracle that the book sets in Arzúa:

> In Villanova [Arzúa], a poor pilgrim begged, for the love of God, from a woman who had some bread which she was heating under some embers. She replied that she didn't have any bread, to which the pilgrim replied: "I hope your bread turns into stone!" When the pilgrim had left and was far from her house, the shameless woman went to the embers to retrieve her bread but found a round stone instead. Truly regretting her actions, she immediately went after the pilgrim but was unable to find him.

Many of the miracles with which *Liber Sancti Iacobi* is sprinkled are set precisely in places which belonged to the Santiago de Compostela Mitre, which may also be the case here.

According to later pilgrims (XIVth – XVth centuries), old Villanova recovered its old name, Arzúa.

Roman bridge in Arzúa.

These itineraries, all of them French, talk about *Arcerouze, dit Villeneufe; Arsetouse, dicte Villeneuve;* and *Alserance, dit la Villeneuve*. This suggests that the main name was Arzúa, but the other designation was also still in use. The process, therefore, would have been parallel to that of Sarria: there was originally a humble town with a name of pre-Roman origin. During the Middle Ages, a new town was founded next to the old one, probably along the Pilgrim Road, and was named *Villanova*. And, finally, for reasons unknown to us, the old name was recovered.

Arzúa.
Parish church main altarpiece.

As mentioned above, Arzúa has two Romanesque churches. The main one, on the square, is dedicated to St James. This could be a sign of the relationship of dependency mentioned earlier in relation to the Church of Santiago de Compostela. It is a building of considerable size, with a rectangular layout, to which a remarkable Baroque tower was added in the XVIIth century. Images of the Apostle, both in pilgrim attire at the top of the high altar, and as a knight and hero of the Reconquest, are housed in this church. Although the church of Santa María must have been older, no remains of its old stonework have survived.

Although no documents have been found to suggest this, the two churches may have had pilgrims' hospitals. In addition to these, the convent of La Magdalena, from which a community of Augustine monks ran a pilgrims' hospital and whose deteriorated remains can still be seen, was founded in the XIVth century.

We know from the existence of the current chapel of San Lázaro in **As Barrosas** outside Arzúa that another pilgrims' hospital, in this case devoted to pilgrims with leprosy or other infectious diseases, used to be here.

Next, we find a series of small hamlets – **Raido, Cortobe, Pereiriña, Calzada** and **Calle** – alternating with eucalyptus plantations on the Road. The names of the last two (meaning "road" and "street") are unequivocal references to their location on the Road to Santiago, the *via publica* mentioned in XIIth century documents.

Close to this last one is the church of **San Verísimo de Ferreiros,** the parish of all these small and spread-out towns. The *Liber Sancti Iacobi* guide mentions Ferreiros as the last Stop of the Road before Santiago de Compostela, a whole thirty kilometres away. *Historia Compostelana* also contains a reference to the Burg of Ferreiros on the Road to

Parish church of Arzúa.

Santiago. In addition, we know that there used to be a pilgrims' hospital which depended on the parish. The significance of all this is that Ferreiros was a Stop of the Road of some importance in the Middle Ages. This is not something you would now guess on the basis of the small and spread-out places which comprise the parish of San Verísimo. The dedication of the church to this martyr from Lisbon is another sign of great antiquity.

The town of Ferreiros, just like other Galician towns along the Road to Santiago which are referred to as "burgs", probably originated when a mass of foreigners started the town anew for purely economic reasons and with no previous local social organisation. In this case, the establishment of a group of craftsmen, mostly the blacksmiths which lend their name to this town of La Coruña, is related to the existence of the public road, the Road to Santiago. The intensive flow of travellers, whether on foot, by horse or carriage, would have created a great demand for this sector of the craft industry. Products in demand would have included nails for pilgrims' shoes, horseshoes, riveting and other reinforcements for carriages, and objects such as farming tools or weapons. The fact that Ferreiros was a place of some importance is further confirmed by the fact that, according to *Historia Compostelana*, it was one of the main stops in the journey of a precious relic, the head of apostle Santiago Alfeo, which had been stolen from Holy Land by archbishop of Braga Maurice (who later became an antipope) and taken to the Clunian monastery of San Zoilo de Carrión. Queen Urraca then took it from there and, to ingratiate herself with her son, the future Alfonso VII, and his tutor Diego Gelmírez, donated it to the Church of Santiago, where it is still worshipped in a reliquary bust.

After Ferreiros is a succession of small places: **Boavista, Salceda, Ras, Xen, Brea** (another Vereda), **Santa Irene, Rúa** (yet another reference to the Road), **Burgo** and **Arca do Pino,** which is the end of this stage.

31   Arca – Santiago de Compostela

As you near your destination, the Trail reaches Monte do Gozo, after leaving behind the numerous hamlets scattered in amongst the woodlands of eucalyptus, and Labacolla airport, and the spires of the Cathedral rise up in front of you.

Monument on Monte do Gozo.

From the Arca hostel you go back 200 m and cross road N-547, to pass through **Burgo, Arca (Pedrouzo),** and **San Antón.** At **Amenal** (km 15), you cross a bridge and the road, and continue across the vegetation to **Cimadevila.** From there you climb up a woodland path which goes around Labacolla airport. At the stone marking km 12 the N-544 emerges, alongside which you descend until you pass a stream and soon afterwards you cross over to the right to turn off towards **San Paio.** On leaving this hamlet you set off on a path which crosses a road and leads into Labacolla. Go down towards the river Labacolla and once over it, you cross the N-534 once more. You then begin to go up a surfaced track, passing through **Villamaior** and, further along, past the Galician and Spanish television studios and a timber factory. After the village of **San Marcos,** from the **Monte del Gozo** itself, and next to the chapel of St Mark (and the monument commemorating the visit of Pope John Paul II), you can finally make out your desired destination of Santiago de Compostela.

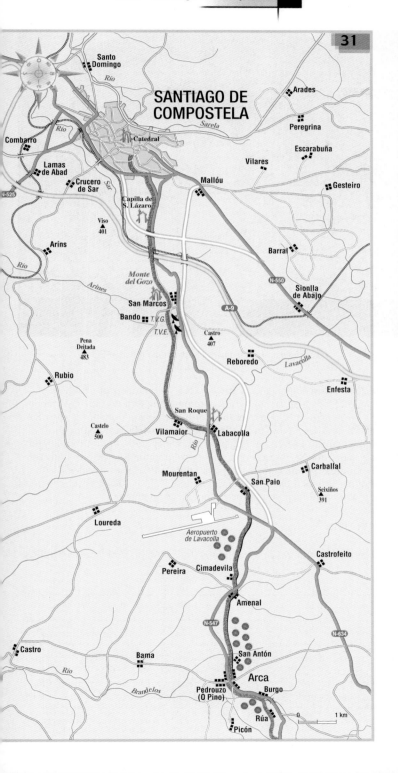

*Top (tympanum) of the central arch of the Portico of Glory
(Pórtico de La Gloria).*

A gentle descent leads you down to the vast number of facilities catering for travellers and you continue along Rúa do Gozo. At the N-544 you cross a bridge over the A-9 highway, the flow of the river Sar and the railway. Now in **Santiago de Compostela,** arriving by the Barrio de San Lázaro, you pass by its chapel and carry on through the areas of Fontiña, Barrio dos Concheiros, and the Rúa de San Pedro. From the Porta do Camiño you take the Rúa das Casa Reais y das Animas to reach the Plaza de Cervantes. The Rúa da Azabachería and the Vía Sacra lead you to the Cathedral of Santiago.

CYCLISTS

The final kilometres of the Pilgrims' Trail pose no problems for cyclists.

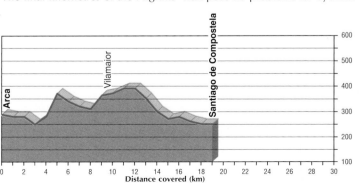

STAGE 31. PRACTICAL INFORMATION

LABACOLLA

HOSTELS

It has a hostel but no telephone.

RESTAURANTS

Casa Lorenzo.
Cruce Aeropuerto. ✆ 981 888 326
Garcas. Lugar de Mourentans, 2.
✆ 981 888 225
Ruta Jacobea. Lavacolla, 41.
✆ 981 888 211

SANTIAGO DE COMPOSTELA

HOSTELS

Acuario hostel. ✆ 981 575 438
Monte do Gozo hostel.
✆ 981 558 942
Seminario Menor hostel in Santiago de
Compostela. ✆ 981 589 200

HOTELS

H* Monte do Gozo.
Ctra. del Aeropuerto, km 2. Bando.
✆ 981 558 942. 1,167 beds. Double
room: € 75/49.
HS*** Hogar San Francisco.
C/ Campillo de San Francisco, 3.
✆ 981 581 600. Double room: € 77/65.
HS* Agusdel.
C/ Pérez Constantí, 7. ✆ 981 585 214.
8 rooms.
HS* La Salle.
C/ San Roque, 6. ✆ 981 584 611
HS* Tambre.
C/ Vista Alegre.
✆ 981 580 046. Double room: € 36/30;
single room: € 18/15; breakfast: € 2,5.
HSR** Alameda.
C/ San Clemente, 32. ✆ 981 588 100.
Double room: € 42/33; single room:
€ 27/21; breakfast: € 2,41.
HSR** Balboa.
A Ponte da Rocha, 8. Conxo. ✆ 981
521 598. Double room:
€ 51/48; single room: € 30/27.
HSR** Fornos.
C/ Hórreo, 7-2°. ✆ 981 585 130.
Double room: € 37/31; single room:
€ 29/22.

HSR** Mapoula.
C/ Entremurallas, 10. ✆ 981 580 124.
Double room: € 31/25.
HSR** México. C/ República Argentina,
33. ✆ 981 598 000. 98 beds. Double
room: € 41/31; breakfast: € 3.
HSR** Vilas. C/ Romero Donallo, 9.
✆ 981 591 150. Double room: € 45/39;
single room: € 27/21; breakfast: € 3.
HSR* El Aparcadero. Aldrei. Marrozos.
✆ 981 539 796. 33 rooms.
HSR* Giadás. Pl. del Matadero, 2.
✆ 981 587 071. Double room: € 34.
P*** As Sirenas. O Roxido. Fecha.
✆ 981 580 310. Double room: € 40/30;
single room: € 30/20; breakfast: € 6.
P** San Paio. A Lavacolla. Sabugueira.
Santiago de Compostela (A Coruña).
✆ 981 888 205. 10 rooms. Double
room: € 36/30; breakfast: € 2,75.
P* José Rey. O Meixonfrío. As Pereiras
de San Caetano. ✆ 981 581 897.
Double room: € 25; single room: € 14.

CAMPING SITES

1.st C Monte do Gozo.
Ctra. del Aeropuerto, km 2. Bando.
1,227 places. ✆ 981 558 942.
2.nd C As Sirenas.
Ctra. Santiago-Carballo, km 11. Fecha.
300 places. ✆ 981 898 722.
2.nd C As Cancelas. Rúa 25 de Xullo,
35. 410 places. ✆ 981 580 266.

MEANS OF TRANSPORT

Monte do Gozo can be reached from
Compostela by bus. This makes the visit
to the city easier for pilgrims.
Santiago de Compostela bus station.
Rúa San Caetano, s/n.
✆ 981 587 700.
RENFE rail station. Rúa Hórreo, s/n.
Labacolla airport information. ✆ 981
597 400. Pilgrims who certify their
arrival in Santiago de Compostela get a
large discount on their Iberia flight.

SERVICES

Amenal has a supermarket, Labacolla
has shops, cafés/bars and
accommodation, and San Marcos has a
shop or two as well. The complex built in
Monte do Gozo includes a restaurant
and café, a camping site, an auditorium
and the European Centre for Pilgrimage
("Centro Europeo de Peregrinación").

A das Burgas

Sanatorio Nosa Sra. da Esperanza

Campo do Cruceiro do Gaio

Campo das Hortas

Rúa de Galeras

Avda. de Pontevedra

Avda. Marques Sargaledos

Avenida de Compostela

Rúa do Pombal

Rúa das Hort

Campiño de Ferradura

Paseo da Ferradura

Paseo das Letras Galegas

Paseo de Bóveda

Igrexa de San Fructuoso

Rúa de Trind

Caballeira de Sta. Susana

Co

Paseo de Santa Susana

Igrexa de Santa Susana

Rúa dos Leóns

Rúa San Clemente

Rúa de Trind

Rúa de Rax

Alameda

Campo San Clemente

Policía Nacional

Colexio de Fonsec

Casas de Compostela

Paseo Central da Alameda

Avenida de Xoán Carlos I

Igrexa do Pilar

Instituto de Bacharelato Rosalía de Castro

Avda. Rodrigo de padrón

Trv. Fonseca

F

Comisaría de Policia

Carreira

do Conde

Campo da Estrela

Rúa de Figueroa

Entrecerc. Ruela

do Franco

Pracíña Franco

R. da R

do

Rúa de Montero

Pardiñas

Porta de Faxeiras

Avda. Peso

R. Bautiza

Rúa

Rúa

do

Casa de Vaamonde

Rúa

Xeneral

Rios

Fonterrab

Pza. Toural

Canton do Toural

Entrerríos

Rúa

Rúa da Senra

Ruela Entremur

Rúa das Orfas

Tras Salon

R. da R. de El Salvador

Doutor

Teixeiro

Porta Mámoa

Convento Igrexa das Orfas

Cardenal Payá

Praza de Galicia

Rúa da Fonte de Santo Ar

Trs. Gramáticos

Ma

Hotel Compostela

Concepción Arenal

Rúa do Salvador

Hórreo

Rúa de Gomez Ulla

Rúa de

Rúa García Blanco

Pitelos

Pitelos

R. Patio de Madres

Ruela do Pisór

do

Rúa

Laverde Ruiz

Rúa de Santiago de Guayaquil

Rúa de Perez Costanti

Rúa de Neira de Mosquera

Parlamento de Galicia

Rúa Irmáns Rei Alvite

Rúa Lopez Ferreiro

Rúa de Curros Enriquez

R. do Castrón Douro

R. do Oliv

Praza da Constitución

Rúa de Ramón

Rúa Eduardo Pondal

Domingo Fontán

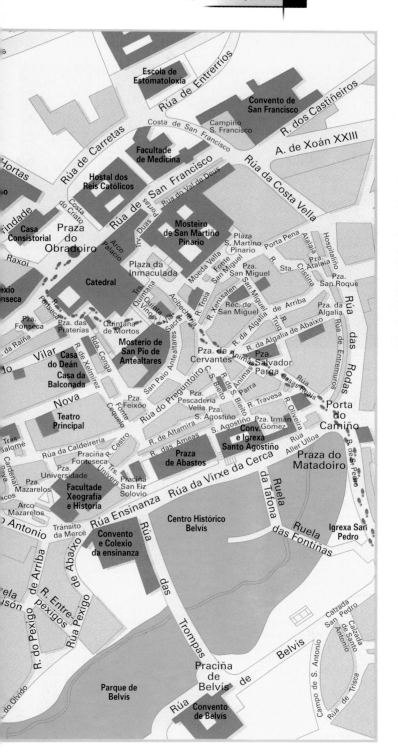

HISTORY AND WEALTH OF THE STAGE 31

Panoramic view of Santiago de Compostela.

THE FRENCH ROAD. ARCA DO PINO – SANTIAGO DE COMPOSTELA

Shortly after leaving Arca, the Road meets the village of **San Antón,** which may be yet another reference to the Order of St Anthony on the Road to Santiago. The place appearing under the name as "Duas Casas" or "Tres casas" in local documents and late mediaeval travellers' reports must have been between **Amenal** (place of "ameneiros", the Galician name for the alder tree) and **Cimadevila.** It was in Amenal, and not in Lavacolla as was almost compulsory, that pilgrim Laffi made his ablutions so that he would be sufficiently clean and tidy to visit the Apostle.

In the village of **San Paio,** a small town which has successfully preserved part of its old appearance, we find, for the first time on the Road, one of the most universal Galician forms of worship: the worship of St Pelayo, the boy from Tuy who was martyred in Córdoba in the Xth century. His martyrdom was so famous in its time that it crossed the Iberian Peninsula frontiers and had the honour of being sung, among other contemporaries and in Latin, by German poet Hroswitha of Gandersheim.

The church of **Labacolla** is also dedicated to St Pelayo, but the fame of this place is due to other reasons, all of them connected to Santiago de Compostela. Although it now lends its name to an airport, in the Middle Ages and later it was the place where the pilgrims would take off all their clothes and bathe in the river to clean off the dirt accumulated in a journey of months, in order to appear clean and decent before St James, to whom they would offer their pilgrimage and on whom they had placed so much hope. The river's Galician name comes precisely from this custom of washing ("lava") one's whole body, including the most intimate parts ("colla"). The author of the *Liber Sancti Iacobi* guide, paraphrasing Roman poet Martial in jest, translated the name of the river as Lavamentula (cf. Latin *mentula,* the male organ of copulation), and described the pilgrims' rite thus:

> "[...] *in a luxuriant place two miles from the city of Santiago is a river called Labacolla [Lavamentula], thus named because this is where French pilgrims on their way to Santiago take off their clothes and, out of their love for the Apostle, wash not only their privates, but the dirt of their whole body.*"

The last obstacle to finish the pilgrimage was, and still is, **Monte do Gozo,** on whose western slope the Apostle's city can be glimpsed for the first time. Its name, already explained in the *Liber Sancti Iacobi* guide ("Mons Gaudium"), is related to the joy felt by pilgrims on seeing the towers of the Cathedral of Santiago de Compostela for the first time. No one else has ever defined the indescribable emotion with which pilgrims are seized at this point like Domenico Laffi did:

> "*We reached the peak of a hill called Monte del Gozo, from which we looked at Santiago, which we had so longed for and which was now only half a league away. When we saw it, we fell to our knees and started crying for joy and singing "Te Deum", but were unable to sing more than two or three lines because the large number of tears emerging from our eyes prevented us from uttering a word. We were forced to interrupt our singing by the emotion which seized our hearts and by our continuous sobs, until we finally felt we had vented our emotion and the crying slowly stopped. We then continued singing "Te Deum" and, singing in this way, we descended towards the burg.*"

Before the wall which gave access to the burg of **Santiago de Compostela,** was the hospital of San Lázaro, founded in the XIIth century for pilgrims with leprosy. This charitable institution is still remembered in the current district and parish of San Lázaro.

The pilgrims' route towards the Cathedral followed the current Los Concheiros quarter. "Concheiros" refers to the pilgrims of St James whose identifying mark was, at least from the end of the XIth century, the shell of St James ("concha" means "shell"). Later on but still outside the old city wall, where we now find Avenida de San Pedro, was the old monastery of San Pedro de Fora, which was already in

Pilgrims in front of Las Platerías square, with the clock tower (Torre del Reloj) in the background.

Typical "souvenirs" for pilgrims and tourists.

existence in the Xth century. Pilgrims on the French Road entered Santiago de Compostela through Puerta del Camino, which the Guide refers to as *Porta Francigena*. Inside the city walls, the route then went along *Via Francigena*, which has now disappeared. Before the Cathedral was a hospital for poor pilgrims and, opposite the northern façade (Azabachería), was a monumental fountain decorated with lions, whose basin was, according to the Guide, large enough to allow fifteen men to bathe at any one time. This is where the so-called "Paraíso de la ciudad" (city's paradise) was. On this place, which was already paved in those days, pilgrims – the tourists of the time – were offered "souvenirs" in commercial stalls.

> *"Shells – the symbol of St James –, wineskins, shoes, saddlebags made out of deer skin, bags, straps, belts and all kinds of medicinal herbs and dyestuffs are sold to the pilgrims there."*

Later, this space devoted to tourism was given the name "Azabachería", because of the jet ("azabache") charms which were sold there and which became a Compostelan speciality which has survived to this day.

Guided by the *Liber Sancti Iacobi* Guide, we have reached the area around the Cathedral, the destination of our pilgrimage and the city of Santiago's centre of activity. Before describing in full detail what was once one of the biggest and finest cathedrals of its time, the worthy reliquary of the remains of one of Christ's apostles and, together with Rome and Jerusalem, one of Christianity's three great pilgrimage centres, the Guide lingers in its surroundings, in the city of Compostela, its rivers, the doors of its walls and, above all, its churches.

Among the churches mentioned by name and which still exist albeit with renovated stonework – are San Pedro de Foras (already mentioned above), San Miguel dos Agros, the monastery of San Martín Pinario, and the churches of Santa Susana, San Fiz (Félix) de Solovio, San Benito del Campo, San Payo de Antealtares and Santa María, which is now the chapel of Santa María de la Corticela and part of the Cathedral.

Among the churches not mentioned in the guide are the church of Santa María Salomé – which already existed in 1145 and which is the only church in the world dedicated to St James' mother –, and the collegiate church of Santa María del Sar, also from the XIIth century. The convent of San Francisco, which may have been founded by St Francis of Assisi in his pilgrimage to Compostela, and Santo Domingo de Bonaval, the burial place of many famous Galicians, were built in later centuries. Some of the city's secular buildings include the Romanesque palace of Gelmírez, which is adjoined to the Cathedral, the schools of Fonseca and San Jerónimo, the Raxoi palace and the great hostal de los Reyes Católicos, although this is only a sample from a list too long to reproduce here.

Santiago de Compostela. Monastery of San Martín Pinario.

But let us return to the Cathedral at the point at which we left it: the northern or Azabachería door (puerta de la Azabachería). Although the *Liber Sancti Iacobi* guide describes its series of icons in detail, the whole façade was unfortunately demolished in the XVIIIth century to be replaced by the neoclassical one which can be seen now and which is the work of Ventura Rodríguez. The statues on the early Romanesque façade were redistributed around the Cathedral and some can still be seen in the Cathedral Museum. The eastern façade, which looks onto plaza de la Quintana, never had a Romanesque portal. The Door of Forgiveness (Puerta del Perdón) was opened on it in 1611. This is always boarded up, except for holy years (those years in which the festival of St James, which is on 25th July, is on a Sunday). Next to it, are 24 statues by master Mateo which were in the cathedral's old choir. From the portals described and interpreted in the guide, only the one on the southern façade, known as Puerta de las Platerías, can be admired today. It is worth standing in front of it with the *Liber Sancti Iacobi* guide text in your hands, and checking it figure by figure to see for yourself how nothing has changed in the last 900 years.

The same cannot be said, however, of Santiago Cathedral's main façade, which faces west on Obradoiro square. It is a late Baroque work erected in 1750 by Galician architect Casas Novoa, who replaced and covered parts of the sober old Romanesque church with his showy Baroque ornaments and crowned its two towers, making them noticeably taller. Let us now go inside: in order to do this, we must ascend the great double steps which archbishop Maximilian of Austria from Jaén ordered

El Obradoiro façade on the Cathedral of Santiago de Compostela.

his fellow countryman Ginés Martínez Aranda, a member of a family of architects based in Castillo de Locubín (Jaén), to build in 1606.

Once inside, we find the Portico of Glory *(Pórtico de La Gloria)*, possibly the Cathedral´s most famous part. It was built in the second half of the XIIth century by master Maestro to replace the old Romanesque portal. It is a triple portal, adorned with an exceedingly complicated collection of over 200 polychrome statues whose expressiveness and dynamism puts them among the best Spanish Romanesque sculptures. A colossal figure of the Saviour, surrounded by the four evangelists and some angels carrying the instruments of the Passion, can be seen on the main tympanum. The twenty-four elders of the Apocalypse, playing all sorts of musical instruments from the time, are crammed onto the archivoltes. The left arch is dedicated to scenes and characters of the *Old Testament,* whereas the one on the right shows the consequences of the Last Judgment, with its corresponding pleasures and torments. On the portals' jambs on the lower level, are the twelve apostles on the left and the prophets on the right. In the centre, just below the Saviour on the mullion that divides the central arch, is the apostle St James depicted as the seated host receiving his guests. Another ancestral pilgrimage rite consists of touching the column which supports the Apostle, and which represents the Jesse tree (Christ's family tree), with the right hand. The five fingers of the cathedral's many visitors who have repeated this rite for centuries have worn the hard marble and left a print several centimetres deep. This is followed by another custom, which has also developed into a rite, consisting of hitting the human head at the foot of this mullion with one's own head, while facing inside. This rite is known by tradition, which would like this figure to be master Mateo, the author

of the portal, as "o santo dos croques" (the saint of the head bumps). Many pilgrims also knock their heads against the bearded figure at the foot of the Jesse tree, which may represent Samson surrounded by two lions in whose open mouths the visitors put their arms while knocking their heads.

Inside the church, we again encounter its original Romanesque style. The building is a church with a Latin Cross layout, three naves and a triforium. The main nave is crowned by a great apse with an ambulatory, which opens up to several chapels, already described in the *Liber Sancti Iacobi* guide.

Behind the main altar is the Romanesque statue of the apostle St James, adorned and surrounded by Baroque excesses, on which the rite/custom of the hug takes place. Below, on an underground level, is the crypt with the chest containing the apostle St James' remains. This is where his burial was found in the IXth century. The existence of a Ist century necropolis before everything that was built later, and which summarises the history of Santiago de Compostela, has been proved by archaeology. Let us go over it very briefly:

In the first third of the IXth century, during the bishopric of Theodomir of Ira Flavia, an old mausoleum from Roman times was found in the forest where the city of Compostela now stands. On the basis of some texts and traditions which asserted that St James had preached in the west and, specifically, in Spain, this was identified as the Apostle's remains. King Alfonso II ordered the first, very modest, basilica to be built, and the new cult, which was favoured by both him and his successors, soon became the most popular in Spain. Its Spanish popularity soon attracted people from other countries who, in ever larger numbers, went to see the Apostle's sepulchre which was buried in what was then the westernmost point of the known world. In view of this success, Alfonso III ordered a bigger and more sumptuous basilica to be built at the end

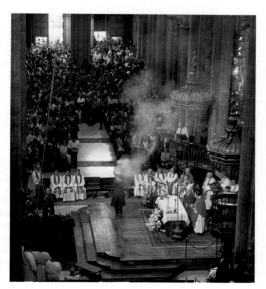

Santiago de Compostela. Above, centre column of the Portico of Glory (Pórtico de La Gloria) on the cathedral; right, the flight of the "Botafumeiro" censer which, due to the action of 8 "tiraboleiros", goes round the lower arm of the cathedral in pendular manner.

of the IXth century. This was destroyed almost a century later by Almanzor who did, however, respect the Apostle's sepulchre. The great bishop Pedro de Mezonzo (who may have written the world famous *Salve Regina* antiphon) undertook the reconstruction of the church around the year 1000. Seventy years later, bishop Diego Peláez started work on the current Cathedral, which was finished off in Gelmírez's time, although additions and alterations have been added to it many times since then.

The treasures housed in the Cathedral are many and very varied. Many, such as the famous reliquary bust of St James the Lesser (Santiago el Menor), the sepulchres of several royal personages, and bishop Theodomir's tombstone, from the time in which the Apostle's grave was found, can be found in the Treasury Chapel (El Tesoro) and the chapel of the Relics (capilla de las Reliquias). A different type of treasure can be found in the capitular archive library. Of particular note among them is undoubtedly the *Calixtine Codex,* a beautiful XIIth century manuscript containing *Liber Sancti Iacobi,* an extremely complex work dedicated to the apostle St James and divided into several parts: it is a very rich liturgical treasure, which includes some of the first known polyphonic

music; the historic explanation for the removal of the Apostle's remains from Jerusalem to Galicia and for the discovery of his sepulchre (which this work attributes to Charlemagne instead of Theodomir); and the description of the Road to Santiago and the City of Santiago itself.

This description of the Road is the well known *Liber Sancti Iacobi* guide which has so often been mentioned in this book and which was the first work to lay down the route of the so-called French Road, which we have faithfully followed with almost no detours.

Above, dressing room and sculpture of the Apostle presiding the Main Altar; below, crypt dominated by the casket containing St James' bone remains as well as those of his disciples Theodore and Athanasius.

The Aragon
Route

1 Somport – Jaca

Our departure point is in the "Pirineo Aragonés", the Aragonese Pyrenees, at a height of 1,632 m between the valleys of Aspe, in France, and that of Canfranc. From here to Jaca you will need to descend southwards, through the long valley of the river Aragón. From Villanúa the horizon widens out and the landscape changes completely, with holm oaks, gall-oaks, and other Mediterranean flora (Villanúa is home to the northernmost holm-oak grove in Europe.

Candanchú ski resort.

Our walk begins on the Puerto de **Somport,** on the French and Spanish border. After a short spell on road N-330, you will see some steps on the left which you need to climb down, following the course of the river Aragón, towards an area of flatland where the hospital of Santa Cristina was once situated. Walk along the road and cross the bridge and very soon you will come to the winter resort of **Candanchú,** facing the monte Tobazo. After a hill you cross the N-330 and the side of the Candanchú castle hill. The trail leads towards the road, at the level of the Ruso bridge, but does not actually reach it. By rough and uneven paths and a surfaced track (which you leave on the right before reaching the Canal Roya campsite), you descend into **Canfranc-Estación,** crossing the river Aragón and arriving finally by road. After passing the large resort, you leave by the same road. Continue until you reach a second tunnel and climb down some steps to the left to cross over to the left-hand side of the river and follow alongside it until you reach **Canfranc.** You enter the village over a stone bridge and leave by crossing the Romanesque Pilgrims' bridge *(Puente de los Peregrinos),* next to the cemetery. You pass under the road twice and before reaching **Villanúa** you are faced with two options:

A) You can follow the Road which leads straight on, without crossing the bridge, through the village of Villanúa and then over farm land. You cross

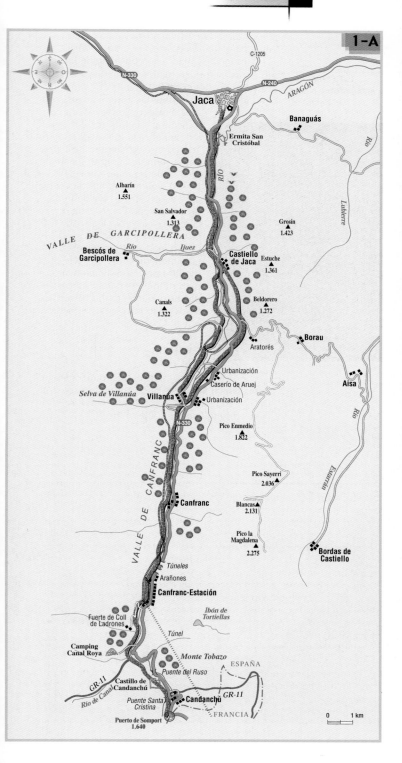

the river and railway track twice and then through an area of gall-oaks up on to a track which crosses the N-330 to reach **Castiello de Jaca.**

Los Peregrinos Romanesque bridge in Canfranc.

B) Cross the bridge (with a recreation area) towards the new part of Villanúa. The arrows take you along the road (there is a fountain and rest area alongside). There is a sign indicating a herding trail on the left, which you follow for 1.5 km. You go through another rest area and a summer camp to reach the area of Borau. Before meeting the N-330, you take a dirt track which, after 2 km reaches **Castiello de Jaca.** Descend via its calle de Santiago and cross the road. You cross the river along the road which leads to Bescós de Garcipollera. Cross the river Ijuez by dirt track. Shortly afterwards a path running parallel to the river passes underneath the N-330 and leads up to **Jaca,** past the hermitage of San Cristóbal.

CYCLISTS

Many parts of this route consist of paths which are quite steep and impossible for cyclists to negotiate. Cyclists are therefore advised to follow the route of the N-330

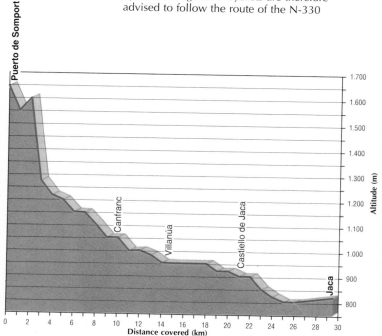

STAGE 1. PRACTICAL INFORMATION

SOMPORT

HOSTELS

Aysa hostel. Puerto de Somport. Ctra. Francia, s/n. It has a dining room, and dinners are served. Closed from 15th to 30th June and October and November. ✆ 974 373 023

CANDANCHÚ

HOTELS

H*** Edelweiss. Ctra. Zaragoza-Francia, km 190. ✆ 974 373 200. Double room: € 37.
H** Candanchú. Ctra. de Francia. ✆ 974 373 025. 108 beds. Double room: € 74/26; dinner: € 6.

CANFRANC

HOSTELS

Canfranc Youth Hostel. ✆ 976 714 797
Pepito Grillo hostel. ✆ 974 373 123
Sargantana hostel. C/ Albareda, 19. 75 beds. Open in July and August, as well as from 1st December to 30th April (groups only). Meals are served. ✆ 974 372 010 / 974 373 217

HOTELS

H** Villa Anayet.
Pl. José Antonio, 8. ✆ 974 373 146. Double room: € 36; breakfast: € 3; lunch/dinner: € 8.
HR* Ara.
C/ Fernando el Católico, 1. ✆ 974 373 028. 40 beds. Double room: € 30.
H* Montanglasse.
C/ Felipe V, 2. ✆ 974 373 311. 60 beds. Double room: € 30.

CAMPING SITES

2.nd C Canfranc.
Ctra. N-330, km 670. ✆ 974 348 354. 90 places.

RESTAURANTS

La Brasa. C/ Fernando El Católico, 11. ✆ 947 373 047. Grilled meat.

VILLANÚA

HOSTELS

DGA Youth Hostel. ✆ 974 378 016
Santa María del Pilar Youth Hostel. ✆ 974 378 016
Tritón shelter. ✆ 974 378 281 / 639 775 117

HOTELS

HS* Alto Aragón. C/ Gabriel Faci Abaad. ✆ 974 486 301. 28 beds. Double room: € 49/36; lunch/dinner: € 10.

JACA

HOSTELS

Municipal Hostel (Albergue Municipal). It has 64 beds and is located next to the Old Hospital (Hospital Viejo), on calle Conde Aznar. It has a kitchen and dining room. Very good facilities. ✆ 974 355 116
Escuelas Pías Youth Hostel. Avda. Perimetral, 6. It has 160 beds. Open all year round. ✆ 974 360 536

HOTELS

H* Alcetania. C/ Mayor, 43. ✆ 974 356 100. 38 beds. Double room: € 48/34.
H* Bucardo. Avda. Francia, 13. ✆ 974 356 363. Double room: € 48/30.
H* Ciudad de Jaca. C/ Sancho Ramírez, 15. ✆ 974 364 311. Double room: € 42/35.
HS* El Abeto. C/ Bellido, 15. 50 beds. ✆ 974 361 642. Double room: € 38/30.
HS* París. Pl. San Pedro, 5. 38 beds. ✆ 974 361 020. Double room: € 28/26.

CAMPING SITES

1.st C Peña Oroel. Ctra. N-330 Jaca-Sabiñánigo. ✆ 974 360 215. 700 places.
2.nd C Victoria. Avda. de la Victoria, 34. ✆ 974 360 323. 288 beds.

MEANS OF TRANSPORT

Jaca has a bus station (✆ 974 355 060), as well as a **RENFE** train station. (✆ 974 360 490). **Canfranc rail station:** ✆ 974 373 029.

HISTORY AND WEALTH OF THE STAGE 1

ARAGONESE STRETCH. SOMPORT – JACA

Somport, whose name *(Summus Portus,* "the highest part of the pass") tells us that we are on a pass on a large hill, is the starting point of our route along the Aragonese stretch of the Road to Santiago. According to the *Liber Sancti Iacobi* guide (c. 1130), French pilgrims used to enter Spain via four roads which crossed France towards the south-west. The three most northern routes *(Via Turonensis* or Tours Route, *Via Lemovicensis* or Limoges Route, and *Via Podensis* or Le Puy Route) had met shortly before entering Spain through the pass of Roncesvals on the Pyrenees. The southernmost and fourth great route is known as *Via Tolosana* (Toulouse Route). It came from Arles, where the pilgrims from Italy had joined the ones from Switzerland and southern Germany, progressed along the "Oberstrasse" (high route) and descended along the Rhone. After Arles, the route went through the cities of Montpellier, Toulouse and Auch, from where it turned south to enter Spain via Somport.

Although the fact that the guide calls the Pyrenean pass on the Toulouse Route *Portus Asperi* seems to suggest that this is the nearby Pas d'Aspe, there are weighty reasons for tipping the balance towards the Somport side. Some of these reasons include, first, the fact that this was the pass on the Roman road that connected Aquitaine with Saragossa and, second, the mention in the guide of the **hospital of Santa Cristina** in the pass in question. The guide even reserves extraordinary praise for this institution, which it puts on the same level as the most important hospitals of the Holy Land and Rome routes: the hospital of Jerusalem and the hospital on the St Bernard mountain pass, which many northern Europeans used in order to enter Italy:

> *"The Lord erected in this world three columns necessary*
> *for the support of the poor: the Hospital of Jerusalem, the*
> *Hospital of Mont-Joux and the Hospital of Sainte*
> *Christine, in Somport. These hospitals are located in*
> *necessary places, holy places, houses of God, for the*
> *restoration of pilgrim saints, the rest of the poor, the*
> *comfort of the sick, the salvation of the dead and the*
> *assistance of the living. Whoever built them will surely*
> *possess the Kingdom of Heaven."*

Unfortunately, nothing but a desolate ruin is left of this extraordinary place. The early decay of this hospital was probably caused by Roncesvals' rapid prosperity. When the guide was written (1130), however, this institution founded by two knights and favoured by the mythical Gaston IV of Bearn and King Alfonso I of Aragon, was in its heyday and dominated, in the form of dependent territories and hospitals, most of the stretch of the Road to Santiago which went through the Bearn area. Like so many other pilgrims' hospitals located on difficult mountain passes, it was run by a community of regular canons. In the late Middle Ages a fortress was erected in the nearby area of "Camp d'Anjou" to protect pilgrims from the many thieves and tax collectors who populated it. In the surrounding area is the modern town of **Candanchú,** which is named after the old castle and is now famous for its ski resort.

After the modern town of **Canfranc-Estación,** which was born around the train station, the Road meets the historic town of **Canfranc,** already mentioned as a Stop of the Road by the *Liber Sancti Iacobi* guide, and by even older documents (1095) which confirmed that it used to include a lodging place for pilgrims. It has been suggested that its name is related to the inhabitants of Canfranc's alleged obligation to keep the road free ("franco") of snow and other obstacles for pilgrims and traders.

In addition to being an important stop for pilgrims, Canfranc had a customs of sorts, established by the kings of Aragon to collect road tolls and goods from travellers. This created a large amount of economic activity (such as markets and currency exchange businesses) in the place. The entry into Spain of the first gypsies, who claimed they were pilgrims to Santiago in order to be exempted from the road toll, is also documented in Canfranc in the XVth century. In addition, King Alfonso the *Magnanimous* of Aragon issued a warrant of protection and safe-conduct to the gypsy patriarch, his "cousin" Thomas, count of Little Egypt (egiptiano < gitano – "gypsy"), valid for the whole of his stay in Alfonso's kingdoms.

Construction near Canfranc.

Among the historic buildings saved from the fire which affected this town in 1944 are the Romanesque parish church, which is dedicated to the Virgin, and an also Romanesque one-span bridge over the river Aragón.

Before entering **Villanúa** *(Villanova),* you can see part of the old road. The parish church of San Esteban houses a Romanesque statue of the Virgin, as well as a sculpture of St James in pilgrim attire. The church of San Vicente, a modest gem of Pyrenean Romanesque art, whose great semicircular apse is particularly remarkable, can be found in **Aruej,** which is slightly away from the Road and now abandoned.

As its name suggests, **Castiello de Jaca** was born around a fortress erected on a hill to defend the northern access to the city of Jaca. Its Romanesque parish church of San Miguel stands out among its other buildings. At the end of the town, after crossing the river Aragón on a mediaeval bridge, is the Romanesque chapel of Santa Juliana.

Inside what is now **Jaca,** although still outside the old city walls, was the La Salud Hospital for pilgrims with infectious diseases, of which some decorative elements have been preserved.

Panoramic view of Jaca.

The *Liber Sancti Iacobi* guide only refers to Jaca as a Stop of the Road, and does not make any comment relating to its status as a capital. It is possible that the city's most splendorous days were over by then (1130). Its best days were during the last quarter of the XIth century, when Sancho Ramírez made it the capital of the new kingdom of Aragon as well as an episcopal see, and granted it a "fuero de Francos" (a privilege designed to encourage foreigners to settle here and to create a bourgeoisie) which enabled it to take off economically. This "fuero", which granted a variety of advantages to foreign traders who settled in this town, was later copied by other towns of the Road such as Estella, Sangüesa, Pamplona or Puente la Reina. The town's layout, which dates from that time, is divided into two parts: the district or "burg" of San Nicolás within the walls, and Burgo Nuovo (the current Burnau) outside them. The current defensive citadel was erected in modern times – as shown by its polygonal layout – on the land where Burnau used to be.

Within the walls, in the old burg of San Nicolás, is the impressive cathedral of San Pedro, which has three naves and a Latin Cross layout. It is a completely Romanesque church, very original in relation to the buildings of that time in Spain and the rest of Europe, and a sign of the Kingdom of Aragon's economic progress at the time. Of particular note

Jaca.
House next
to the Citadel.

Jaca. Above, citadel; below, interior of the cathedral's central and side naves.

inside the church are its magnificent sculptures, which are closely connected to the ones in the church of San Martín in Frómista. In addition to its remarkable technical quality, the church is remarkable for the richness of the contents depicted on the tympani and capitals which are inspired on the Bible as well as on other literary works such as the great Spanish Paleochristian poet Prudentius' *Psicomaquia*. The statues on the southern door, one of which has been identified as representing St Peter (to whom the church is dedicated), are particularly outstanding among the round statues.

Inside the church are the relics of St Indaletius, one of the seven apostolic men, ie. the Apostles' (or, according to another version, St James') disciples, whose mission it was to evangelise Spain. St Indaletius was the first bishop of Urci (now called Pechina, in Almería). His remains were taken to San Juan de la Peña in 1084 and subsequently to Jaca Cathedral, where they can still be found today. Together with his remains are those of St Voto (Odón) and St Felix, San Juan de la Peña's founders. The Cathedral Museum houses a large collection of Romanesque paintings, mostly from the church of San Salvador. The magnificent sarcophagus of doña Sancha, one of the daughters of Ramiro I, the first king of Aragon, was brought from Santa María de la Serós to the Benedictine monastery of Jaca, where it remains to this day.

Jaca's references to St James include the now destroyed church of Santiago (which lent its name to a district of the city) some of whose ruins are in the current church of Santo Domingo; and the several hospitals which used to be in the city, such as the hospital of San Andrés or the hospital of San Juan de Jerusalén.

2 Jaca – Arrés (Puente la Reina de Jaca)

The route veers westward as does the river Aragón, the course of which has followed out the ground to form the corridor of the Canal de Berdún. Unlike the day before, the ground you come across is almost always flat, with cereal fields and very few trees. To the south of the route are the Peña Oroel and the sierra of San Juan de la Peña.

Cloister of San Juan de la Peña monastery.

To leave **Jaca** you take the Paseo de la Constitución and once you have crossed the gardens, the route leads on to the Camino del Monte Pano (or de Mocorones), which passes alongside an area of houses. On arriving at the cemetery, 2 km further on, you will meet road N-240, which you walk along for a few metres and then continue along a herding trail running parallel. Cross the river Gas (after 1.5 km) and once past a building materials factory, you come to a path on the left which takes you to San Juan de la Peña. A little further on you pass through a poplar grove (Casa del Municionero), on the right of the N-240, and an old military camp. Cross over to the left 1 km further on. Negotiate your way across the Atarés gulley to return to the main road via the one leading to Atarés (3 km). A path running parallel to the main road takes you up into oak and pine trees and goes down to the old San Juan de la Peña road, along which you walk a few steps and turn off onto a path which emerges on the right. After another gulley, continue on past the rear of a hotel (the old Venta de Esculabolsas). After crossing the new road, carry on towards the road to Binacua, where you come back to the San Juan de la Peña road. Continue until you see a path on the right between bushes and farm land. Cross the road to come into **Santa Cilia** (3 km from the hotel). Leave by a path running parallel to the road by the fields of cereals. When level with a rivulet, you cross to the left-hand side of the road. At km 302 there is sign directing you to a path leading to the Arrés hostel, thus avoiding a bend in the road, but returning to it at km 303. From there you can see **Puente la Reina de Jaca,** which you reach by turning right and crossing the bridge. Before this you have two options:

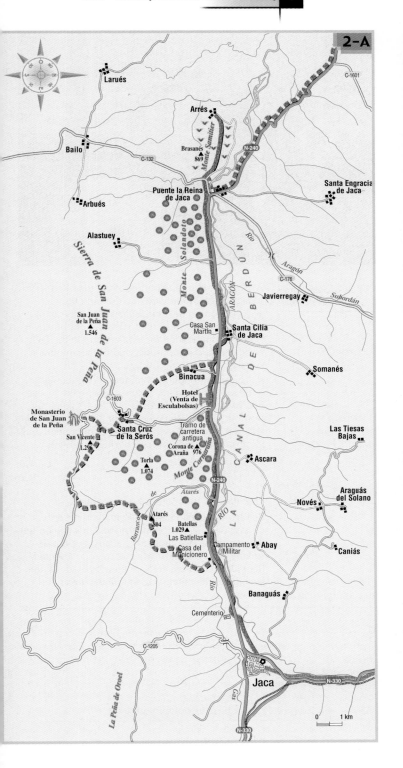

View of Santa Cruz de la Serós.

A) You can continue on from Puente la Reina along the N-240 towards Berdún and then proceed for the next two stages along the right-hand side of the Yesa dam. This option, however, is not recommended for walkers due to the lack of hostels and signposting, and to the amount of surfaced route.

B) The second option continues along the left-hand side of the dam. Before crossing the bridge you proceed towards **Arrés** (3.5 km), taking the turn-off and walking along it for a while until you take a narrow path which appears on a bend and climbs up the hill, through bushes, mainly box.

CYCLISTS

This stage of the route is quite negotiable.
Before you reach Puente la Reina you need to choose whether to continue on to Arrés (which is the recommended route for walkers, but not so suitable for cyclists) or whether to go to Puente la Reina and continue on from there towards Berdún, keeping to the national road to Pamplona.

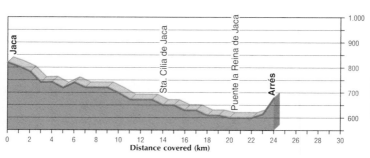

STAGE 2. PRACTICAL INFORMATION

SANTA CRUZ DE LA SERÓS

HOTELS

H** Aragón.
Ctra. N-240, km 295. ∅ 974 377 112.
44 beds. Double room: € 39/32;
breakfast: € 3,75; lunch/dinner: € 11.

SANTA CILIA DE JACA

HOSTELS

Municipal Hostel (Albergue Municipal).
C/ Del Sol, 8. 20 beds, a kitchen and
living room. Open all year round.
∅ 974 377 063

HOTELS

H* El Bosque.
Ctra. N-240, km 300. ∅ 974 377 351.
18 beds. Double room: € 45/36.

CAMPING SITES

1.st C Pirineos. Ctra. N-240, km 300.
∅ 974 377 351. 720 places.

PUENTE LA REINA DE JACA

HOTELS

HS* Del Carmen.
Ctra. N-240, km 285. ∅ 974 377 005.
60 beds. Double room: € 36/33;
breakfast: € 4,75; lunch/dinner: € 11,5.

RESTAURANTS

Mesón Anaya. Ctra. Nacional 240, km
303. ∅ 974 377 194

Mesón de la Reina. Ctra. Tarragona.
San Sebastián. ∅ 974 377 004

ARRÉS

HOSTELS

The Federation of Road Associations
(Federación de Asociaciones del
Camino) has adapted a beautiful stone
house. 20 beds, a kitchen, bathroom and
large amounts of hospitality are on offer.

MEANS OF TRANSPORT

The Alosa Group runs regular lines
between Pamplona and Jaca, through
Venta de Esculabolsas, Santa Cilia de
Jaca y Puente la Reina de Jaca.

SERVICES

During this stage you will only find one
hotel, before crossing towards Santa
Cilia de Jaca, which has some services.
There are more services in Puente la
Reina de Jaca. Arrés, a small township
which is now coming back to life, only
has one café/bar.

HISTORY AND WEALTH OF THE STAGE 2

ARAGONESE STRETCH. JACA – ARRÉS

Pilgrims leaving Jaca are offered an interesting variation to the Road's straight layout. It is a detour to the left, known as Monte Pano Road (Camino de Monte Pano) or San Juan de la Peña road (Camino de San Juan de la Peña), which leads precisely to the great National Monument of the **monastery of San Juan de la Peña.** Although it has been said that it was never related to the pilgrimage to Santiago, some documents and traditions state the opposite. Among these is St Francis of Assisi's well known – although unfortunately undocumented – pilgrimage in 1213. According to Franciscan Order tradition, after Jaca he visited San Juan de la Peña, where the monks gave him a plot of land which they owned in Jaca, on which to build his convent. What we do know from documents, however, is that a few years after the saint of Assisi's death, his co-religionists were begging for money to finish the church and convent of Jaca.

San Juan de la Peña monastery.

Many pilgrims other than St Francis took the detour to San Juan de la Peña, which housed such glorious relics as the Apostolic Male Indaletius' remains or a fake "Holy Grail", a chalice alleged to have been used by Jesus in the Last Dinner and which has inspired much literature, music and cinema since Wolfram von Eschenbach's *Parsifal*. In addition to the miraculous relics, pilgrims were also perfectly aware of the existence of a Benedictine community in San Juan de la Peña, whose rules bound it to offer hospitality to outsiders and people in need.

According to the monastery's chronicles, San Juan de la Peña originated as a refuge for brothers Voto and Felix, who fled Saragossa when it fell into Muslim hands. Three centuries later, Navarrese King Sancho III *the Greater* brought a Clunian community to the place where the brothers had erected their hermits' residence, and dedicated the sanctuary to San Juan de la Peña, possibly because a nearby chapel was dedicated to San Juan de Atarés. As well as being the bridge on

San Juan de la Peña monastery. Above, church; below, cloister.

which the Clunians started to impose Roman rites in Spain, San Juan de la Peña is also the place where the old Mozarabic liturgy was replaced by the Gregorio-Roman one in the Iberian Peninsula in 1071.

San Juan de la Peña's impressive architectural collection is divided into two levels. The lower level includes the church from Mozarabic times (Xth century), and the council room. The upper level contains the Romanesque church, the pantheon of the Kings of Aragon and, above all, the open air cloister, which is protected by nothing but the rock ("Peña") which lends its

name to the sanctuary and whose capitals – of remarkable quality – show scenes of Christ's life.

Later on but still on the same San Juan de la Peña detour, we find another National Monument, the church of Santa María de la Serós, in **Santa Cruz de la Serós.** This Romanesque church was once part of a female monastery, whose occupants were known as St John's sisters (hermanas de San Juan) due to its link to the monastery of San Juan de la Peña. This designation applied to the nuns may come from the name Serós (sorores "sisters" < *sero[r]es < Serós).

Panoramic view of Santa Cruz de la Serós.

The monastery's most splendorous time was, similarly to the monasteries of Jaca and San Juan de la Peña, the last quarter of the XIth century. In 1070, doña Sancha Ramírez, the daughter of the first King of Aragon Ramiro I, joined this monastery after the death of her husband, the count of Urgel, thus joining her sisters Urraca and Teresa, who were already there. The gifts made by doña Sancha, whose sepulchre we saw on our way through Jaca, made the community noticeably richer, and enabled the building of the church, which has a rectangular layout divided into three naves and crowned by a semicircular apse, and whose architecture and statues are very similar to those of Jaca Cathedral and San Juan de la Peña.

As was the case with Santa María, the small church of San Caprasio is all that is left of the ancient monastic complex. What is particularly

Santa Cruz de la Serós. Church of Santa María de la Serós.

striking about this church, also built in the latter part of the XIth century, is the fact that it was dedicated to Caprasius, the bishop of Agen, who was linked to one of the Road's most important forms of worship: that of the Virgin Faith (Sainte Foi), whose relics were worshipped in Conques.

From Santa Cruz, travellers can return to the straighter road via **Binacua.** The most important reference to the pilgrimage on the stretch of the Road between Jaca and the next town, **Santa Cilia,** is Venta Esculabolsas, famous for the bad treatment received by pilgrims and other travellers, whose bags were emptied by their hosts.

Puente la Reina de Jaca is the Stop that the *Liber Sancti Iacobi* guide calls *Osturit,* although other documents from that time refer to it as *Asturito.* It is a highly strategic place, where the Aragonese route's main road converged with a smaller one which had crossed the Pyrenees via Puerto de Palo. In addition to having a privileged position, it was also, according to the documents, a royal residence. It did indeed belong to King Alfonso I of Aragon, who had bought it for his mother, Queen Felicia, and who later donated it to San Juan de la Peña. For these reasons, *Osturit*-Puente la Reina de Jaca deserves to be mentioned in the guide as a the Stop of the Road. We do not know when the old name was replaced by the new one, which is related to the bridge over the river Aragón.

On leaving the town, travellers face a choice: the first option – which was chosen by the author of the *Liber Sancti Iacobi* guide – involves following the road, whereas the second route runs parallel to it to the South and also has some references to the pilgrimage. The end of our stage is precisely in **Arrés,** the first town in the second option.

3 Arrés (Puente la Reina de Jaca) – Ruesta

The route continues along the river Aragón, towards the controversial Yesa dam, and the solitary landscape is predominantly agricultural until you reach Artieda. You will then be in sight of the woodlands of the sierra de Peña Musera.

Bridge over the river Aragón in Puente la Reina de Jaca.

You leave **Arrés** by a path to the left of the road which takes you down from the village. On descending you will see the same vegetation of bushes (box) as you did on arrival. Once at the bottom, you cross a track which you will rejoin soon after. You then walk to the left, westwards, with the river Aragón on your right and the cereal fields on your left. You will see **Berdún** on the other side of the bank. After around 6 km you will need to traverse several gulleys until you meet the road running between Berdún and Martes (to the left of the route). Here you turn left and go up the road until you see a track on the right. You walk up this northwards until you reach a farmyard and then turn left, parallel again to the river. A little further on the track comes out onto a cart track which you follow for a few metres, and then let it carry on to the river, while you turn westward once more. Shortly afterwards you cross the boundary between Huesca and Zaragoza. Until you reach the level of Mianos (also on the left), the path meanders, crossing several gulleys (Sobresecho and Calcones) and some strange gravel mounds. You walk for a while through holm oaks, and after these 6 km, you take a tree-lined track which passes a farmyard. Before climbing to Mianos, you must go towards a path on the right which leads to the road going up to **Artieda.**

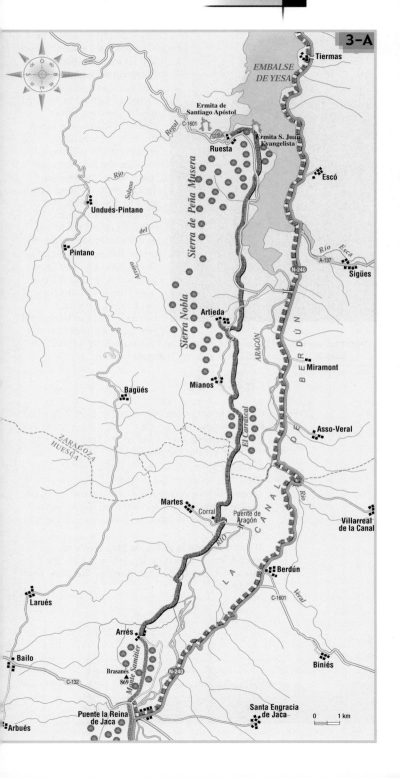

3-A

Tiermas

EMBALSE DE YESA

Ermita de Santiago Apóstol

Regal

C-1601

Ermita S. Juan Evangelista

Ruesta

Escó

Río Solano

Undués-Pintano

Río Esca

Pintano

Arroyo del

A-137

N-240

Sigües

Sierra de Peña Musera

Sierra Nobla

Artieda

ARAGÓN

Miramont

DE BERDÚN

Bagüés

Mianos

El Carrascal

Asso-Veral

ZARAGOZA

HUESCA

LA CANAL

Río

Martes

Corral

Puente de Aragón

Villarreal de la Canal

Larués

Berdún

C-1601

Veral

Arrés

Bailo

Monte Samitier

N-240

Brasanés 869

Biniés

C-132

Puente la Reina de Jaca

Santa Engracia de Jaca

0   1 km

Arbués

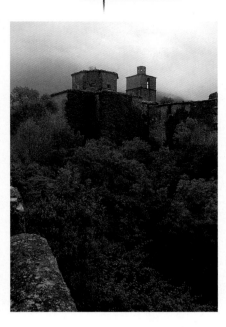

Once you have passed the cemetery, you leave the road and go into the village. Climb up through its streets and then descend via the calle Luis Buñuel to the road which takes you out of Artieda. Go down as far as the junction and a few metres on you will see a track on the left when you reach some warehouses. This leads to the road which goes to Sos del Rey and passes through Ruesta, between cereal fields and woodland. A path appears on the left, which you go up. Once at the top, you cross the road to go into the oak trees. The wood stretches out to form a passage between the farm lands, and pine trees abound. You

Panoramic view of Ruesta.

come to the San Juan Bautista hermitage and further on you reach **Ruesta** by road.

CYCLISTS

Cyclists may choose between the route described for those travelling on foot, which takes them as far as **Sangüesa** on the left of the Yesa dam, and the route on the right-hand side:

A) After coming down from **Arrés,** the terrain is quite flat, although full of gulleys. The wood appears before you reach Ruesta. If you wish, on leaving Artieda you can take road C-137 in the direction of Sos del Rey, which passes through **Ruesta.**

B) From **Puente la Reina de Jaca** (without proceeding to Arrés), at km 303 you take the N-240 which passes through **Berdún, Tiermas, Yesa** and **Javier.**

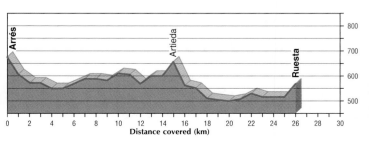

STAGE 3. PRACTICAL INFORMATION

ARTIEDA

HOSTELS

Pilgrims' Hostel (Albergue de peregrinos).
C/ Luis Buñuel, 10. It has 20 beds.
Lunch and dinner are served.
Open all year round.
∅ 948 439 316 / 669 270 318

RUESTA

HOSTELS

Municipal Hostel (Albergue Municipal).
It has 62 beds, a kitchen, dining room,
restaurant, heating and camping site.
Open all year round. ∅ 948 398 082 /
620 831 925

BERDÚN

HOSTELS

"Rincón de Emilio" hostel.
Private hostel. It doesn't have a
telephone.

HOTELS

HS* Rincón de Emilio.
Pl. Martincho, 1.
∅ 974 371 715. 14 beds.
Double room: € 38,5; breakfast: € 4;
lunch/dinner: € 13.
P Berdún.
C/ Medio, 3.
∅ 974 371 748. 14 beds.
Double room: € 23;

MEANS OF TRANSPORT

Alosa buses go through Berdún, Sigüés
(at the junction), Escó and Tiermas.

SERVICES

The Road goes past several small towns,
which it ignores, before reaching
Artieda. Artieda only has one café/bar.
Ruesta is a town which is coming back
to life thanks to the General Workers
Confederation (Confederación General
del Trabajo – CGT), although as far as
services are concerned, all it has is a
camping site.
If you follow the other route, Berdún has
a selection of accommodation and other
services, and Sigüés y Tiermas have
camping sites.

Panoramic view of Berdún.

ARAGONESE STRETCH. ARRÉS – RUESTA

As mentioned at the end of the previous stage, after leaving **Puente la Reina de Jaca,** the Road divides into two paths, both of which can be considered historic Roads to Santiago. Pilgrims, especially on stretches without important towns, did not follow a specific road or physical path, but used a sort of corridor of varying width which included several towns and a whole web of small paths. Although these may not have allowed huge detours, they did allow the pilgrims to zigzag widely and choose between different small places which were close to each other and offered similar services.

This is the case that concerns us. The Road continues on two parallel variants, and similar references to the pilgrimage can be found in the small towns which form the milestones of each route. In order to describe them, since these two variants do not join again until the next stage (Aragon 4. Ruesta-Sangüesa), we shall designate them A and B.

A) On the North Road, which now runs on road N-240, the first town is **Berdún,** at the top of Canal de Berdún, a large plain with a cereal tradition in the Aragón Bajo Valley, already classified as a geographical entity in Roman times. The town of Berdún, whose Celtic-sounding name contradicts the basically Iberian past of this land, has preserved its layout and ancient appearance. Its location on the flat peak of a hill would seem to confirm the presumed Celtic etymology of its name, since the Celtic word *dunum,* meaning "castle" or "fortress", can be guessed in it.

Still in Canal de Berdún, this variant of the Road goes through the now abandoned towns of **Sigüés, Escó** and **Tiermas.**

This last town is one of the Stops highlighted in the *Liber Sancti Iacobi* guide, which even includes a small description, pointing out its royal bath characteristics:

> *"Next comes Tiermas, which has some royal baths whose waters are always hot."*

Indeed, both the etymology of the name and the documentation and archaeology point to the existence of Roman baths, built to take advantage of the hot and sulphurous water sources near the river. Some remains can still be seen when the drought causes the Yesa reservoir water level, on the foot of the hill where the town of Tiermas is built, to decrease.

It was only relatively recently that Tiermas was abandoned by its inhabitants, when the Yesa reservoir, which makes the most of the water from the river Aragón, was built. Although the city is at the top of the hill and wasn't in itself affected by the water, the lives of its inhabitants were affected, because they were based on the cultivation of the lands in the valley, and the people had to leave their homes and find a new place to settle in. Only the buildings, also destined to slow decay and which include a sector of the town's great mediaeval wall, the castle, the parish church of La Trinidad and a large proportion of its houses, were left.

B) The second variant of this region runs south of the river Aragón. After Arrés and opposite Berdún, is **Martes.**

The church of **Artieda,** the next town, once belonged to the hospital of Santa Cristina de Somport, whose presence, in the form of priories and other properties, was very important in this area. For this reason, we can guess that Artieda may have had a pilgrims' hospital.

Although the existence of a pilgrims' hospital in Artieda in the Middle Ages is no more than an educated guess, the presence of a

Above, Artieda street which runs concurrently with the Road to Santiago; below, Yesa reservoir and Tiermas (abandoned village).

hospital in **Ruesta** is confirmed by documents. In the XIth century, this town had a church dedicated to St James, as well as one dedicated to St Mary and one to St Peter. We also know that there was a lodging place which depended on this latter church. All these religious institutions in Ruesta, together with the church of Tiermas, were given to the Benedictine abbey of La Sauve-Majeure *(Silva Maior),* near Bordeaux, by King Sancho Ramírez in 1087. Those were the most prosperous days for this Aquitaine abbey, whose founder, St Gerald of Corbie, was still alive. It was closely connected to the Road to Santiago, of which it was an important Stop. From this we can infer that the Benedictines set up a priory in Ruesta in which they assisted, as they were bound to, the pilgrims who came this way.

4   Ruesta – Sangüesa

The first part of this stage passes through woodland (the foothills of the sierra de Peña Musera), with the Yesa reservoir lying to the north. Before reaching Undués de Lerda the scenery changes as the land flattens out and becomes more humanized, with fields planted with cereals.

View of Javier castle.

To leave **Ruesta** you go down through the village and take a path which, with the dam on your right, crosses the bridge over the river Regal. You then climb up, leaving the campsite to one side. Cross the campsite track to reach the Santiago hermitage. Meeting this track again, climb up it through a reforestation of conifers towards the regional Ruesta road, but a track then takes you off to the right, climbing upwards and westwards once more. On a small plain, surrounded by cereal crops, you will come to another path which you follow up and through the pine trees (this point also marks the start of the P. R.-10 path to Yesa). Once at the top, you turn left and take a track on the right. You leave behind you the woodlands of the sierra de Peña Musera and the Ruesta boundary. From here you need to descend in a south-westerly direction towards the Sangüesa valley, between farmed land on the one side and thicket on the other. From time to time you will see the odd holm oak. Now nearing Undués de Lerda, you climb over a hill and, via the Roman road (which is not in very good condition), you cross the Molinar stream to climb up to **Undués.** On leaving you take a path down and once past the last building, now in ruins, there is a path leading off to the left. You come out onto a track which passes through farm land and

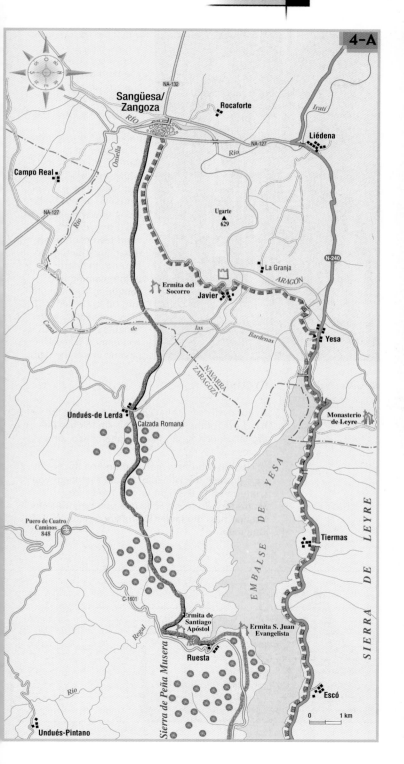

4-A

Sangüesa/
Zangoza

NA-132

Rocaforte

Irati

Liédena

NA-127

Río

Onsella

Campo Real

NA-127

Río

Ugarte
629

N-240

La Granja

ARAGÓN

Ermita del
Socorro

Javier

de

las

Bardenas

Yesa

Canal

NAVARRA
ZARAGOZA

Undués-de-Lerda

Calzada Romana

Monasterio
de Leyre

EMBALSE DE YESA

Puero de Cuatro
Caminos
848

SIERRA DE LEYRE

Tiermas

C-1601

Regal

Ermita de
Santiago
Apóstol

Ermita S. Juan
Evangelista

Ruesta

SIERRA de Peña Musera

Río

Escó

0   1 km

Undués-Pintano

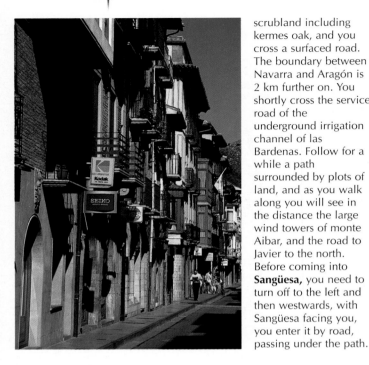

scrubland including kermes oak, and you cross a surfaced road. The boundary between Navarra and Aragón is 2 km further on. You shortly cross the service road of the underground irrigation channel of las Bardenas. Follow for a while a path surrounded by plots of land, and as you walk along you will see in the distance the large wind towers of monte Aibar, and the road to Javier to the north. Before coming into **Sangüesa,** you need to turn off to the left and then westwards, with Sangüesa facing you, you enter it by road, passing under the path.

Sangüesa high street (Calle Mayor).

CYCLISTS

A) For cyclists who have carried on along the left-hand side of the Yesa dam, this stretch has the drawback of not offering any alternative surfaced routes.

B) Cyclists who have gone around on the N-240 pass through the village of **Yesa.** From there you can turn off to the right to visit the **Leyre Monastery.** To reach Sangüesa you turn off to the left and pass the **Javier Castle** and continue on to **Sangüesa.**

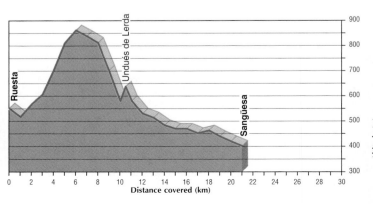

STAGE 4. PRACTICAL INFORMATION

UNDUÉS DE LERDA

Hostels

It has 56 beds. ∅ 948 888 105

LEYRE

Hotels

H** Hospedería de Leyre.
Monastery of San Martín de Leyre.
∅ 948 884 100. 60 beds. Double room:
€ 60/26,5; single room: € 45/39;
breakfast: € 5; lunch/dinner: € 10,5.

YESA

Hotels

HS** El Jabalí. Ctra. Pamplona-Jaca,
km 49. ∅ 948 884 042. 42 beds.
Double room, with ensuite bathroom:
€ 38/24; single room: € 21/18;
breakfast: € 3,5; lunch/dinner: € 10.

Restaurants

Arangoiti. C/ René Petit, 23.
∅ 948 884 122. Regional cuisine.
Average à la carte price: € 24-12.

El Jabalí. Ctra. de Jaca, km 49.
∅ 948 884 042. Regional cuisine. It is
also a hostel. Average à la carte price:
€ 16-9.

La Boya. Ctra. Pamplona-Jaca, km 49.
∅ 948 398 054

Yamaguchy 2. C/ Confederación.
∅ 948 884 102. Average à la carte
price: € 24-12.

JAVIER

Hotels

H** El Mesón. Pl. de Javier.
∅ 948 884 035. 16 beds. Double room:
€ 52; breakfast: € 5; lunch/dinner:
€ 12,5.

SANGÜESA

Hostels

Sangüesa municipal hostel.
C/ Enrique Labrit, 26. 12 beds and a
kitchen. ∅ 948 870 042.

Hotels

H** Yamaguchi.
Ctra. de Javier. ∅ 948 870 127. 80
beds. Double room: € 62/54; single
room: € 37; breakfast: € 6,5;
lunch/dinner: € 23.

HS** J. P.
P.º Raimundo Lumbier, 3.
∅ 948 871 693. 14 beds. Double room:
€ 44; single room: € 35; breakfast: € 4;
lunch/dinner: € 12.

P** Las Navas.
C/ Alfonso el Batallador, 7. ∅ 948 870
077. 12 beds. Double room: € 36; single
room: € 18; lunch/dinner: € 9.

Camping sites

2.nd C Cantolagua. Camino Cantolagua.
∅ 948 430 352. 220 places.

Restaurants

Acuario. C/ Santiago, 9. ∅ 948 870 102.
Roasts and fish. Average à la carte
price: € 24-12.
Ciudad de Sangüesa. C/ Santiago, 4.
∅ 948 871 021. Regional cuisine.
Average à la carte price: € 24-12.
Hotel El Mesón. Javier tourist area.
∅ 948 884 035. Stone building with a
careful and modern décor. Home-made
Basque and Navarrese cuisine. Average à
la carte price: € 25-12.
Las Navas. C/ Alfonso el Batallador, 7.
∅ 948 870 077. Regional cuisine.
Average à la carte price: € 24-12.
Mediavilla. C/ Alfonso el Batallador, 15.
∅ 948 870 212. Roasts. Average à la
carte price: € 42-24.

Means of Transport

The Jaca-Pamplona line goes through
Yesa.
Several bus lines go through Sangüesa.
Pamplona bus station: ∅ 948 223 854.

History and wealth of the stage 4

Leire Monasteries. Apse area.

Aragonese Stretch. Ruesta – Sangüesa

Remember that, until the end of this stage, the Road remains divided into two parallel branches, A and B:

A) After Tiermas and the frontier between Aragon and Navarre, the Road comes to **San Salvador de Leyre,** one of the oldest and most outstanding monasteries in Spain. The first document we have relating to this monastery was provided by the great Mozarabic writer St Eulogius of Cordoba (800-859), who tells us in his *Apología de los Mártires* about how he found a biography (or, rather, an autobiography) of Muhammed in a cupboard in Leyre. Let us read the brief but delicious document certifying how, even in those difficult times, the monastery already had a good library:

> *"Some time ago, during my stay in the city of Pamplona, I was compelled by my curiosity to spend some time rummaging in the unknown documents in the monastery of Leyre. I suddenly found, as part of a book, a brief biography of the abominable prophet."*

Shortly after St Eulogius' life, the best known of Leyre's abbots, St Virila (870-950) was thriving. The fame of his name is associated with a legend which is a metaphor of the mystical trance and is repeated in many places with different protagonists: St Virila, lulled by a little bird's sweet song, falls into a pleasant sleep from which he only awakens three hundred years later.

The famous crypt of San Babil is formed by four naves divided by arches, and is the oldest preserved part of the monastic complex at Leyre, possibly from Eulogius and Virila's time, or slightly later. The arches rest on gigantic capitals, supported in turn by cylindrical pillars. The worship of *St Babylas,* a martyr and bishop of Antioch, to whom the crypt is dedicated, was particularly strong from the VIIth century onwards in what is now Andalusia. It may be possible to make a connection between Eulogius' visit to Leyre and the start of the worship of St Babylas in this northern place, to which a relic of his saved from a southern sanctuary may have arrived at this time.

In spite of its old importance, the monastery's boom of wealth and power was linked to the Kingdom of Navarre's time of greatest splendour, during the reigns of King Sancho III *the Greater* (1000-1035) and his successors. During this time Leyre received generous gifts, and its Romanesque church was built. The most noteworthy aspects inside the church, which was

Leire monastery. Crypt of San Babil.

consecrated to the Saviour in 1057, are the three apses at the front (of which the middle one is bigger than the lateral ones), which are characterised by half-point arches, and the chapel, which is also the burial place of the first kings of Navarre. The most striking feature of the exterior is, without a doubt, the main portal, known as *Porta Speciosa (Puerta Hermosa)*, whose motley statues have recently been linked to the portal of San Isidoro de León.

This branch of the Road has always followed the route on the right of the river Aragón, via **Yesa,** and crossed the river Irati, in the outskirts of Liédena, through Foz de Lumbier, which was crossed on a spectacular one-span bridge which is now half torn down. This means that it did not go via Sangüesa, which is the end of this stage. Many pilgrims, however, took a detour to Yesa to visit this important city full of references to the pilgrimage. In order to do this, they had to cross the river Aragón by means of a mediaeval bridge of which some arches on either side of the river can still be seen today.

This detour includes **Javier** castle, whose name is a dialectal variation of the Basque "Etxa berri" (new house). Today, Javier (Xavier) is one of the most popular boys' names, not only in Navarre and the Basque Country but also in the rest of Spain and worldwide. The name's success was due, not only to its pleasant sound, but also to a modern time character, jesuit St Francis Xavier (1506-1552), who was born in this castle and took its name. He was an apostle in India and Japan and his worship in the Catholic world is exceedingly widespread. Javier castle is currently the destination of a massive pilgrimage, known as "Javierada", which takes place on the first Sunday of March.

B) Before Sangüesa, where it meets the first branch, the second branch only goes through the town of **Undués de Lerda.**

Although mysteriously ignored by the *Liber Sancti Iacobi* guide, **Sangüesa** is an important part of the Road. As mentioned above, archeology shows that the path followed by pilgrims did not take a detour to Sangüesa, but went straight towards Monreal, yet Sangüesa is a town born for the Road to Santiago and full of references to the pilgrimage, as we will now see. The city now known as Sangüesa, however, is not the same as the one which bore that name in the ancient world *(Sancosa)*. The old Sangüesa was what is now Rocaforte, a pre-Roman *oppidum* built on a hill on the strategic piece of land between the rivers Aragón and Irati. Due to its proximity to the Road to Santiago, King Sancho Ramírez granted "fueros" (codes of law or privileges) to anyone who came to live here. However, old Sangüesa's inconveniently high position prompted Sancho's son Alfonso I *the Warrior* to build a new town on the plain around the palace they owned (which was located before the river Aragón), and granted it the Jaca "fuero de francos" (a privilege designed to encourage foreigners to settle here and to create a bourgeoisie) in the year 1122.

The new city or "New Burg" (Burgo Nuevo) of Sangüesa was built according to the rectangular model which enables the land to be divided between its new inhabitants in equal parts. The perpendicular axis of this rectangle, the current Rúa Mayor, was the Pilgrim Road which lead the pilgrims from the city's entrance to its exit. The latter was on the bridge over the river Aragón, exactly after a model in Puente la Reina. The new settlers, most of whom came from France, settled on either side of the street to offer various services to the pilgrims. It may have been their disagreements with the "Old Burg's" (Burgo Viejo) native population which caused them to build a wall with six doors.

Sangüesa. Church of Santiago.

The town's prosperity was evidenced in the six parishes it had at one point, and the thirteen hospitals which existed in the city provide proof of its certain relationship with the pilgrimage to Santiago. The most important of these was, without a doubt, the hospital of the Hospitaller Knights of St John (hospital de los Caballeros Hospitalarios de San Juan), to whom Alfonso I, a great patron of this order, donated his palace at the start of the bridge over the river Aragón, in 1131. He also gave them the church of Santa María, on whose land they later built the impressive building now known as the collegiate church of Santa María la Real. It is a church with a Latin Cross base, three naves and three apses, built in the second half of the XIIth century and beginning of the XIIIth. Its large tower, which is crowned with an arrow, is also from this time. The best part of this church is certainly the statues on the southern façade, which comprise one of the best Romanesque sculpture collections in Spain. It seems that the statues from the first stage (c. 1130), must be related to the ones in San Juan de la Peña and other parts of Aragon. Those of the second stage, signed by a master by the name of Leodegarius (c. 1200), seem to have been directly inspired by Chartres and other French churches, especially from Bourgogne. The group formed by a smith forging a sword and a warrior using it to kill a dragon is famous among the many motifs depicted on this

Sangüesa. Collegiate church of Santa María la Real.

façade, and may be related to the legendary story, translated by Wagner into music, of the Germanic hero Siegfried.

The church of Santiago, which has three naves with their respective apses, is also from the XIIth century. On the tympanum of its main façade is a polychrome statue of St James dating from the XVIth century. Inside is a very large Gothic statue of the Apostle, which was discovered in 1965.

Other old churches in Sangüesa, which have not been preserved, include the church of San Nicolás, which belonged to Roncesvals, and the church of La Magdalena, which was annexed to a lepers' hospital outside the city walls.

Among the more recent monuments, the bulk of the Príncipe de Viana palace and the Rectory, which is adorned with references to St James, are particularly noteworthy. In the area around Sangüesa, the Romanesque chapel of San Adrián de Vadolunego in the Sos del Rey Católico direction, is worth a visit.

5   Sangüesa – Monreal

Both options available offer views of great beauty. If you choose to pass the Alto de Aibar, the stretch between Rocaforte and Izco is uninhabited and you run the risk of losing your way if you do not follow the signs carefully. The other option keeps close to the road and its main attraction is the pass through the Foz de Lumbier.

Panoramic view of Liédena.

You leave Sangüesa by the calle Mayor, passing Santa María la Real, towards the bridge of the same name. Once you are on road NA-127 you have two options:

A) There is a turning off to the left to Rocaforte, from which a path in turn leads off to the right and passes the Papelera (paper mill) and the sown fields up to **Rocaforte.** From there you descend (there is a sign for Alto de Aibar) via a path shaded by black poplars and one or two dwarf oaks, in a landscape of scrubland (with hawthorn and box). Once you arrive at the Cañada Real you begin to climb passing the ruins of Santa Cilia, alongside a stream and crossing under the Aibar road through a tunnel. A path takes you off to the right and after passing an opening, and descending for a while parallel to the road, you go down again to the right and cross an enclosed field. After going through a pine grove, on the descent, you take a surfaced track, on the right of which you take a path through pines, box and juniper on the side of the hill. By another path you cross a stream to walk up another hill, where you follow a path off to the left. You skirt the hillside, walking parallel to this stream for 2 km, until you take a new track up through conifers, moving away from the lowland, to the site of Olaz (a village which disappeared in the 14th century). Further up you take another track and then a path which goes down to the left. From here you can now see Izco, which is reached by crossing cereal fields.

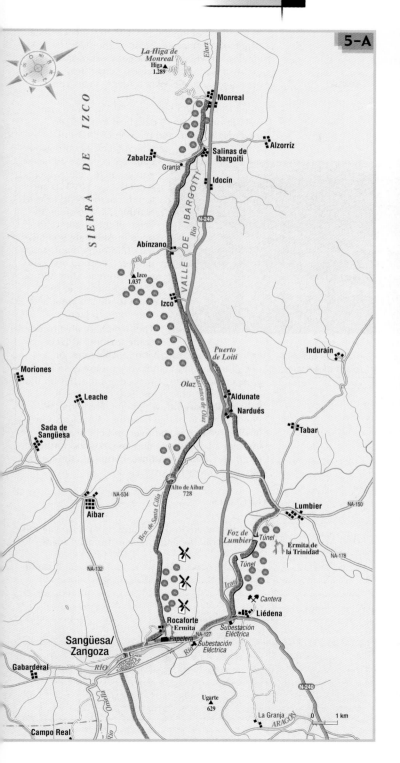

B) Continue along the NA-127 towards **Liédena,** which you enter after crossing the river Irati. On leaving the village a track goes westward, as does the river Irati, through vines, cereal fields and olive trees. After 2.5 km a tunnel takes you into the amazing gorge of Foz de Lumbier, along a green route. With vultures circling above, you walk through kermes oak, box and juniper, towards the dam, and then on to the tunnel which takes you out again. **Lumbier** is the next place you come to, after which you take the NA-150 and turn off at the bend towards **Nardués.** Leave along the verge of the N-240, and once in **Aldunate** you take a path through maple trees, past an oakwood and pine grove. To reach the Alto de Loiti, you return to the main road, and via a path you come to **Izco.**

The two alternative routes come together at Izco.

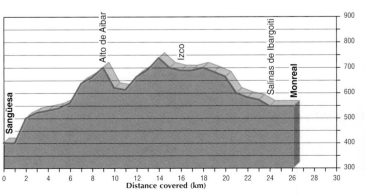

Alto de Loiti and village of Aldunate.

From here you walk 2 km to **Abinzano,** on a track through farm land, with mountains of greenery to the left. The road approaches on the right. After another 5 km, you will come to **Salinas de Ibargoiti,** which you enter via the Puente Grande bridge over the river Elorz. On leaving, you cross the river and climb a hill, through a pine wood, and an oakwood further on. Before entering **Monreal** you pass the football pitch and cross the river Elorz.

CYCLISTS

Cyclists are advised to choose option B, which is more negotiable and closer to surfaced roads.

STAGE 5. PRACTICAL INFORMATION

LIÉDENA

HOTELS

HS** Latorre.
Ctra. Pamplona-Huesca, km 40.
𝄐 948 870 610. Double room: € 48;
single room: € 30; breakfast: € 5;
lunch/dinner: € 11.

IZCO

HOSTELS

San Martín hostel. C/ Mayor, s/n. It has
20 beds and a kitchen. Open all year
round. 𝄐 948 362 210 / 948 362 129

MEANS OF TRANSPORT

The Jaca-Pamplona line stops at
Liédena, Aldunate and Monreal.

SERVICES

In Izco, the hostel itself sells food and
drink. Once you reach Monreal, there
are quite a few services available.

MONREAL

HOSTELS

The hostel is next to the church on C/ De
la Corte, 1. It has 26 beds, a kitchen and
a washing machine. Open all year round.
𝄐 948 362 081

HOTELS

HS** Unzué.
Ctra. Huesca. 𝄐 948 362 008. 22 beds.
Double room: € 75/42; breakfast: € 3;
lunch/dinner: € 10.

HISTORY AND WEALTH OF THE STAGE 5

ARAGONESE STRETCH. SANGÜESA – MONREAL

Just like Puente la Reina's high street (calle Mayor), Sangüesa's rúa Mayor used to lead to a bridge, which is mentioned in the "fuero" (charter) granted to the city in 1122 by Alfonso I *the Warrior*. The bridge, one of whose buttresses contains a Roman inscription, has unfortunately not survived, although we know from descriptions of it that it was a magnificent seven-span example.

Shortly after crossing the metal bridge that replaced it, we find the chapel of San Nicolás, part of an old Cathedral Treasury of the same name belonging to Roncesvals. The capitals of its magnificent but now ruined Romanesque church were saved and can now be seen in the Museo de la Cámara de Comptos in Pamplona.

Panoramic view of Rocaforte.

Rocaforte is the "Old Burg" (Burgo Viejo) of Sangüesa, as well as being the town that bore that name *(Sancossa)* from pre-Roman times until the "New Burg" was founded. Its current descriptive name comes from its location at the top of a hill with a view to a wide landscape, and its fortified character. However, Rocaforte's main glory does not relate to fighting but to the fact that St Francis of Assisi went through it in his pilgrimage to Santiago de Compostela. Although, as we have already seen, tradition has it that St Francis stopped in Jaca and San Juan de la Peña, chronicles of the Franciscan Order in Spain affirm that his first foundation was in Rocaforte. According to them, St Francis retired to a chapel dedicated to the apostle St Bartholomew, which became the first Franciscan building in Spain. In addition to the hermit residence of St Bartholomew, northwest of Rocaforte, the area around the town is full of references to scenes of St Francis' every-day life during his stay here, such as the fountain of St Francis ("Fuente de San Francisco"), where he used to go to quench his thirst, or St Francis' stone rest ("Piedra del descanso de San Francisco"), on which he used to sit down to rest.

Franciscan Order chronicler Wadingo also tells us how the saint planted an orchard which included a mulberry tree with healing properties. Years later, when the Franciscans left Rocaforte, the mulberry tree dried out, but it grew green again when the religious order returned. There are a few more legends about St Francis' possible stay in Rocaforte and Sangüesa, although they were all written many centuries after the time to which they relate. As we will see in later stages, many places of the Road to Santiago have similar references to the ones in Rocaforte, as well as many legends and anecdotes which turn around St Francis in his pilgrimage to Santiago. There are no documents confirming the angelic patriarch's probable journey to Compostela, but what we can say is that the Franciscan foundations in the Road to Santiago, many of which were created during the

Roman village of Lumbier.

saint's life, are among the first in the Iberian Peninsula.

Sangüesa and its environs are full of Roman and even earlier remains. Of particular note among these were the bridge of Sangüesa, some stretches of Roman road and, above all, the town of **Liédena,** just outside the old road. It is a sumptuous late-Roman (IVth century) rural town and a good example of the Romanisation levels of this area close to the Pyrenees. In close proximity to this village, on the road which pilgrims used to follow before Sangüesa was founded, and which may have been an old Roman road, is the impressive **foz de Lumbier,** an exceedingly rugged natural gorge created by the river Irati's erosive action on the limestone. A bridge – which was no less impressive than the gorge itself – was built in the Middle Ages to cross the gorge. It had a single very high arch and was known as puente del Diablo (the Devil's bridge).

Many legends (with small variations) attributing the work – normally a bridge – to the devil, have been created around here, just like in many

River Irati in Foz de Lumbier.

House and church of Idocin.

other landscapes which were either difficult or impossible to get through but which were solved by a highly technical work of engineering. Their general plot is as follows:

A community is suffering because nature has created difficulties, which it cannot overcome, in its area. The devil, always on the lookout for human need, offers his technical assistance to overcome them, but asks for a very high price in exchange: he wants either the next newborn within the community or the first living being that crosses the bridge. The men accept the deal and the devil diligently carries out his work, but when the time to be paid comes, he is disappointed to see that the cunning men, although not in breach of their promise, offer him a small kid instead of the human offering he was expecting.

Slightly away from foz de Lumbier, to the south, the Road crosses some desolate places leading to Alto de Aibar. At its foot is the deserted spot of **Santa Cilia,** a now abandoned mediaeval village. "Cilia" is the contracted from, typical in this area, of the name Cecilia, a Roman martyr from early Christian days and patron saint of musicians since the late Middle Ages. The extent and strength of her worship in the area of Jaca and its outskirts is probably due to the presence of a relic of hers, which made her the object of remarkable worship.

The same reasoning applies to St Babylas, whose name, which is also under the typically contracted form of Babil, can be found, after Alto de Aibar, in the names of a gully and a hill. The chapel dedicated to him, whose portal is now in the chapel of Santa Bárbara at the top of Higa de Monreal, must have been in that area too. The special devotion to this eastern martyr, since Mozarabic times, in the area of Leyre and Sangüesa prompted King John II and his mother Doña Catalina to bring the saint's relics to Sangüesa as late as the XVth century, where a basilica was erected in his honour.

The parish church of San Martín, a late Romanesque / early Gothic building erected in the XIIIth century – although quite seriously renovated – stands out among the few but beautiful houses of **Izco.** The dedication of the church to St Martin of Tours can be considered as one of the many infiltrations of French forms of worship into Spain via the Road to Santiago.

The parish church of **Abínzano,** dedicated to St Peter the Apostle, is also from the XIIIth century. Just like the church of San Martín in Izco, its old stonework was seriously renovated in later years (XVIth-XVIIth centuries).

On a slight detour from our route, at the edge of the road, is **Idocin,** a small town whose main glory stems from being the hometown of Francisco Espoz y Mina, one of the most famous Spanish guerrilla fighters who headed the popular resistance against Napoleonic occupation during the war for independence. Its biggest and oldest

Mediaeval bridge of Monreal.

monument, however, is the church of San Clemente. Just like most churches in these small towns around Monreal, the church of San Clemente was built in the Middle Ages, between the XIIth and XIIIth centuries, and was the object of a harsh modern time reform which gave it its current appearance.

The same happened to the parish church of **Salinas de Ibargoiti,** which is dedicated to the archangel St Michael. The name of the town comes from its salt wells.

Monreal is mentioned in the *Liber Sancti Iacobi* guide as a Stop of the Road to Santiago, the end of the second stage of the Aragonese stretch, and the beginning of the third stage. This is not without reason, since Monreal is yet another town born and developed thanks to the Road to Santiago. The name Monreal is relatively recent – the earliest reference to it is in a document from 1132 – and clearly refers to the town's Royal foundation. The kings did not, however, grant it a "fuero" (charter) until almost twenty years later, in 1149. Before the French settled here, there was a town called Higa either on this land or on a spot close to it. This is now part of the name of the great calcareous cone, Higa de Monreal, on whose foot the current town can be found.

Monreal's layout is the typical layout of Navarrese-Aragonese towns created around the Road to Santiago: a long street (in this case, calle del Burgo), with the town's houses laid out rationally along it. The parish church of Santa María del Burgo, which was dedicated to St Martin of Tours in early days and which houses an image of Santa María del Burgo, is of particular note among its buildings.

Its most important reference to the pilgrimage is a document from 1144 confirming that there used to be a pilgrims' hospital here, which depended on the Church of Pamplona.

6   Monreal – Puente la Reina

This stage takes you along the northern side of the sierra de Alaiz, over the cereal plain of the river Elorz valley to Tiebas (from where you can see Pamplona to the north). Once you have negotiated the motorway, the N-120 and the railway track, you enter into the area of Valdizarbe. From there, the river Robo guides you to Puente la Reina.

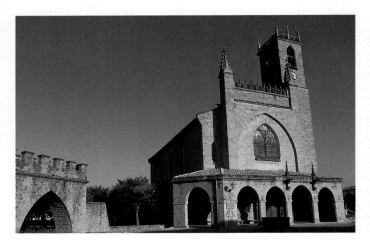

Obanos. Church and square.

The calle del Burgo leads you to the edge of **Monreal** (an arrow pointing towards the church actually indicates the way to the hostel), from where you take the Camino de los Carros through fields of cereals. The road runs to the right and on the left is the Higa de Monreal mountain. Now nearing the river Elorz, you walk through corridors of hawthorn and other bushes, until you cross a bridge, to proceed towards the sierra de Alaiz and continue along the mountainside through holm oaks and box. After 4 km you come to **Yárnoz.** Pass the church and leave by the cemetery path. Continue skirting the mountainside and via an extremely steep path you reach **Otano.** Shortly afterwards (1.5 km) and with an old quarry at its entrance, you come to Ezperun. A corridor of maple trees takes you to **Guerendiain** (1 km), and you leave by passing the church of San Juan. Keep skirting the mountainside, this time through holm oaks and common oaks. You then have almost 4 km to go before you reach **Tiebas,** which is on the sierra, between quarries. You enter the village by a path which appears on the right. You must then choose between two routes to travel from here to Enériz:

A) If you leave by passing the school, where the hostel is, you need to cross the local road and descend, leaving the quarry to your left and the football pitch to your right. As you approach the motorway, walk alongside it until you can cross underneath it through a tunnel. You will also need to cross the N-121 and the railway track. After **Muruarte de Reta** you go on to **Olcoz,** where you take a path on the right which will take you up a hill. Descend to the river Robo and follow its course. You

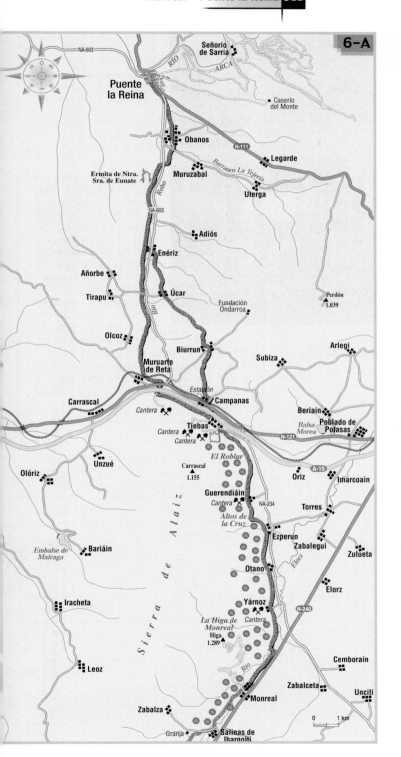

6–A

Enériz street.

then cross the Úcar road, and enter into **Enériz** along its calle San Juan.

B) Leaving Tiebas via its local road, you cross the motorway, go around the station and walk in the direction of **Biurrun.** From there you take a path leading to **Úcar,** which you leave towards **Enériz.**

The two alternative routes now come together and you continue along the course of the river Robo. When you reach the point where the path veers away from the river, turn towards the church of **Eunate.** You pass through a recreational area. If you wish to climb up to **Obanos,** you will need to cross the N-601, pass some vineyards, cross the road leading to Muruzábal and climb a steep slope. From Obanos you descend and cross the road again. First of all you continue parallel, and then take a path through orchards to come onto the road to **Puente la Reina.**

CYCLISTS

If the route appears too difficult you can leave Monreal via the N-240 and take road NA-234 which turns off to the left. On crossing the motorway, you go round on the N-121 for a short while, until you see the NA-601 on the right, which comes out on to the N-111 to take you into Puente la Reina.

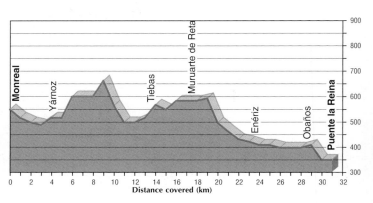

STAGE 6. PRACTICAL INFORMATION

TIEBAS

HOSTELS

Municipal Hostel (Albergue Municipal). There is a shelter in the old schools. It has a single lounge with mats, and a toilet with no shower. There is a pelota court close by, where you can have a shower.

RESTAURANTS

Casa Tere. Campanas. Ctra. Zaragoza, km 15. ✆ 948 360 020
Jiménez. Ctra. Campanas.
✆ 948 360 012
Venta Úcar. Úcar. Venta de Úcar.
✆ 948 350 094

EUNATE

HOSTELS

There is a small building for pilgrims next to the chapel.

OBANOS

HOSTELS

Usda hostel. Located next to the church. It has 36 beds and a kitchen. Open from 1st November to 1st March. Closed on Tuesdays. ✆ 676 560 927

RESTAURANTS

Ibarberoa. C/ San Salvador.
✆ 948 344 153. Average à la carte price: € 18-12.

PUENTE LA REINA

HOSTELS

Hotel Jakue. Located at the entrance. It has 40 beds, a kitchen and washing machine.
The **Priests of the Sacred Heart of Jesus** (PP Reparadores) have a hostel on C/ Crucifijo, which is open all year round. It has 80 beds, a kitchen, a dining room and a washing machine.

The owners of the camping site have adapted the "Santiago Apóstol" hostel in Paraje el Real with 100 beds. Washing machine.

HOTELS

HR** Bidean. C/ Mayor, 20. 38 beds. ✆ 948 341 156. Double room: € 80/48; single room: € 50/40; breakfast: € 6.

H** El Peregrino. Ctra. Pamplona-Logroño, km 23. ✆ 948 340 075. 28 beds. Double room: € 180/72; breakfast: € 9. lunch/dinner: € 48.

RESTAURANTS

Hotel Jakue. C/ Irunlarrea.
✆ 948 341 017. Average à la carte price: € 18-11.

La Conrada. Paseo de los Fueros.
✆ 948 340 052. Average à la carte price: € 12-6.

La Plaza. Pl. Mayor, 52.
✆ 948 340 145.
Average à la carte price: € 12-6.

Lorca. Pl. Mayor, 54. ✆ 948 340 127. Average à la carte price: € 24-12.

Sidrería Izarbe. C/ Irunbidea. Ctra. Pamplona-Logroño, km 23.
✆ 948 340 434. Roasts.

Mesón del Camino.
Enériz. C/ Mayor. ✆ 948 350 170

MEANS OF TRANSPORT

The Pamplona-Puente la Reina-Estella-Logroño line, run by the La Estellesa company, goes through Puente la Reina.
✆ 948 222 223.

HISTORY AND WEALTH OF THE STAGE 6

ARAGONESE STRETCH. MONREAL – PUENTE LA REINA

From the Middle Ages until recently, travellers left Monreal via a beautiful paved bridge over the river Elorz which, although still standing, can sadly no longer be used, since the old pilgrims' road leading to the bridge no longer exists due to the current concentration of smallholdings.

Also in the middle of a field is a Gothic stone cross called "Piedra de San Blas" (St Blaise's stone), which may be a reference to an old lepers' hospital located on the outskirts of Monreal.

At the other side of the river Elorz are the ruins of the chapel of **Garitoain,** which was demolished in 1942. This was the last remaining part of an old priory belonging to the French Benedictine abbey of Sainte-Foi de Conques, which used to have a church and a pilgrims' hospital. Before the Benedictines settled in, there used to be a village whose freedom was declared by Sancho III *the Greater* in 1032.

The next town of the Road is **Yarnoz,** between the cereal plains and the first spurs of the Alaiz mountain range (Sierra de Alaiz). The town is comprised of a small and homogeneous group of stone houses, with which the parish church of La Natividad subtly blends in. A larger square defence tower dating from the XIVth century stands out on the town's higher part.

Very close by and still at the foot of the mountain range, is **Otano.** Its parish church, dedicated to the Ascension, was erected in the Middle Ages and subsequently renovated in the XVIth and XVIIth centuries.

The images seen in Yarnoz and Otano are practically repeated in the next two towns, **Ezperun** and **Guerendiáin,** in the form of an old but renovated mediaeval church (dedicated to the Conception and St John the Baptist respectively), and a small but elegant group of houses (some of them abandoned) between the foot of the Alaiz mountain

View of the mediaeval church of Guerendiáin.

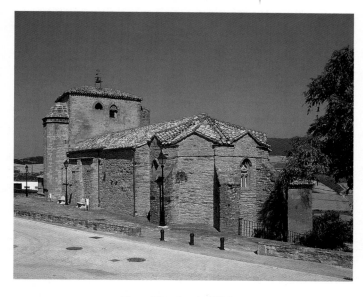

View of the church of Tiebas.

range and the cereal plains of the Elorz valley. In spite of their proximity to the Road to Santiago, none of these small towns show any signs of owing their origin or wealth to the Road. As suggested by their Basque names, they were born as modest rural villages which prospered thanks to agriculture. Their image and presence is useful for explaining the contrast there was in the Kingdom of Navarre during the XIth, XIIth and XIIIth centuries, when it was divided into two realities which, although physically close to each other, were completely opposite due to their kings' opposite wills: there was rural Navarre, whose population was dominated by Basque-speaking natives, and urban Navarre, which was represented by all the French burgs created at this time (Monreal, Sangüesa, Puente la Reina, Estella, the French burgs of Pamplona, etc.) and populated by foreigners, craftsmen and traders who originally lived exclusively off the great pilgrimage route and the need for services which emerged from it.

This simple sketch of the contrast that existed at the time helps us understand the insults directed by the author of *Liber Sancti Iacobi* at the Navarrese people, that rural population which, due to its economic activity, ignored the pilgrims; which, due to its tongue, could not understand or make itself understood by the pilgrims; and which felt disregarded in its own land by the new colonists from the French burgs, to whom the Navarrese kings themselves had granted privileges and exemptions denied to their old subjects. All this resulted in an atmosphere of antagonism and mutual contempt, often translated into genuine civil wars – as was the case in Pamplona during the whole mediaeval period – which can help us understand the reasons behind the insults to the Navarrese in *Liber Sancti Iacobi*, certainly created in this context.

Although **Tiebas** is also at the foot of the Alaiz mountain range, we find in it a very different reality to the one in the Elorz valley. Tiebas

View of Biurrun.

was a residence of the Navarrese kings of the House of Champagne, troubadour Theobald I and his son Theobald II (XIIIth century), who had a castle built here and in which they spent long periods of time. At one point, the kingdom's royal archives were kept here, showing the importance of this place at that time. Tiebas' other important building is its Romanesque parish church of Santa Eufemia. King Theobald may have chosen Tiebas as a place of residence because of its strategic position, on a crossroads near Pamplona, whose valley – the "Cuenca" – it towered over.

Those wishing to follow the Road have two parallel options (A and B) between Tiebas and Enériz, which run separately for about eight kilometers.

A) The first option, on the right hand side, first goes through **Campanas,** the first Aragonese Road town in El Valdizarbe. This place's pilgrimage tradition can be seen in the existence of a chapel dedicated to St Nicholas of Bari, which lets us know that there was once an old pilgrims' hospital here. There was also a lodging place for travellers in modern times, called "Venta de las Campanas", which lends its name to the current, fairly modern, village.

The solid parish church of El Rosario can be found in **Biurrun,** a town comprised of large rural houses typical of the Valdizarbe area. In addition to this, two chapels – dedicated respectively to St Martin of Tours and St Christopher – tell us about this town's mixed character – mostly agricultural but with some Road to Santiago influences –, in contrast with the small towns at the foot of the Alaiz range. Indeed, the presence of the worship to St Martin of Tours can be seen as the infiltration of a cult which, in spite of its worldwide spread, has a markedly French character and was brought here via the Road to Santiago. As to St Christopher, although his worship in the Road to Santiago is not particularly common, he is a traditional protector of wayfarers and travellers in general.

In **Úcar** we find, in addition to the parish church of La Asunción, a chapel dedicated to St Michael, another protector of Christianity by right, in the outskirts of the town. We cannot be sure, however, that his worship was associated with any kind of hospitality or pilgrims' service rendered in this town.

B) The second possible way to get from Campanas to Enériz first goes through **Muruarte de Reta,** which has a beautiful Gothic church dedicated to St Stephen.

Another beautiful Romanesque church, this time dedicated to St Michael, can also be admired in the next town of this branch, **Olcoz.** The ornaments on its portal have recently been linked to the one in Santa María de Eunate.

In **Enériz,** where the two branches of the Road which split up in Campanas meet again, we find

Image of the Virgen of Eunate.

the town's parish church, a Neoclassical building dedicated to the Magdalene, which is almost certainly a sign that there used to be an old hospital here.

Before meeting and becoming one with the road from Roncesvals, the Aragonese Road reaches the last, and possibly most famous, monument on its route: the **chapel of Santa María de Eunate.** The origin of its name is not clear, although the suggestion that it relates to

Chapel of Santa María de Eunate.

Monument to the Pilgrim near Puente la Reina.

the arches which surround the building (in Basque: Eun- "hundred", -ate "doors") has been widely publicised. Neither have its peculiar constructive form, its presence in this remote location or its exact function been satisfactorily explained, in spite of the amount of ink used writing about this original building. It is a small Romanesque building with an octagonal layout and unequal sides. The chapel's pentagonal apse starts from one of these sides. The church is surrounded by a sort of corridor or uncovered cloister, concentric in relation to the temple, bordered on the inside by the church and on the outside by an arcade, and surrounding the whole complex. This has traditionally been linked to the Order of the Templars, on the basis that its circular shape and the corridor which surrounds it could be an imitation of the Holy Sepulchre in Jerusalem, which is also circular and surrounded by an ambulatory. In spite of the lack of reliable documentary proof, however, it is more likely that the chapel of Eunate belonged to the Knights of St John, as suggested by some documents. As to its function, in addition to providing a possible meeting place for the Knights of St John, it was definitely a burial place for members of this Order as well as for the many Santiago pilgrims who died on the way through here. This has been confirmed by the scallops among the remains found in the ossuaries (which were between arches, at the foot of each arch).

Slightly further on, the place where the roads from Somport and Roncesvals merge is now marked by a modern iron statue by Gerardo Brun. This is next to Road N-111 before it enters Puente la Reina.

The other roads

1 Extension: Santiago – Padrón

Exterior of the collegiate church of Iria Flavia.

The route running from Santiago to the village of Padrón begins at the Plaza del Obradoiro. Along the Rúa do Franco you come to the Porta Faxeira and from there via the Carreira do Conde or the calle Xoán Carlos I you take the calle Rosalía de Castro which takes you out of the city and into the district of A Choupana. Cross the bridge over the river Sar and continue towards the ruins of **A Rocha Vella.** Over the hill of **Agro dos Monteiros** and after a continuous series of ascents and descents, you reach the town of **Rúa de Francos,** on the outskirts of which you will see the ruins of **Castro Lupario.** Passing the **Pazo do Faramello, Areal** and **Angueira de Suso,** and after leaving a pine grove behind you, you come to the church of Santa María de Cruces and shortly afterwards the Santuario de Nosa Señora da Escravitude. From there you continue on through **Loureiro, Vilar, Tarrío, Anteportas, Cambelas, Rueiro, Souto, Quintáns** and **Pousa** until you reach **Iria Flavia,** by now very close to **Padrón.**

EXTENSION 1.
PRACTICAL INFORMATION

HOSTELS

Teo:
There is a hostel with 28 beds on the old N-550 road. ✆ 981 815 700
Padrón:
It has a pretty renovated house, with 44 beds, on Rúa Costiña do Carme. ✆ 981 810 044

HOTELS

Biduido:
H** Milladouro. Rúa Anxeriz, 12. 0 Milladouro. ✆ 981 536 623. Double room: € 61/27; single room: € 49/38.

Iria Flavia:
H** Rosalía. C/ Maruxa Villanueva. A Matanza. ✆ 981 812 490. Double room: € 50/43; lunch/dinner: € 9.

Padrón:
HR** Rivera. C/ Enlace Parque, 7. ✆ 981 811 454. Double room: € 45/34; breakfast: € 3.

RESTAURANTS

Padrón:
Mesón Gaucho Rois. Avda. Compostela, 53. ✆ 981 810 190
Santiaguiño. Praza de Macías, 8. ✆ 981 810 023

1–P

Ponte Valga

Campaña

Sta. Martiña
de Barcala

ULLA

Enfesta

Pontecesures

C-550

Lestrove

Souto

S. Miguel
de Barcala

Herbón

Padrón

RÍO

VR-G1-1
Extramundi

Colegiata de Sta.
María de Iria

Iria

Carcacía

Couso

Río

Rumille

Reis

Seira

Lampai

Rarís

Escravitude

C-541

Santuario de Nosa
Señora da Escravitude

Ramallosa

Cruces

Sorribas

Sta. María
de Cruces

Luou

Lispasande

Francelos

Ribasar

Faramello

S. Xulián de
Bastavales

Recesende

A-9

Cacheiras

Calo

N-550

Rúa de Francos
Castro
Lupario

Sebaxáns

Osebe

S. Salvador
de Bastavales

Balcaide

Raices

Milladoiro

Biduido

Tarrío

Bugallido

Ortoño

Crujeiro

Paramuiño

Os Ánxeles

Combarro

A Rocha
Vella

Framil

Torrente

Laraña

Bertamiráns

Conxo

Santo
Domingo

Pardiñas

C-543

Pedrouzos

Paredes

Sar

Vidán

Barcia

Lamas

Roxos

Sarela

Sarela de
Abaixo

Carballal

Portanxil

Catedral

Quintáns

Ponte Sarela

**SANTIAGO DE
COMPOSTELA**

Lombao

Aguapesada

Río

Raxos

0   1 km

Pedrouzos-
Vilar

HISTORY AND WEALTH OF THE EXTENSION 1

After succeeding in such a long and hard pilgrimage, many refuse to see Santiago de Compostela as their journey's definitive goal, so they seek to prolong the experience by visiting two emblematic places, Padrón and Finisterre.

The first of these, Padrón, is closely related to the worship of St James; since this is where his relics were disembarked after their journey from Jerusalem, it forms a substantial part of the sacred geography linked to the apostle St James. Although lacking in such significant monuments as this, the second destination, Finisterre, is the place where the ancients located the western confines of the known world with the immeasurable and mysterious ocean.

EXTENSION 1. SANTIAGO DE COMPOSTELA – PADRÓN

According to the *Liber Sancti Iacobi* guide, pilgrims on their way to Padrón left Santiago through the Fajeira door (puerta Fajeira), which was at the end of rúa del Franco. Judging by the text of the guide, which refers to it as *porta de Felgariis,* its name seems to be related to the ferns which probably grew around it.

The guide also explains how, once outside the old city walls, the road to Padrón first lead to the church of Santa Susana, a building which still stands today in the park of La Herradura, a beautiful green area in the modern city. The church was consecrated in 1105 to the Holy Sepulchre by the then bishop Diego Gelmírez, who very solemnly deposited a beautiful relic taken from the Church of Braga: the body of St Susan (Santa Susana), the Old Testament character whose story is told in the prophet Daniel's book.

The milestones of the short way between Santiago and Padrón are the so-called **A Rocha Vella** (the Old Rock), the ruins of a castle of the archbishop of Santiago de Compostela next to the Road. Later on, after going through **Biduido** (whose plant-based name refers to the birches which grow there) and **Osebe,** you reach **Rúa de Francos,** at whose entrance travellers are welcomed by a beautiful Gothic stone cross. Very close by, and in addition to the remains of a Roman road and a graceful one-span mediaeval bridge, the **Castro Lupario** enclave, a pre-Roman ruin associated with the legend of St James, can be found. According to a tradition which is already reflected in *Liber Sancti Iacobi,* this is where Mrs Lupa, a matron who was asked by the disciples of St James – who had brought their master's body from Palestine to Galicia – to give them her property (which eventually became Compostela) so that they could bury the Apostle, lived. After several vicissitudes, Mrs Lupa, who had previously devoted herself to idolatry, converted to Christianity and gave the disciples of St James the estate which she owned so that they could bury the Apostle in it.

The Road continues through Faramello and **Cruces,** whose parish church of Santa María still preserves its old Romanesque façade. Within the territory of Cruces is the Baroque sanctuary da **Escravitude.**

Following the course of the river Sar towards the sea, the road goes through the hamlets of **Vilar, Tarrío, Anteportas, Cambelas, Rueiro, Souto** and **Quintáns,** and reaches the very old **Iria Flavia,** which is now included within the town of **Padrón,** but whose name has been preserved in the collegiate church of Santa María de Iria.

View of Padrón.

This place's great importance in the context of the legend and worship of St James stems from the fact that it is the capital of the diocese in whose territory the Apostle's body was found, and of the port in which his remains were disembarked. This locality had the status of Roman city since Vespasian's times – hence its surname "Flavia" – and it was the capital of a legal jurisdiction in early Roman times and had an episcopal see from Ancient times. Its Cathedral was originally dedicated to Mérida martyr St Eulalia, but this was later changed to the current denomination of Santa María. The body of the apostle St James was found inside its territory in bishop Theodomir's times (XIth century). In time, this fact caused the old see's decline.

Indeed, the great strength of the new "holy place" of Santiago de Compostela gradually pushed Iria away from the limelight, to the point that, in 1095, the bishops of the see replaced the old title of Bishop of Iria with the new name of Bishop of Compostela. In addition, Iria was demoted to a simple collegiate church. The old city of Iria's change of name in favour of the new name Padrón was also a consequence of this ousting, and the reason for the new name was the fame attained by the crag ("padrón" in Galician means "large stone, usually of a commemorative character") to which the ship from Jaffa which was carrying St James' body was tied up when it reached land.

This "padrón" is now identified – although other versions do exist – with a Roman altarstone which started its life as the inscripted base of a statue but was then used as a footing for the altar – whose construction was ordered by bishop Theodomir as early as the IXth century – of the church of Santiago de Padrón. Today it can be seen in the current church's Neoclassical style chancel.

Another reference to St James' presence in Padrón is the Carmen fountain *(fuente del Carmen),* which miraculously sprang up when the Apostle intervened by hitting a rock with his staff. The fountain contains reliefs referring to the transfer of the Apostle. The El Carmen convent, built in the early XVIIIth century, stands there.

However, of particular note among Padrón's monuments is the collegiate church of Santa María de Iria, although this is due more to its honourable past than to what it can offer visitors today: a collection of buildings whose current aspect was conferred by Baroque style and which has been remodelled in successive stages.

2 Extension: Santiago – Fisterra – Muxía

View of Cee in Corcubión estuary.

Taking the Plaza del Obradoiro as your starting point, you leave **Santiago de Compostela** by the Rúa das Hortas, Poza de Bar, San Lorenzo and la Robleda (next to the convent of San Lourenzo de Transouto), from where you leave the city. After passing **Ponte Sarela,** you continue through the many villages in the municipality of **Ames** until you reach the medieval bridge of **Augapesada.** Climb up the Alto do Mar das Ovellas and further on you cross the flow of the river Tambre at **Pontemaceira Vella.**

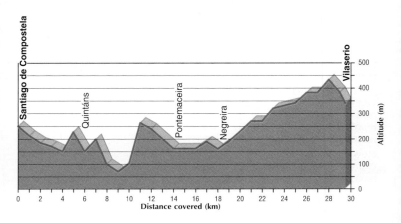

EXTENSION 2.
PRACTICAL INFORMATION

HOSTELS

Negreira: 22 beds and a kitchen.
Olveiroa: 44 beds and a kitchen.
Fisterra: It offers shelter (C/ Real, 2),
48 beds and a kitchen. ∅ 981 740 781
Dumbría: Shelter in the sports centre. The
parish church in Grixá takes in pilgrims.
Muxía: In the municipal sports centre.

HOTELS

Santiago de Compostela:
HS* La Salle. C/ San Roque, 6.
∅ 981 584 611
Cee: H** Larry. C/ Magdalena, 8.
∅ 981 746 441. 21 rooms.
Fisterra:
H* A Langosteira. Avda. Coruña, 57.
∅ 981 740 543. Double room: € 38/28.

Muxía: HS** La Cruz. Avda. López
Abante, 44. ∅ 981 742 084. Double
room: € 45/33; lunch/dinner: € 11.

RESTAURANTS

Bertamirans: Mi Tasca. Avda. de la
Mahía, 21. ∅ 981 584 449
Negreira: Casa Barqueiro. Avda. de
Santiago, 13. ∅ 981 818 234
Cee: O Galego. C/ Rosalía de Castro,
33. ∅ 981 746 654
Corcubión: San Martín. Avda. da
Mariña, 4. ∅ 981 746 601
Fisterra: Apalaxa. C/ El Muelle.
∅ 981 740 569
O Centolo. C/ del Puerto.
∅ 981 740 452
Muxía: La Sirena. C/ Condes de
Maceda, 13. ∅ 981 742 007

Now arriving in **Negreira,** you cross the river Barcala (leaving behind you the Pazo do Cotón and the Chapel of San Mauro) and continue along the mountainside in the direction of Terra de Xallas. After the flatlands you climb the hillside of Monte Aro, from where you can make out the Fervenza dam and you descend, skirting the Serra do Castelo, into the valley of the river Xallas, which you cross in **Ponteolveiroa.** You then take a surfaced road to **Olveiroa,** and leave it in the direction of **Hospital,** which you reach once you have crossed the flow of the river Logoso. After passing the Ferroatlántica factory the road forks and you then need to decide whether to go to Muxía or Fisterra:

A) The route to Fisterra passes the hermitage of Nosa Señora das Neves and the Fonte Santa, and shortly afterwards the hermitage of San Pedro Mártir. Before descending through the pine groves of Alto do Cruceiro da Armada, the sea appears before you. You need to continue towards it in order to come to **Cee** and then **Corcubión.** Once past **Sardiñeiro** you take the promenade alongside the Lagonsteira beach, which takes you directly to **Fisterra.** The Rúa de Santa Cataliña and the Rúa Real take you to the church of Santa María das Areas and from there you take the road towards the Finisterre lighthouse.

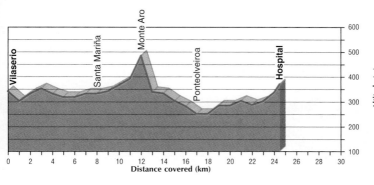

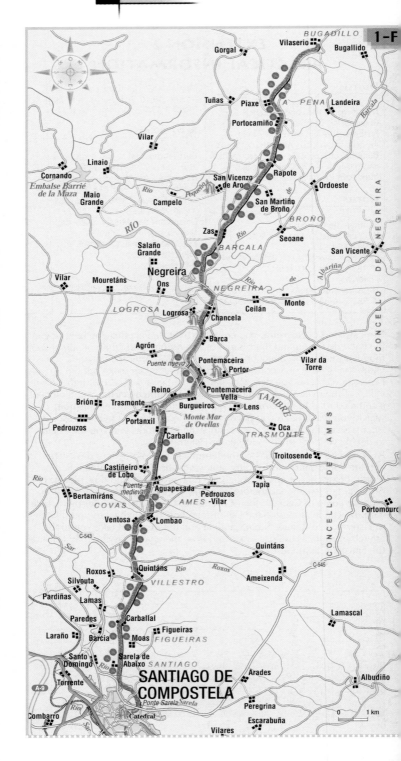

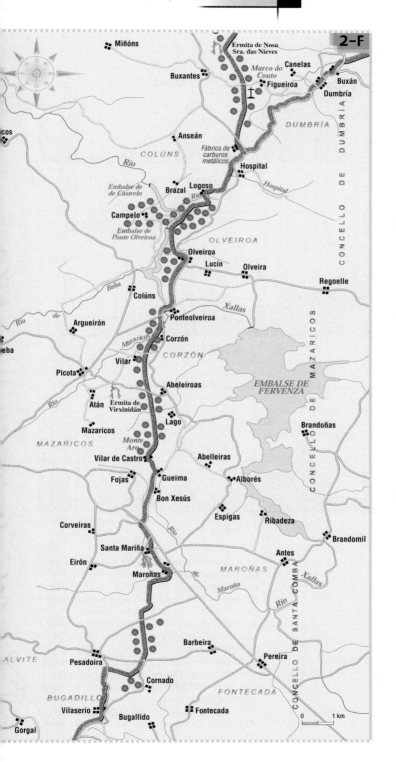

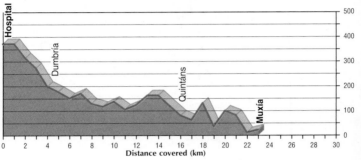

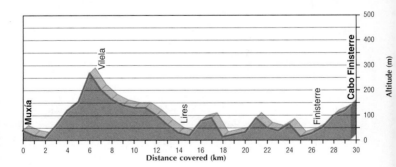

To go to Muxía from Fisterra, you pass **San Martiño de Duio** and travelling northwards you come to Punta de Rostro. You reach the **Lires** estuary by dirt tracks and, after passing near to cape Touriñán, you climb the Facho de Lourido. After descending you come into Muxía, from where you reach the Sanctuary of Nosa Señora da Barca.

B) To take the alternative route to Muxía you need to proceed in the direction of Dumbría, skirting round the Pena do Corvo. From there you continue northwards along surfaced roads and dirt tracks, passing the monasteries of San Martiño de Ozón and San Xián de Moraime, to reach **Muxía** along the Espiñeirido beach.

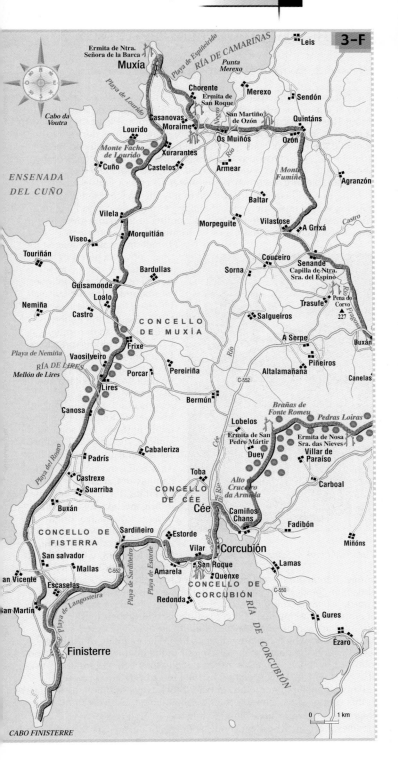

3-F

HISTORY AND WEALTH OF THE EXTENSION 2

EXTENSION 2. SANTIAGO DE COMPOSTELA – FISTERRA AND MUXÍA

The extension of the Road to Santiago to *Finis terrae* doesn't have as many St James related monuments as the French Road or any other Road. There is documentary evidence dating from at least the early XVth century, however, that, once in Santiago, many pilgrims decided to continue the Road of Stars (Camino de Estrellas) which guided them from the firmament towards the West, until one of the confines of the known earth, the place where the land was interrupted by the immeasurable and unknown Western sea: Fisterra or Finisterre.

In order to complete this appendage to the pilgrimage, Mediaeval pilgrims would cross the wall of Santiago through the Santo Peregrino door (puerta del Santo Peregrino) – according to the name given to it in the *Liber Sancti Iacobi* guide – or La Trinidad door (puerta de la

Trinidad), located between the place now occupied by the Raxoi palace and the Reyes Católicos hostel, to continue westbound along the current Huertas street (calle Huertas).

In this road to the boundaries of the earth, XVth century Gascogne pilgrim Nompar de Caumont only mentioned two interim stops: the as yet unidentified *Salhemana* and the place of Maroñas. Other reports point out the difficulty involved in following the Road until Finisterre, and some of the authors, such as XVth century Sebastian Ilsung, even got lost.

After going through the modest hamlets of **Carballal** y **Quintáns,** the Road encounters, in **Augapesada,** an interesting bridge of mediaeval origin. From here, pilgrims continue via the towns of **Trasmonte, Ponte Maceira,** which owes its name to a XIVth century

Fisterra. Church of Santa María das Areas.

bridge, **Barca** and the country house of **Chancela** (pazo Chancela), already at the doors of Negreira. One of the episodes of the apostle's transfer as narrated in *Liber Sancti Iacobi* is depicted on the town's coat of arms: after asking doña Lupa for a place to bury their master, St James' disciples are sent by this lady to *Dugium,* an old city located in Finisterre and which has now disappeared. The evil king of this city secretly plots the death of the disciples but the divinity warns them and, followed by the king and his armed people, they flee. During the pursuit, at a point which is not specified by the text, a bridge miraculously collapses beneath the impious pursuers' feet. Local tradition, as reflected in this coat of arms, attempts to place the miraculous event here.

Negreira is the most important town in this road. It is a town of mediaeval origin, whose most outstanding monuments are the mediaeval

Lighthouse of Cape Fisterra or Finisterre.

country house of Cotón *(Pazo do Cotón)* and an adjoining chapel dedicated to St Maurus.

After **Portocamiño** is **Maroñas,** which Nompar de Caumont went through in his pilgrimage. The mediaeval church of Santa Marina can be admired here.

The pilgrim faces a choice, either in **Olveiroa** or in **Hospital,** between a road which leads directly to Cape Finisterre (A), and one which runs parallel to this towards Muxia (B).

A) Between Hospital and Finisterra, the road goes past the Neoclassical church of La Virgen de las Nieves and, on reaching **Cee,** the sea can be seen for the first time. Once you reach **Corcubión,** the Gothic parish church of San Marcos, which houses an Italian origin XVth century sculpture of St Mark *(San Marcos),* is of particular note among the town's well preserved houses.

The old understanding of the world, according to which this was one of its terrestrial boundaries, explains the name **Fisterra** or Finisterre. The ancestral Indoeuropean myths relating to the death of the Sun in the West are expressed by the ancient geographer historians and the Greek and Roman historians who mention the religious fear which seized Junius Brutus' legionaries on observing the gigantic red sun impressively diving into the Ocean's waters, with the resulting impression that the latter were on fire.

The Latin name Finisterre was distorted by popular etymology into "Finstersterne", meaning something like "dark star", by many of the German pilgrims who arrived here, and who may have been influenced by the fact that the Atlantic Ocean was referred to in mediaeval times as the "dark sea".

The old city of *Dugium,* which is remembered in the saint-based names of San Martiño de Duio and San Vicente de Duio, was located near Finisterre.

The Romanesque church of Santa María das Areas (of the sands) can be found, together with the remains of an old pilgrims' hospital, in the centre of the town. A beautiful Gothic sculpture of the Holy Christ of Fisterra *(Santo Cristo de Fisterra),* one of the most popular forms of worships in the whole of Galicia – to a great extent due to the pilgrims – can be found inside the church. In addition to the Holy Christ, a

Renaissance image of the Virgen del Carmen and a sculpture of the apostle St James are worshipped in this church.

Many pilgrims documented the existence here of a monastery dedicated to St William but which is no longer in existence after its destruction by Breton pirates in the XVIIth century. The fact that Nompar refers to it as *Saint Guilhames du desert* tells us that this is the same form of worship as the one we found in several points, such as Gellone (Herault) and Obanos (Navarre), of the Road to Santiago. According to their respective legends, after his pilgrimage, Duke William X of Aquitaine withdrew as a hermit in each of these three places, where he finished his days in odour of sanctity.

B) From Hospital to Muxia, the road first goes through **Dumbría,** and then runs through **Sanande** and **Quintáns** before reaching the church of **San Martiño de Ozón,** which still retains its early Romanesque apse. A bit later, the road goes through **Muiños,** which owes its name to the large number of mills which can be found there. In **Moraime,** the monastery of San Julián, which contains some Gothic mural paintings, offers another good example of the area's Romanesque art.

Muxía owes all of its fame to its sanctuary dedicated to the Virgin of the Boat (Virgen de la Barca), which is also related to the worship of St James. According to the legend, when St James was preaching the Christian gospel in these lands before returning to Jerusalem, the Virgin Mary put into port at this coast to encourage him in his preaching, and her stone boat was tied to that shore forever. That place is now the destination of one of Galicia's most popular pilgrimages. Some pilgrims, such as XVth century Sebastian Ilsung, went as far as stating that this was where the most important miracle of the whole of the Road to Santiago took place.

Sanctuary of Nosa Señora da Barca in Muxía.

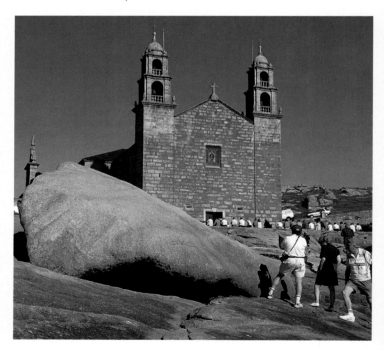

3 Via de la Plata

Roman road entering under the arch of Cáparra.

The Via de la Plata runs from south to north, starting in **Seville** (although you can also begin the walk, signposted as the "Camino Mozárabe", in **Granada**), and either linking with the Camino Francés (the French Way) in Astorga, or entering into Galicia after passing Puebla de Sanabria.

The Vía de la Plata begins by passing along the Sierra de Sevilla, a cattle grazing terrain full of holm oak groves and cork trees. Cross the Sierra Morena mountains and proceed into the lands of Extremadura via **Monesterio.** Walk through the agricultural area of Tierra de Barros **(Zafra),** and the lowlands of the river Guadiana **(Mérida).** Over pasture land you come to **Cáceres** and cross into the province of Salamanca over the sierra de Béjar, where common oaks begin to appear alongside holm oaks. After **Béjar** you come into **Salamanca,** and further on you reach the province of **Zamora,** through Tierra del Vino. After passing through the city of Zamora, and leaving Tierra del Pan behind you, you have two options:

A) Continue towards **Puebla de Sanabria,** passing through **Santa Marta de Tera,** and enter into Galicia by the province of Orense.

B) Go towards **Benavente** and **La Bañeza,** now in the province of León, towards **Astorga.**

There are hardly any hostels until you reach Galicia, although in many places pilgrims are welcome to stay in the town halls or parish churches.

In Galicia there are hostels in **A Gudiña, Laza, Vilar de Barrio, Xunqueira de Ambía, Verín, Monterrei, Sandiás, Ourense, Cea, Bendoiro, at the Medelo campsite,** and finally in **Monto do Gozo,** before reaching **Santiago de Compostela.**

Vila Nova de Foz Côa
SALAMANCA
N-501
N-620
San Pedro de Rozados
Alba de Tormes
N-630
GUARDA
Ciudad-Rodrigo
Fuenterroble de Salvatierra
Guijuelo
Sª. de Gata
La Calzada de Bejar
Béjar
N-110
Covilhã
Las Hurdes
Aldeanueva del Camino
Hervás
Sª. de Gredos
Fundão
Arenas de San Pedro
Villar de Plasencia
Carcaboso
Plasencia
Jaraíz de la Vera
Coria
Navalmoral de la Mata
PORTUGAL
Río Tajo
Cañaveral
Casar de Cáceres
CÁCERES
Trujillo
San Vicente de Alcantara
Valdesalor
N-V
Cruce de las Herrerías
Vegas del Guadiana
Villanueva de la Serena
Mérida
Guadiana
BADAJOZ
Río
Don Benito
Elvas
N-432
Olivenza
Cabeza del Buey
Almendralejo
Tierra de Barros
N-502
Hinojosa del Duque
Zafra
Jerez de los Caballeros
N-432
N-630
Monesterio
N-433
N-435
Río Guadalquivir
N-IV
Valverde del Camino
Carmona
Écija
SEVILLA
A-49
HUELVA

HISTORY AND WEALTH OF VIA DE LA PLATA

OTHERS 1. VÍA DE LA PLATA OR MOZARABIC ROAD

The Road from Sevilla to Santiago de Compostela uses to a large extent – until its end in Astorga – an old Roman road described in a much older work than the *Liber Sancti Iacobi* Guide (XIIth century) which documents the French Road. The work in question is *Itinerario de Antonino*, a "road guide" written in the IIth century, possibly in Emperor Antoninus Pius' time, which described all the roads in the Roman Empire in existence at the time. The description of the roads consisted of a list of the cities, mansiones and stops along them, as well as the distances between them, which were taken directly from the large milestones with inscriptions which were located on the sides of the road.

In the case that concerns us, *Itinerario de Antonino* describes the stretches of Vía de la Plata in sections: *Ab Hispali Emeritam* (from Sevilla to Mérida), *Ab Emerita ad Ocelum Duri* (from Mérida to Zamora) and *Ab Ocelo Duri Asturicam* (from Zamora to Astorga). According to this old guide, the towns along this route were the following: *Hispalis* (Sevilla), *Italica* (today Santiponce), *Monte Mariorum* (possibly Guillena), *Curica* (Monesterio), *Contributa* (possibly Villafranca de los Barros), *Perceiana* (possibly Almendralejo), *Emerita* (Mérida), *Ad Sorores* (near Casas de Don Antonio), *Castris Caecilii* (Cáceres), *Turmulos* (possibly in the area which is now water-logged by the reservoir of Alcántara II, in the municipal district of Garrovillas), *Rusticiana* (municipal district of Galisteo), *Capara* (Ventas de Cáparra), *Caelionicco* (Ventas de Montemayor), *Ad Lippos* (Valverde de Valdelacasa), *Sentice* (Pedrosillo de los Aires), *Salmatice* (Salamanca), *Sabaria* (municipal district of San Cristóbal del Monte), *Ocelo Duri* (Zamora), *Vico Aquario* (Castrotorafe, near San Cebrián de Castro), *Brigeco* (Villabrázaro, near Benavente), *Bedunia* (possibly La Bañeza) and *Asturica* (Astorga).

Sketch of the construction of a Roman road and its elements.

Roman theatre in Mérida.

This is, at least in some stretches, the best preserved Roman road in the whole of the Iberian Peninsula, and was in use until the XIXth century. Its current name, Vía de la Plata, is the result of a relatively modern popular etymology which slightly modifies the phonetics of the name "Bal'lat", meaning "paved way", given by the Arabs to this road and which is a certain reference to the path's beautiful paving of the time.

It was in use during the whole of the Middle Ages, especially from a military point of view, and successive raids took place on the Vía both from South to North, especially during the caliphate and Almanzor times in the IXth-XIth centuries and, later, from North to South, when the Reconquest was unstoppable in its advance, from Fernando I and Alfonso VI until Fernando III *the Saint,* the conqueror of Sevilla (XIth-XIIIth centuries). The road was not of course used solely by enemies exchanging blows, but also by neighbours exchanging commodities. In this respect, neither Visigoths nor Muslims or Christians added, by their use, anything to the aims for which its Roman builders had created the Via.

However, when the apostle St James' sepulchre was found in Galicia in the IXth century, Vía de la Plata started to be used by Mozarabic pilgrims from the south-east of the Peninsula, large numbers of whom undoubtedly directed their steps towards Compostela. At the beginning of the year 1000, when Almanzor destroyed the city and cathedral of Santiago, he left the Apostle's sanctuary, in relation to which he had received reports from many of these pilgrims, untouched. We must admit, however, that the documentary reports of Mozarabic pilgrimages to Santiago are almost non-existent, and that the vestiges of a hospitality and services network for pilgrims along its path are likewise scant.

The fact that it was an old road, whose path was covered in important cities and stops, may mean that these services had already been created a very long time ago and that, in a way, they had been preserved in Visigothic and Arabic times. In addition, the Vía had probably already been used as a pilgrimage road by worshippers of St Eulalia, the patron saint of Mérida and one of the most popular paleochristian Spanish martyrs of her time (as you may remember, the Cathedral of Iria Flavia was dedicated to her). We know that in the VIth century the archbishop of the city, Masona, had a "xenodoquio" (pilgrims' hospital) built to shelter the many visitors who came here attracted by the valued relic of St Eulalia or St Olalla.

Triumphal arch in Cáparra.

Although this route contains many signs of devotion to the apostle St James, this fact must be understood in the context of the Reconquest rather than in that of the pilgrimages, since the territories on the route, which belonged to the Kingdom of León by right of conquest, were one of the main scenes for the activities of the Military Order of St James.

There is little we can say in these tight lines about cities as old and magnificent as Seville, Mérida, Cáceres, Salamanca or Zamora which, unlike so many historic towns on the French Road, owe nothing or little of their birth and historical development to the worship of St James. Any reference to St James in these cities can be said to have been added on with time as an adornment and, to a great extent, contemplated, rather than because of the cities' location on a pilgrimage road, from the point of view of the war patronage conferred in the Middle Ages on the apostle St James.

We will, however, highlight four milestones in this long path which display an old (and by this we mean early mediaeval) link to the worship of St James or to *Liber Sancti Iacobi*, the work which served as an important vehicle for its publicity.

The first of these milestones is **Cáparra.** Although this is naturally an old city, whose origin has little to do with St James, it is the subject of a curious mention in *Pseudo-Turpin,* the fourth book of *Liber Sancti Iacobi,* an imaginative chronicle aimed at explaining the finding of the apostle St James' body, the creation of his road (the French Road, of course) and, by extension, the Reconquest of Spain. That work mentions Cáparra as a city condemned to remaining forever inhabited by reason of its unrelenting resistance to Charlemagne, which tells us that the city was already in ruins at the time (XIIth century). The fact that Cáparra is used as a cursed city in *Pseudo-Turpin's* fanciful fantasy may have been a wink at the pilgrims who went up Vía de la Plata, or at the knights who went down it during their raids and who, within the current municipality of Oliva de Plasencia, found the magnificent remains of the ancient Caperenses' city. Its extraordinary triumphal arch, with four sides open to each of the cardinal points, is

Above, milestone near Navarredonda de Salvatierra; below, Torre del Gallo in Salamanca Cathedral.

particularly noteworthy. Its magnificence and originality were such that its fame reached the author of *Pseudo-Turpin,* who included Cáparra in the settings of his work.

The second milestone can be found in **Salamanca,** which is also closely connected with *Pseudo-Turpin.* The milestone in question is one of the capitals in the city's Old Cathedral (Catedral Vieja), which represents a motif we have found up to four times on the French Road (Estella, Irache, Villamayor de Monjardín and Navarrete): the episode, told in chapter XVIII of *Pseudo-Turpin,* of the battle on horse between Roland and Ferragut. The capital was built in the second half of the XIIth century and bears the signature of its sculptor, one *Petrus Petriz.*

The third milestone is not on Vía de la Plata itself but on one of its detours, which goes up the river Tera up to lake Sanabria before reaching Benavente. The milestone, a parish church dedicated to the Astorgan martyr who lends her name to the town, can be found in **Santa Marta de Tera,** a small town in the valley of this river.

Above, panoramic view of lake Sanabria; below, front of the apse in the monastery of San Martín de Castañeda.

Its architecture, dating from the late XIth century, bears some resemblance to the collegiate church of San Isidoro de León. Two aspects make this church extraordinary. The first one is a capital depicting angels carrying a naked sexless body – representing the soul of the martyr to whom the church is dedicated –to the heavens on a round shield. This admirably sculpted scene is wonderfully highlighted twice a year: in the spring and autumn equinoxes, the rays of the morning sun which find their way through a gap in the apse illuminate the capital like a floodlight, leaving the viewer with the impression that it is the sun, symbol of divinity, that is taking St Martha's (Santa Marta's) soul with it. The second reason for Santa Marta de Tera's special significance is the Romanesque sculpture of St James adjoined to the church's southern façade, which is the oldest representation of St James in pilgrim attire. The Apostle is holding his staff on his right hand while blessing with the left. A pilgrim's "escarcela" (a bag symbolising the way of the pilgrim) adorned with a shell, just like the one carried by "Jesús peregrino en Emaús" (Pilgrim Jesus in Emaús) in the cloister of Santo Domingo de Silos, can be seen hanging from the Apostle's shoulder across his chest and falling on his left side.

There is a legend, originating from the pilgrimages relating to lake **Sanabria,** on the same stretch; this is the legend of Villaverde or Valverde de Lucerna, a city submerged in the waters by a curse. Jesus, in pilgrim attire, arrives at this town in search of food and accommodation but, barring one exception, the inhabitants of the town fail to duly assist the pilgrim, who punishes the town with being flooded by a large volume of water, which is the current lake Sanabria.

This legend, which can also be found in *Pseudo-Turpin* in a different setting: El Bierzo (lake Carucedo, Ventosa) and with another protagonist (Charlemagne instead of Jesus), and which originated in Switzerland (hence the name Lucerna – Luzern), was brought to this land by the Cistercian monks of San Martín de Castañeda, who depended on Santa María de Carucedo. The fact that Jesus appears as a pilgrim must be taken as an indication that pilgrims went through this area.

4 The Northern Roads

The great appeal of the routes which run across the north of Spain towards Santiago de Compostela is their proximity to the sea and the spectacular scenery viewed along the route. Rocky cliffs, beaches, coves and estuaries, valleys, countless rivers, Atlantic forests, or woodlands of pines and eucalyptus, and meadows all contribute to the beauty of the route. On the other hand, the rough terrain over which you must continuously climb up and down, together with a lack of clear signposting and dangerous stretches along winding roads with little visibility, means that both the level of difficulty, and the level of satisfaction you feel once the journey is achieved, are greater.

You begin the route by crossing the Santiago bridge from **Hendaya** to **Irún** and continue in the direction of Cantabria. There are no pilgrims' hostels in the Basque Country, although in addition to other types of accommodation, there are youth hostels in **Fuenterrabía, San Sebastián,** and **Zarauz.** On crossing the hill of la Haya de Ontón, you come into the lands of Cantabria, where you will now find pilgrims' hostels in the towns of **Castro Urdiales, Laredo, Santoña, Santander, Comillas** and **San Vicente de la Barquera.** From **Unquera** you pass into Asturias by crossing the **Bustio** bridge over the river Deva. The first pilgrims' hostel you come to is the one in **Piñeres** (in the municipality of Llanes), which is followed by the hostels in **Leces** (Ribadesella), **La Isla** (Colunga) and **Sebrayo** (Villaviciosa). The hostel in **La Vega** (Sariego) is on the way to **Oviedo,** where you will also find refuge. Other hostels on the route called "El Camino Primitivo" (the Primitive Way), or the inland route, from Oviedo to Santiago, are in **Villapañada** (Grado), **El Escamplero** (Las Regueras), **Salas, Borres** (Tineo), **Peñaselta** (Allande), **La Mesa** (Grandas de Salime) and **Grandas de Salime.** Now in Galicia the chain of hostels run by the Xunta (the Galician autonomous government) offer refuge in **O Cadavo** and **Lugo** before linking into the "Camino Francés" (the French Way) at **Melide.**

San Sebastián. View of the façade of the church of Santa María.

If you keep to the coast, the hostels which welcome pilgrims are in **Avilés, Soto de Luiña** (Cudillero), **Almuña** (Valdés), **Piñera** (Navia), **La Caridad** (El Franco), **Tapia de Casariego** and **Tol** (Castropol). Crossing the river Eo you come into Galicia, which has hostels in **Ribadeo, Lourenzá, Mondoñedo, Vilalba, Baamonde,** and **Sobrado dos Monxes.** Then from Arzúa onwards the route coincides with the "Camino Francés".

In the Basque Country there is an alternative route which crosses Guipúzcoa and Álava, passing through **Vitoria** and linking into the "Camino Francés" at Santo Domingo de la Calzada or at Burgos. On this route there are no pilgrims' hostels either.

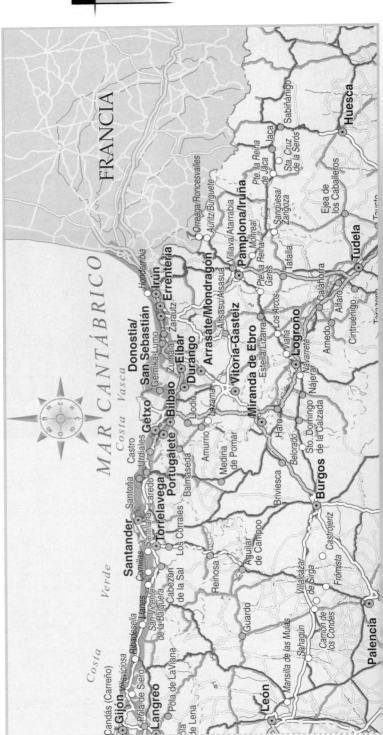

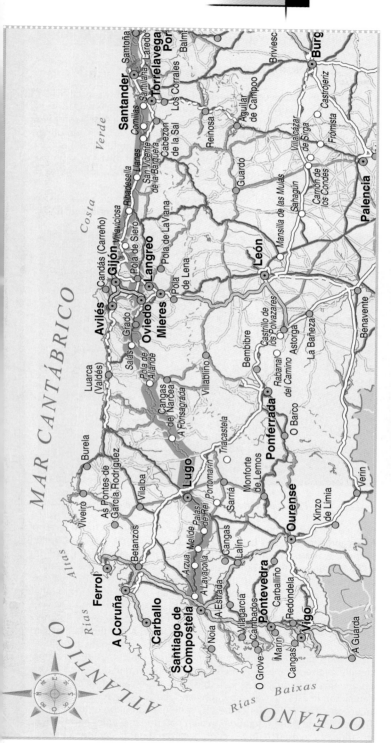

HISTORY AND WEALTH OF THE NORTHERN ROADS

OTHERS 2. THE NORTHERN ROADS

It is now widely believed that before the French Road was established in the XIth century, early pilgrims to the sanctuary of Compostela took a path that went along the Cantabrian coast. This reasonable assumption, based also on comments from texts such as *Historia Silense* and other mediaeval chronicles, fails, however, to find other architectural or documentary evidence, such as hospitals, important towns or simply a large communication artery for an accident-free journey, to allow us to reliably reconstruct its path.

The comment, mentioned above, in *Historia Silense*, which was followed by other works, reveals that king Sancho III *the Greater* of Navarre

Panoramic view of San Vicente de la Barquera.

diverted the old pilgrim road towards Nájera through the rough lands of Álava and Asturias. This has lead many to assume that the oldest Road to Santiago was a path which came from Bayonne, entered Spain via Irún and went through the territories of Guipúzcoa, Vizcaya, Álava, Cantabria and Asturias. As mentioned, this supposition has not been confirmed by either archaeology or documents, and neither of these allow us to reliably reconstruct a great itinerary on these lands. This is not to say, however, that such itinerary did not exist. In the XIIth century one of the authors of *Historia Compostelana*, who was forced to travel along this road, stated that pilgrims – whether mounted or on foot – avoided going through these lands, since traversing them caused great difficulties (the author literally referred to them as "a chaos") to whoever dared attempt it. We assume that such difficulties were basically those caused by the Cantabrian coast's uneven orography and the sea's large inland incursions. The difficulties caused by state of civilisation of these areas (Basque Country and Cantabria), which had no large cities and hardly any monastic presence, in the centuries from the IXth century and

*San Salvador
de Valdediós
or Conventín.*

stretching to the end of the XIIth century, was probably no less significant. From the pilgrims' point of view, this translated itself into dangers and lack of assistance, as reported in some XIIth century sources.

The situation, however, changed in the late XIIth and the XIIIth century, when the large towns of the eastern Cantabrian coast, such as **Irún, San Sebastián, Guetaria, Guernica, Bilbao, Castro Urdiales, Laredo, Santoña, Santander** or **Santillana del Mar,** were either born or started to undergo considerable development. However, the first reports of pilgrims making their journey on the coastal route, such as bishop Mártir de Arzendjan's narration, go as far back as the XVth century.

San Vicente de la Barquera does, however, have some relatively old (XIIIth century) evidence of the passing of pilgrims through here on their way to Oviedo and Santiago. This evidence is both architectural – such as the Pilgrim's door (puerta del Peregrino) and the hospital of La Concepción next to the church of Santa María de los Ángeles – and documentary. This is also the case in **Llanes,** as far as Asturias, whose lodging house we know was founded in 1330.

As the road approaches Oviedo, the references to the pilgrimage become ever more frequent. This can be seen in **Ribadesella, Colunga, Lastres** and **Villaviciosa,** although there is always some uncertainty when interpreting these traces. To give two examples, the river of Los Romeros next to **Caravia,** or the Pilgrims' Fountain (Fuente de los Peregrinos) which can be found before reaching Villaviciosa, are related to pilgrims who were either going to Santiago or were on some local pilgrimage. In the case of Caravia, there are reports of Templar presence and of a monastery of Santiago, founded in the XIIth century.

Between Villaviciosa and Oviedos we find **Valdediós** where, in addition to the famous church of San Salvador, we know that there once was a Cistercian community. Further on is **Narzana,** whose Romanesque church of San Pedro is attributed to the Knights of the Templar. The next important town on this route, **Pola de Siero,** was founded precisely around a hospital for "pilgrims and the poor", the San Pedro lodging

San Salvador Cathedral in Oviedo.

house, a gift made to the monastery of San Vicente in Oviedo in 1142. Since several hospitals outside the Santiago pilgrimage route were created in Asturias at that time, we must again query whether or not we are in the presence of a fundamentally St James-related charitable institution. After **Noreña, Argüelles** and the monastery of Santa María de la Vega, pilgrims entered **Oviedo.** As mentioned above (see the León-Villadangos stage), Oviedo was, for several centuries starting from the XIIth, the second most important pilgrimage centre in the Iberian Peninsula after Santiago de Compostela. However, as we also mentioned above, what we know of the pilgrimage to Oviedo mostly relates to a variant of the French Road, many of whose pilgrims decided, on reaching Leon, to take a detour from the straighter path in order to visit the spectacular relics housed in Oviedo's Cathedral of San Salvador. From the capital of Asturias, these pilgrims went to Santiago de Compostela via the following route, which has a better selection of archaeological and written documents.

The first of these tells us how, on being informed of the lucky finding of St James' body in his kingdom, Asturian King Alfonso II promptly set off towards Galicia, thus becoming the first known pilgrim. The first town on his route must have been **Escamplero,** where the monastery of San Martín and a lodging place were later erected. There was also a hospital, founded by Alfonso VII in 1144, and an important bridge, in **Peñaflor. Villapañada** had a territory which depended on the Knights of St John of Jerusalem, who had many possessions both here and in **Grado** as well as a pilgrims' hospital in Villapañada.

Taking into account the close link between the Cluniac order and the Road to Santiago, the fact that the only Cluniac monastery in Asturias was in **Cornellana** is very significant. Although the earliest evidence of its lodging house dates from the XVth century, it must already have been in existence much earlier. The Road continued via **Salas** and **La Espina,** where there were two hospitals, one of which belonged to the Church of Santiago de Compostela.

A document from the early XIIIth century talks about a "Franciscan road" through the village of **Tineo,** and establishes that such a road must go through **Obona.** Carrying on through Grandas de Salime, pilgrims entered Galicia via the pass of Acebo, which was similar to the one at

El Cebreiro, and encountered a hospital which depended on the territory of Portomarín, which in turn depended on the Order of St John.

After going through numerous villages, many of them with important references to the pilgrimage, the Road enters the important and ancient town of **Lugo,** the Roman city of *Lucus Augusta,* through the door of San Pedro (puerta de San Pedro), one of the doors in its famous Roman wall.

The two great objects of devotion which pilgrims found in Lugo were the Santísimo Sacramento (Holy Sacrament), on permanent display since the XIIth century, and a very beautiful Gothic sculpture of the Virgin, known as the Virgin of the Big Eyes (Virgen de los Ojos Grandes). Both of these are housed in the

Monastery of San Juan de Cornellana.

Cathedral, a Romanesque building – although with many extensions and coverings – whose most outstanding feature is a magnificent Pantocrator sculpted on the northern façade. Pilgrims left Lugo through the Carmen door (Puerta del Carmen), the Roman wall's oldest door, crossed the river Miño by means of its Roman bridge and, after going past a hospital for pilgrims with leprosy which has lent its name to the current quarter of San Lázaro, went towards Melide, where this northern road met the French Road.

In this chapter we have reconstructed an ideal layout of a possible northern route of which not all its stretches are well documented. A possible variant to this great East-West axis is the route which goes down from Bayonne to Burgos via the amazing **San Adrián** tunnel, where it would join up with the French Road.

Another possibility, which is not evidenced until somewhat late times (XVth century) is the route which, without going through Oviedo, followed the Asturian route through the cities of **Gijón, Avilés, Luarca** and **Ribadeo.** After crossing the river Eo, on the frontier between Asturias and Galicia, this northern Road reached the old monastery of **Vilanova de Lourenzá,** as well as the important town of **Mondoñedo,** which became an episcopal see in the IXth century, when the very old Portuguese see of Dume was moved. The most important stop between here and Arzúa, where this branch meets the Road to Santiago, is the great monastery of **Sobrado dos Monxes.**

Gothic sculpture of the "Virgen de los Ojos Grandes" (Virgin of the Big Eyes) in Lugo cathedral.

5 Portuguese Roads

Lisbon. Southern façade of the Jerónimos monastery.

There are many routes in Portugal which lead to Santiago de Compostela and each of them offers variations and detours. From southern Portugal the routes run up towards **Lamego** or **Lisbon.** From there, and passing through **Coimbra,** you continue towards **Oporto,** from where there is a route which is totally signposted. The route as far as Galicia is as follows: **Oporto-Braga** or **Barcelos-Ponte de Lima-Valença do Minho.** Once in Galicia you continue on through **Tui** towards **Pontevedra** and from there to **Padrón** and **Santiago de Compostela.**

If you choose to undertake the pilgrimage through Portugal you will encounter substantial difficulties due to the lack of hostels (**Ponte de Lima** and **Valença do Minho**) and to the fact that a large part of the route is on the road. Once you have crossed the border at the river Miño, you will again find hostels belonging to the chain sponsored by the Xunta de Galicia. As per the rest of the Galician routes, these hostels are either in new buildings or in old ones which have been renovated. They are located in the following towns: **Tui, O Porriño, Redondela, Pontevedra, Porta, Padrón,** and **Teo.**

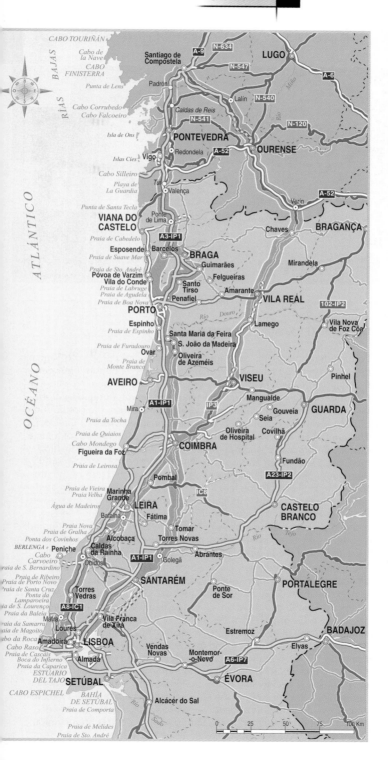

HISTORY AND WEALTH OF THE PORTUGUESE ROADS

Évora. Templo de Diana.

OTHERS 3. THE ROADS IN PORTUGAL

Portugal has a very old, constant and intense relationship with Santiago de Compostela, which is the logical result of the continuity between Portugal and Galicia, whose only physical barrier is the river Miño. In fact, there was no administrative frontier separating Portuguese from Galician land until the XIIth century: in Roman times, the northern part of what is now Portugal was part of the Roman province of *Gallaecia.* This continued into Suevan and Visigothic times in the form of a large diocese with *Bracara Augusta* (Braga) as its head. After the Muslim invasion, the Asturian and Leonese kings attacked and reconquered Portuguese cities and territories as an undifferentiated part of the old Visigothic kingdom. In the late XIth century, King Alfonso VI created the counties of Galicia and Portugal, and bequeathed them to his sons-in-law from Burgundy, Raymond and Henry. The latter's son, Alfonso, attained definitive autonomy with respect to the kingdom of León and created a new separate state which took care of the reconquest of the western part of the Peninsula: the land that is now Portugal.

The Portuguese reconquest, like the Spanish one, is also associated to a great extent with the figure of the apostle St James. So, for example, the episodes of the reconquering of two of the impost important cities in Portugal – Coimbra and Lisbon – are repeatedly evoked in St James' icons and worship history. The first description of the Apostle as *Miles Christi* which, in terms of iconography, is translated into the famous "Matamoros" (Moor Killer) figure, can be found for the first time in the report of Fernando I's conquest of Coimbra, which is told in *Historia Silense* and *Liber Sancti Iacobi*. The crusaders who took part, almost a century later, in the conquest of Lisbon, had made a pilgrimage to Santiago de Compostela. The memory of the bloody battle which preceded the taking of the city and whose most decisive part took place in the quarter of Alfama has been preserved in the form of worship of this popular quarter's parish church, which is, of course, dedicated to St James.

The presence in Portugal of the worship of St James, with its derivations, is widespread and significant. An example of this is the presence, in the monastery of Alcobaça, of one of the oldest and most complete copies of *Liber Sancti Iacobi*. The presence of *Liber Sancti Iacobi's* genuinely Xacobean texts left their mark in the homiletic work of two of Portugal's most important mediaeval preachers: Franciscan St Anthony of Lisbon (better known as St Anthony of Padua) and Dominican monk Paio de Coimbra. Unrelated to this is the famous tax of St James (voto de Santiago) under which Spanish towns had to pay the Church of Santiago a periodic tax, and which was also in force in Portugal during the whole of the Middle Ages, just like in the kingdoms of Castille and León. As our last example, we can mention the fact that many Portuguese monarchs were great worshippers of St James. Some of them, such as Queen Isabel the "Saint" in the XIVth century and Manuel I, even made the pilgrimage; others, such as the above mentioned Manuel the Fortunate at the end of the XVth century, helped finance the building of the great Royal Hospital of Santiago de Compostela.

Don Manuel's contribution to the building of a work of international interest like the Royal Hospital of Santiago is an indication that there was a high number of Portuguese pilgrims who benefited from this St James related institution. Judging by the scattered traces left in Portugal by the pilgrimage, the roads followed by the pilgrims to get to Santiago must also have been very varied.

From the Algarve, Portugal's southernmost point, pilgrims either went north towards Lisbon via **Alcácer do Sal** and **Setúbal;** or took an inland route via **Beja, Évora, Guarda** and **Lamego.**

Two great routes, presumably old in spite of the lateness of their documentary evidence, started from **Lisbon:**

Lisbon. Sepulchre in the Jerónimos monastery.

Coimbra.
University
Courtyard on
Queima das
Fitas day.

A) The first of these ran next to the Atlantic Ocean coast and is full of
monuments of extreme importance in the history of Portugal. After
leaving Lisbon and the royal palace of Sintra behind, you reach **Mafra,**
a grandiose convent built in the XVIIIth century by the Portuguese
Crown for a community of up to 300 monks. After this, the road is
marked out by the Romanesque fortress of **Torres Vedras** and the
equally fortified city of **Óbidos.** North of these is **Alcobaça,** the most
important monastic centre in Portugal, which was entrusted to the
Cistercian Order in the XIIth century. The importance of this great
monastery can be seen in the fact that its abbot was one of Portugal's
spiritual guides. We must assume that within it, the Cistercian monks
practised charity towards the pilgrims, although we know of no texts
dating before the XVIIIth century which can confirm this. As
mentioned above, the relationship between this monastery and the
worship of St James can be seen in the presence of an old and
beautiful complete copy of *Liber Sancti Iacobi* in Alcobaça's great
library. If we follow this route we reach **Aljubarrota.** This is where, in
1385, the Portuguese troops defeated those of John I of Castille, who
sought to annexe the Portuguese Crown to his own states. The
magnificent monastery of Santa María de la Victoria of **Batalha** was
built as a consequence of this battle. After going past two more famous
places, **Leiria y Pombal,** the Road went somewhat inland and entered
Coimbra, another Xacobean milestone in Portugal. In gratitude to the
Apostle (who had appeared to him as a knight in a nocturnal vision)
for his help conquering the city in 1064, Fernando I ordered the
church of Santiago to be built.

B) The first place reached by the other road which leaves Lisbon to go
towards Santiago is **Santarém,** which used to have two assistance
institutions which may have been related to the Road to Santiago. This
is at least what their respective names, Hospital do Palmeiro and
Hospital de Rocamadour, suggest. Later on, the road stops in **Golegâ,**
whose name (from the Latin word *Gallecianus*) may be related to the
road that lead the pilgrims to Galicia. The next stop, **Tomar,** is more
significant since it has one of the most important monasteries that the
Order of the Templars ever had. After the Order was dissolved, the
Portuguese Templars continued to act as such, although they renamed
their institution to Order of the Christ. The central chapel, whose
round shape was built in imitation of the Holy Sepulchre church which
lent its name to the Order, is the monastery's most noteworthy

Pomar church and castle.

architectural element. As mentioned above, this variant and the one described before, both of which came from Lisbon, meet again in the beautiful city of **Coimbra.**

Here, pilgrims encounter another choice: either to return to the coast via Oporto, or to take a path inland via Viseu, Lamego and Chaves.

A) The main milestones on the first option are, of course, the old city of **Oporto,** which lent its name to the Kingdom of Portugal *(Portu Calle)*; the small but beautiful Romanesque church of **San Pedro de Rates;** and **Barcelos,** where the most famous monument in the Portuguese Road to Santiago, the "cruceiro do Senhor do Galo", which commemorates a Xacobean miracle similar to the one in Santo Domingo de la Calzada, can be found. After going through **Ponte de Lima** and **Valença do Minho,** which contain many references to St James, the Road enters Spain via **Tui,** yet another very old episcopal see of the old province of Braga. The Road continues all the way to Santiago through the towns of **Redondela, Pontevedra** – where the beautiful Baroque sanctuary of La Peregrina with its layout in the shape of a"vieira" (scallop shell) can be found –, **Caldas de Rei** and **Padrón.** We must point out that this variant has an alternative detour, at Oporto's exit, which allows a visit to the very important city of **Braga** instead of Barcelos with its many references to St James.

B) The second road from Coimbra runs inland, through the very old cities of **Viseu, Lamego** and **Chaves,** enters Spain via **Verín** and continues towards Santiago via **Ourense,** joined to a broken Vía de la Plata variant.

Braga. Bom Jesús.

6 The English Road

Hércules tower in A Coruña.

The Camino Inglés has two ports as starting points: **Ferrol** and **A Coruña.**
The route starting in Ferrol and passing through **Pontedeume, Miño** and
Betanzos runs close to the sea and passes estuaries and inlets before
turning inland towards Santiago de Compostela. The route beginning in
Coruña is shorter and you can reach **Bruma** within a day. The two routes
meet here to continue on to Santiago de Compostela, just over 40 km
away.

The hostels on this route are in **Neda** (on the Ferrol route), **Miño** and
Bruma.

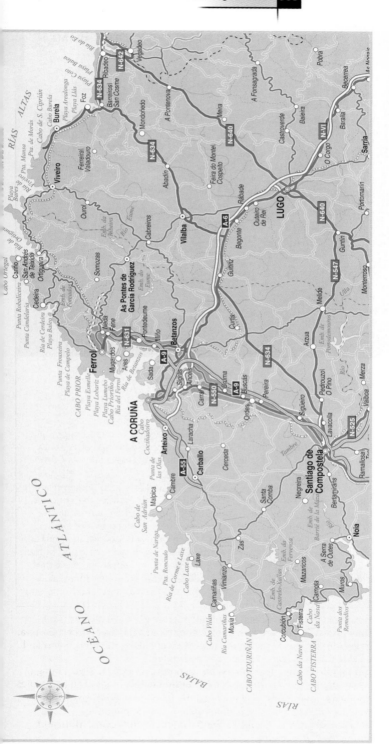

HISTORY AND WEALTH OF THE ENGLISH ROAD

———— *View of A Coruña from the air.* ————

OTHERS 4. THE ENGLISH ROAD

This is the name that currently describes the short overland pilgrimage journey (approximately 100 km) made by those who had arrived at different points of the Galician Cantabrian coast, especially La Coruña and Ferrol, by boat.

The origins of this pilgrimage are very old and are documented from the XIIth century. According to the Chronicle which narrates the conquest of Lisbon by King Alfonso Henriques with the help of a contingent of British and Northern crusaders, the crusaders – forced by the elements – made a stopover in Galician land, which they used to visit the Lord St James, before heading towards Lisbon. We also know that many of the pilgrims who had arrived by boat – people from Hansa and the British Isles as well as Scandinavians – made a pilgrimage to the three great Christian sanctuaries of the time, – Santiago de Compostela, Rome and Jerusalem – in the same crossing.

However, and even though maritime pilgrimages have always taken place, we will later see how King Henry II of England's pilgrimage project in the late XIIth century actually went along the French Road, starting from his French properties in Aquitaine.

The outbreak of the Hundred Years' War (1339-1453), however, meant that it was no longer advisable for English pilgrims to go via their old Aquitaine possessions, and thus had the immediate consequence of drawing large numbers of people to the maritime pilgrimage, which saw its best years in the second half of the XIVth century and especially during the XVth century.

Some remarkable artistic works, such as the beautiful Goodyear altarpiece or the Cross of the Pearls (Cruz de las Perlas), both of which are now housed in Santiago Cathedral Museum, bear witness to the British pilgrimages of this time. The first of these is a small portable polychrome alabaster altarpiece divided into five panels with five scenes of the Life of St James sculpted on them. This was a gift made in 1456 by English pilgrim John Goodyear, the parson of Chale (Isle of Wight, Winchester Diocese). The second testimony is the Cross of the Pearls, an exquisite piece of craftmanship donated by King James IV of Scotland in the late XVth century.

We also have literary testimonies which tell us about some of the details and peculiarities of this type of pilgrimage. Of particular value among these is the report written by William Wey, a clergyman who belonged to England's most exclusive intelléctual circles of his time and who was a founding member of the Royal College of Eton. Master Wey made his pilgrimage, just like John Goodyear, in the year 1456, so it wouldn't be surprising if they had coincided in the same St James expedition, chartered in Plymouth on 16th May 1456. According to Wey's report, the expedition was comprised of six pilgrims' boats which had come from different ports of southern England (Bristol, Weymouth, Limyngton, Portsmouth y Plymouth) and had joined up in Plymouth to set sail together towards Santiago. The crossing took five days, at the end of which the boats sighted cape Ortegal and, from there, sailed to La Coruña. At La Coruña harbour, Wey counted up to 37 English pilgrims' boats from a total of 80 ships from Wales, Ireland, Normandy, Brittany, France and other places.

Unfortunately, Wey does not tell us about his journey from La Coruña to Santiago de Compostela, which he covered in a single day.

In **A Coruña,** the church of Santiago, built in the early XIIth century by Alfonso IX of León (a great benefactor of the city), is of particular interest in relation to the pilgrimage. Much later, in the XVth century, Wey tells us about a remarkable liturgic celebration performed in the church of Santa María del Mar, a most beautiful Romanesque church located in the heart of *Cidade Vella,* the oldest part of La Coruña. He also tells us how

A Coruña. Collegiate church of Santa María.

Ferrol. View of the Armas Square dominated by the Town Hall.

English pilgrims could enjoy religious services in their own language in a Franciscan convent which no longer exists.

Once you leave the city, the first relevant St James milestone is **Sigrás,** which used to have a pilgrims' hospital and a Romanesque church dedicated to the apostle St James. Very close to Sigrás, although on a slight detour, is the magnificent church of Santa María de **Cambre,** which may have had links with the Order of the Templars. The road continues via **Anceis** and, after a series of hamlets, some of which have an unquestionable road-related character – Rua, Calle, Carral –, it reaches **Bruma,** where there used to be another hospital.

From here the road goes to **Buscás, Poulo** and **Pereira,** where a mediaeval bridge must be used. After leaving **Sigüeiro** behind, the river

Pambre is crossed by means of a bridge of mediaeval origin. Between here and Santiago, the most remarkable pilgrimage monument is the so-called Fonte do Inglés (the Englishman's Fountain), which is located after **Barciela** and provides reliable evidence of the dominant nationality among those who took this road. English pilgrims entered Santiago via La Peña door (Puerta de la Peña).

In **Bruma,** those pilgrims who had disembarked at **Ferrol** harbour met the ones who came from A Coruña. The most important places through which they had to go in this stretch of the road were certainly the Cluniac monastery of **San Martín de Xubia** and the city of **Betanzos.**

Betanzos. Detailed view of the façade of the church of San Francisco.

SPANISH TOURIST INFORMATION OFFICES ABROAD

CANADA. Toronto
Tourist Office of Spain.
2 Bloor Street West Suite 3402.
Toronto, Ontario M4W 3E2.
℘ (1416) 961 31 31.
Fax (1416) 961 19 92.
www.tourspain.toronto.on.ca
e-mail: toronto@tourspain.es

GREAT BRITAIN. London
Spanish Tourist Office.
22-23 Manchester Square.
London W1M 5AP.
℘ (44207) 486 80 77.
Fax (44207) 486 80 34.
www.tourspain.co.uk
e-mail: londres@tourspain.es

JAPAN. Tokyo
Tourist Office of Spain.
Daini Toranomon Denki Bldg.4F. 3-1-10.
Toranomon. Minato-Ku.
TOKYO-105.
℘ (813) 34 32 61 41.
Fax (813) 34 32 61 44.
www.spaintour.com
e-mail: tokio@tourspain.es

RUSSIA. Moscow
Spanish Tourist Office.
Tverskaya – 16/2 Business Center
"Galeria Aktor", 6th floor.
Moscow 103009.
℘ (7095) 935 83 97.
Fax (7095) 935 83 96.
www.ru.tourspain.es
e-mail: moscu@tourspain.es

SINGAPORE. Singapore
Spanish Tourist Office.
541 Orchard Road.
Liat Tower # 09-04.
238881 Singapore.
℘ (657) 37 30 08.
Fax (657) 37 31 73.
e-mail: singapore@tourspain.es

UNITED STATES OF AMERICA
Los Angeles
Tourist Office of Spain.
8383 Wilshire Blvd, Suite 960.
Beverly Hills, California 90211.
℘ 1(323) 658 71 88.
Fax 1(323) 658 10 61.
www.okspain.org
e-mail: losangeles@tourspain.es

Chicago
Tourist Office Of Spain.
Water Tower Place, suite 915 East.
845 North Michigan Avenue.
Chicago, Illinois 60 611.
℘ 1(312) 642 19 92.
Fax 1(312) 642 98 17.
www.okspain.org
e-mail: chicago@tourspain.es

Miami
Tourist Office of Spain.
1221 Brickell Avenue.
Miami, Florida 33131.
℘ 1(305) 358 19 92.
Fax 1(305) 358 82 23.
www.okspain.org
e-mail: miami@tourspain.es

New York
Tourist Office of Spain.
666 Fifth Avenue 35th floor.
New York, New York 10103.
℘ 1(212) 265 88 22.
Fax 1(212) 265 88 64.
www.okspain.org
e-mail: nuevayork@tourspain.es

EMBASSIES IN MADRID

CANADA
Núñez de Balboa, 35 – 3ª planta.
℘ 914 233 250. Fax 914 233 251

GREAT BRITAIN
Fernando El Santo, 16.
℘ 913 190 200. Fax 913 081 033

JAPAN
Serrano, 109.
℘ 915 907 600. Fax 915 901 321

RUSSIA
Velázquez, 155.
℘ 915 622 264. Fax 915 629 712

UNITED STATES OF AMERICA
Serrano, 75. ℘ 915 872 200,
fax 915 872 303

CONTENTS

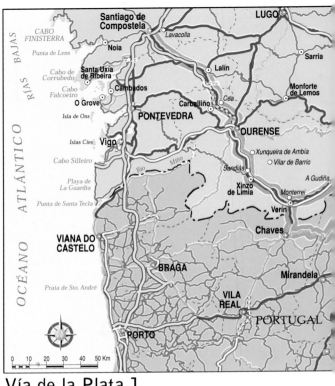

Vía de la Plata 1

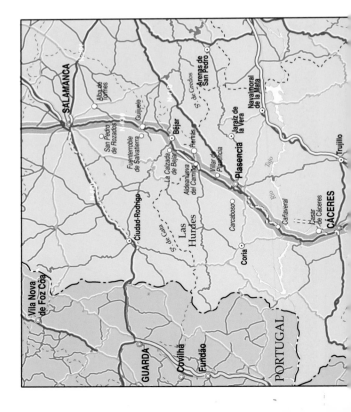